The Politics of Inclusive Development

The Politics of Inclusive Development

Interrogating the Evidence

Edited by
Sam Hickey, Kunal Sen, and Badru Bukenya

OXFORD
UNIVERSITY PRESS

Great Clarendon Street, Oxford, OX2 6DP,
United Kingdom

Oxford University Press is a department of the University of Oxford.
It furthers the University's objective of excellence in research, scholarship,
and education by publishing worldwide. Oxford is a registered trade mark of
Oxford University Press in the UK and in certain other countries

Published in the United States of America by Oxford University Press
198 Madison Avenue, New York, NY 10016, United States of America

British Library Cataloguing in Publication Data
Data available

Library of Congress Control Number: 2014943260

ISBN 978-0-19-872256-4

Printed and bound by
CPI Group (UK) Ltd, Croydon, CR0 4YY

This book is dedicated both to the future of our latest arrivals, Noah Jem, Shawn Michael, and Matthew Francis, and in memory of the late Adrian Leftwich, a greatly valued colleague and friend.

Foreword

The Effective States and Inclusive Development (ESID) Research Centre strives to create knowledge that contributes to making states more effective and committed to achieving social justice. This is a grand goal but our partnership of academic and research institutes—across Africa, Asia, Europe, and North America—works at local, national, and international levels to deepen the understanding of governance in the developing world in ways that impact on policies and practices so that peoples' lives and livelihood are improved. Our partnership is multinational, multidisciplinary—and examines development from a multidimensional perspective!

This book is ESID's first major academic collection and draws on a large numbers of studies that partners have provided (see <http://www.effective-states.org> for full details). Its title—*The Politics of Inclusive Development*—would have appeared an oxymoron to earlier generations of those engaged in the policy and planning of development. For many involved in development when it was focused on foreign aid, 'politics' was a catch-all term for the processes that stopped detailed technical plans (and the theories underpinning them) from achieving their stated goals. It was always a negative force: the idea of 'politics' delivering growth or human development was risible. But, times have moved on. The pretence, and futility, of the assumption that 'development' occurred in some rarefied, apolitical context has been laid to rest as growing numbers of studies have demonstrated that 'politics matters', indeed 'institutions matter'.

For those of us who spent our early careers at the grassroots level in development practice the initial findings of these erudite studies has not been a surprise: we had always known that our operational work was embedded in political processes that might block achievement but could, when conditions were supportive, facilitate economic and social advancement. What we needed was advice and guidance about what could be done to make political contexts more responsive to inclusive development (usually labelled as 'rural development' in those dim and distant days). The research in this book represents a significant step in making the understanding of development more politically savvy by developing the theoretical apparatus and knowledge base to support better-informed development policy and practice.

This book provides:

1. a detailed and original theoretical framework that shapes ESID's work and, we hope, that of other researchers;
2. a systematic review of the evidence about the politics of 'what works' in achieving inclusive development;
3. a set of clear and concise propositions about how to advance such knowledge in a policy relevant fashion.

Its editors—Sam Hickey, Kunal Sen, and Badru Bukenya—are to be congratulated for succeeding in editing a volume that is both grounded in the classic tomes of social science theory and highly topical.

Over the last ten to fifteen years the context for development has changed profoundly and that change continues at a phenomenal rate. The geography of wealth is shifting east to Asia. Sub-Saharan Africa, long viewed through a lens of Afro-pessimism, is tipped for investors as a future growth pole. The majority of the world's extremely poor people now live in countries classified as middle-income. Connectivity grows at unprecedented rates, raising the prospects for improved transparency of public and private actors—perhaps, even improved accountability. And, with the rise of remittances and new sources of development finance, traditional foreign aid increasingly seems like a minor factor in the development arena.

But, not all is good news. Two particular issues stand out. First, economic inequality is reaching unimaginable levels, with Oxfam reporting that the world's eighty-five wealthiest people own the same as the three billion poorest. Economic power and political influence are increasingly concentrated in the hands of small numbers of supranational mega-billionaires far removed from contact with the day-to-day problems and opportunities of the majority. Just as alarming, it is clear that the global capitalist system that produces and distributes wealth is environmentally unsustainable. The system that has underpinned economic growth and human development will have to be transformed if future generations are to have a chance of experiencing a 'good life'.

In such a context, the theoretical contribution of this book is of particular significance, as it moves the focus from statics and equilibria to change and dynamics. It takes us beyond the 'new' new institutional economics of growth to understanding how dynamic political settlements shape patterns of accumulation, social provisioning, and social recognition as they impact on state capacity and elite commitment (or lack of commitment) to development. Building on the work of Douglass North, Daron Acemoglu, James Robinson, and Mushtaq Khan, the book's analytical framework integrates critical additional elements: the role of ideas (alongside incentives); the possibility of popular agency; the influence of transnational factors;

the opportunity for emerging coalitions to promote inclusive development; and the dynamics of political regime change in growth processes. Beneath this framework lies the constant interplay of politics and power relations, as those with power seek to maintain the status quo and new actors and emerging coalitions seek change.

While this book is a scholarly output, it identifies implications for policy and practice (for ESID outputs targeted on policy audiences, see the Briefing Papers on our website). The universal prescriptions of the original new institutionalism—democracy, decentralization, strengthening the demand side, and so on—are shown to be double-edged: they may weaken rather than strengthen development outcomes. While the volume critiques 'one size fits all', it does not shift to the other extreme—'context is everything'! It identifies a typology of political conditions that, in the future, will seek to generate type-specific findings to stand alongside case-specific conclusions. Whether these findings will be able to overcome 'the barriers' that political analysis faces in aid agencies remains a question for future analysis.

As CEO of ESID, I want to wholeheartedly thank the book's editors, contributors, and all those who have contributed to its production (ESID and BWPI's excellent support staff, scores of reviewers, research assistants, and partners on four continents) for their efforts. I hope you enjoy reading it—even more, I hope it contributes to deepening your understanding of the politics of inclusive development.

David Hulme

This document is an output from a project funded by the UK Aid from the UK Department for International Development (DFID) for the benefit of developing countries. However, the views expressed and information contained in it are not necessarily those of, or endorsed by, DFID, which can accept no responsibility for such views or information or for any reliance placed on them.

Contents

Contents

List of Figures

List of Tables

List of Abbreviations

ACA	Association of Water Committees (Angola)
AIM	Alternative Investment Market, part of London Stock Exchange
APPP	Africa Power and Politics Programme
AR	Acemoglu and Robinson
ARENA	Nationalist Republican Alliance (El Salvador)
Busan HLF	Busan High-Level Forum (South Korea)
CADFund	China–Africa Development Fund
CAFTA-DR	US-Central American Free Trade Agreement
CAITEC	Chinese Academy of International Trade and Economic Cooperation
CEDAW	Convention on Elimination of All Forms of Discrimination
CEPAL	Economic Commission for Latin America
CFG	Community Forest Groups
CFS	Centre for the Future State
CIF	China International Fund
CNPC	Chinese National Petroleum Company
CPA	Comprehensive Peace Agreement (Sudan)
CPC-ID	Communist Party of China's International Department
CPP	Convention People's Party (Ghana)
CSG	Child Support Grant (South Africa)
CSO	Civil Society Organization
CSR	Corporate Social Responsibility
CSRC	Crisis States Research Centre
CSWI	Commission on the Status of Women (India)
DAC	Development Assistance Committee
DFID	Department for International Development (UK)
EAM	East Asian Model
EFA	Education for All
EGDI	Expert Group on Development Issues (Sweden)

List of Abbreviations

EITI	Extractive Industries Transparency Initiative
ELF	Ethnolinguistic Fragmentation
EPRDF	Ethiopian Peoples' Revolutionary Democratic Front
ESID	Effective States and Inclusive Development
FDI	Foreign Direct Investment
FISP	Farm Input Subsidy Programme (Malawi)
FMLN	Farabundo Martí National Liberation Front (El Salvador)
FOCAC	Forum on China–Africa Cooperation
FRIDE	Foundation for International Relations and Foreign Dialogue
GEG	Global Economic Governance Programme
GNI	Gross National Income
GNPOC	Greater Nile Petroleum Operating Company
GRN	Gabinete de Reconstrução Nacional (Angola's Reconstruction Office)
ICMM	International Council on Mining and Metals
ICRG	International Country Risk Guide
ICSD	Integrated Child Development Scheme (India)
ICSID	International Centre for the Settlement of Investment Disputes
IDS	Institute of Development Studies (UK)
IFAD	International Fund for Agricultural Development
IFC	International Finance Corporation
IFI	international financial institution
IFPRI	International Food Policy Research Institute
ILGI	informal local governance institution
ILO	International Labour Organization
IMF	International Monetary Fund
JFM	Joint Forest Management Groups (India and Nepal)
KDP	Kecamatan Development Program (Indonesia)
LBC	Licensed Buying Companies (Ghana)
LDC	less developed country/ies
MDG	Millennium Development Goal
MEMVR	Routine Road Maintenance Microenterprise (Peru)
MMCP	Making the Most of Commodities Programme
MOFCOM	The Ministry of Commerce of the Government of the People's Republic of China
MOU	Memorandum of Understanding
NAFTA	North American Free Trade Agreement

NDC	National Democratic Congress, formerly PNDC (Ghana)
NGO	non-governmental organization
NIF	National Islamic Front (Sudan)
NREGA	National Rural Employment Guarantee Act (India)
NRM	National Resistance Movement (Uganda)
NSAP	National Social Assistance Programme (India)
ODI	Overseas Development Institute
PBF	Performance-Based Financing initiative
PCR	Rural Roads Program (Peru)
PDS	Public Distribution Scheme (India)
PNDC	Provisional National Defence Council, later NDC (Ghana)
PRSP	Poverty Reduction Strategies Papers
ROL	Rule of Law
RPC	Research Programme Consortia
RPF	Rwandan Patriotic Front
SEA	Strategic Environment Assessment
SERNAM	Servicio Nacional de la Mujer (Chile)
SEZ	Special Economic Zones (Africa)
SfL	School for Life (Ghana)
Sida	Swedish International Development Cooperation Agency
SME	small or medium-sized enterprise
SOE	state-owned enterprise
SPLM/A	Sudan People's Liberation Movement/Army
TNC	transnational corporations
TSX	Toronto Stock Exchange
TVE	township–village enterprise
UNDRIP	United Nations Declaration on the Rights of Indigenous Peoples
UPA	United Progressive Alliance (India)
VDC	Village Development Committees (Malawi)
WDR	World Development Report
WHO	World Health Organization
WID	Women in Development

List of Contributors

Armando Barrientos is Professor and Research Director at the Brooks World Poverty Institute at the University of Manchester in the UK. He is also co-director of the International Research Initiative on Brazil and Africa. His research interests focus on the linkages existing between welfare programmes and labour markets in developing countries, and on policies addressing poverty, vulnerability, and population ageing. His most recent book is *Social Assistance in Developing Countries* (Cambridge University Press, 2013).

Anthony Bebbington is Higgins Professor of Environment and Society and Director of the Graduate School of Geography, Clark University, USA. He is also a Research Associate of the Centro Peruano de Estudios Sociales, Peru and a Professorial Research Fellow at the University of Manchester. His work addresses the political ecology of rural change, with a particular focus on extractive industries and socio-environmental conflicts, social movements, indigenous organizations, and livelihoods, particularly in South and Central America. His most recent book is *Subterranean Struggles: New Dynamics of Mining, Oil and Gas in Latin America* (University of Texas Press, 2013) with Jeffrey Bury.

Badru Bukenya is a development analyst and practitioner. He completed his PhD at the Institute of Development Policy and Management (IDPM) and then worked as a Research Associate with the Effective States and Inclusive Development Research Centre (ESID), both at the University of Manchester. He is currently a lecturer in the department of Social Work and Social Administration at Makerere University Kampala. He has previously worked with Uganda's largest NGO, The AIDS Support Organisation (TASO). His research focuses on the politics of civil society, service delivery, social protection, state-building, and citizenship formation in Africa.

Deval Desai is a research associate at the School of Oriental and African Studies (SOAS), University of London. He also works with the World Bank on justice and equity for the poor, where he helped establish a justice and conflict programme. He currently advises the UN on rule-of-law issues in the post-2015 Agenda, and is an invited member of the UN roster of experts on the rule of law and legal empowerment. He has published on these issues in a range of academic and policy fora. He is a member of the Bar of England and Wales.

Arjan de Haan is a development expert who focuses on public policy and poverty in Asia. He leads the IDRC programme Supporting Inclusive Growth, based in Ottawa, Canada. He has previously worked at the Institute of Social Studies (Erasmus University Rotterdam) in The Hague, where he was convenor of the master's programme in social policy and led the development of a database called Indices of Social Development. He has published widely and is co-editor of the *Canadian Journal of Development Studies*.

Sam Hickey is Professor of Politics and Development. He is currently the joint Director of Research within the DFID-funded Effective States and Inclusive Development (ESID) Research Centre (<http://www.effective-states.org>) and Associate Director of the Brooks World Poverty Institute. His research examines the politics of development and poverty reduction, with specific reference to sub-Saharan Africa, and has been has published extensively in the leading development studies journals. This includes work on natural resource governance, social exclusion and adverse incorporation, citizenship and participation, social movements and NGOs, the politics of social protection, and the use of political analysis in international development.

Matthias vom Hau is an assistant professor of comparative politics at the Institut Barcelona d'Estudis Internacionals (IBEI). A political sociologist by training, he has a PhD from Brown University and previously held a postdoctoral fellowship at the University of Manchester. Matthias' research is on the intersection between identity politics, state formation, and development, with a regional focus on Latin America. He has published widely on nationalism and state formation, and the historical roots of social provision and growth in the region. His current work investigates how ethnic-based collective action affects the institutional competence of states to provide public goods and promote development.

Simeen Mahmud is Lead Researcher at the BRAC Institute of Governance and Development (BIGD), at BRAC University. Her past research focused on citizenship and participation, education and gender, and women's work and empowerment in Bangladesh. She is currently working on social policy, with a focus on health and education; the construction of citizen identity and practice in difficult environments; and the effect of health and micro-credit interventions on women's well-being.

Claire Mcloughlin is a Senior Research Fellow based in the International Development Department, University of Birmingham, where she undertakes research for the GSDRC and the Developmental Leadership Programme (DLP). Her recent research has focused on the politics of service delivery, and the effects of service provision on state-building processes in post-conflict states. She is completing her doctoral research in IDD on the relationship between education and state legitimacy in Sri Lanka.

Giles Mohan is Professor of International Development for the Open University. His work concerns the politics of development, particularly the intermingling of territorial scales and transnational networks. He was a handling editor of the *Review of African Political Economy* and a member of the editorial boards of *Political Geography, Antipode, Geography Compass*, and the *International Development Planning Review*. His most recent work concerns the role of China in African development and has been funded by a series of ESRC grants. Giles has published extensively in geography, development studies, and African studies journals and has consulted for a range of BBC documentaries on issues of international development. His book, with Marcus Power and May Tan-Mullins, entitled *China's Resource Diplomacy in Africa: Powering Development?* was published by Palgrave Macmillan in 2012. Zed Books published his latest book, entitled *Chinese Migrants and Africa's Development* in 2014.

Paul Mosley is Professor of Economics in the Department of Economics, University of Sheffield. His main research interests are in economic development, with related interests in economic history, social policy, and the politics of economic policymaking. His recent publications include *Out of the Poverty Trap: Overcoming Financial Exclusion in the Inner City* (Routledge, 2011), *The Politics of Poverty Reduction* (Oxford University Press, 2012), and *Sir Arthur Lewis: A Biography* (Palgrave Macmillan, 2013).

Sohela Nazneen is a Professor at the Department of International Relations, University of Dhaka and a lead researcher at BRAC Institute of Governance and Development (BIGD), BRAC University. Her research mainly focuses on institutional analysis of gender, particularly in the areas of governance, rural and urban livelihoods. Her latest publication is *Voicing Demands: Feminist Activism in Transitional Context* (Zed Books, 2014), a co-edited book with Maheen Sultan.

Sony Pellissery is Associate Professor at the National Law School of India University, Bangalore. Previously he was with the Institute of Rural Management, Anand, India. He is a public policy specialist with particular interest in the politics of service provision in developing countries. His 2009 monograph on the politics of social protection in rural India is a treatise on the implementation of welfare state policies at the local level. In 2009 he was awarded the India Social Science Research Award by the International Development Research Centre, Canada.

Kunal Sen is Professor of Development Economics and Associate Director of the Brooks World Poverty Institute at the University of Manchester. His current research is on the political economy determinants of inclusive development, particularly within the DFID-UK-funded Effective States and Inclusive Development Research Centre, based in the University of Manchester, of which he is the Joint Research Director. Professor Sen's most recent books are *State-Business Relations and Economic Development in Africa and India* (Routledge, 2012) and *Trade Policy, Inequality and Performance in Indian Manufacturing* (Routledge, 2008). He has also published over sixty articles in leading economics and development journals. He won the Sanjaya Lall Prize in 2006 and Dudley Seers Prize in 2003 for his publications.

Prerna Singh is Assistant Professor at the Department of Government at Harvard University. She is also a Faculty Associate at the Weatherhead Center for International Affairs and the South Asia Initiative at Harvard. Her research and teaching interests encompass the field of comparative politics, with a regional specialization in South Asia. Prerna's work is centrally concerned with questions of identity politics. Specifically, she seeks to understand the causes and consequences of the various manifestations of identity and to explore the relationship of identity politics with institutions and development.

Ward Warmerdam is a PhD candidate at the international Institute of Social Studies (ISS) in The Hague. His thesis examines China's engagement with Africa, the lessons from China's own development experience, and how these inform China's aid principles and practices.

Michael Woolcock is Lead Social Development Specialist in the World Bank's Development Research Group and a (part-time) Lecturer in Public Policy at Harvard University's Kennedy School of Government. He is a founder of the World Bank's Justice for the Poor programme, and has published extensively in fields ranging from history and law to the social sciences and humanities. His current work focuses on building strategies for effective implementation in low-income countries and for assessing the generalizability of claims regarding the impact of development interventions in novel contexts and at larger scales of operation.

Part I
Introduction

1

Exploring the Politics of Inclusive Development: Towards a New Conceptual Approach

Sam Hickey, Kunal Sen, and Badru Bukenya

Introduction: The Politics of Inclusive Development

The recognition that politics plays a central role in shaping the prospects for development in poor countries constitutes one of the most significant advances that development theory and practice has made since the turn of the millennium. From being a marginal concern that the often technocratic world of international development struggled to deal with (Carothers and de Gramont 2013), there is now widespread acceptance that politics is critical to both the reduction and reproduction of poverty. This holds across all dimensions of development, including the delivery of basic services and social protection, the promotion of job-creating forms of growth, the governance of resources and the extension of recognition to marginal people and places, including women. Politics is now seen as a significant force at each stage of the development process, from shaping processes of exclusion and inequality to raising awareness and recognition of these as problems of (in)justice, and from determining which policies get adopted through to if and how they get implemented. Indeed, all of the most influential analyses of long-run development to emerge of late have argued strongly that politics is the critical factor (Acemoglu and Robinson 2012; Fukuyama 2011; Khan 2010; North et al. 2009), albeit with differing approaches as to what 'politics' might consist of.

This recognition has catalysed a widening and deepening of research into the specific role that politics plays in shaping development. In an effort to offer a systematic survey of the growing field of politics and development, and to relate this to the emergence of new theoretical approaches, this collection draws from the initial research findings of the Effective States and Inclusive Development (ESID) research centre, which exists to identify and investigate the kinds of politics that can help to secure inclusive development and how these can be promoted.[1] Authors were charged with systematically exploring the evidence from the available literature on how politics shaped the delivery of development in their specific domain, including growth, the governance of natural resources, basic services and social protection, the rule of law, the politics of recognition, and the influence of transnational factors. Alongside this inductive approach, ESID also reviewed the main conceptual contributions to understanding the politics of development, both in general terms and with specific reference to the concepts of state capacity and elite commitment which had been identified as critical in many studies of the politics of development. This introduction brings together the main conceptual and empirical insights from this body of work, and uses it as the basis for suggesting some next steps for building a theoretically informed and policy-relevant programme of research that can help take the growing field of politics and development forward in coherent ways.

The remainder of this section briefly defines what we mean by 'politics' and 'inclusive development', before the next summarizes the key findings of our studies according to the following domains of development: accumulation and growth, including through the exploitation of natural resources; the promotion and protection of social and civil rights through basic services, social protection, and the rule of law; the recognition of difference and inequality; and finally the transnational politics of development. We then attempt to synthesize across these findings to identify the broader themes and issues that emerge, and to put these into conversation with the current literature on how we should conceptualize and theorize the politics of development. This involves a critical engagement with the most influential body of thinking on this at the current time, namely work that seeks to go beyond the dominance of new institutionalist thinking over good governance debates, including the 'political settlements' perspective recently developed by Mushtaq Khan (2010), the major contributions of North et al. (2009) on 'violence and social orders', and also Acemoglu and Robinson's (2012) work on 'inclusive institutions'. Whilst noting the many points of convergence between the findings of our systematic reviews and this new perspective, our findings suggest the need to extend these neo-institutionalist approaches to incorporate a broader view of how politics shapes development agendas, processes, and outcomes. This leads us to tentatively propose the

---

[1] For more details, see <http://www.effective-states.org>.

outlines of a new conceptual approach that goes beyond institutional and behavioural studies of politics to include a deeper sense of the forms of politics and power relations that underlie the critical issues of state capacity and elite commitment that our chapters draw attention to. The final section uses these combined insights to suggest the conceptual and methodological contours for the next phase of primary research into the politics and development.

Some definitional questions first. In terms of 'politics', we follow Adrian Leftwich's (2004) definition of politics as 'all the processes of conflict, co-operation and negotiation on taking decisions about how resources are to be owned, used, produced and distributed', although we also consider the struggle over *ideas* (as well as resources) to be a fundamental and significant element of politics, an issue to which we return below. We define inclusive development as a process that occurs when social and material benefits are equitably distributed across divides within societies, across income groups, genders, ethnicities, regions, religious groups, and others. These benefits necessarily comprise not only economic and material gains but enhanced well-being and capabilities as well as social and political empowerment being widely experienced. This definition involves at least two important moves. The first, and most familiar, is to go beyond a narrow understanding of development as a primarily economic process to one with an integral focus on the achievement of equity and the rights and status of citizenship. This is important here not just in ethical terms but also because comparative historical evidence suggests that the forms of politics that have underpinned inclusive forms of development (e.g. Evans 2010; Sandbrook et al. 2007; Walton 2010), differ in significant respects from those associated with economic growth (e.g. World Bank 2008a). The second move is to shift the focus beyond 'poverty' and 'the poor'. As argued elsewhere (Hickey 2008), this discourse can make it difficult to think politically and may distract from a focus on achieving the fuller goal of social justice implied by the term 'inclusive development'. For example, people rarely self-identify or organize themselves as 'the poor', which makes it difficult to appreciate popular agency through a poverty lens. Most poverty analysis relies on an analytical separation of the poor from the rest of society that tends to become moralized (Rothstein 2002), often in ways that cast responsibility for both poverty and poverty reduction on the poor themselves and to therefore undermine the case for elite groups to support large-scale public action.

However, it is important here to go beyond the notion that 'inclusion' is uniformly a 'good thing': a misconception that a good deal of critical thinking on poverty analysis has sought to problematize (Green 2009; Hickey and du Toit 2007; Mosse 2010). It is now acknowledged that being included on adverse terms in dominant political, economic, and social orders can be disempowering for weaker groups, including women (Jackson 1999) and minority ethnic groups (Masaki 2010), who become incorporated on subordinate terms and may be denied the agency that can come from operating beyond the confines of hegemonic formations. The focus on equity and empowerment within the definition we adopt represents a relational understanding of how development unfolds (Mosse 2010), one that avoids simplistic readings of inclusion and insists that sustainable and inclusive forms of development involve progressive changes to the power relations that underpin poverty and exclusion. The intention, then, is to develop a more encompassing and relational view of development that problematizes the workings of societies rather than the characteristics of particular groups and involves thinking in broader terms around how to achieve social justice, towards which poverty reduction is an essential but insufficient step. There is also a more instrumental argument for focusing on inclusion rather than poverty, in that it enables development thinking and strategy to include but extend beyond a focus on 'the poor' to include the non-poor whose political support may be required to sustain broader-based and more sustainable interventions (e.g. Nelson 2003). Bringing better-off groups into the equation means including those citizens who are often more adept at attracting public goods provision and at maintaining a better quality of service delivery through social accountability mechanisms.

What Does the Evidence Tell Us about the Politics of Inclusive Development in Different Domains?

This definition of inclusive development leads to a focus on at least three domains: economic, social, and political, and the collection we present here is organized in these terms. Drawing on insights from theories of social justice (Young 1990; Fraser 2009; Lister 2008), this means we need to understand not only the politics of accumulation and growth, but also of both redistribution and recognition. Whilst the former allows us to deal with the material aspects of development, the focus on recognition reflects the extent to which cultural and political forms of exclusion and inclusion also matter for development. Working across these different dimensions and domains of development also extends both the range of policy areas the collection talks to and enables us to engage with and critically assess recent conceptual advances from a greater range of perspectives. This section sets out the key findings from each substantive section of the book in turn, starting with accumulation and growth.

The Politics of Accumulation

Compared to other domains, there is a relatively rich literature on the politics of economic growth and development, most notably around the role of developmental states. Although work in this tradition has recently been extended to include more social aspects of development (e.g. Evans 2010; Leftwich 2008), the main focus remains firmly on economic growth and development, usually in the form of industrialization (Evans 1995; Johnson 1982; Kohli 2004; Leftwich 1995; World Bank 2008a; Vu 2007). Centred mainly on the post-war success stories of South East and East Asia, and to some extent Latin America, the generic lessons have tended to focus on the role of highly competent and committed bureaucrats and political leaders with the capacity to deliver certain public goods, to work closely with and to discipline capital on the basis of its 'embedded autonomy', and to place limits on the potentially fragmentary demands of disparate social groups. Contextual factors have also emerged as significant, as with the threat of violence and disorder from either within or without (Henley 2014; Routley 2012). More recently, the field has moved to examine some of these features in more depth, as with the role of state–business relations in shaping economic policy (Sen 2012), and both intra-elite and elite–mass relations (Vu 2007). However, stronger moves are required in this direction in order to attain the level of depth and nuance required to generate more insightful and actionable findings. As well as exploring the political factors in more depth, there is also a need to disaggregate and differentiate between the different types and levels of development involved here, whether in terms of the rate and type of growth that is pursued or the domain within which growth strategies are located.

For example, Kunal Sen argues in his chapter that the forms of politics that are associated with the initial stages of take-off are likely to be different to those associated with sustaining growth over a longer period. This chapter is informed by the insight from the development states literature that growth often precedes the advent of democracy, and the work of Mushtaq Khan (2006) which shows that no countries in the developing world have achieved economic take-off as a result of first establishing institutions associated with good governance. Rather, what matters more for growth accelerations are informal institutions such as patron–client networks that are capable of securing credible commitment amongst a limited number of elites, rather than more open and formal institutions such as laws and regulations. However, for economic growth to be maintained over time would seem to require that such deal-making becomes more open and ordered, and also a commitment amongst elites to invest in the forms of state capacity that can allow for the provision of high-quality public goods that matter for growth and structural transformation (e.g. infrastructure) and the overcoming of coordination failures (Evans 1995). Therefore, while clientelist political settlements (Khan 2010) with predominantly informal institutions would be more likely to characterize growth accelerations, hybrid contexts with a mix of informal and formal institutions would be more likely to characterize growth maintenance. This has important implications for development policy, and strongly suggests that efforts to implant Western-style institutions in developing countries during the take-off phase are misplaced. Sen notes that current theoretical contributions to the politics of economic growth, including those by Acemoglu and Robinson (2012) and Khan (2010) do not offer a unified theory of the underlying political dynamics of the 'stop and go' economic growth that one observes so frequently in developing countries, or a convincing account of the political drivers of institutional change from growth stagnation or collapse to growth acceleration, and then on to growth sustenance, and that this should be the key focus for future research in this area.

There is also a growing awareness that the main sector/s which stimulate growth in particular economies is of great political as well as economic significance for inclusive development. This is particularly important in terms of shaping the relative levels of labour/capital-intensity associated with a growth strategy, which goes a long way to defining how inclusive such strategies will be. Recent research has shown that the choice of such strategies is closely shaped by the bargaining power of key economic and social actors and the relationships they have been able to forge with the state and parts thereof (e.g. see Nattrass and Seekings 2010 on South Africa). Further research along the same lines within ESID argues that firms put different kinds of pressures on governments to act in particular ways depending on the extent to which the firms are producing for domestic or international markets, and the availability of rent-seeking opportunities in the relevant sector. For example, whereas manufacturing capital may lobby governments to invest in infrastructure and human capability-building that requires heavy investments in public infrastructure and which has large spillover effects for the rest of the economy, rentier forms of capital that rely on exports for growth is likelier to request more enclave-based forms of support (Werker and Pritchett 2012). In its most extreme form, found most clearly in states that rely heavily on natural resources, this can lead to both economic and political versions of the resource curse (Ross 2012). Given that growing numbers of developing countries have recently discovered often large levels of natural resources, it is particularly important to understand the politics of natural resource governance.

Tony Bebbington's chapter analyses the institutional and political relationships that govern the interactions between natural resource extraction, economy, and society, relationships that will help define the implications of resource extraction for democracy and the qualities of growth. With a focus on the mining and hydrocarbon sectors, he explores the conditions under which these relationships are likely to be reproduced or changed, and the ways in which they might mediate the interactions between extraction and inclusion. The framework used to understand these processes is grounded in two perspectives, the first of which draws on the literature on political settlements, contentious politics, and the politics of ideas, placing particular emphasis on the role of social mobilization and political coalitions in processes of institutional change. The second perspective engages with the particular relationships of scale, space, and time that characterize the natural resource sector and give it specificity. He emphasizes that these questions of space and time are especially important in influencing how the growth of an extractive economy shapes the relationships between growth, redistribution, and the politics of recognition. The implication is that any effort to understand the governance of extraction and of its relationships to development must be spatially and historically explicit. In light of these arguments the chapter closes with a discussion of the conditions that might favour the emergence of institutional arrangements under which resource extraction is more likely to foster inclusive development.

The focus on coalitions and the linkages across the different domains of development also features strongly in Paul Mosley's chapter on the fiscal politics of development, which acts as a bridge between this and the next section of the book on social provisioning. Mosley argues that although the poor, acting on their own, are politically weak, there are, nonetheless, ways in which they can make themselves essential to the elite. The most prevalent form of this is through forming coalitions with them that are mutually beneficial, either through the promise of electoral support or threat of unrest. This political process, which for Mosley can be seen playing itself out in relation to particular policy processes and through the establishment of particular institutions, has enabled poverty in some countries and regions (e.g. Ghana, Uganda) to fall dramatically. Informed by his earlier work on the politics of poverty reduction (2012), Mosley analyses the distributional impact of public expenditure and taxation, with an emphasis on the sectors of agriculture and social protection, and on the instruments of input subsidy and 'progressive' export taxation. Here direct spending on agriculture as well as spending on complementary sectors such as rural infrastructure and education have been found to offer critical escape routes out of poverty by 'increasing the productivity of the rural poor in the short term and, in the medium term, paving the way for the possibility of small-scale-based industrialization for export'. Mosley also tackles the issue of how to make taxation pro-poor in low-income countries, inspired by the cases of Uganda and Ghana, where the focus was shifted away from levying taxes on exports to imports, thus enabling governments of these counties to shift some of the tax burden away from the rural poor and onto comparatively wealthier urban consumers. The decision by the Zambian government to impose a tax on the profits of mining companies, which was earmarked for social protection programmes, is flagged as a key strategy for joining up processes of accumulation with progressive forms of redistribution. Such moves send strong 'signals' to poorer groups and facilitates their inclusion within 'pro-poor coalitions', and reflects the growing sense in which policies play intensely political functions in developing countries (Henley 2014).

The Politics of Social and Legal Citizenship: Promoting and Protecting the Rights of the Poor?

Although not as extensive as the literature on economic development, a growing number of studies have examined the role of politics in shaping the provision of services aimed at protecting and promoting the social and civic rights of marginal groups. This has been particularly the case with social service provision, whether directed at raising human capabilities in general terms (e.g. Carbone 2009a; Evans 2010; Nelson 2007), or in relation to specific sectors such as education (e.g. Grindle 2004; Kosack 2012; Stasavage 2005) and the fast-growing literature on the politics of social protection (e.g. Graham 1995, 2002; Hickey 2009; Nelson 2003). The literature has become increasingly nuanced and also divided in recent years, particularly concerning whether processes of democratization help or hinder the delivery of services, between bottom-up versus up-down forms of accountability and concerning the centralized or decentralized shape of the state. Our systematic reviews of the available evidence engage directly with these debates and show the need to move beyond often-redundant conflicts between apparently polarized positions by drawing attention to the deeper forms of politics and power relations at play.

Our chapters strongly support the general thesis that politics closely shapes the effectiveness and quality of service delivery and social protection. Claire Mcloughlin reviews eight successful cases of delivery drawn from seven countries, namely Bangladesh, Rwanda, Ghana, Ethiopia, Indonesia, Malawi, and Peru, and across four sectors: maternal and child health, basic education, rural roads, and agricultural marketing. The chapter traces the main characteristics of the political environment for these cases at three levels, from the national political context through the politics of sector policy-making to the micro politics of implementation, and links them directly to levels of performance and outcomes at the point of delivery. In their chapter, Armando Barrientos and Sony Pellissery examine the significance of politics in the rise of social assistance programmes in developing countries in the last decade, and argue that politics has been crucial to the adoption, design, and implementation of social assistance programmes. They develop a framework for distinguishing the different dimensions of influence, including the role of democracy, the bureaucracy, and civil society, which is then applied to the development of social assistance in India, Brazil, and South Africa. This comparative perspective is particularly helpful in exemplifying the framework from different contextual viewpoints, and contributes new insights into the specific forms of politics that shape social assistance.

Both chapters join broader calls for a move beyond the presumption that civil society and bottom-up pressures can play a critical role in improving the responsiveness and accountability of governments with regards to service delivery (e.g. World Bank 2003). So, although the role of civil society and an active media was found to be important in catalysing state responsiveness in some cases, the available evidence on the political drivers of social provisioning strongly suggests that the often unqualified support for bottom-up pressures is misplaced, both in terms of overlooking the role of more top-down pressures and for obscuring the forms of popular politics that may make a difference. In terms of the latter, Mcloughlin suggests that pro-poor service provision might occur where there are forms of social accountability that draw on moral norms of reciprocity, are locally grounded, and build on a culture of participation, rather than being driven by the more professionalized and technical worlds of NGOs promoting particular social accountability mechanisms or 'widgets' (Joshi and Houtzager 2012). Importantly, both chapters also point to the significance of more political and top-down drivers of performance. For Mcloughlin, strong top-down authority and leadership are critical in ensuring that policies are carried through from their adoption to actual implementation. Barrientos and Pellissery observe that the expansion of social assistance from small privileged groups to broader target populations in line with universal principles, does not emerge easily, and often involves intense political struggles. Whereas civil society actors played a key role in expanding social assistance in India, it was political parties who were the critical actors in Brazil and South Africa, a finding which echoes the wider calls to look beyond civil to political society when it comes to the politics of poverty reduction (Houtzager and Moore 2003; Hickey and Bracking 2005). Again, coalitions between such actors may be required to realign policy adoption and implementation in favour of more marginal social groups (Leftwich 2010). Such findings are closely aligned with the growing evidence that citizens may lack the power to alter the incentives which shape the capacity and commitment of governments and elites at both national and local levels (Booth 2005), and support the growing emphasis on identifying ways of promoting different modes of accountability (e.g. Joshi and Houtzager 2012; Deveranjan et al. 2011).

This debate overlaps to some extent with increasingly contentious discussions concerning the links between democracy and the delivery of social services. For example, Mcloughlin draws on recent research into the politics of improving maternal health services and outcomes in Rwanda to suggest that a powerful and ideologically committed political party or leader may be able to enforce high-quality forms of service delivery even in the context of limited democratization and bottom-up pressures. This finding is at odds with much of the literature on the politics of service delivery which suggests that democratization is a critical factor here. However, this literature is itself increasingly split between those who associate the increased regularity of elections with increased levels of social provisioning (e.g. Stasavage 2005) and those who point out that political party competition can reduce the extent to which the voice of marginal groups is influential over public policy, and also that political competition in many poor countries has had the damaging effect of driving up the intensity of clientelist forms of politics (Carbone 2009b). Within such contexts, and in line with the chapter from Mosley in this collection, it may be that increased social provisioning reflects the power of poor groups to present a credible threat to leaders and/or form a coalition with elites (Kosack 2012). Our contributors find evidence to support both sides of this debate. For example, Mcloughlin notes that political party competition has driven up provision for child and maternal health in Bangladesh, as successive ruling parties attempt to scale up provision in order to outperform their opponents. However, the downside is that increased party control over the distribution of resources has increasingly politicized service delivery at local levels and reduced the extent to which the bureaucracy is delivering public goods on an impersonal or universal basis. What may matter most here are the particular constituencies that a regime is seeking to woo. Levels of 'political will' for primary education in Ghana, for example, have been shown to fluctuate over time according to the extent to which the ruling party has been dependent on the support of the poor, and the extent to which the interests of the poor were articulated by a political entrepreneur (Kosack 2012). Similarly, Mcloughlin shows that agricultural policies gained particular political salience in Ghana and Malawi under regimes that courted the support of farmers, and continued to be a central source of state legitimacy where they subsequently attracted a large basis of citizen support.

This evidence therefore tends to suggest that discussions over top-down and bottom-up forms of accountability and between democratic and more 'authoritarian' forms of rule are hinged in the wrong place. What matters here is not so much the presence of formal political institutions such as parties or elections but rather the underlying forms of politics and power relations which shape their operation, driven to some extent by calculations around political returns that are made by political actors at all levels. This perspective is gaining ground (e.g. Kjær and Therkildsen 2012), and is increasingly summarized in the language of 'political settlements', a concept we return to below in more depth.

The final issue covered with regards to how politics shapes the delivery of services and social protection concerns the structural form that the state takes, and particularly the degree of decentralization. Barrientos and Pellissery argue that the level of decentralization does not appear critical in explaining the success or failure of social assistance programmes, a finding supported by other work on the politics of social protection (Hickey 2009). In some countries, like India and Brazil, decentralization offered great promise whereas in South Africa it was the centralization of authority that was associated with numerous advantages for the programmes there. This observation means that social protection programmes are likely to be influenced by the particular context in which they emerge and therefore likely to produce dynamics that are difficult to compare across time and space.

Although the majority of the literature in this field to date has focused on how politics shapes social provisioning, increased attention has started to fall on the political impacts of social provisioning, including on state capacity and legitimacy (Bukenya 2013; van de Walle and Scott 2011) and the broader social contract (Barrientos 2013; Hickey 2009). The importance of this new agenda emerges strongly from our chapters here, and forms a central part of the conceptual framework that we propose at the end of the chapter. For example, Barrientos and Pellissery show how long-established programmes of social assistance have a feedback effect on politics at both local and national levels. At the national level for instance, incumbent politicians and parties obtain significant political support as a result of introducing such programmes. Similarly, some political elites at the local levels have managed to manipulate the programmes to serve their political interests, suggesting that such programmes may in some contexts deepen regressive forms of politics rather than the more progressive building of social contracts.

A rich territory for exploring the forms of politics that underlie and help to shape the rules of the game concerns the rule of law, which Deval Desai and Michael Woolcock define as a system that informs people of what to expect from others through durable and enforceable rules applying equally to all constituent members of a given juridical space. In their thorough examination of 'the politics of what works' with regard to the rule-of-law interventions in developing countries, Desai and Woolcock explore how contests among elites and between elites and end users shape institutions through a contested, iterative, and dynamic process that, in any given setting, is likely to yield an idiosyncratic outcome borne of a unique hybrid mix of local and external inputs. They present the politics of the rule of law as deeply complex and inherently multi-directional: elites, for example, certainly use the rule of law, but legalization is powerful and can be used in unpredictable ways against elites by other elite groups or by non-elite actors. They also argue that the political salience, legitimacy, and action-ability of such understandings must be negotiated anew in each setting, between different epistemic groups (professions, users, policymakers) and across divides of gender, ideology, and class. More broadly, their chapter reveals something of the tension between the workings of political settlements and how the rule of law becomes established. One of the key insights from recent work on political settlements (Khan 2010) and limited access orders (North et al. 2009) that we discuss in more detail below, is that elites will only agree to the establishment and functioning of institutions, including and perhaps particularly around the rule of law, if such institutions ensure the distribution of resources and status in their direction. To the extent that the rule of law can act as a constraint to elite behaviour, then elites may have good reasons to restrict the establishment of the rule of law and particularly its progressive roll out beyond the limits of the initial elite bargain (cf. North et al. 2009). Much of this interplay between the rule of law and the type of political settlement will be determined within specific contexts, and involve the specific interests and ideas that elites have around the rule of law systems, and cannot be collapsed into a deterministic or *ex ante* model.

Our chapters in this section offer important and innovative suggestions concerning the role of future research in the field. As Mcloughlin notes, the widespread consensus that politics matters for effective service provision needs to be matched by studies that systematically integrate political analysis to produce robust evidence that can inform policy and practice. Similarly, Desai and Woolcock find that 'more research' as conventionally understood will only yield marginal improvements in conceptual clarity and to our cumulative empirical knowledge of the dynamic relationship between rule of law, politics, and development. Rather, they offer concrete ideas on how the rigour and relevance of rule-of-law interventions from both an analytical and practical standpoint could be enhanced. First, they propose the need, by scholars and practitioners, to invest in richer data-gathering exercises, in empirical tasks that de-homogenize people based on conceptual as well as material differences. Secondly, they suggest that more investment in the monitoring and *real-time* evaluation of rule-of-law interventions is needed. Third, and cognizant of the fact that rule of law reform is inherently a site of contestation among social groupings, they recommend that greater effort needs to be extended to invigorating programmes by supporting the construction of spaces for public engagement and discursive participation.

The Politics of Recognition

Whilst the material aspects of development might be delivered through more inclusive forms of growth and the redistributon of goods and opportunities through social provisioning, this does not guarantee that resources will be distributed equitably amongst different socal groups or that each will acheive a full or equal range of human capability development. As feminist theorists of social justice argued some time ago (Young 1990; Fraser 1995), addressing issues of inequality and exclusion involves engaging with the politics of recognition as well as the politics of redistribution. 'Poverty' involves deprivations in terms of status and powerlessness (Mosse 2010) and it is now broadly recognized that any fuller sense of human flourishing needs to take into account the right to have a voice and be represented. This is particularly important in countries where there is a high degree of bivalence (Kabeer 2000) or 'intersectionality' (Collins 2000) across different forms of disadvantage, such as where cultural forms of identy overlap with markers of class as with lower caste groups in India and most indigenous groups in Latin America. In response to social movement (and other) pressures around these issues, there has been an increasing tendency to promote the political representation of marginal groups—whether through quotas for representatives of marginal groups in legislatures at local and national levels, constitutional changes and anti-discrimination legislation, the creation of new states or provinces for marginal regions, or the creation of specific government agencies to act on behalf of marginal groups (e.g. ministries of gender). These forms of 'descriptive' representation are seen both as rights in themselves and as important means through which the status and resources associated with citizenship can be re-allocated and redistributed, thus achieving 'substantive' representation (Waylen 2007).

The conditions under which the politics of recognition becomes recognized and instituted, and the impact that this has on both inclusive development policies and outcomes, remain poorly understood. Taking the case of women, who not only constitute the vast majority of the world's poor but who also continue to face serial injustices across multiple dimensions of development (Jackson 1999), Sohela Nazneen and Simeen Mahmud explore women's political empowerment, drawing on a selection of country cases to analyse the gendered nature of political and policymaking processes and identify the different contextual and structural factors that promote gender-inclusive development policies and outcomes. In terms of gaining political representation for women, they find that the political history of countries matters here, with women's political entitlements often secured at key moments of state formation. This could result from the role played by women's movements in anti-colonial struggles or by women in the conflicts that lead to new regimes being installed. The commitment of political leaders to support women's political rights, for instrumental and/or ideological reasons, is often a critical factor here. Although increasing attention is now falling on whether the increased participation of women in politics has had any direct impacts on processes of governance and development (e.g. Agarwal 2011), the evidence base here is particularly weak. Few analyses of when gender-equity policies become adopted and get implemented include an analysis of the politics involved in these processes. From what little we do know, Nazneen and Mahmud conclude that coalitions involving multiple actors (movements, politicians, bureaucrats/'femocrats') are required to overcome resistance to promoting gender equity, and that transnational discourse and actors can also help create the political and policy space required to promote gender equity policies. The informal modes of politics that often prevail within developing countries, including clientelism, tend to disadvantage women who may lack the resources and connections to play the patronage game effectively. Women's representatives face particular challenges in contexts where traditional leaders and dominant ideologies perpetuate patriarchal notions of gender roles. In general, our findings support the suggestion that enquiries into what shapes the politics of gender equity needs to be framed in terms of broader state–society relations (Htun and Weldon 2010).

Still less is known about what, if any, institutional effects unfold once the politics of recognition becomes institutionalized within political systems. Much of the broader literature on this question tends to assume a negative relationship between the politics of difference and the capacity of states to effectively deliver development, whether specifically in terms of the way in which systems of affirmative action may undermine the capacity of the state to deliver public goods (Gerring et al. 2005) or the more general sense that polities based on multiple identities find it harder to achieve effective forms of governance (Alesina et al. 1999). In their chapter, Prerna Singh and Matthias vom Hau show how scholars have developed sophisticated arguments about how variations in the quality and reach of state services have shaped ethnic-based identification and mobilization (Fearon and Laitin 2003; Yashar 2005), and that there is now a large and growing literature on how ethnic identities influence state capacity outcomes. Most prominently, a large and influential body of scholarship argues that ethnic diversity undermines public goods provision, with Banerjee, Iyer, and Somanthan (2005, p. 639) claiming that the negative relationship between ethnic fractionalization and public goods provision constitutes 'one of the most powerful hypotheses in political economy'.

Singh and vom Hau directly challenge these assumptions and argue that the politics of recognition, in the form of collective ethnic mobilizations, may actually increase rather than diminish the capacity of the state to promote development. Drawing on a systematic review of the available literature, they argue that the current literature is flawed in several respects, including its simplistic definition of what constitutes ethnicity and a conflation of state capacity with public goods provision. They instead propose an alternative analytical framework which incorporates a variety of different conceptualizations of ethnicity (cognitive, behavioural, and institutional), shifts the analytical focus from public goods provision to state capacity, and draws on a broader variety of causal mechanisms that detail how ethnicity might influence state capacity.

The Transnational Politics of Development

The tendency within most of politics and development literature to cast development as an essentially national project reflects a limited understanding of the multiple ways in which the capacity of states and commitment of elites to deliver development is closely shaped by transnational factors. Not only has the politics of the post-colonial world always been heavily transnationalized, from imperialism through to the creation of 'governance' states under influence of global governance institutions (Harrison 2004), these processes have both deepened and extended since the first wave of developmental states in the South emerged in the 1950s and 1960s. The deepening of global flows—of capital, labour, ideas—has meant that the strategic choices available for developing countries today are closely shaped by prevailing global orders, both material and ideological. Examining the politics of development in developing countries thus necessarily involves looking at how transnational processes, factors, and ideas shape politics, not least as the international context also produces a number of drivers of bad governance in developing countries (Unsworth and Moore 2006). Elites may face few incentives to build effective bureaucracies or promote inclusive development in conditions where, for example, banking systems, tax havens, and the arms trade encourage forms of corruption and extra-state violence that undermine state-building processes. Importantly, whilst development studies has tended to presume that aid and international development agencies are the key 'external' factors we need to explore the broader range of transnational actors and processes that constitute and shape the politics of development. The new 'Rising Powers' are busy reshaping this context, bringing in new resources and ideas around how development can be done and new modalities of engagement. Traditional donor agencies remain a part of this picture, but their mixed record of promoting good governance (World Bank 2008b) and the ways in which rising powers have introduced new drivers of governance and development (Power et al. 2012) means we must include but also look well beyond the role of aid.

In their chapter Arjan De Haan and Ward Warmerdam set out to analyse the relationship between aid and state capacity for development along four dimensions. Given that corruption is frequently cited as the most pressing political problem that has stalled development, their first task is to explore the causal relationship between aid and levels of corruption. However, the available literature is unclear on this, and points to a number of contested and/or untested assumptions regarding the potential role of aid to reducing corruption without offering enough conclusive evidence either way. On the one hand, the rules and conditionalities associated with aid may deter public officials from engaging in corrupt practices and the presence of donor aid may enhance governments' ability to pay regular salaries, which may in turn reduce the corruption of public officials. However, there is also evidence to support the view that higher levels of aid have the potential to create 'Dutch Disease', and some which suggests that community-driven models of aid delivery tend to undermine the role and accountability of the state. Given the lack of systematic empirical research that directly relates specific types and levels of aid to specific governance indicators, we are left with a contested and often untested set of assumptions.

Looking beyond corruption, there are grounds for claiming that donor practices may be undermining the capacity of states to deliver development. The most commonly identified issues include claims that: donor procedures tend to be cumbersome and time-consuming; aid flows are often unpredictable and often follow the financial cycles of donors rather than those of recipients; there are too many donor agencies working in uncoordinated ways, while donor priorities also change frequently; and that aid is not always driven by developmental objectives but rather motivated by a variety of factors, including being used as an instrument of foreign policy and geo-strategic purposes. The impact of aid on state capacity depends on several factors, including the levels and modalities of aid delivery as well as the duration of aid dependency. In particular, project-mode aid delivery, which remains the most popular among donors, has been heavily criticized in the literature for reasons such as constraining opportunities for scaling up of good practices, the proliferation of projects, and possible drain on local administrative capacity. De Haan and Warmerdam also highlight 'real' determination to achieve change on the part of partners and a strong donor understanding of local context as critical conditions for successful (institutional development) projects.

Inspired by the observation that China is the major 'new' player in Africa and therefore likely to impact on development and politics in numerous ways, Giles Mohan sets out to identify the channels through which China engages with African development and the role the African state plays in mediating these interactions. Recognizing the importance of context, and particularly the extent to which different political systems shape the encounter with China (Alden 2007), Mohan examines the role of China in three different types of state in Africa, namely pariah states (Sudan), illiberal regimes and weak democracies (Angola), and democratic countries with diversified economies (Ghana). His analysis reveals that China impacts on African development in multiple ways that go well beyond aid and cuts across contexts, regardless of the nature of the African state. A key feature of this engagement is inter-elite brokerage which tends to bypass domestic channels of accountability and potentially undermines good governance by serving to entrench existing forms of patrimonialism, although this has increasingly been challenged by civil and political society actors in Africa through the promotion of transparency. China's emphasis on supporting high-profile infrastructure projects promises to deliver gains for both development and the state, in terms of enhanced legitimacy in the eyes of its citizens. Its preferred mode of delivery, namely the project-based approach criticized here by De Haan and Warmerdam for its negative effects on governance, may actually offer greater control over corruption than other forms (including general budgetary support) since there is less free-floating cash to be siphoned off. Another source of controversy around Chinese projects has been around the importation of labour and the environmental effects of such investments. Following Chen and Orr (2009), Mohan argues that the evidence around investment and labour suggests that labour importation varies according to the nature of the project, the Chinese firm involved, and the labour market conditions in Africa. As far as the environment is concerned, Mohan finds that the environmental impacts of Chinese activities in Africa are poorly understood since much focus has been on a few high profile cases. Generally, and whereas the African state is often reflected in the literature as vulnerable in face of the powerful international actors, Mohan is careful not to rule out African countries' room for manoeuvre. He notes that, in particular, the discovery of strategic minerals in several countries has given them a degree of space to negotiate or even play donors and investors off against one another.

Broader Lessons from the Politics of What Works: From Evidence to Theory-testing

What, then, can we draw out from across these systematic reviews of the available evidence on how politics shapes development? Clearly, there are significant risks involved in trying to draw out cross-cutting findings from such a broad range of work. The forms of politics associated with delivering growth may be very different from those aligned with developing human capabilities (Evans 2010; Khan 2005), and the problem may be even more fine-grained than this. As Sen argues here, different forms of growth are associated with different political drivers. Mcloughlin (2012) similarly argues that the forms of politics that matter for social provisioning will differ by sector. Importantly, the evidence that could be drawn on by our authors came from a wide variety of sources, contexts, and perspectives, and not all of it had thoroughly integrated a political perspective. Furthermore, the cases available to our authors were chosen on what they could reveal about the politics of what works rather than on rigorously comparative grounds in terms of their contextual setting, a point we return to below in propos- ing a methodological as well as conceptual way forward. As such, rather than seeking to aggregate insights from this diverse evidence base, we find it more useful here to put these findings into conversation with the most recent conceptual and theoretical developments within the field of politics and development, and to explore the extent to which our findings fit the prevailing wisdom on this issue. This theory-testing approach (George and Bennett 2004) is intended to be both critical and constructive in that it should also suggest the conceptual groundings for a rigorous and coherent research agenda on the politics of development moving forward.

The New Turn to Politics within Mainstream Development Theory

In recent years there has been a significant shift within the mainstream of development theory and policy towards taking politics more seriously. In part, this can be characterized as a shift away from the dominance that new institutional economics had over the good-governance agenda throughout the 1990s and for much of the early 2000s. For critics, this conceptual focus on 'the rules of the game' (North 1990) only ever offered a limited and often technocratic understanding of how politics shaped development (Harris et al. 1997). It has been notable, then, that the most influential recent stud- ies of long-run development to emerge in the past few years have placed politics at the heart of the story (Acemoglu and Robinson 2012; Fukuyama 2011; Khan 2010; North et al. 2009), in an apparent recognition that what lies behind the emergence and functioning of institutions is the complex world of politics and power relations, a finding that historical institutional thinkers had already come to in their framing of institutions as crystalliza- tions of (past) power struggles and key to the maintenance of power distribu- tion in society (Mahoney and Thelen 2010). There is a particular focus here on the role of inter-elite relationships as a causal factor that underpins the emergence of stability and functioning institutions. For North et al. (2009, p. 159) 'political and economic development result from creating more sophisticated and durable institutions to structure elite relations within the dominant coalition'; as such, the differences between developed and developing countries is attributable to 'the pattern of social relationships' in each, but particularly within the elite. This move from institutions to politics and certain forms of power relations marks a potentially significant ontological shift within mainstream analyses of governance and development, and chimes closely with other recent advances highlighted here, including the revival of relational approaches within studies of developmental states and state capacity (Evans 2010; vom Hau 2012; Vu 2007) and those emphasizing that state–society relations are critical to shaping the politics of development (IDS 2010; Sandbrook et al. 2007; Walton 2010).

The notion that institutional functioning and the underlying conditions for development are established first and foremost by the character of intra-elite relations forms the central concern of both Mushtaq Khan's work on 'political settlements' and North et al.'s (2009) idea of 'limited access orders' and how they might become 'open access orders'.[2] The '"political settlement" refers to the balance or distribution of power between contending social groups and social classes, on which any state is based' (di John and Putzel 2009, p. 4). Arrived at through a process of struggle and bargaining between elite groups, this settlement establishes the basis for institutional arrangements to take shape. Critically, institutions must be arranged to distribute enough resources to powerful organized groups in society, otherwise 'these groups will strive through different means including conflict to change institutions till they are satisfied or they give up' (Khan 2010, p. 4). This resonates with North et al.'s (2009) explanation that social order can only exist once elites have reached an agreement amongst themselves over the centralization of violence and the operation of institutional constraints around a limited set of property rights.

Taken together, these approaches suggest two main and inter-related transmission mechanisms through which political settlements and limited access orders shape developmental forms of state capacity and elite commitment. The first flows from the stability of institutional arrangements, the second from the nature of ruling coalitions. Political stability and order is critical not only for the simple reason that it allows institutions to function but also because stability enables elites to engage in the type of long-term thinking and planning required for growth to emerge (Kelsall et al. 2010).[3] Where elites are

---

[2] Despite important intellectual differences between the two approaches, they derive from similar ontological priors, particularly concerning their shared rational-actor perspective on political behaviour, and are more complementary than contradictory to each other.

[3] The resolution of conflict, particularly in ways that offers the emerging ruling coalition the legitimacy to make difficult decisions and the space to do so without significant opposition (generally made more possible under conditions of elite polarization rather than elite compromise, see Vu 2007).

constantly struggling to assert the legitimacy of a prevailing order, the incentives are to undertake short-termist measures designed to maintain order and keep the regime in power. In a context of personalized deals between elites, this involves both creating rent-seeking possibilities for potentially troublesome elites and securing their support for 'limited access' (and usually clientelist) institutional arrangements that can help offer greater returns than they could attain through violent means (North et al. 2009).

A more distinctive contribution concerns the role played by coalitions in shaping state capacity and elite commitment. In terms of state capacity, political settlements analysis suggests that state organizations are unable to act effectively unless the nature of the political settlement within which they are located permits them to do so: from this perspective, the political coalitions at the heart of political settlements are thus historically and logically prior to the emergence of state capacity, which in turn precedes the effective formulation and delivery of policies. The capacity of the state to act, and whether or not effective state institutions get built and are allowed to function, is therefore determined by the character of the players, coalitions, and agreements made around the operation of power—not about formal Weberian forms of state capacity per se. So, it would be feasible to imagine a state with high levels of bureaucratic capacity and infrastructural power, but which was prevented from acting in certain policy domains due to the lack of an agreement between dominant groups. For Khan, what is particularly important in shaping the capacity and commitment of governments to deliver development is the need within ruling coalitions to maintain certain types of relationships both horizontally (with other elite factions) and vertically (with organized social groupings) in order to preserve regime stability and survival will create strong incentives to act in particular ways. For Khan (2010, p. 64): 'The relative power of productive interests and their technological and entrepreneurial capabilities can determine the incentives and opportunities of ruling coalitions to pursue particular institutional paths'. This focus has strong echoes of recent work on state–business relations (e.g. Sen and te Velde 2009) and of earlier work on the 'embedded autonomy' of developmental states (Evans 1995; Routley 2012; vom Hau 2012), including the focus on whether patron–client politics tend to be *predatory* as opposed to *productive* in particular contexts. Even within clientelistic political settlements, the presence of a political leadership with long-term time horizons, in alliance with centralized control over rent-seeking, can enable patrimonial settlements to be developmental, whereas a tendency towards decentralized rent-seeking and short-term exigencies within the political settlement is likely to be predatory and unproductive (Kelsall et al. 2010).

To date, there have been fewer efforts to extend this approach beyond issues of conflict and economic growth and productivity to the delivery of social and political rights. Aside from vague assertions that elites will extend benefits to non-elite groups once they are satisfied with the division of spoils amongst themselves (Khan 2010; North et al. 2009), or when elites perceive it to be essential for regime survival (Bates 2005; Whitfield and Therkildsen 2011), there remains a gap in the literature concerning the role of political settlements in shaping the politics of social provisioning.

A political-settlements perspective offers some powerful insights regarding the emergence of developmental forms of capacity and commitment, many of which resonate with other recent work on the politics of development. In particular, the idea that 'the overall causality runs from conflicts to coalitions to state capacity' (vom Hau 2012, p. 11) is increasingly popular within studies of state capacity, and, as we argue below, resonates with the findings we present in this collection. In terms of elite commitment, political settlements research is aligned with recent research into the politics of development (IDS 2010) in framing this question primarily in terms of incentives, whereby the underlying distribution of power generates incentives that shape elite behaviour. However, it is in this insistence that incentives are all that matters, a perspective which locates political elites as purely instrumental actors working to secure their own interests, that the limitations of the political settlements (or limited access orders) perspective become most apparent, and where our own findings start to diverge from where a pure political settlements approach would lead us. As discussed below, our chapters suggest that ideas matter as well as interests, and also that both the 'incentives' and the 'ideas' that shape elite behaviour are not necessarily endogenous to the political settlement but may derive from further afield, including the arena of transnational flows.

Our Findings: From Coalitions to Commitment and Capacity

Our chapters offer strong evidence that the processes of elite bargaining, informal politicking, and coalitional dynamics play a key role in shaping the capacity and commitment of the state and elites to deliver development in specific domains. In terms of growth, Kunal Sen argues that whereas a 'deals' environment can offer the groundings for the take-off of economic growth, a movement to a 'rules'-based institutional environment, or at least a context of 'ordered deals', is likely to be required for growth to be sustained (Pritchett and Werker 2012). The arrangements governing the exchange of power within different political settlements can directly shape social provisioning, including a distinction that can be drawn between the relative power and stability accorded to dominant leaders who may be committed to delivering development over the long run as against the often short-term horizons engendered by intense political party competition within clientelist contexts (Levy 2012). Mcloughlin shows how these dynamics can strongly shape the delivery of public goods such as health and education, particularly in terms of the quality of these services. The inclusion of poor and marginal groups in ruling coalitions is deemed critical in Mosley's work on how the links between fiscal and social policy play out in practice, whilst Nazneen and Mahmud's chapter on the gendered politics of development argues persuasively that much of the gap between women's political inclusion and their influence over pro-women policies can be explained by the workings of the political settlement, particularly in terms of how informal/patronage-based forms of politics weaken the power of female agency in the political realm. It is perhaps Tony Bebbington's chapter on natural resource governance which illustrates most clearly the convergence of our findings with that of the political-settlements approach, whilst also revealing some important points of divergence.

Bebbington offers a clear and current example of Poteete's (2009) insistence that the emergence and building of coalitions is of both chronologically and analytically prior to the development of institutions and policies, and shows that how the politics of coalition-building plays out has important implications for the prospects of inclusive development. In the case of El Salvador during the mid-1990s, mining companies had begun to conduct geological explorations, largely with the complicity of a coalition of national economic and traditional political elites and in the context of a pro-business government. Mining companies were progressing their activities in ways that outstripped the capacity of the state to regulate mining investment, ensure environmental protection, establish tax and royalty systems, and so on. It was only when rural groups in the affected areas started to protest against these activities, and to build a coalition with sympathetic national and international actors, that the government suspended all activities, before its more left-wing successor went further and set in place a process through which El Salvador could develop the institutional capacities required to govern the mining industry before any further exploitation could take place.

For Bebbington, this 'reflect(s) the importance of understanding the institutional relationships through which resource extraction is governed as endogenous to an existing political settlement, while also exploring the processes through which both endogenously and exogenously driven institutional change might occur'. This implies a more dynamic view of how political settlements emerge and might be transformed than is often the case in the current literature, one where change can be driven from those excluded from power and from transnational as well as national actors. It also implies a greater role for agency than the path-dependent approach which characterizes much current political-settlements analysis, whereby policy coalitions involving a range of actors (including popular ones) can have an important influence on the prospects for inclusive development (Leftwich 2010) rather than this simply being read off the structural nature of the political settlement or the incentives within ruling (or political) coalitions. Importantly, it also shows the importance of ideas, both in terms of the ideological persuasion of governments and the ideas that both drive the activities of civil society and transnational actors and are used by them to win certain political struggles. This and other chapters therefore start to reveal the limitations of relying on a political-settlements approach alone, without taking account of the role played by ideas, popular actors, and transnational factors, three issues that we return to shortly.

Which Forms of State Capacity Matter Most?

Our findings thus chime with perhaps the most consistent message to come from the growing literature on the politics of development over the past decades, which has centred on the centrality of state capacity and elite commitment in securing inclusive development outcomes. High levels of state capacity have been a central feature in all successful cases of long-run development witnessed in the post-Second-World-War era, across all domains of development. In terms of economic growth, the initial findings of the developmental-states literature on this have been further strengthened by the rise of new economic powers, all of which have involved a central role for a capable, committed, and credible state (World Bank 2008; also Vu 2007). In terms of redistribution, 'the state remains the only entity with the legitimacy and capacity to capture and redirect the wealth that society produces' (Sandbrook et al. 2007, p. 253), including through social provisioning (Leftwich 2008; Walton 2010). Finally, it has also become clearer that the state also closely shapes the possibilities for political inclusion and empowerment amongst citizens (Houtzager and Moore 2003; IDS 2010). Given that states can be highly capable without necessarily being committed to development, the commitment of political elites to delivering development has also been identified as a critical element of the politics of what works (Booth 2011d; Hossain 2005; Leftwich 1994; Vu 2007).[4]

Our findings largely concur with these conclusions, and, in linking this to the underlying role of politics and power relations through the political-settlements perspective, starts to suggest how the conditions within which developmental forms of state capacity and commitment

---

[4] For example, Vu's seminal (2007) comparative study of developmental states in Asia distinguishes between the 'structure' of the state and state–society relations that is required to generate the capacity to deliver development and the 'role' that elites chose to play in committing to this.

might emerge, and to reveal the specific types and forms of capacity and commitment that matter. Drawing on vom Hau's earlier (2012) work, Singh and vom Hau define state capacity as 'the ability of states to apply and implement policy choices within the territorial boundaries they claim to govern', and comprises three distinct, but interrelated dimensions: the state's embeddedness with non-state actors; the organizational competence of state agencies; and the territorial reach of state institutions (vom Hau 2012). This approach goes beyond standard Weberian approaches and situates the state as a more relational phenomenon that is embedded within the broader society, albeit with varying degrees of autonomy (Evans 1995). Several of our contributors identify one or more of these dimensions as critical. For example, and in terms of the politics of accumulation, the capacity of the state to govern its relationships with capital (both national and transnational) in the national interests is critical, both in general (Sen) and in the specific case of natural resources (Bebbington, Mohan). The relational dimension of state capacity also shapes the politics of social provisioning, particularly concerning the depth and extent of relationships between civil and political society (Mcloughlin, echoing Evans 2010). In terms of the politics of recognition, Nazneen and Mahmud argue that 'the state remains the critical institution for the promotion of women's rights and gender justice in the contexts of poverty, global financial flows, and rising religious fundamentalism'. Again, the state's relational capacities are essential here, in terms of the links between political actors, key bureaucrats, and women's movements.

Political Commitment: From Incentives to Ideas?

As suggested earlier, the ability of the political-settlements approach to generate clear insights into the emergence of elite commitment is more limited.[5] Although the role of interests in shaping elite behaviour is clearly important, our sense is that to position development as purely a survival strategy for elites to maintain regime continuity in the face of elite competition and/or the threat of disturbance from popular groups (Henley 2014; Whitfield and Therkildsen 2011) is too limited a perspective. Barrientos and Pellissery argue strongly that to focus only on the incentives that elites respond to is much too limited: social contracts and pacts, key events, ideology, and knowledge are important too. In particular, our authors suggest that ideas also matter a great

---

[5] Political commitment has proved a tricky concept to define. In a narrow sense, one approach is to simply define it as 'the extent of committed support among key decision makers for a particular policy solution to a particular problem' (Post et al. 2010, p. 569). However, this remains an under-theorized and loosely defined concept, with our studies unable to draw out of the existing literature a strong sense of the underlying drivers of this commitment and how it becomes sustained over time.

deal here, including the different ideological standpoints of regimes concerning the governance of natural resource governance, with more social democratic regimes willing to both exert stronger control over capital and consider linking natural resource extraction more clearly to social provisioning than more market-friendly, conservative regimes (Bebbington, also Mosley). How resources should be accumulated and redistributed is thus shaped by particular ideas around development that are linked to the maintenance of particular coalitions but which are not reducible to them. Nazneen and Mahmud similarly emphasize the extent to which discourses of women's right and gender equity, often drawn from transnational debates and mobilized in partnership with global civil society actors and agencies, have been influential in securing women's empowerment. For Mohan, the capacity of elites to govern their relationships with external forces may depend on their vision of the national interest as well as any bargaining power derived from more material sources.

The Transnational Politics of Development

Whereas most of the political settlements literature remains tightly focused to the nation state as the primary focus of analysis, our chapters suggest that developing countries in particular need to be framed in broader, more transnational terms. This is perhaps particularly the case in countries with new natural resource finds, and which find their national political community subject to particularly deep forms of transnationalization via the role of oil companies (Watts 2004) but also global regimes of transparency and accountability. Although still critical in several respects, aid agencies are increasingly finding themselves displaced in such contexts, as aid dependency is reduced and aid replaced by flows associated with oil and gas finds and related investments. This not only reduces the influence of aid efforts to restructure and reform the state (de Haan) but also introduces new players such as China whose modes of engagement seem different in both form and effect. As Mohan points out, there is often more heat than light in such debates. However, there is growing evidence that China's emphasis on supporting the sovereignty of states around their political orientation and their backing for the type of major infrastructural projects often preferred by national political elites is introducing different kinds of incentives and ideas when it comes to the capacity and commitment to deliver development.

The Importance of Popular Agency

Our final point of divergence concerns the somewhat exaggerated emphasis that the political settlements approach, and perhaps particularly North et al.'s work on limited access orders, places on the elite-led nature of politics and development in developing countries. Our chapters on the rule of law, gender, and natural resources show how popular movements play a critical role in establishing and driving the kinds of coalitions which are required for inclusive forms of development to become seen as possible and to be delivered. This accords with recent comparative insights into the historical process through which developmental regimes emerge, and includes but also goes beyond the sense in which popular uprisings, or at least the threat of them, can also shift elite commitment towards more popular concerns (e.g. Slater 2010; Henley 2014). Concerned specifically with how social democratic regimes have developed in the global periphery, Sandbrook et al. (2007) identify an earlier role for subordinate groups in accessing and shaping the political settlement. Critical here is the emergence of new configurations of class power as a result of processes of capitalist development, particularly the displacement of landed elites by lower- and middle-order classes.[6] This is clearly not an easy process. Barrientos and Pellissery observe that the expansion of social assistance from small privileged groups to broader target population, in line with universal principles, does not emerge easily but can involve intense political struggles, something perhaps belied in the limited attention given to precisely how and why regimes move from 'closed' to 'open access orders' (North et al. 2009).

Overall, then, our findings resonate strongly with the new literature on political settlements, particularly in terms of the significance of coalitions in shaping the capacity and commitment of governments to deliver development. Importantly, this holds across each of the domains we investigate here. However, our findings also suggest that there are serious shortcomings with the political-settlements approach and suggest numerous ways in which our conceptual basis moving forward needs to be both broadened and deepened to take adequate account of the ways in which politics shapes the prospects for inclusive development. This includes adopting a more dynamic and transnational perspective, and recognizing the importance of ideas and ideology as well as the more instrumental drivers of political

---

[6] This move beyond intra-elite relations to take greater cognizance of links with broader social groupings helps move the focus onto the broader realm of thinking around state–society relations (e.g. Migdal 1988). This includes work within the social contract tradition, which for some is a more useful term than 'political settlements', particularly when taking popular agency more seriously and including social as well as economic aspects of development. For example, Michael Walton's (2010) essay on the politics of human development over the long run also examines the importance of both intra-elite relations and state–society relations as establishing 'political equilibria' or 'social contracts' and comes to much the same conclusion as Mushtaq Khan concerning 'a central channel of causation, from underlying social, economic and political processes through social contracts and institutions to human development outcomes' (Walton 2010, p. 38).

behaviour. The final section seeks to move us from these insights into a more holistic and integrated conceptual and methodological way forward for future research on the politics of development.

Moving Forward: Beyond the 'New' New Institutionalism

The theory-testing enabled by this interplay of our evidence base and recent thinking within politics and development inevitably falls short of generating a clear theoretical route forward. What it offers instead is a stronger sense of the range of variables, relationships, and processes that are likely to matter, which in turn can be mapped into a broad conceptual framework for understanding the politics of inclusive development. Figure 1.1 lays out the main variables and relationships that we consider to be worthy of investigation; it does not constitute a model, still less a theoretical explanation of how things actually work. It simply sets out the key variables that need to be tracked in order to test which offers the greatest traction on the outcomes to be explained, but without (at this stage) over-specifying the precise relationships and mechanisms at play. Later work by ESID will, we hope, elaborate this more fully.

Under this schematic representation of the links between politics and development, the underlying conditions for development are established by formation of particular types of political settlements, a process which occurs in a continuous interplay with institutions, changes in the political economy and also the initial conditions within any given society. This draws on Khan's (2010) emphasis on how capitalism shapes political settlements but also Sandbrook et al.'s (2007) findings on the initial conditions that are required for social democracy to emerge, including insertion within the global political economy and state formation. This places the relationship between state capacity and political settlements as central to determining the underlying conditions for development, with further empirical research required to establish the precise sequencing involved here. Moving rightwards, the diagram seeks to make explicit the ways in which underlying power relations shape the more proximate worlds of policymaking and implementation, as mediated through the work of policy-level coalitions that can involve a range of actors: elite and popular, from state, civil society, and the private sector, and from transnational as well as national contexts. Such coalitions form a critical bridge between the underlying and proximate politics of development and closely shape the possibilities for inclusive development. The driving force for such coalitions can come from beyond the ruling coalition, including the ways in which certain civil society movements have driven the creation of new and developmental forms of policy

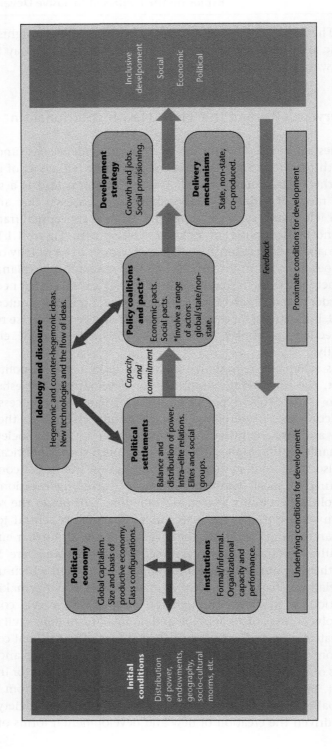

Figure 1.1. Thinking about the politics of inclusive development: a relational approach

Source: Authors.

coalitions by building relationship between local communities, bureaucrats and local politicians (e.g. through the co-production of services, Mitlin 2008). Transnational actors such as donor agencies may be closely involved in policymaking coalitions, from the role of international financial institutions in establishing macroeconomic strategy through to the promotion of social protection strategies and interventions. Transnational and national forms of capital are often closely entwined in both formal and informal relationships with political elites, in ways that can have different impacts on state capacity and commitment to deliver development according to the characteristics and sectoral location of particular firms. Indeed, the influence of transnational factors are emphasized throughout the approach, including the ways in which colonialism helps establish initial conditions, the character, and timing of how countries are inserted into the global capitalist political economy and the influence of transnational flows of ideas.

Finally, the diagram is also intended to capture the dynamism that characterizes the politics of development, including through the identification of critical feedback mechanisms. For example, when governments build roads they are also effectively building state capacity, particularly in terms of its 'infrastructural power'. State legitimacy matters for economic growth (Engelbert 2002), and the effective delivery of basic services both requires and helps to build political legitimacy. Perhaps most important is the extent to which development outcomes, particularly in terms of growth and economic transformation,[7] will reshape class configurations and the size and character of the formal economy in ways that may re-order existing political settlements and introduce new or newly empowered players into coalitions at different levels. One of the more important contributions made by the political-settlements work of Khan has been to remind us that these forms of structural transformation may be required to establish the conditions through which more effective and legitimate forms of governance arise.

There are also important methodological issues to address, and we would argue that the shift from theory-testing to theory-building proposed here can be achieved most persuasively through comparative case-study research. This is generally considered the most robust and insightful means of both testing the veracity of particular theories within and across different cases, and also building new theories through examining the interplay of particular variables within and across particular contexts (George and Bennett 2004). Such an approach, based on a carefully selected set of

---

[7] See Sandbrook et al. (2007), also Poteete (2009, p. 546): 'Economic growth generates structural changes, increases the variety of interests in society, and opens up possibilities for new coalitions. Likewise, constraints and opportunities change with regional political and global economic developments'.

countries, should enable the building of mid-level theoretical generalizations that have relevance to policy actors working across different contexts. This in turn requires the development of a typology capable of classifying different contexts as representatives of specific types of political settlement, from which comparative cases can be selected (e.g. Levy 2012). Inspired by telling insights that have been generated from recent research on the politics of development that has adopted a comparative perspective (e.g. Kohli 2004; Henley 2014; Vu 2007), ESID is adopting this approach in its work and will be sharing the results in future volumes.

Conclusion

The understanding that politics shapes development processes and outcomes has become a commonplace within development theory and practice. This collection offers a wide range of insights into the ways in which politics matters within and across several domains of development, from growth through basic services, social protection and justice to recognition, and at multiple levels, including the transnational. Although much of what we find chimes with recent conceptual developments that place politics at the heart of new understandings of how long-run development comes about, our evidence also reveals some shortcomings in such accounts. The burgeoning field of politics and development research has reached a stage of conceptual development which demands that influential theoretical propositions are thoroughly and critically tested across a range of contexts and different domains of development, and through a mixture of different epistemological, disciplinary, and methodological perspectives. It is not possible at this stage to predict which approaches, or mixture thereof, will generate the strongest insights into the politics of development, and this may well vary across the broad range of phenomena we propose to investigate. What matters is that future research seeks to leave the field of politics and development not only more empirically rich and theoretically robust than it currently stands, but also, and in so doing, to generate a more useful guide to building routes towards social justice.

Part II
The Politics of Accumulation and Growth

Part II
The Politics of Accumulation and Growth

2

The Political Determinants of Economic Growth: An Analytical Review

Kunal Sen

Introduction: The Politics of Growth

This chapter is an analytical review of what we know about the political economy determinants of economic growth. The process of economic growth and why there are such significant differences in living standards across countries is one of the most important and challenging areas of research in development studies. An early tradition in the very large literature that exists on the determinants of economic growth mostly focused on understanding the proximate determinants of economic growth, and in particular, the role of human and physical capital accumulation, technological change, and productivity growth in explaining economic growth. However, as North and Thomas (1973) noted, such proximate determinants or correlates of economic growth 'are not causes of growth; they are growth' (p. 2). In the theoretical literature on the determinants of economic growth, institutions—defined as 'the rules of the game or, more formally, the humanly devised constraints that shape human interaction' (North 1990, p. 3)—are now widely regarded as the fundamental cause of economic growth, the fundamental cause being 'the factors potentially affecting why societies make different technology and accumulation choices' (Acemoglu 2009, p. 20). This literature argues that better functioning regulations and laws provide firms with incentives to invest in productive activities and to develop new goods and production technologies, which lead to greater factor accumulation and technological change that bring about economic growth (Hall and Jones 1999; Acemoglu et al. 2005).

Parallel to the developments in our theoretical understanding of the causes of growth, there has been a realization in recent years that the emphasis in the previous growth empirics literature on long-run growth or levels of income (such as in the report of the Commission for Growth and Development, 2008) is not compatible with the 'stylized facts' of economic growth (Pritchett 2000). As Jones and Olken (2008, p. 582) point out:

> Almost all countries in the world have experienced rapid growth lasting a decade or longer, during which they converge towards income levels in the United States. Conversely, nearly all countries have experienced periods of abysmal growth. Circumstances or policies that produce ten years of rapid economic growth appear easily reversed, often leaving countries no better off than they were prior to the expansion.

Long-run growth averages within countries mask distinct periods of success and failure, and while the growth process of all 'developed' economies is well characterized by a single growth rate and a 'business cycle' around that trend (at least until the recent crises), this is not true of most countries in the world (Kar et al. 2013a, 2013b). Massive discrete changes in growth are common in developing countries, and most developing countries experience distinct growth episodes: growth accelerations and decelerations or collapses (Jerzmanowski 2006). The recent empirical literature has highlighted the need to differentiate between different phases of growth in a particular country—that is, our understanding of the causes of growth needs to take into account the fact that the causes of growth accelerations may well be different from the factors that maintain growth, once it has ignited in the country (Rodrik 2004).

The chapter is structured as follows. As a prelude to our review of the theoretical and empirical literature, we sketch out in the next section a conceptual framework by which to understand the political channels of economic growth, where we view economic growth as switches between growth regimes, differentiating between the determinants of growth accelerations and of growth maintenance. In the third section, we review the recent contributions to the theoretical literature on the politics of economic growth through the lens of our conceptual framework. Similarly, the fourth section discusses the empirical literature on the political determinants of economic growth. The chapter concludes with a section presenting a set of research questions that can help guide future research on the politics of economic growth.

The Political Channels to Economic Growth

As the recent empirical literature on economic growth shows, economic growth in many developing countries involves discrete and quantitatively massive transitions between periods of high growth, periods of negative

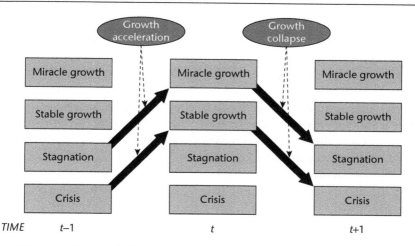

Figure 2.1. Transition paths between growth phases
Source: Author.

growth, and periods of stagnation. To fix our ideas on transition paths around growth regimes, we provide a simple sketch of these transition paths in Figure 2.1. Using a rough-and-ready way to demarcate growth regimes, we classify growth regimes into four categories: i) a growth regime which we call 'miracle growth' where the average increase in per capita income is 5 per cent per annum or more; ii) a growth regime which we call 'stable growth', where the average increase in per capita income is between 0 and 5 per cent per annum; iii) a growth regime which we call 'stagnant growth', where the average increase in per capita income is around 0 per cent per annum; and iv) a growth regime we call 'growth crisis' where the average change in per capita income is negative. Figure 2.1 makes clear that a complete characterization of the growth process in any particular country needs an understanding of the factors that lead to growth acceleration—that is, the transition from stagnation or crisis to stable growth or miracle growth—as well as the factors that lead to the avoidance of growth collapses and the maintenance of positive growth—that is, the ability of the country to stay in stable growth or miracle growth in period $t+1$ per cent if it has experienced the same in period t. It is not obvious that the factors that lead to growth acceleration will lead to growth maintenance as well—as Rodrik (2004, p. 3) argues:

> Igniting economic growth and sustaining it are somewhat different enterprises. The former generally requires a limited range of (often unconventional) reforms that need not overly tax the institutional capacity of the economy. The latter challenge is in many ways harder, as it requires constructing a sound institutional underpinning to maintain productive dynamism and endow the economy with resilience to shocks over the longer term.

In our view, the *key research problem* on the political drivers of economic growth should be to understand the political dynamics around the transition from one growth regime to another, and the political economy determinants of growth accelerations, growth maintenance, and growth declines/collapses. The *overarching research question* then is: what determines the *political transitional dynamics* around *growth regime traverses*—that is, the move from one growth regime to another growth regime? In this section, we sketch out a framework which makes an attempt in this direction and that we will use as a way to embed our review of the theories and empirics of the politics of growth within the context of the overarching research question.

We identify three distinct political channels to growth. The first is *credible commitment* by the state. That is, the state needs to credibly commit to potential and current investors that it will not expropriate most or all of the profits that may accrue from the production process or the means of production themselves. Credible commitment can be both motivational and imperative. Credible commitment is motivational if it is in the interest of both the state and the investor to adhere to the rules (both formal and informal)—that is, the state will commit to not expropriating rents over and above which may be considered to be 'fair' if it wants to make sure that investors commit to the investment decision and engage in production, so that rents can be generated through the production process. This commitment needs to be seen as credible by investors in that they believe that the state will not renege on its implicit or explicit promise not to expropriate all or most of the rents accruing from the production process in the future, especially after investment decisions involving sunk costs in fixed capital have been taken. Investors also need to commit to share a part of their rents to the state (or its constituents, such as politicians) and when states raise revenues from taxes, to pay the state the necessary taxes. Credible commitment can also be imperative if politicians bind themselves to certain rules (both formal and informal), and there is a reputational cost for reneging, such as a weakening in the state's legitimacy, or a loss in the support of important factions that may support the state.

Credible commitment can be seen as both a necessary and sufficient condition for capital accumulation to take place or for entrepreneurs to make the necessary investments in productivity enhancing changes in their enterprises. Most investment activities take time and there are lags between the time period when investment in land and machinery is made, and the time period when profits can be obtained from the sale of the product in the market. Investment decisions are by their nature lumpy and may have large sunk costs—that is, the costs of certain investments cannot be recovered in full if the investment decision turns out to be less profitable than anticipated. By credibly committing *ex ante* to not extracting most of the proceeds from the investment decision, the state provides the incentive for the entrepreneur to make the investment and production decision and can extract a part of the proceeds from the investment *ex post*. In this sense, credible commitment is incentive-compatible both for the state and the entrepreneur. However, it follows from the nature of credible commitment that the state has to take a reasonably long view in that reneging on the commitment not to fully extract the rents from investment in one period can lead to a loss in credibility on the part of the state, and for investors not to trust the state when it comes to future investment decisions, leading to a fall in investment, and, consequently, in rent extraction in future periods.

Credible commitment can, however, be obtained through both formal and informal institutions. Formal institutions such as laws which prohibit the expropriation of private property (which investors believe will be implemented), courts that provide sanctions against the firm's customers when there is a non-payment of dues, and bankruptcy procedures which protect financiers such as bondholders when a firm enters into bankruptcy are all examples of formal institutions of credible commitment.

But informal institutions such as kinship structures, social norms, and patron–client networks can also act as institutions of credible commitment, especially in environments where formal institutions do not exist or are not well functioning. For example, in a patron–client network, where the patron is the politician and the client is the domestic entrepreneur, the politician may protect the entrepreneur and provide him or her with access to funds and certain privileges (such as licenses for production or imports) in return for the rents that accrue from production which may be used in part for financing the political machinery. Entrepreneurs too will have an incentive to find political patrons who may be keen to protect them, in exchange for economic and political support. Therefore, the existence of informal institutions of credible commitment can be both necessary and sufficient for an episode of growth acceleration, especially in a low-income country where formal institutions have not developed or do not function effectively. As long as the informal institutions that exist can address at least in part the credible commitment problem in the investment decision, entrepreneurs will be willing to invest, and economic growth will result.

A second political channel to economic growth is *the provision of public goods*. Among the determinants of economic growth that have been identified in the empirical growth literature are public goods such as primary and secondary education and provision of health services that are both available to a broad cross section of the population, and infrastructure such as roads and electricity, that are seen as being crucial enabling factors for economic growth to occur. The literature on the provision of public goods generally sees these goods being produced when the state has enough capacity both to raise taxes to finance large-scale provision of public goods and to administer the effective delivery of these goods. The dimensions of state capacity that may matter here are bureaucratic and infrastructural power—the capacity of the state to implement decisions and exert its authority over the national territory. Clearly, the more capable the state is in its ability to raise taxes (which is also a function of how legitimate the state is perceived to be in the eyes of its citizens) and in its ability to use these taxes to provide high-quality 'productive' public goods to the majority of the population, the larger will be the growth-enhancing effects of public goods provision (and arguably, the more broad-based economic growth will be). But bureaucratic and infrastructural power need a certain degree of bureaucratic professionalism, and it is more likely that the formal institutions that underpin such bureaucratic professionalism (such as meritocratic recruitment and merit-based promotion) will emerge later in the growth process. Therefore, the provision of public goods will be less important as a political channel to growth accelerations and may be more important for growth maintenance. However, not all public goods need a critical level of bureaucratic professionalism for their provision, and it is possible that some local public goods which may be important for growth take-offs such as the creation of an export processing zone or an industrial estate (that allows for pockets of growth to develop in the economy) and the infrastructure associated with these public goods can be provided even within clientelist and neopatrimonial contexts (Kelsall et al. 2010).

The third political channel to growth *is the overcoming of co-ordination failures in investment decisions.* These coordination failures often result from the high costs of collecting and processing information for new products, technologies, and industries in low-income countries. By investing in new information collection and processing and making information about the relevant new industries freely available to firms, the state can play a facilitating role in the introduction of new products and the move to new industries, and as a consequence, in bringing about structural change and technological upgrading in the economy (Lin and Monga 2011). Coordination failures also result from the fact that private returns to investment in sectors that offer the potential of dynamic comparative advantage in low-income countries may be less than social returns, as firms need to go through a learning process to build the capabilities to become competitive in new industries (Whitfield and Therkildsen 2011). Since this learning process may involve substantial financial losses at least at the initial stage, the private return to such investment may well be negative, even the investment may lead to significant positive spillover effects and the building up of social and human capital. Risk-averse entrepreneurs with low wealth endowments may not be willing to invest in such investments that have high sunk costs and prefer to invest in activities with a high short-term possibility of profits but which offer fewer possibilities for technological upgrading.

The divergence of the private and social returns to investment may be particularly evident in more modern manufacturing activities or in knowledge-based services as compared to unskilled labour-intensive manufacturing or primary commodity production. As the economy moves into these modern sectors, economies of scale and scope become more important, and there is a greater reliance of firms on highly skilled labour and access to long-term finance to make the lumpy investments in equipment, working capital, and export financing. Thus, there is a need for the state to play a coordinating role in directing scarce investible funds and limited foreign exchange (to purchase imported capital goods and technology from abroad) to the most productive firms and facilitate the upgrading and diversification of individual firms (Lin and Monga 2011).

But the overcoming of coordination failures needs both a political elite that is committed to a long-term vision of economic development (since the growth pay-offs to technological upgrading and industrial diversification may take time to occur) and the presence of an economic bureaucracy that is staffed by relatively competent individuals who are insulated from the pressures of special interests. Such bureaucracies are characterized by a high degree of well-institutionalized and organizationally consistent career ladders which bind them to corporate goals while simultaneously allowing them to acquire the expertise necessary to perform effectively (Evans 1995). The relative autonomy of the bureaucracy allows them to intervene selectively in favour of certain firms, sectors, and industries in a market-conforming way and to provide incentives to capitalists and to discipline them (Harriss 2006). Based on the East Asian successes in how governments in these countries successfully overcame coordination failures, Evans (1995) has argued that another important attribute of bureaucracies in these countries that allowed them to address coordination failures effectively was their 'embeddedness', that is, 'the dense set of concrete interpersonal ties that enabled specific agencies and enterprises to construct joint projects at the sectoral level' with local capitalists (Evans 2011, p. 47). Both embeddedness and autonomy were essential features of the state's ability to address coordination failures effectively in the East Asian 'growth successes'. As Evans (2011, p. 47) argues, 'avoiding capture and being able to discipline entrepreneurial elites is a defining feature of the "embedded autonomy" of East Asian developmental states, distinguishing them from less successful states in Asia and Africa'.

How important would the overcoming of coordination failure be as a political channel to growth across different growth regimes? Our discussion of how coordination failures may arise in developing countries indicates that it is more likely to be evident in the later stage of structural transformation when the economy has started the transition from activities that are less human-capital intensive and technologically less sophisticated to more complex activities. Thus, the state's role in overcoming coordination failures will be more important when growth has already ignited than in a context where growth is yet to accelerate. Further, as we have argued earlier, the level of capacity and autonomy of the bureaucracy that may be needed to address the complex interventions necessary for resolving all but the most basic coordination failures would be more likely to emerge at a later stage of the growth process. A possible hypothesis is whether the lack of ability of the state to resolve coordination failures plays a causal role in why some states cannot successfully transform their economies to more productive and technologically advanced activities. This may also explain why some countries are able to maintain high growth if they are able to successfully transform their economies, while growth dies out in other countries which cannot manage this transformation.

To summarize, in this section, we have sketched out a framework of analysis that has related the three political channels that we consider to be key to economic growth to different phases of economic growth. We have argued that the first political channel we discuss—institutions of credible commitment—may be a necessary and sufficient channel to growth accelerations while contributing to growth maintenance as well, and that informal institutions of credible commitment may play a more important role in growth accelerations, as opposed to formal institutions which may be more important in growth maintenance. We also argued that the second political channel we discuss in this section—the provision of public goods—would be more important in growth maintenance and in the avoidance of growth collapse, though it can also play some role in growth accelerations. Finally, we argued that the third political channel we discussed—the overcoming of coordination failures—would be more important in growth maintenance, and can be expected to play an insignificant role in growth acceleration.

Reviewing the Theories on the Politics of Growth

In this section, we will review the major theoretical and empirical literature on the politics of economic growth, and assess the strengths and weaknesses. We will deliberately be selective in our review, concentrating on recent contributions which help us to understand the political determinants of economic growth across different phases of growth. The three major theoretical bodies of literature that we will discuss are the work of: i) Daron Acemoglu and James Robinson (Acemoglu and Robinson); ii) Mushtaq Khan (and the work of the Africa Power and Politics programme, which draws some of its central propositions from Khan's work); and iii) the set of literature on coalitions and development leadership (including the work of the Centre for the Future State). We begin with a review of the work of Acemoglu and Robinson.

The Politics of Growth Maintenance: Acemoglu and Robinson

As with much of the recent literature on the politics of economic growth, Acemoglu and Robinson (AR)'s starting point is the work of Douglas North, who brought into the literature on the determinants of economic growth the key insight that institutions are the fundamental cause of economic growth (Acemoglu et al. 2005; Acemoglu and Robinson 2008, 2012). The set of institutions that matter for broad-based economic growth, according to AR, are inclusive economic institutions and inclusive political institutions. Inclusive economic institutions are secure property rights for the majority of the population (such as smallholder farmers and small firms), law and order, markets that are open to relative free entry of new businesses, state support for markets (in the form of public goods provision, regulation, and enforcement of contracts), and access to education and opportunity for the great majority of citizens. Inclusive political institutions are political institutions that allow broad participation of the citizens of the country and uphold the rule of law, and place constraints and checks on politicians along with the rule of law. AR argue that together with political pluralism, some degree of political centralization is also necessary for the states to be able to effectively enforce law and order. In contrast to the growth-enhancing effects of inclusive economic and political institutions, AR argue that extractive economic institutions such as insecure property rights and regulations that limit entry to markets and extractive political institutions that concentrate power in the hands of a few, with limited checks and balances, are not likely to lead to broad-based and sustained economic growth (i.e. growth can occur for some time under these institutions but is not likely to last and will benefit a narrow set of elites rather than the majority of the population).

But what determines the set of economic and political institutions prevailing in the country at a particular point of time? Economic institutions are not distribution neutral: they not only determine the aggregate growth potential of the economy but also the distribution of resources in the country. This implies that economic institutions are *politically determined*, as the prevalent power relations will determine which set of economic institutions are more likely to emerge. A similar argument can be made for political institutions, and AR argue that these are determined by the political power of different groups in society. Political power can be both *de jure* and de facto. *De jure* political power refers to power that originates from the political institutions in society. *De jure* political institutions determine the constraints on and the incentives of key actors in the political sphere and could be both formal (i.e. whether the political system is democratic or autocratic) or informal (i.e. the set of informal constraints on politicians and political elites). De facto political institutions, on the other hand, originate from the possibility that important social and political groups which hold political power may not find the distributions of benefits allocated by *de jure* political institutions and by economic institutions acceptable to them, and may use both legal and extra-legal means to impose their wishes on society and try to change these institutions (e.g. they may revolt, use arms, co-opt the military, or undertake protests).

AR argue that the degree of de facto political power originates from the ability of some groups to solve their collective-action problem and from the economic resources available to the group (which determines their capacity to use force against other groups). In the ultimate analysis, therefore, the initial distribution of economic resources and the nature of *de jure* political institutions determine both *de jure* and de facto political power and these in turn determine the set of economic institutions and political institutions that are likely to emerge in the economy, which in turn determine economic performance and the distribution of resources that are compatible with the distribution of political power. This can be seen in the schematic representation in Figure 2.2.

While AR do not directly invoke the concept of political settlement in their discussion of how political factors determine the form and functioning of economic institutions, and by doing so affect economic growth, they introduce the concept of *political equilibrium* which is similar to the manner in which the concept of political settlements has been used in the literature, particularly, as we will see later, by Mushtaq Khan. According to AR, the political equilibrium is the set of political and economic institutions compatible with the balance of de facto political power between groups. The key point here is that it is the political equilibrium that determines the institutional arrangements in society and the manner in which economic

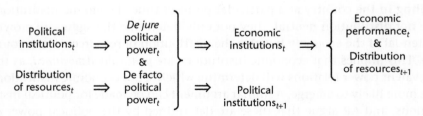

Figure 2.2. The evolution of political and economic institutions in Acemoglu and Robinson
Source: Acemoglu and Robinson (2008).

institutions function. Therefore, as AR argue, 'making or imposing specific institutional reforms may have little impact on the general structure of economic institutions or performance if they leave untouched the underlying political equilibrium'. An example of this was in Argentina during the imposition of Washington Consensus-type economic reforms in the late 1980s when Menem and the Peronist party after 1989 recognized that the policies of the Washington Consensus could be bent to function as 'politics as usual', and there was little change in the underlying political equilibrium even though the instruments that the Peronists used after 1989 were different (Acemoglu and Robinson 2008). AR point out that the reason the reforms failed was not due to the nature of the reforms but that the political equilibrium would have to change if the reforms were to succeed.

An important implication of AR's theory is that bad political equilibrium that leads to poor economic performance may persist over time, and economic growth may stagnate in a country for many years as a consequence. Since the distribution of political power determines the evolution of economic and political institutions, political elites who hold power will always have an incentive to maintain the political institutions that give them political power, and the economic institutions that distribute resources to them. Furthermore, the initial distribution of resources enables elites who have access to these resources to increase their de facto political power, allowing them to push for economic and political institutions favourable to their interests, reproducing the initial disparity in political power (Acemoglu et al. 2005). Therefore, there will be a persistence of extractive economic and political institutions in societies with such institutions, since the elites who benefit from these institutions would have no incentive to change them. Conversely, inclusive and political institutions will be more likely to prevail, once they emerge, as the emergence of such institutions (e.g. democratization and secure property rights for the majority of the population) will be likely to result in strong economic performance, reinforcing the welfare-enhancing effects of these institutions and allowing states to become more credible via greater legitimacy to the commitment of these institutions.

But what explains the switching from one growth regime to another; say, from stagnant growth to miracle growth? AR argue that while bad political equilibrium tends to persist, change is possible. With time, institutional drift may occur, leading to a critical juncture where there may be institutional divergence. This is shown in Figure 2.3.

Many factors can contribute to this divergence. For example, new economic elites may emerge who challenge the existing balance of power and demand change in economic institutions from extractive to more inclusive institutions. There is also the possibility of revolt from citizens excluded

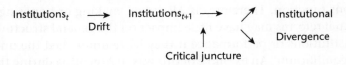

Figure 2.3. Institutional change in Acemoglu and Robinson
Source: <http://economics.mit.edu/files/7850>.

from current political institutions, and the elite may respond with greater political pluralism. AR view these critical junctures as 'stochastic' and therefore, to a large extent, exogenous, and they state that it is not clear 'under what circumstance political equilibria that lead to economic growth will arise' (Acemoglu and Robinson 2008, p. 10). Therefore, it is not clear how a country will move from a bad political equilibrium associated with growth stagnation/crisis to a good political equilibrium associated with stable or miracle growth, where the political drivers of this move are endogenously determined, and not due to external events or to exogenous factors.

The political channels that are evident in AR's theory of growth are formal institutions of credible commitment (as in the rule of law that leads to the security of property rights) and public goods provision. There is less recognition in their theory of the important role the state can play in overcoming coordination failures, and that the emergence of formal institutions of credible commitment and the provision of high quality public goods may not be enough to bring about the structural transformation that has been evident in the successful cases of economic growth in East Asia. Notwithstanding this omission, AR's theory is more a theory of growth sustenance (and by association, also a theory of long-term growth stagnation) than a theory of growth acceleration or of growth collapse. Once growth has ignited in a country, the emergence of inclusive economic and political institutions may lock in the growth process, and also by implication, broaden the process of growth to make economic growth inclusive. Also, while AR do not directly state that the inclusive economic and political institutions they take to be correlated with sustained economic growth are formal institutions, the specific examples they provide of inclusive economic institutions, such as contract enforcement and state regulation of markets, and inclusive political institutions, such as the rule of law for all citizens, suggest that these are more likely to be formal institutions. This also suggests that AR's theory of growth may be more relevant in the understanding of growth maintenance rather than growth acceleration, as the formal institutions that AR take to be crucial to economic growth need a sufficient level of state capacity for enforcement and for their effective functioning, and these enforcement capabilities (and the commitment of the ruling elite to enforce these institutions) are unlikely to be observed in the very early stages of economic growth when growth has begun to accelerate. To understand the political drivers of growth acceleration, we need a theory that can help us understand how economic growth occurs even without the presence of well-functioning formal institutions. We now discuss the work of Mushtaq Khan which, as we will argue, provides such a theory.

The Political Foundations of Growth Accelerations: Mushtaq Khan

Like AR, Khan starts with the proposition that institutions are the funda-mental cause of economic growth (Khan 2010). Also like AR, Khan takes institutional performance to be a function of the distribution of power between important groups in society. Khan (2010, p. 4) argues that the polit-ical settlement—defined as 'the interdependent combination of a structure of power and institutions at the level of a society that is mutually "compat-ible" and also "sustainable" in terms of economic and political viability'—is the key determinant of institutional performance and consequently, eco-nomic growth. While there are strong similarities here in Khan's notion of political settlement and AR's concept of political equilibrium (both take political power and institutions to be interdependent and both take insti-tutional form and functioning to be determined within the political settle-ment/equilibrium), there are differences as well—Khan's treatment of the way a political settlement emerges suggests a more dynamic view of how elites come to a settlement on the type of institutions that are compatible with the balance of power, and how these institutions may be enforced. In Khan, a political equilibrium which leads to very poor economic per-formance is not likely to last, and there would necessarily be a move to an equilibrium which is compatible with an institutional configuration that delivers better economic performance. In this sense, Khan truncates the set of AR political equilibria if ordered continuously from bad to good equilibria (from left to right) on the left—bad equilibria, while a theoretical possibil-ity, is not likely to persist, and therefore, not an equilibria in the dynamic sense. Khan does not define what the minimum level of economic viability for a political settlement may be, which suggests that the difference between the two concepts will not differ greatly in empirical terms (and as AR would argue, bad political equilibrium has shown a tendency to persist for a very long time in history).

In Khan's notion of political settlements, institutions and the distribu-tion of power have a circular and interdependent relationship. Khan defines power as holding power—that is, 'how long a particular organization can hold out in actual or potential conflicts against other organizations or the state' and where holding power is 'a function of a number of characteristics of an organization, including its economic capability to sustain itself during conflicts, its capability to mobilize supporters to be able to absorb costs and its ability to mobilize prevalent ideologies and symbols of legitimacy to consolidate its mobilization and keep its members committed' (Khan 2010, p. 20). The relationship between holding power and institutions is two-way. The configuration of holding power at the level of society is supported by a range of formal and informal institutions that reproduce and sustain the specific configuration of relative power between organizations by enabling a consistent set of economic benefits to be created and allocated. In turn, relative power determines which institutions emerge, whether institutions are enforced, and what their effect is on economic performance. If the distribution of benefits by a particular institution is not accepted by groups who have high holding power, there would be opposition to the introduction of the institution or its enforcement would be contested, leading to a possible increase in political instability, even though the institution may be growth-enhancing.

An important contribution of Khan is the primacy he accords to informal institutions in the beginning of the growth process. Khan argues that the inherited distributional power cannot be supported by the incomes generated by formal institutions alone, and that 'informal institutions play a vitally important role in all developing countries because informal institutions are the only feasible mechanism for sustaining economic benefits for powerful groups who would otherwise have lost out' (Khan 2010, p. 26). The reason why formal institutions play a less important role in developmental transitions is that those with holding power will have few of the capabilities that could benefit from protection of property rights and the rule of law, and would therefore have little interest in enforcing these institutions. It is informal institutions, then, that are compatible with the incentive structure of powerful elites, who can use these institutions to have continued access to incomes through 'political accumulation'.

Khan defines a clientelist political settlement as a political settlement where significant holding power is based on sources outside the incomes generated by formal institutions. Khan contrasts this with a capitalist political settlement, where capitalist profits are the dominant source of holding power, and argues that clientelist political settlements are likely to be the type of political settlement prevailing in developing countries, where the formal sector tends to be small, and much of the holding power of important groups are held outside the formal sector. While capitalist political settlements are more of a heuristic device for Khan since they are not likely to emerge in most developing countries until a late stage of economic development, it is more realistic to see political settlements in developing countries as hybrid in nature, with a combination of elements of both clientelist and capitalist settlements. This is for two reasons—one, in many developing countries, there are already existing productive formal sectors for reasons of history (due to colonization strategies and past import-substituting industrialization policies), and two, with some economic growth occurring, there would be demand for formal institutional change (or the enforcement of formal institutions where they exist) originating from many new agents in the productive sectors of the economy.

However, clientelist political settlements are more likely to characterize growth accelerations. Under these settlements, patron–client networks—informal relationships or organizations that involve individuals with different degrees of power—are likely to provide the institutional context within which credible commitment problems to do with investment can be addressed in an environment where formal institutions of property rights are either not there or are not likely to be enforced. In a typical patron–client network, the patron (who could be a politician or a local mafia, for instance) is an organizer of power who organizes group of clients 'who offer their organizational support in exchange for the benefits that the patron offers' (Khan 2010, p. 60). Patron–client networks can operate as informal networks or be within formal organizations such as political parties. Khan suggests that patron–client networks can be organized as pyramids, with an individual or faction being a patron of one network and client of another network. The hierarchical structure of these networks and the elements of control exercised in each level of the pyramid allows for patron–client networks to be self-sustaining and therefore credible to productive entrepreneurs in the sense that the rents from the investment process will not be completely expropriated. Therefore, patrons in the network offer local enforcement and dispute resolution activities to their clients—the investors—in return for political support and the rents that accrue from the production process.

But why do patron–client networks not degenerate into predatory networks, where the level of rent extraction is so high, that investors have little incentive to invest, or where patrons expropriate the productive assets of investors (or where investors fear that expropriation will occur at any point in the production process). Khan extends his analysis of patron–client networks and clientelist political settlements in two important ways to address this issue. Firstly, Khan argues that the structure of the ruling coalition is important in explaining why some patron–client networks have greater enforcement capabilities than others. Two dimensions of power matter in understanding these capabilities. First, the horizontal distribution of power, which is the power of the ruling coalition relative to the power of excluded coalitions. Second, the vertical distribution of power, which is the relative power of higher- compared to lower-level factions within the ruling coalition.

The most favourable combination in terms of the enforcement capabilities of the ruling coalition is when the ruling coalition faces low opposition from excluded factions so as to take a long-term view, allowing patron–client networks to be self-sustaining and growth focused. With limited power from lower-level factions, the ruling coalition is able to exercise control across the entire pyramidical structure of the network to make sure that the network does not turn predatory. A concentrated horizontal distribution of power coupled with dispersed vertical distribution of power leads to a vulnerable authoritarian coalition that is always in the danger of being overthrown, while a concentrated vertical distribution of power coupled with dispersed horizontal distribution of power leads to a weak dominant party that may be growth oriented, but is unable to obtain 'buy-in' from the different lower-level factions in using rents productively for growth. Finally, dispersion in both horizontal and vertical distribution of power can lead to 'competitive clientelism', prompting cycling of factions in power and the shortening of the time horizon of patrons, leading to possible predation and a lack of economic growth.

The second way Khan explains why some patron–client networks are growth conforming while other networks are not is to do with the capabilities and organizations of emerging capitalists. There are two dimensions of organizational capability that matter here—the technological and entrepreneurial capabilities of the emerging capitalists and the holding power of productive investors. Khan argues that investors with high capability can drive accumulation if they are politically networked, and who are able to use their political power to gain access to resources or government contracts such that they are able to accelerate their accumulation and technology acquisition strategies. On the other hand, high-capability entrepreneurs who do not have significant holding power are more amenable to discipline by a developmental coalition, allowing for effective industrial policy to be implemented, as in Korea in the 1960s to 1980s. Entrepreneurs with low to moderate capability who are politically networked can drive accumulation in the early stages, especially in low-technology industries. Finally, entrepreneurs with low to moderate capability and who are politically weak are the ones who will face most constraints on accumulation, and growth occuring in this context would depend on whether a developmental ruling coalition is in place or not.

While Khan provides a powerful theory on why patron–client networks can be growth enhancing, and not degenerate into rent-dissipating entities as often viewed in the governance literature, there are also some limitations in Khan's theory of economic growth. Firstly, it is not clear how a dominant ruling coalition which has both significant vertical and horizontal power would necessarily be growth oriented. What prevents the coalition from using its considerable power to use extractive institutions for its own ends and to maintain an optimal rate of rent extraction which may not lead to a growth collapse, but will not lead to stable/miracle growth as well? The sanction mechanisms here are weak in the absence of a third-party enforcer and the ability of the ruling coalition to be growth oriented would depend on the coalition's own long-term self-interest to maximize wealth, or in the vision of long-term development among the elites who constitute the coalition (and, therefore, exogenous to Khan's theory). Secondly, it is not obvious why competitive clientelism—that is, the cycling of factions in power—would necessarily lead to poor growth outcomes if it is a high-expectations political equilibrium, where citizens expect certain critical public goods such as education and health to be provided, regardless of the faction in power, such as that occurred in the state of Kerala in India, leading to high rates of pro-poor growth (Besley et al. 2006). Thirdly, it is not clear how technological upgrading and the overcoming of coordination failures can take place in pure clientelist political settlements when the ability of the state to 'pick winners' and to monitor the performance of firms needs a certain degree of bureaucratic capacity, and a relative autonomy of the state from the investor class (Evans 1995). It is more likely that the character of the political settlement underpinning economic growth changes from a pure clientelist political settlement to hybrid political settlements where formal institutions (e.g. the setting up of joint economic councils between the business sector and the government) and formal organizations (both an effective economic bureaucracy and well-organized and representative business associations) are increasingly important in resolving coordination failures (Bräutigam et al. 2002). Finally, Khan downplays the role of high-quality public goods provision (including a literate and skilled workforce and no infrastructure constraints) that have been seen as important determinants of economic growth in the empirical growth literature, and it is difficult to see how public goods such as education, health, and infrastructure can be provided through patron–client networks which by their very nature are exclusionary.

The above discussion suggests that Khan's theory of the politics of growth is a more convincing theory of growth acceleration than it is a theory of growth maintenance. Informal institutions and patron–client networks may be crucial in igniting growth and formal institutional reform may have little growth-enhancing effect in clientelist political settlements. But as economic growth progresses, hybridity would be a feature of political settlements, and there would be an interplay of both formal and informal institutions in the growth maintenance process. While clientelist political settlements with predominantly informal institutions would be more likely to characterize growth accelerations, hybrid political settlements with a mix of informal and formal institutions (along the lines of AR's notion of inclusive economic and political institutions) would be more likely to characterize growth maintenance.

Developmental Patrimonialism

Recently, a set of scholars working in the Africa Power and Politics Programme (APPP) has argued that neo-patrimonialism, a system of personal rule held together by the distribution of economic rents to clients and cronies, can be *developmental* in that neo-patrimonialism can be compatible with rapid pro-poor economic growth, and under certain conditions, may even help the climate for business and investment (Kelsall 2011b). The work of the APPP may be seen as an application of Khan's theory in the African context (though with some important modifications as well). The central hypothesis of the APPP is that a personalized system to manage rents centrally and to orient rent-generation to the long term can bring about strong economic performance, along with other enabling factors such as a strong, visionary leader, a single or dominant party system, a competent and confident economic technocracy, a strategy to include (at least partially) the most important political groups in some of the benefits of growth, and broadly pro-capitalist pro-rural policies (Kelsall et al. 2010). Like Khan, the APPP stresses the importance of centralized rent-management built around patronage systems as key to economic growth, in contexts where formal institutions are yet to develop or are not well-functioning, and Weberian bureaucracies are yet to emerge.

However, many of the features that the APPP considers to be characteristics of development patrimonialism are also seen as features of predatory states, such as a high degree of concentrated political power and economic discretion, and the undermining of formal or customary political processes by endemic corruption. The key variable that seems to distinguish predatory states from developmental patrimonialism is the long-term vision of the ruling elite which is absent in the former regime and present in the latter regime (see Bavister-Gould 2011 and Bratton and Masunungure 2011 on the typology of predatory states and a case study of Zimbabwe). It is not clear from the APPP's work what factors explain the stretching of the time horizon of the ruling elite to the long term—is it the level of produced output (i.e. the size of the productive economy) such as those not obtained from natural resources or foreign aid but from manufacturing and agriculture? Is it the lengthening of the discount rate of the ruling elite if they see themselves as less vulnerable to a coup or revolt in the country? Is it the temporal characteristics of the production process—that is, the longer the timescale of production (such as the production of tree crops like coffee), the fewer the incentives of the elite to engage in predation? Is it the nature of the technology in productive sectors—that is, the more sophisticated the technology, the more difficult it is to master that technology and consequently, the less is the incentive of ruling elites to expropriate output in the short term? Further sharpening of the hypothesis on how long-termism in elite commitment to the productive economy may occur would provide a better sense of how long-termism may emerge in specific contexts, and help one understand under what conditions a long-term vision would not depend on the specific qualities of the leader in charge but would be institutionalized, and so would be self-sustaining.

Coalitions and Developmental Leadership

A recent strand of work has stressed the importance of developmental leadership, understood as the political processes that mobilize people, organizations, and resources through collective action, as important catalysts for economic growth (Leftwich 2010). An earlier literature by scholars such as Deborah Bräutigam has also highlighted the role of 'growth coalitions', which are coalitions of business and political elites that are underpinned by synergistic relations and which mobilize institutions and resources for economic growth, in explaining the growth successes of countries such as Mauritius in the African context (Bräutigam et al. 2002).[1] More recently, Abdel-Latif and Schmitz (2010) look at sectoral differences in investment and growth outcomes in Egypt and find that the key contributory factors to making alliances between business and policymakers growth-oriented and not predatory was: i) common interest in the sector's growth; ii) common understanding of its problems; and iii) translating willingness into an ability to take action. They find that growth alliances were often rooted in informal linkages between economic and political elites, though there were differences in how these linkages came out in pre-existing sectors such as the food industry where most of the linkages were built around strong social ties coming from the same extended family, school, or city, while in emerging sectors such as communications, information, and technology, the roots lay in a more common professional background. The finding of Abdel-Latif and Schmitz supports the proposition that informal institutions are going to be

---

[1] One important criticism of the growth coalitions and developmental leadership literature is that it pays insufficient attention to issues of causality—do growth coalitions and development leadership cause economic growth, or do they tend to emerge once economic growth accelerates due to institutional reforms and exogenous factors such as changes in the world trading regime (Brady and Spence 2009)? Jones and Olken (2005) address this issue by using death of leaders as a source of exogenous variation in leadership and find robust evidence that leaders matter for economic growth. They also find that the effects of leaders are strongest in autocratic settings where there are fewer constraints on a leader's power.

more important in growth accelerations, and especially in bringing about 'pockets of growth' in an otherwise stagnant economy.

The literature on coalitions and developmental leadership contributes to our understanding of the politics of economic growth in two important ways. Firstly, it provides us with micro-level reasoning that is missing to a large extent in the work of AR and Khan. As Bates points out in his review of North, Wallis, and Weingast (2009), an emphasis on agency in a theory of growth allows one to 'be introduced to active agents, be they politicians, merchants, farmers or kinsmen', and to be 'informed about the problems they faced, the constraints they encountered, the beliefs they entertained and the strategies they devised' (Bates 2010, p. 755). Such micro-level reasoning allows a more nuanced and sophisticated understanding of how elites behaved in particular contexts, and what their responses and strategies were when faced with a 'critical juncture'—a threat or challenge, both internal and external—which may explain the political processes around growth accelerations and the prevention of growth collapses. Secondly, an understanding of the political processes around effective state–business relations and growth coalitions allows us to understand why growth accelerations and growth collapses occur in some countries and not in other countries with very similar initial conditions. That is, a focus on the actions of agents and organizations—the players of the game—allows us to trace out in sharper detail the move from one to another political equilibrium that may occur in a growth regime switch.[2]

Reviewing the Empirical Literature of the Politics of Economic Growth

A recent set of papers in the empirical growth literature has tried to go beyond the proximate determinants of economic growth (such as macro-economic stability and trade openness) to study the fundamental causes of

---

[2] There is a danger is some of the literature on coalitions to overstate the case for the characteristics of political coalitions as a sufficient explanatory variable for economic growth. For example, using Botswana as an example, Poteete (2009) gives primacy to the nature of the political coalition over structural factors as the key explanatory variable for economic growth to occur, particularly in resource-rich countries. That is, according to Poteete, the inclusivity and stability of the coalition was important to Botswana's economic growth in the immediate post-independence period. However, Poteete underplays the role of institutional pre-conditions and the manner in which the structure of the economy was aligned with the incentives of political elites to invest in the productive sector at the time of independence (cattle farming), while in Zambia, with a similar economic structure, this did not occur (Robinson and Parsons 2006). Furthermore, it is arguable how important are characteristics such as inclusive and stability of coalitions to explain economic growth—as Haber et al. (2003) show, after the fall of the Porfirio Diaz dictatorship in 1911 in Mexico, there was significant political instability but also strong economic growth—and the experience of Indonesia during the oil price boom years shows

economic growth across countries, and in particular, the importance of economic and political institutions.

Much of this literature has mostly focused on the determinants of long-run per capita income differences and less on determinants of why countries switch from one growth phase to another. Starting with the seminal piece by Acemoglu, Johnson, and Robinson—AJR—(2001), the empirical literature in this tradition shows that institutional quality matters for long-run economic growth, more than other 'deep determinants' of economic growth such as geography or culture. However, while measures of institutional or governance quality used in this body of work may be strong, positive correlates of long-run per capita income, they appear to be less important in explaining why some countries experience economic growth and not others. As Khan (2012) notes, for the same level of institutional quality, we see very different growth experiences among developing countries. Since the measures of institutional quality used in the AJR genre captures in essence how well formal institutions are functioning, what the cross-country econometric work in the AJR tradition establishes is the strong positive relationship between the quality of formal institutions and long-run economic growth, but not necessarily of growth transitions within countries. The implication of this literature from our perspective is that while well-functioning formal institutions may not be important determinants of growth accelerations, these institutions may be important in the growth-sustenance process, and in the long-run evolution of per capita incomes.

Finally, it is worth noting that while the cross-country econometric literature on the institutional determinants of economic growth have gone beyond the earlier focus on proximate determinants of growth such as macroeconomic stability, trade openness, and human-capital formation, and have been able to bring in an emphasis on economic and political institutions as the fundamental cause of economic growth, they still leave open the question: what is the underlying political equilibrium/settlement that generates growth-enhancing institutions, and are there specific characteristics of settlements within which growth-enhancing institutions emerge? To address this question, it will be necessary to both deepen the cross-country quantitative research by analysing the political equilibria around growth regime traverses and to complement the quantitative research with historical case studies that analyse the changes in and within political settlements around growth regime switches, with a specific focus on the political process that shapes the emergence of growth coalitions.

that a narrowly based ruling coalition (led by Suharto) can deliver significant pro-poor growth as a significant proportion of the oil revenues were channelled into a major school-building programme that had a significant poverty reduction impact (Hill 2000).

The Political Determinants of Growth Regime Switches

What do we know about the political drivers of growth regime switches? An emerging literature has examined the determinants of growth accelerations, and why some countries maintain high growth while growth declines in other countries. With respect to growth accelerations, Hausmann et al. (2005) find that standard growth determinants such as major changes in economic policies, institutional arrangements, political circumstances, or external conditions 'do a very poor job of predicting the turning points' (p. 328). They argue that growth accelerations are caused predominantly by idiosyncratic and often, small-scale changes, and suggest that further research is needed to identify the common elements in these idiosyncratic elements. Pritchett (2000) points out that slow moving determinants of growth such as improvements in the quality of institutions or time-constant factors such as geography (land-lockedness, distance from the equator), resource endowments (e.g. minerals), ethnic diversity, culture, and colonial experience are less likely to explain the frequent shifts from one growth regime to another that we observe in many developing countries and the wide variations in within-country economic growth. Jones and Olken (2008) show that growth accelerations are accompanied by increases in productivity and not investment, and with increases in trade, suggesting that reallocation of resources from less productive to more productive uses are an important part of growth accelerations. Growth declines, on the other hand, are associated with monetary instability and increases in inflation, along with higher frequency of military conflict, and trade does not play an important role in growth declines as it does in growth accelerations. Jones-Olken also find changes in institutions are not associated with either growth accelerations or declines, where institutional quality is measured by a lower level of corruption and the rule of law. However, they find that growth accelerations and declines are more likely to occur in autocracies than democracies, and in political interregnum or transition periods. On the other hand, Berg et al. (2012) find that growth duration (i.e. the avoidance of growth collapses) is positively related to the presence of democratic political institutions in the country, along with the degree of equality of income distribution. Finally, Jerzmanowski (2006) finds that better institutional quality improves the possibility that a country will remain in a stable or miracle growth phase and will be less likely to suffer a growth collapse.

The findings from the empirical literature reinforce the conclusions that we have drawn from the theoretical literature, and support the proposition that the political drivers of growth acceleration are different from the political determinants of growth maintenance. But it still leaves open the question: how does a country move from the set of institutions that are causal to a growth acceleration to the set of institutions that allow growth to be maintained, and given the high number of growth-acceleration episodes which do not sustain, why do countries exhibit differential success in the transition path from one growth regime to another? In the concluding section, we attempt to draw both the theoretical and empirical literature together to develop a set of research questions around the political dynamics of such transition paths that can help explain the stylized facts of economic growth.

Conclusions and a Set of Research Questions

In this chapter, we provided an analytical review of the theoretical and empirical literature on the politics of economic growth. We noted that the focus in much of the literature on rates of *average* growth of per capita income has obscured the fact that most countries observe dramatic fluctuations in growth of per capita income—most developing countries tend to observe stop–go growth episodes, with growth accelerations followed by growth decelerations or collapses. Thus, to understand the political drivers of economic growth, we need an explanation of the political dynamics around the transition from one growth regime to another, and the political economy determinants of growth accelerations, growth maintenance, and growth declines/collapses.

We then sketched out a framework that can take us closer to an understanding of the political determinants of growth regime traverses. We proposed three key political channels to economic growth—institutions of credible commitment, provision of public goods, and the overcoming of coordination failures. We argued that these three channels play out differently across different phases of economic growth. Institutions of credible commitment—may be a necessary and sufficient channel to growth accelerations while contributing to growth maintenance as well, and that informal institutions of credible commitment may play a more important role in growth accelerations, as opposed to formal institutions which may be more important in growth maintenance. The provision of public goods would be more important in growth maintenance and in the avoidance of growth collapse, though it can also play some role in growth accelerations. The overcoming of coordination failures would be more important in growth maintenance, and can be expected to play an insignificant role in growth acceleration.

We then reviewed the two dominant theories of the politics of growth— the theories of Acemoglu and Robinson (AR) and Mushtaq Khan. We argued that there are strong similarities in both theories in their emphasis on the political settlement/equilibrium as the key political driver of economic growth.

However, the theory of AR, with its emphasis on inclusive economic and political institutions, may be more relevant for growth maintenance, while the theory of Khan, with its emphasis on informal institutions and patron–client networks, is more relevant for growth acceleration. We also reviewed the literature on coalitions and developmental leadership and argued that they contribute to our understanding of the politics of growth in two important ways: by providing micro-level reasoning on how political settlements arise, and how they relate to economic growth, and by allowing for the possibility that not all switches in growth regimes can be attributed to incentive structures and power relations, but can be due to agential factors as well.

The empirical literature on the political and institutional determinants of economic growth complements the main conclusions that we have drawn from the review of the theoretical literature. While the cross-country econometric literature on institutions and growth suggest that there is a positive relationship between institutional quality (usually measured by the quality of formal institutions such as Weberian bureaucracies) and the level of income, there is less support for the proposition that better formal economic and political institutions or a good property rights regime or the prevalence of democracy are either necessary or sufficient to obtain growth accelerations.

Our review of the literature on the determinants of growth accelerations and growth maintenance also support this conclusion—these studies find that reforms in formal economic institutions do not seem to be associated with growth accelerations, and that the latter is more likely in a country with a non-inclusive political institution such as autocracy. However, this literature finds that a country which has witnessed growth acceleration is more likely to stay in a high-growth regime and not suffer a growth decline if better quality formal institutions were to emerge and develop in the growth process.

We end with a set of research questions that we suggest can frame future research on the politics of economic growth:

- What are the political drivers of growth accelerations? Are these more related to informal institutions/patron–client networks, development patrimonialism, and clientelist settlements?
- What are the political drivers of growth sustenance and growth collapses? Are these more related to the emergence (or non-emergence) of inclusive institutions and hybrid settlements? Do growth maintenance processes need the emergence of Weberian characteristics in bureaucracies?

- What explains the transition from political settlements characterizing growth accelerations to political settlements characterizing growth sustenance? To what is the transition endogenous? To what extent is the transition exogenously determined?

- What role do growth coalitions and developmental leadership play in growth accelerations and growth maintenance? Are the formation of growth coalitions and developmental leadership causal to the growth process, or are they enabling factors?

- How do growth coalitions and development leadership emerge, and how are they sustained? What are the structural factors and initial conditions that explain developmental leadership from predatory leadership?

- How do institutions interplay with coalitions and leadership in bringing about political equilibria conducive to economic growth?

3

The Politics of What Works for the Poor in Public Expenditure and Taxation

Paul Mosley

Making States Developmental and Pro-poor: The Evolution of Thinking

'What forms of state capacity and political commitment are required to underpin sustainable levels of growth and employment?' asks the prospectus of the Effective States and Inclusive Development (ESID) research programme (University of Manchester 2011, p. i). This chapter is concerned with the state's *fiscal* capacity—its ability to raise revenue and to spend it in a way that sustains growth and eliminates poverty—which is certainly one of the key functionings required to enable a state to work. We are concerned, in particular, with the political feasibility dimension of fiscal policy.

The first section of this chapter presents a brief historical review of approaches to these issues. This section exposes three key building blocks related to the construction of the fiscal component of an effective state on which our knowledge is still insufficient. These building blocks, examined in the remaining sections, are, first, how to make public expenditure and taxation pro-poor, second, how to build effective pro-poor coalitions, and finally, how to build tax structures which facilitate escape from a low-tax, weak-state equilibrium. In these sections, we seek to highlight gaps in research that need to be filled.

The Politics of Pro-poor Fiscal Policy: The Evolution of Thinking and Policy Priorities

During the second half of the nineteenth century, we see for the first time fiscal policy being used, particularly in what were then the newly industrializing countries of Germany, Russia, and Japan, not just to meet governments' financial requirements, but as a developmental instrument designed to transform the structure of the economy, and specifically to overcome market imperfections which prevent the economy from evolving in the way desired by the government. Amongst the activist fiscal policy instruments used to achieve this objective, four are particularly important: government investment in strategic sectors, especially infrastructure; subsidy for specific inputs (notably loanable funds) for which markets are missing or at any rate not providing the necessary support for re-equipping the economy; development of new sources of finance to overcome a government financing constraint, such as the tax on the value of unimproved land implemented by the Japanese government in 1870, which financed much new infrastructure construction; and not least, infant-industry protection, first given its developmental rationale by the German political scientist Friedrich List in 1841[1] and since then possibly the commonest and certainly the most controversial instrument of pro-developmental fiscal intervention. An important rationale for this more interventionist stance after 1850 was the belief that, in the new world where many players were competing for control over the global economy, the old laissez-faire approach to policy and to finance could, in the absence of such purpose-built intervention, no longer deliver industrialization in the manner that had worked for Britain and the United States (Gerschenkron 1959).

After the First World War, indeed from the 1920s right through to the 1970s, this activist approach to fiscal policymaking in emergent countries received considerable support from comparative economic development experiences. During the inter-war depression Brazil under President Vargas, notably, joined the group of countries practising activist fiscal policies for industrial development, and as a consequence was able during that period to record higher rates of economic growth than any country except Russia, now itself implementing five-year plans within a completely socialized economy (Hilton 1975). After the Second World War, in defiance of a liberalizing General Agreement on Tariffs and Trade agreed within the Bretton Woods agreement of 1944, what has become known as the *dirigiste* ('controlling' or 'directive') approach to economic policy (Lal 1983) was expanded to encompass a majority of developing countries. Especially in the fields of input subsidy and export taxation, as well as orthodox protectionism, we see the state's fiscal role being expanded in pursuit of faster development.

By the mid-1970s it was clear that this pattern of interventionist fiscal policy was impacting on developing countries in two radically different ways. In one group of countries, principally the 'tigers' of South East Asia

---

[1] A good account of List's political economy is provided by Payne and Phillips (2010, pp. 37–43).

(South Korea, Taiwan, and later Malaysia, Thailand, and Indonesia), but also including Brazil and arguably northern Mexico, non-traditional, and in particular manufacturing, exports expanded rapidly through the 1950s and 1960s, and this fed through into a rapid growth in the economy as a whole. In these countries and northern India, a green revolution was also beginning, enabling them to achieve self-sufficiency in food. And as a consequence of both these trends, tax revenue was able to grow in a broad-based manner and escape the straitjacket imposed on all poor countries by the dominance of taxes on foreign trade,[2] revenue from which is unstable and constrained by the long-term adverse trend in the terms of trade of primary commodities. In these countries, a positive interaction between policymaking and the diversification of the economy had become visible, leading their governments to become celebrated as 'developmental states'—most of them, at this stage, not democratic, still less corruption-free, but nonetheless able to manage a break-out into autonomous self-sustained development such as Japan and their other nineteenth-century predecessors had achieved. In the other group, comprising at this stage all other developing countries including India and China, neither a break-out into the development of manufactured exports nor the development of a fiscal base which would enable this break-out to take place was occurring. There were numerous reasons for this bifurcation, but one of them—the tendency for state intervention to be used in many countries not to promote development but to protect the special interests of 'rent-seekers'—emerged from the shadows at this time, notably in the work of Little et al. (1975) and Krueger (1979).

At this point, we become able to fit poverty, on which we are beginning to have usable data, into the picture. Policymakers had always been aware that objectives other than growth of output, and in particular individuals' standard of living, were relevant to development; but in early global development policy manifestos, such as the very first (United Nations 1951), low standards of living are equated with unemployment, and the assumption is made that a combination of policies which achieve high growth and policies which will achieve low unemployment will be enough. By 1973, however, it was clear that they were not enough. In Ethiopia and Bangladesh, after a quarter of a century in which the world had hoped that it might have been freed from starvation,[3] famine had once again recurred, and in many parts of the

[2] In the 1970s, revenue from taxes on foreign trade in developing countries averaged about 40% of total domestic revenue (World Bank, *WDR 1979*, appendix tables). But in many countries the proportion was far greater than this. In Uganda, export taxes on coffee alone accounted through the 1970s for more than 80% of total domestic revenue (Bowden and Mosley 2011, using Uganda *Annual Trade Reports*).
[3] The horrifying Chinese famine of 1958–62, which killed between thirty and fifty million people, was not known to the world until the 1990s.

62

world growth was leading to inadequate, indeed in some places near-zero, increases in productive employment. The World Bank's chief economist, Hollis Chenery, estimated that 'a decade of rapid growth in underdeveloped countries has been of little benefit to perhaps a third of their population' (Chenery et al. 1975, p. xiii).

This awareness brought about a reappraisal of development policy—in the Bank under its new president, Robert McNamara; amongst like-minded donor agencies, and amongst governments and, incipiently, NGOs in developing countries. This reappraisal (much of the intellectual substance of which is to be found in the World Bank/IDS document *Redistribution with Growth* (Chenery et al. 1975)) had two main axes, which correspond to the two dimensions of pro-poor action delineated earlier. In terms of the *optimality* criterion, we encounter through the 1970s a shift towards 'pro-poor spending policies', especially in favour of agriculture and in particular smallholder agriculture, implemented through new modalities such as integrated rural development projects—but also, in urban expenditure policies, a recognition of the economic importance of the informal sector and a shift towards policies for the benefit of low-income people such as site and service housing schemes. However, the Bank, correctly acknowledging the importance of the political–economy dimension, also took the further step of asking under what circumstances pro-poor expenditures and tax policies would be *feasible* (Bell 1975). Bell noted two important channels, beyond altruism, why a self-interested elite might wish to adopt pro-poor policies, namely the desire to buy off a rebellion of the dispossessed and the need of an insecure elite to bolster its position by finding allies—who might in some cases be found amongst the poor (Bell 1975, pp. 54–5)—motives which we characterize respectively as the *precautionary* and the *reactive* motivations for pro-poor action (Mosley 2013). In practical terms these ideas were embodied into the Bank's spending programmes through measures such as land reform, especially in Latin America, and financial support for the informal sector (Chenery et al. 1975: especially chapters 4, 6, and 7). These ideas have abiding relevance to the construction of an inclusive, pro-poor fiscal research programme.

Much, though not all, of the pro-poor thrust of the 1970s was aborted by the global recession of the 1980s, and by the tide of liberalization and retrenchment that stemmed from it. But the retreat from the 'poverty focus' policies of the McNamara era, of course, proved to be only temporary. What began in the 1980s as a protest against the social costs of adjustment (Cornia et al. 1987) was to grow into one of the most influential of the *World Development Reports* (World Bank 1990), which rested its analysis of poverty on a 'three-legged stool'—labour-intensive policies, investment in the human capital of the poor, and social safety nets. This was no ordinary humanitarian manifesto, but eventually grew, through the Millennium Development Goals (MDGs), into a global anti-poverty crusade (Hulme 2010). The idea of poverty reduction, or putting it more positively 'inclusive development' remains, twenty years later, the primary goal of international development efforts.

What Types of Expenditures and Taxation Will Have the Strongest Effect on Poverty Reduction?

Public Expenditure

Appended to the World Bank's 1990 *World Development Report (WDR)* was a new wave of analytical work on poverty reduction, of which a particularly significant component was Ferroni and Kanbur's paper (1990) on 'Poverty-Conscious Restructuring of Public Expenditure'. Ferroni and Kanbur divide the 'poverty impact' of a specific anti-poverty initiative, or expenditure on a specific sector, into three elements: gross impact, poverty focus (the proportion of persons affected who are poor), and the social valuation (the assessor's weighting between different criteria of well-being). Ferroni and Kanbur's work signals a new stage in the analysis of distributional impacts of expenditure, with gross impact decomposed into production and consumption components, the pathways of impact formally specified and, even at the beginning of the 1990s, sensitivity shown to the existence of multiple poverties each of which might require a different response. The commonest way of developing this approach has been not to look at public expenditure as a whole, but to focus on a particular anti-poverty idea, from malaria eradication to agricultural extension to village savings and loan associations, or a particular expenditure programme, or sector of the economy, and applying some variant of the Ferroni–Kanbur analysis to that. In what follows we shall concentrate on studies of the developmental and poverty impact of four sectors of expenditure: agriculture; human capital (health and education); social protection and subsidy; and military expenditure. In conclusion we shall summarize the studies which compare across different categories of public expenditure.

Agriculture

Because most of the poorest people live in rural areas and derive livelihoods only from agriculture and agriculture-related labour, it follows almost axiomatically that the major route to poverty reduction in most areas (excepting Latin America, where much poverty is urban rather than rural) is an increase in agricultural productivity, and expenditures which will make that possible. This was acknowledged by the first great development economist, Arthur Lewis (1953), in a report on the industrialization of Ghana which can be read as a forewarning of the flaws in Ghana's own import-substituting industrialization strategy;[4] it was reiterated in Ferroni and Kanbur's review of poverty-conscious expenditure strategies, which argues that 'agriculture is a key sector to be promoted, since no other sector is capable of comparably participatory growth' (1990, p. 5); and more recently it has been given quantitative teeth by a series of studies mounted under the auspices of the International Food Policy Research Institute (IFPRI), which focus on India and China (Fan et al. 2000; Fan et al. 2004; Fan 2008). The IFPRI study of India by Fan et al. (2000) finds that investment in rural roads and in agricultural research achieve far and away the most significant impacts on poverty, with education in a fairly distant third place and 'other investments, including irrigation, soil and water conservation, health, and rural community development, achieving only modest impacts on growth and poverty per additional rupee spent' (Fan et al. 2000, p. 1038). Feeder roads and agricultural research, Fan et al. argue, achieve big impacts because they impact on poverty through multiple channels: by increasing food production, by reducing the price of food grains to urban consumers, and by improving the distribution of income (Fan et al. 2000, p. 1040). In China (Fan et al. 2004) the results similarly show that the impact of agricultural research on poverty is crucially important, especially in the remote western areas where the worst poverty still persists. However, by contrast with India, they find education to be an even more powerful way of reducing poverty in rural areas. As in India, investment in irrigation and in dedicated area-based poverty reduction programmes are found to have an insignificant effect on poverty. The only African country investigated by the IFPRI studies is Uganda, and there also (Fan and Rao 2008) agricultural research is the dominant poverty-reducing influence, with feeder roads and education once again significant negative influences on poverty, although with a much less dramatic effect than research spending.[5] Because of data problems, studies of the impact of public expenditure in Africa are relatively sparse by comparison with Asia and Latin America. However, across four case-study countries of Africa (Uganda, Ethiopia, Malawi, and Zimbabwe), Mosley and Suleiman (2007) find, in similar vein to the IFPRI studies, that infrastructure and

[4] 'The surest way to industrialise the Gold Coast would be to multiply by four or five the resources available to the [Agriculture] department for fundamental research into food production' (Lewis 1953, para. 24).

[5] The number of poor reduced per million Ugandan shillings of public expenditure is given as follows: agricultural research and development, 58.39; feeder roads, 33.77; education, 12.81 (Fan and Rao 2008, pp. 82–3).

education spending are an important influence on rural poverty in addition to direct spending on agriculture. In addition, the Mosley and Suleiman study finds that the stability of pro-agriculture expenditure, as well as its level, is a significant influence on rural poverty levels.

Health and Education

Since the *Redistribution with Growth* studies of the 1970s the World Bank has been enthusiastic about human capital spending as a potential route out of the 'Baldwin trap',[6] providing, in principle, both a way of increasing the productivity of the rural poor in the short term and, in the medium term, paving the way for the possibility of small-scale-based industrialization for export (e.g. Chenery et al. 1975, chapter IV). Reflecting this, aid donors have moved a large part of their incremental disbursements in pursuit of the MDGs away from project aid (physical capital) and towards human capital, in the shape of technical assistance expenditures designed to build the human capital of the poor. Both in relation to education and health, however, the Bank has warned that in order to achieve maximum rates of return, as well as in order to reduce poverty, it is necessary to slant the pattern of public spending towards primary education and health, and away from universities and referral hospitals (e.g. World Bank 1990, 1991, 1995a[7]). Health and education also were included in the IFPRI comparative review of public expenditure and poverty (Fan et al. 2004), which finds that the Bank's warnings were well founded. 'The distributional effect of expenditures is low', they report (Coady 2008, p. 125). The benefits of public expenditures were found to be progressive in only three or four out of twelve countries analysed (i.e. Argentina, Uruguay, Malaysia, and Chile). However, where education and health were administered, as especially in Latin America, through means-tested conditional cash transfers (e.g. *Oportunidades*, formerly PROGRESA, in Mexico and *Bolsa Familia* in Brazil), the results have been promising (Coady 2008, pp. 128, 136; de Britto 2008).[8] The impact

[6] The 'Baldwin trap' is named after the path-breaking analysis of Robert Baldwin (1963), who argued that the two main strategies for development from a subsistence level both suffered from fatal flaws: mining generated potential spin-offs into industrialization but was capital-intensive and therefore generated few income opportunities for the mass of the population; whereas, conversely, smallholder agriculture generated multiple income opportunities for the mass of the population but few technological spin-offs.

[7] The World Bank's 1990 *WDR* (World Bank 1990, box 5.2) found the rate of return to primary education to be 26% across the developing world as a whole, compared with a return of 16% to secondary education and 14% to tertiary education. Across a sample of two industrialized and ten developing countries, the Bank's 1991 *WDR* (table 3.2) finds that an additional year of schooling raises male wages by an average of 9% and female wages by an average of 13%.

[8] In recent years a specialized literature has emerged on the form of the conditional cash transfer, with a particularly lively advocacy of school feeding programmes (Powell et al. 1998;

of conditional cash transfers in Latin America is also considered in detail by Haggard and Kaufman's comprehensive study of welfare spending in middle-income countries (Haggard and Kaufman 2008, p. 216). The inference seems to be that in a number of developing-country environments, as in industrialized countries (where the principle is known as 'Director's Law'),[9] political pressures cause the benefits of health and education spending to be concentrated on the middle class and the poor to remain marginalized, *unless* effective targeting procedures are implemented. How these pressures arise and can be circumvented calls for more research, and we consider them further in the third section of this chapter.

Social Protection and Subsidy

Here we consider three kinds of public expenditure on subsidy, or transfer payment. *Food subsidies*, as shown by the Ferroni and Kanbur study and also by Coady (2008), emerge as not only an inefficient but not even an equitable instrument of social protection, which have a deterrent effect on food production, and generally fail to reach vulnerable groups, partly because as in Côte d'Ivoire they are awarded principally on commodities such as wheat and rice which are not salient in the consumption of the poorest people. *Other instruments of social protection expenditure* are also examined by Coady et al. (2004), Barrientos and Hulme (2008), and Coady (2008), including social funds, cash transfers, and rural public works. In Coady's sample, the average degree of targeting effectiveness, or poverty focus, which as we have seen was 0.93 for food subsidies, is measured as 1.2 for social funds, 1.4 for cash transfers, and 1.85 for public works. Thus, in these cases, social protection expenditures were at least doing their fundamental job of redistributing from richer to poorer, and in the case of cash transfers some of the reasons for this relative success have been examined above. But the most successful of all are an ancient expedient, *public works*, used indeed by industrialized countries to avert famine in the nineteenth century.[10] An important reason for the targeting effectiveness of such schemes is that they make abundant use of what is often the only thing that poor people are able to sell—labour. Because

Daelmans et al. 2003; De Britto emphasizes that, although conditional cash transfers are a valuable expedient, they do not reduce poverty on their own, and complementary actions to stabilize the macroeconomy and remove deeply rooted inequalities are often also necessary (2008, p.191)).

[9] After the American political scientist Aaron Director, who 'almost a decade ago . . . proposed a law of public expenditures: Public expenditures are made for the primary benefit of the middle classes, and financed with taxes which are borne in considerable part by the poor and rich' (Stigler 1970, p. 1).

[10] For example, several of the main roads of northwest Scotland such as that from Dingwall to Ullapool were 'destitution roads', built in the late 1840s, an extension of those built by Thomas

the wage offered on such schemes is low, they are able to 'self-target'—only the poor wish to take up such employment offers, and therefore no expensive arrangements are required to achieve effective targeting. Public works programmes are particularly useful in addressing vulnerability and at times of emergency. As Coady (2008b, p. 153) notes, 'community involvement has been found to be important in increasing overall effectiveness', and this of course raises issues of intra-community political motivation and incentives. We return to this issue in the third section of this chapter.

Input subsidies have, as discussed in our historical review, been used since the nineteenth century both as an instrument for accelerating the rate of industrial development and, indeed, for rebalancing the whole pattern of growth from consumption towards investment. Rigorous studies of the specific developmental effectiveness of input subsidies are surprisingly scarce, but it appears likely that, especially among smallholders, they played an important part both in accelerating the rate of adoption of new technology by smallholders and thereby in reducing rural poverty in South East Asia.[11] In Africa, growth has been less than in Asia, fiscal constraints bite more tightly and subsidy is a less feasible option failing the possibility of collusion with aid donors, and largely for this reason[12] less use has been made of agricultural-input subsidy as an instrument of raising productivity and reducing poverty. Two places where this instrument, exceptionally, has been employed are Ghana and Malawi, and we believe that a great deal can be learned from both experiences. In both cases the input subsidized has been fertilizer, a key element in agricultural productivity.

The political and economic contexts differ greatly between the two cases. In Ghana, fertilizer subsidy is only available for growers of the country's main cash crop, cocoa. Cocoa productivity, especially during the middle 2000s, has increased sharply; and poverty during the period 1990 to 2005 has halved, in large part because of increased labour demand driven by this expansion of cocoa production (Nsowah-Nuamah et al. 2010). However, even though fertilizer subsidies in Ghana are now targeted through the use of a voucher system, with the intention of progressivity,[13] and even though

Telford in the earlier part of the century, to obviate the risk of a famine amongst rural subsistence cultivators such as had occurred in Ireland in 1846. See Devine (1995) and Richards (2002).

[11] On the role of subsidies in bringing about growth with equity in South East Asia see World Bank (1990); on subsidies and agricultural development strategy in China, see Fan, Zhang and Zhang (2002); on South Korea, see Moore (1985); on Indonesia, see Djurfeldt and Jirstrem (2004, chapter 4); specifically on BIMAS, the programme of multiple input subsidies adopted by the Indonesian government in the 1970s, see Barker et al. (1985).

[12] But also for political reasons, including the greater persistence of 'urban bias' (South Africa is a notable example, but Ghana is also a case in point).

[13] 'Almost all . . . fertiliser subsidies of the 21st century pronounce goals of being targeted to poor farmers' (Banful 2011, p. 1168).

Ghana has been spectacularly successful in making the transition to democracy and reducing many dimensions of corruption, some observers see the allocation of fertilizer vouchers as having been politicized[14] and, as a consequence, still inefficient (Branoah-Banful 2011).

In Malawi, by contrast, subsidized fertilizer is applied principally to maize, the country's main foodcrop, again in the form of vouchers which entitle the user to one 50kg bag of 23:21:0 (nitrogen: phosphate: potassium) basal fertilizer and one 50kg bag of urea, as part of a 'Starter Pack' input package, comprising new seeds as well as fertilizer, and designed to launch the smallest-scale and most vulnerable farmers into the market (Harrigan 2003). The introduction of Starter Pack, prima facie, was highly effective, as it led to a sharp increase in production; the three-year average of maize yields has now risen to around 2 tons/hectare, or about twice the African average (Mosley 2012, chapter 5). The need to import maize has diminished greatly, with an export surplus in 2006/2007, providing additional food security; however, at the same time, the price of maize has increased, which has altered the profile of poverty, decreasing it for producers but increasing it for consumers, especially consumers who do not have jobs or assets to draw on[15] (Dorward and Chirwa 2011, p. 232). At the time of writing, Malawi had experienced major governance problems in 2010 and 2011 which put aid flows, and thus the continuance of the fertilizer subsidy, at risk, but there is hope, with the election of a new president in 2012, that these problems may have been resolved.

In both these cases, there is non-rigorous evidence that even the subsidies currently in position have had an important role in raising productivity and, thereby, reducing poverty. However, in both cases political factors have had a leading role in the design of the subsidy package and some commentators have stated outright that the new, targeted, systems of input allocation by voucher are still politically tainted. We therefore believe that there is a strong case for a study of the political and economic rationale for agricultural-input subsidies, which examines the possibilities for increasing the effectiveness of input subsidies by making them 'smarter' and in particular by making them performance-based in a way that is conscious of the distortions which have entered the new voucher systems. Just as performance-based subsidies helped to create the developmental states of South Korea and Indonesia in the second half of the twentieth century, so we feel that the proto-developmental states of Africa in the twenty-first

---

[14] In particular, Banful (2011, p. 1166) alleges that 'more vouchers were targeted to districts that the ruling party has lost in the previous presidential elections and more so in districts that had been lost by a higher percentage margin'.

[15] Especially this has caused suffering in the south of the country in districts such as Ngabu, where a quasi-South Asian problem of landlessness is beginning to emerge.

could be assisted by a better understanding of what this instrument of economic policy has achieved and could achieve.

Taxation

The incidence of taxation on the poor has been very thinly studied: a 2001 report to DFID (Gemmell and Morrissey 2001, p. 1) records that 'poverty and/or inequality considerations have received little if any attention in LDC tax reforms', and indeed there exists something of a conventional wisdom, with which we disagree, which suggests that fiscal redistribution should only be carried out on the expenditure and not on the tax side. Some of the few studies of this issue that have been done, both officially by the IMF (e.g. Cubero and Hollar 2010, on Central America) and by NGOs (e.g. Lashari and Sharpe, 2011, on Pakistan) suggest that the incidence of taxation as a whole is regressive, for familiar political reasons: the rich in developing countries, because of their control over power-structures, global reach, and knowledge, are very good at tax evasion, and more broadly at manipulating governments so that they are not even required to pay taxes. The valuable work on taxation of the two DFID RPCs so far established, the Centre for the Future State (CFS) and the Crisis States Research Centre (CSRC), does not get to grips with this research gap. Here, we take a case-study approach to five countries comparatively: three African cases (Ghana, Uganda, and Zambia) and two Latin American cases (Bolivia and Argentina). The thrust of the argument is that although, indeed, there is a tendency for LDC tax systems to be regressive, this tendency has been successfully resisted in a number of countries through the incorporation into elite bargains of a number of imaginative ideas which suggest that it may be good politics to be pro-poor.

African Cases: Uganda, Ghana, and Zambia

In Uganda, Ghana, and indeed all the African countries which developed on a basis of African smallholder exports,[16] the colonial authorities originated in the 1930s and 1940s, as described earlier, the practice of diverting a portion of the on-farm price of export crops away from farmers and into the country's treasury to finance development—a practice which was continued after independence in the 1960s. The proportion thus retained varied according to the state of the international market but in some boom years rose to over 90 per cent of the export price. This rake-off was never described by governments of the time

---

[16] 'Peasant export economies' as described by Myint (1976); this economic structure also developed in Malaysia, Indonesia, and other countries of South and South East Asia.

as a tax, rather as a 'development levy' or equivalent phrase,[17] but so effectively did it function as one that, in Uganda at the end of the 1980s, three-quarters of the government's total public revenue was accounted for by export duties on coffee alone. All exports other than coffee were wiped out by this export taxation,[18] which at the same time, being targeted on labour-intensive and mostly low-income rural producers, was highly regressive.

In 1991, Uganda grasped the nettle of eliminating the export tax and creating in its place a structure of import duties, initially at high rates which were then gradually lowered over the later part of the 1990s. In the process, the structure of taxation has been shifted from one almost exclusively targeted on smallholder rural producers, the majority of whom were poor at the beginning of the 1990s, to one much more oriented towards urban consumers, a good number of whom are well off. Thus not only has the 'tax trap' been sprung, but sprung in a pro-poor manner: Chen et al. (2001) show that the tax changes of the 1990s led to an increase in the progressivity of the tax system in Uganda.[19] In Ghana, the process of liberalization, again by contrast with Uganda, has involved not the total removal of the export tax but rather its gradual easing to a level of about one-third of the export price, by comparison with 80 per cent at the beginning of the 1980s. Notwithstanding this, there has been a distinct reduction, since the end of the 1980s, of Ghana's dependence on primary exports for its revenue and a reduction in particular of the fiscal pressure on the cocoa producer, which suited well the political imperatives bearing on the PNDC (later NDC) governments of Ghana in the 1990s, namely above all to capture and retain support in rural areas.[20] Much more than in Uganda, the diversification of tax revenue has been not just into the building up of VAT revenue but also into collections of direct tax from individuals as well as companies.[21] There

---

[17] Governments still using this system of taxation in the 1980s included, in addition to Uganda and Ghana, Cameroon, Benin, Togo, Nigeria, Côte d'Ivoire, Congo, and Congo DRC; see Mosley and Chiripanhura (2009).

[18] 'For example, tea production fell from a peak of 20,000 tons in the early 1970s to around 2,000 tons by the early 1980s, and cotton production fell from 87,000 tons to 2,000 tons' Reinikka and Collier (2001, p. 31).

[19] See Chen et al. (2001). Liberalization of taxes on smallholder exports has in other African countries with a similar productive structure (in particular Cameroon, Benin, Togo, Madagascar, and Côte d'Ivoire) had a much lesser impact on poverty. We investigate this difference in poverty impacts in Mosley and Chiripanhura (2009) and give, provisionally, three reasons for it: better infrastructure, enabling the benefits of crop-price liberalization to be transmitted to small-scale producers; better chemistry with the aid donors, enabling a more stable and productive flow of aid money; and, deriving from this, a more pro-poor expenditure pattern, which built upon a pro-poor asset structure inherited from colonial times (Bowden and Mosley 2012).

[20] 'The NDC . . . was aware that it was not especially popular in the cities where structural adjustment had produced the greatest pain, but it also knew that the elections would be won and lost in the countryside' (Nugent 2001, p. 410).

[21] In 2003, tax collections from the personal sector in Uganda were 19 billion shillings out of total direct tax revenue of 276 billion shillings, or 6.8%. In Ghana they were 1,535 million cedis out of total direct tax revenue of 3,401 billion, or 45% (Mosley 2012, table 5.6).

has even been a broadening of taxation into previously untapped bases such as the informal sector (Joshi and Ayee 2008).

By contrast with Uganda and even Ghana, Zambia's economy and therefore its tax system is much more heavily dependent on mining. The President, Levy Mwanawasa, imposed a new windfall tax in 2008 on the profits of the copper companies, explicitly earmarked to be spent on social protection expenditures (Cheeseman and Hinfelaar 2009, p. 65; Lungu 2009), which was suspended in 2009 and then restored in 2011 in the form of a 3 per cent duty on mineral royalties, proceeds from which were earmarked 20 per cent for government spending on health and education[22] and 20 per cent for local councils, with the balance going to community development. In other words, Zambia, having embarked on a promising quasi-Latin American path (some Latin American cases are considered below) of linkage between windfall export taxes and social protection, now appears to be experiencing a 'mineral taxation political business cycle'. It would clearly be to the advantage of investment and poverty reduction if this cycle could be stabilized, and we believe that a great deal can be learned from the experience of Latin American countries, including Argentina, Bolivia, Venezuela, and Ecuador, which have also experimented with export taxation partly or wholly earmarked for progressive expenditures and in particular social protection. Taxes of this sort have for the last decade been an important element in providing an economic and social basis for the anti-neoliberal, left-of-centre political movement known in Latin America as *neodesarrollismo*: of course they represent a direct challenge to the 'Washington Consensus' which is based on the opening of closed economies and, since exports are seen by the Consensus as the key to growth, on the removal rather than the imposition of taxes on exports. Much more covertly and with less use of anti-Washington rhetoric than Latin America, several African countries have also experimented with earmarked export taxes of this sort, again with progressive and sometimes also with decentralizing intentions. These countries include Zambia, as discussed above; Ghana, whose attachment of cocoa export duties to 'new-style' import subsidies was also earlier described; and Mauritius, where taxes on sugar exports until the 1990s[23] played a major part in achieving the transition from a primary product-based economy and tax system to a more diversified economy (Bräutigam 2008, chapter 6). Bräutigam describes the political and governance advantages of the Mauritian export taxes as follows:

> Although the sugar industry benefited from extensive rents . . . these rents never became a resource curse, because they were *earned* by the tens of thousands of

---

[22] *The Courier*, issue no. XXIII (May/June 2011).
[23] In 1994, the sugar export tax was replaced with a value-added tax on consumption.

sugar planters, collected by the government through the export tax and used to build capacity in the state and in society. The export tax helped the private sector to organise, and it built their capacity to interact with the government. It helped both state and society to solve some of the collective action dilemmas they faced in building skills and supporting research on sugar. It served to underpin the demands by taxpayers for voice and for state employment, leading to a state that was unusually democratic and with an unusually high proportion of local officials at independence. (Bräutigam 2008, p. 158; emphasis in original)

The significance of this achievement, of course, does not relate to tax structures only. Mauritius is the closest thing to a developmental state in Africa: much closer than the more analysed cases of Botswana and South Africa, neither of which has been able to achieve a breakout into export-based manufacturing. These results have not been achieved by adherence to the Washington Consensus, but through a structure of performance-based protection which closely approximates the model of the East Asian developmental states (Gulhati and Nallari 1990). Indeed, although most progress towards the remaking of the 'Washington Consensus' has consisted of a broadening of the range of policy instruments rather than of new theory, we believe that if it turns out to be possible, under this programme, to design 'smart' export taxes which deal with the revenue problem, the distributional problem, and the incentive problem at the same time, orthodox trade theory, which outlaws export taxes, will have to be remade. Of course, the politics associated with export taxes on minerals, as in Zambia and Latin America, differs from the politics associated with export taxes on primary exports, as in Ghana and Mauritius. We develop this point further later.

Although the general political advantages of export taxation of this sort have been discussed by a number of commentators,[24] no study of any country, to our knowledge, has yet analysed their distributional impact, nor has any study examined the potential trade-offs between short-term political and distributional impact and long-term impact on distribution and growth, and whether this trade-off can be finessed in any way.

We may summarize this discussion of pro-poor expenditure and taxation options as follows:

1. The main sectors of public expenditure where there is evidence of high leverage on poverty globally are agriculture (and specifically

---

[24] In particular, the IMF has become very interested in the issues associated with export taxation of minerals including oil (Hossain 2003; Sala-i-Martin and Subramaniam 2003; Daniel et al. 2010; IMF 2011: appendix VII). But in general, its analysis is of taxation only, and not of taxation linked to public expenditure; nor are the political consequences of different incidences of taxation and expenditure, and their political impacts on political stability, factored in.

agricultural research and development), rural infrastructure (and specifically rural roads, including emergency social protection expenditure), and primary education. Increases in military expenditure have a negative impact on poverty.

2. Putting these things together, pro-poor expenditure has a positive impact on poverty and aid effectiveness. Research is needed to understand the way in which input subsidies can be configured in a 'smart' manner so as to reduce poverty in a targeted manner whilst at the same time maximizing investment.

3. The instability of expenditure, as well as its composition, impacts on the well-being of the poor. Research is needed on how elements of public expenditure and the influences on it, such as overseas aid, impact on expenditure instability, and on how such instability could be mitigated.

4. Information on the distributional impact of taxation is particularly thin. In some cases, precisely because the political thrust of taxation in colonial and post-colonial times was urban-biased and anti-poor, the reforms of the 1990s can be seen even without elaborate analysis as pro-poor.

5. The imposition of taxes on large-scale corporations, and the removal of exemptions, is, providing that it does not damage investment, good for poverty reduction; as illustrated by reductions in poverty consequent on amendments to the export tax regime both in Africa (Ghana, Uganda, and Zambia at least) and Latin America (Argentina, Bolivia, and Ecuador). In the case where these corporations deplete non-renewable natural resources, such taxes provide an environmental as well as a poverty dividend.

6. Building on point 5 of this list, it is important to research the impact of linkages between export taxation on large companies and the kind of targeted pro-poor payments described above, and the implications of 'smart' export taxes of this sort for trade and development theory.

How Do Pro-poor Coalitions Form and Hold Together?

The very idea of 'pro-poor political action' is a little paradoxical because, as individuals, poor people have little ability to change the world by influencing others; nor, as we have discussed, do they anywhere form a coherent or united class with an idea of their common interests and the ability to advance them as a group (Bell 1975, p. 53; Haggard et al. 1996, p. 120). Often, indeed, as recent surveys have pointed out, the interests of different groups within the poor are in fact opposed.[25] And yet, political action on behalf of the poor has often been successful, witness the dramatic fall in poverty that has occurred over the last twenty years,[26] which has benefited not only the urban groups where development theories of the 1960s and 1970s assumed that power in developing countries was concentrated (Lipton 1977), but poor rural people also. How has this happened?

Our story emerges from the two answers originally given by Bell (1975, p. 53):

1. *The precautionary motive: the elite may fear that, unless they incorporate the poor in their policymaking, they will be pushed out of power.* As DFID note (2011, p. 13) 'exclusionary politics are associated with high levels of violence and poor development outcomes', and the elite, perceiving this, may choose to pre-empt such outcomes by means of inclusive policies. However, if inclusion is wise and exclusion is foolish, even from the point of view of self-preservation, the question then arises why so many elite leaders opt for exclusion rather than inclusion (amongst twenty-first-century examples, Indonesia under Suharto 1997–2000, Bolivia under Sanchez de Losada 2003, and now Libya, Egypt, and Syria 2011–13 are relevant cases). As shown by Hesselbein (2011) the elite bargain is by no means always an inclusive one, and the decision to be inclusive is a gamble; we need to understand better why those who take the conciliatory rather than the hawkish option choose to do so.

2. *The reactive motive: the elite may be weak, unable to govern on its own without support, and look to the poor for support.* In cases where (1) does not apply, a weak elite may nonetheless decide that a coalition is the best bet since they reason that otherwise they cannot hold on to power,[27] and this focuses our attention on when it is a low-income group that is sought out to be a member of that coalition, and what enables coalitions with low-income groups to endure rather than collapse.

Most of the literature which speaks to these hypotheses is of a case-study, rather than a globally comparative, nature[28]—there is still very little material

---

[25] The most eloquent demonstration of this is by Anirudh Krishna (2009, p. 954), who shows, with the help of data from Andhra Pradesh, that the entrepreneurial poor who expect to escape from poverty soon tend to make fiscal demands on the state which correspond to their expected future livelihood (including demands for education, transport, and other infrastructure such as irrigation), whereas the newly poor make different demands, in particular for better health care, whereas the chronic or persistent poor make demands which are different again, in particular wage labour.

[26] See Hulme (2010).

[27] As noted by DFID (2011, p. 64): 'It is usually broad based coalitions, not just "the poor" or "civil society" that bring about change.' The remarks by Krishna about variations in motivation amongst the poor are also relevant here.

[28] Case-study literature which examines the scope for forming pro-poor coalitions includes the essay on Tanzania by Therkildsen (2008) which argues that the ruling party, CCM, can be

on what causes weak elites to look to poorer groups to consolidate their position, and what factors successfully enable them to do that.[29]

In Mosley (2012) we show that elites, even if they do not directly identify with the interests of lower-income groups, may still see them as enough of a threat (Indonesia and Russia) or a potential asset (Uganda, Bolivia, Argentina, Ghana) to implement policies which have those lower income groups' interests in mind. We also know that, in some cases, recent experience of conflict (Uganda, Bolivia, Argentina, and Indonesia) or simply of economic underperformance and political turbulence (Ghana) can serve as a salutary shock which crystallizes a decision by the policy authorities to work within a more inclusive institutional and decision-making framework. However, the sample from which our observations are drawn is quite small, and biased towards countries who have been successful in learning from experience, which argues for caution in making inferences.[30]

However, one gap in our knowledge is pretty clear. This is that, although Argentina, Bolivia, Uganda, Ghana, and Indonesia may have learned effectively from misery in the 1990s and 2000s, other countries confronted with identical shocks have not done so, and we do not yet know why. Within the fiscal area, we therefore need to research why elites, confronted with a challenge to their authority:

- sometimes 'take the risk' of sending tax and expenditure signals which are intended to be inclusionary, and sometimes not;
- sometimes send institutional signals (e.g. the creation of the Argentinian *Mesa de Dialogo*, and the Bolivian *Asemblea Constituyente*) which are intended to be inclusionary, and sometimes not.

To send a signal, of course, is not a guarantee that it will be accepted, and if we are to understand why coalitions form, we also need to understand not only why representatives of low-income groups, on receiving such a signal, decide to

regarded as 'a pro-poor distributional coalition', and this author's essays on politics of poverty reduction (Mosley 2012, 2013).

[29] Studies which have attempted to generalize concerning the factors which cause weak elites to look to the poor for support remain uncommon. One study which does attempt this is the paper by Moore and Putzel (2001), which insists that there is scope to increase the political capabilities of the poor at the macro (central government), meso (sectoral or regional), and micro (project) levels, and in particular emphasizes that the poor and middle-income strata often have common interests. This point has been taken up by observers especially in Latin America, such as Schneider (2004), who additionally argues that innovation in the formation of coalitions is more likely to come about in circumstances of economic crisis 'because the status quo is seen as intolerable', an observation borne out by our discussion of the cases of Argentina, Bolivia, and Uganda below. On Latin America, see also the papers by Birdsall et al. (2011) and Lopez-Calva and Lustig (2010).

[30] A particular merit of Hesselbein's analysis of elite bargains (2011) is that she examines cases of states which have fallen apart, such as Afghanistan and the DRC, as well as the usual cast of success cases.

accept it or reject it. In other words, our research needs to try and understand the bargaining process which leads to a political settlement, and thereby to frame workable generalizations about what kind of atmosphere leads to an inclusive political settlement in which fragile coalitions can become stronger. In terms of likely explanatory variables, this requires us to investigate the role of:

1. Inequality, 'especially horizontal', as stated by DFID's review of politics and governance research (DFID 2011, p. 34). Langer (2009, pp. 544–5) shows that the possibility of violent political mobilization in northern Ghana was obviated by the efforts made by successive (southern-based) regimes to conciliate the north and in particular to encourage the political inclusion of the northern elites. He draws an explicit parallel with Côte d'Ivoire, where the northern elites were excluded rather than coopted and where there has been severe conflict from 2002 to the beginning of the current year (Langer 2009, p. 545).

2. Democratic political institutions. Ghana and Mozambique are the prime African illustrations of this, and the theme connects in an obvious way to institutions and legitimacy.[31]

How Can Bottom Billion Countries Escape from the Low-tax, Low-income, Weak State Trap? (And the Role of Aid in this Trap)

We conclude by examining the politics of the 'tax trap', which is the problem that weak states have weak tax systems, and so cannot easily afford the spending which is required to strengthen the state. As shown by Moore (1999) the lowest-income ('bottom billion') group of countries have not only the lowest tax ratios but also, very possibly because they dare not embark on the politically risky measures required to increase them, the lowest rate of increase of tax revenue. Without escape from this trap, of course, there is no possibility of building a developmental state.

However, escape from the trap is possible. We have seen this in the second section of this chapter, in our discussion of Ghana and Uganda. These countries, in spite of being low-income countries with an average per capita income of around $500, nonetheless managed to more than double their tax ratios between 1990 and the present,[32] and then to convert that into a

---

[31] DFID, however, warn (p. 14) that 'elections may not be an effective vehicle to achieve lasting elite bargains'.

[32] The tax ratio of Uganda was just under 5% in the late 1980s, but increased from this to a stable level of about 12% by the mid-2000s, at which point it has stalled (as discussed further below). In Ghana, the tax ratio increased from 11% to 22% between 1990 and 2007. Data from IMF *Government Expenditure Statistics*.

pattern of public expenditure which yielded rapid pro-poor growth (Osei et al. 2005; Stotsky and Woldemariam 1997; Gupta 2007). What enabled them, and other such exceptional cases, to do this? In particular, did they confront the political risks associated with increasing the ratio of tax revenue to national income, or did they find a way of finessing those risks?

In Table 3.1, we categorize developing countries by income and tax ratio. The poorest countries, on average, have the lowest tax ratios (about 13 per cent, by contrast with almost twice that in the upper-middle-income category), but the dispersion around the average tax ratio in the bottom income group is considerable, and we now focus on the 'outliers' in the lowest-income group: the ones who, although poor, have been able to escape from the low-tax trap. These include, in addition to Ghana and Uganda, Kenya and Zambia.

A key determinant of success for the poorest countries has been *ability to escape from a limited tax structure dominated by trade taxes*. In colonial times, the revenue base of developing countries was derived mainly from duties on exports and imports, which were the simplest revenue source to administer. Forty years after the end of colonialism, revenue from trade taxes still accounts for around half of all state revenue in many bottom billion countries, and this has been a major constraint on development, as the commodities

Table 3.1. Tax ratios by income category (with 'outstanding performers' separately listed)

	Per capita GDP($) 2009	Tax ratio (average 1980–2009)	Trade taxes share of tax revenue (average 1980–2009)	Independent revenue authorities	Aid/GDP% (average 1980–2009)
Upper middle-income (per capita income>$4000) (n=5)	5456	23.4	10.4		1.8
Lower middle-income (per capita income $1000-$3000) (n=5)	2394	15.2	12.7		6.1
Low income (per capita income<$1000) (n=21)	500	13.2	22.1		11.1
Low income outliers:					
Ghana	670	17.1	24.4	yes	9.0
Kenya	770	18.3	12.0	yes	7.0
Uganda	420	11.0	17.0	yes	12.2
Zambia	950	18.7	16.3	yes	19.5

Source: World Bank, *World Development Indicators.*

which are most salient in the trade of developing countries have low income elasticities, hence revenue from them cannot be expanded rapidly as the economy expands; also, because their prices are volatile, tax revenue derived from this source is unstable, which is damaging both for the effectiveness of public expenditure and for political stability (Greenaway and Milner 1993). Therefore, a crux for expanding the tax base is the ability to diversify out of trade taxes into a broader mix of revenue sources, in particular taxes on sales, income, and capital. This structural shift was more effectively achieved by the four 'outliers' than by low-income countries as a whole. (It still has a long way to go: e.g. in most of low-income Africa and Latin America, taxation on capital assets has made very little progress.)

The 'outliers', of course, like the rest of the world, had to find a way round political opposition to the introduction of new taxes, and the fascinating question for future research is how this was achieved. We have already observed three ways in which this was done:

- *sequencing* of new taxes so that they were brought in at times when taxpayers were, as much as they would ever be, in a receptive mood because they have just received broad-based cuts in real income, some of them consisting of cuts in trade taxes. Thus, there was little political opposition to the wide diffusion of value added tax (VAT) in Uganda and Ghana in the 1990s, because at the beginning of the decade producers of export crops (cocoa in Ghana and coffee and cotton in Uganda) had received a substantial dividend from an increase in on-farm prices consequent on reduction in export taxation on those crops. This in turn derives from the fact that Uganda and Ghana, in the late 1980s and 1990s, achieved political settlements in which smallholder producers were very well represented;

- *earmarking* of taxes to expenditure, in particular to social security (Argentina, Bolivia, Zambia, also Mauritius, which made the link between tax payment and the receipt of benefits visible and justifiable to taxpayers);

- *introduction of a progressive rhetoric and ethos* into the tax system which encouraged compliance (the approach previously described as 'tax signals', in which the link between tax payments and the benefits derived from expenditure is publicized and illustrated, and the social contract between taxpayers and the state is presented as a necessary part of the construction of a developmental state).

In addition to these three approaches, experiments have been made in tapping new taxes by initiating a dialogue between taxpayers and government, as described for the case of the Ghanaian informal sector by Joshi and Ayee

(2008). Beyond changes in tax rates and bases, complementary policies are relevant to explaining these levels of tax effort, for example, exchange rate flexibility: African countries with flexible rates have been much more successful than countries with fixed rates in generating increases in tax revenue. Equity is also as a background factor which encourages compliance, just as it encourages the achievement of political stability (see third section of this chapter).

In many cases, the heavy lifting that made possible an increase in tax effort was achieved by reforms of *institutional structure* rather than by changes in policy. For example, the creation of independent revenue authorities, as we saw from our Latin American cases in the second section, have been associated with increases in tax ratios. In Africa, the introduction of internal revenue authorities is more recent but is also making progress especially in 'outlier' cases (Zambia, Uganda, Ghana; see Table 3.1). In addition, where closing of loopholes permitting rich people and corporations to go tax-free has been politically feasible (Kenya since 2002, Ghana), that has been very important not only in increasing revenue but in building a pro-compliance ethos (or social contract) that has facilitated further governance reforms.

So, on the evidence of Table 3.1, a part of the story is that in the countries we have identified as outliers, governments have escaped from the tax trap by finding it in their long-term interest to vary both the structure of taxation and its administrative environment. As part of the strategy used to achieve this, some agricultural taxation, as in Ghana, Uganda, and other countries based on smallholder exports, was radically *cut*. The pill of an increased average tax burden was sugared both by policy and administrative devices, and in both cases the establishment of an ethos of fairness was, we argue, of great importance.

But the question remains, why did some countries find it in their interest to broaden the tax base in this way, and others not? Underlying this question are two political developments of great importance of the last thirty years: the ability of some states (the ones conventionally treated as proto-developmental states) to adopt a long-term time perspective, which acknowledges, for example, the value of building up a domestic tax base to finance development expenditure rather than depending on aid flows; and the ability of these same states to construct elite bargains which, being broad-based, are able to stand up to rather than surrender to the special, often urban-based, interests whose dominance makes the state weak. These issues have been investigated on a case-study basis by, for example, Bräutigam et al. (2008), di John (2008), Hesselbein (2011), and Mosley (2012). However, there exists as yet no general story concerning the politics of building developmental states out of weak low-income states.

Part of this process, of course, is the transformation of aid donors from a liability into an asset for the government revenue base, and this is by no means easy. In Bräutigam and Knack (2004) it is suggested that increased aid flows are associated not only with lower tax receipts but also with worse levels of another indicator of state capacity, namely the ICRG index of corruption. Grossman (1992) has also suggested that 'by making control of the government a more valuable prize, aid may even increase political instability' (quoted in de Haan and Everest-Phillips 2007, p. 10). The line of thought that emerges from all this is that aid flows, whatever good they may do in the short term, may do harm in the long term by undermining institutions. An argument of this sort can be used to underpin some disturbing recent findings about aid impact, for example the contention of Rajan and Subramaniam (2008) that aid and growth are not correlated, whatever the length of lag that is used.[33] Indeed, the whole horizon of aid-effectiveness studies has recently become clouded, in part by this suggestion that aid may in some inescapable way undermine governance.

Does aid in fact undermine long-term fiscal capacity in this way? If this question could be answered this would contribute not only to our understanding of what determines tax capacity but to our broader understanding of the causes of poverty. In the background paper, Mosley (2011), we begin from one of the fundamental insights of the Haggard and Kaufman (2008) study—that tax capacity determines the ability of governments to finance social programmes and thus reduce poverty. To that idea we add two findings from earlier on in this paper, namely that expenditure composition is important in determining poverty impact (2008, pp. 6–12) and that, as just discussed, the composition of taxation and in particular the ability of governments to diversify out of their traditional dependence on trade taxes may be important for determining governments' ability to expand public revenue. These ideas can be assembled to generate Figure 3.1.

In common with de Haan and Everest-Phillips (2007) we feel it is important to see donors as political agents, and we would add on the basis of the preceding discussion that it is important to see taxpayers also as political agents in order to understand the possibilities for escape from the tax trap and in particular the reasons why some very poor countries, in spite of the temptation to substitute aid for tax effort, spurn that temptation and manage to escape. We find that various political–economy factors, including the shock of recent conflict, the inclusiveness of the elite (as previously discussed) and the quality of the technical-assistance relationship with the IMF and other parties, help to determine tax effort, which in turn determines

---

[33] We stress that Rajan and Subramaniam do not use this argument to explain their findings. In Rajan and Subramaniam (2009) they suggest instead a Dutch-Disease causal mechanism.

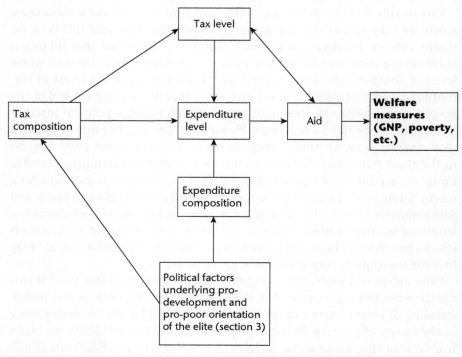

Figure 3.1. Causal links in a model of aid, expenditure, and taxation
Source: Author.

expenditure possibilities, which determines growth and the effectiveness of aid as in Figure 3.1. Our analysis, still highly provisional, indicates the following preliminary conclusions (Mosley 2011, tables 2–4):

1. Growth and poverty reduction capacity are influenced by the composition, as well as the level, of expenditure flows (following the argument of the second section of this chapter).

2. Expenditure capacity is influenced by revenue generated, holding constant other determinants of expenditure ceilings including macro-budget constraints, democracy, and strategy factors determining the ability to government to chart a palatable way around the inevitable opposition to increased taxes.

3. Tax revenue is determined, following the argument of this section, by tax composition and administrative capacity. It is also influenced by aid; however, the impact of aid on tax is much more complex than the simple crowding-out effect visualized by Bräutigam and Knack. The relationship is a two-way, interactive one, and its outcome is determined not only by the Knack-Bräutigam crowding-out effect, but also

by the magnitude of two more positive impacts, namely the direct effect of technical assistance by donors into tax design, the strategy factors discussed in point 2 of this list, and the indirect effect of aid on tax revenues via growth.

4. Therefore, the size and composition of taxation and their consequent impact on public expenditure are crucial to understanding the impact of aid on growth, including that part of the impact which works through the link from aid to tax revenue. As it happens, we arrive, using plausible lag-structures, at a more optimistic estimate of the impact of aid on growth than do Rajan and Subramaniam. In common with other commentators such as Arndt et al. (2009) and Minoiu and Reddy (2010), we find a mildly positive long-run effect of aid on growth.

However, the crucial issue is not this soundbite, but the dependence of the size of the impact on fiscal behaviours. We hope that our exploration of these behaviours can help make aid donors, including DFID, more effective in their operations.

Conclusion

A key challenge within international development is how to identify the political processes which will enable developing countries to achieve improved access to services, and more committed and accountable states. This chapter has focused on the fiscal element of those processes, and has identified three major territories needing to be researched: effective targeting of public expenditure, the creation of coalitions which include the poor, and ways of exiting from the 'low-tax, weak-state' trap. Within these territories we have identified, having regard to ongoing complementary research, eight pieces of work which fill gaps in that research. Below we list these tasks in the form of propositions needing to be tested, and show how they emerge from the existing literature.

In the first territory, *making public expenditure and taxation more pro-poor in their impact*, we have seen that where markets for critical inputs fail, subsidies which make those inputs available have been a critical tool in creating the developmental states, first of Japan and Brazil in the first half of the twentieth century, and then in the Far East in the second half. In bottom billion countries, subsidies have been less effective; but they are now proving their worth. The challenge for the future (task 1) is to *design them in forms which strengthen the state by allocating subsidy in forms which are 'smart', that is, improve equity and efficiency at the same time*. Another strand we have observed in the expenditure literature is that, as noted in the case of Malawi, expenditure instability damages effectiveness and indeed may make the state itself more fragile. A part of making the state more stable in a political sense, indeed, consists (task 2) of *making it more stable in an economic sense by reducing the volatility of government expenditure.* Since, in bottom billion countries, a large part of public spending is financed by aid, this task inevitability brings the issue of controlling aid volatility into play.

In the last ten years there has been a great upsurge of literature on taxation and its role in securing the state and making it developmental. However, very little of this literature has been explicitly devoted to the redistributive role of taxation. The recent experience of Latin America in particular, has shown that export taxes, however, can both be revenue-increasing, progressive, and at the same time 'smart', by introducing appropriate efficiency incentives. *A main research challenge facing this research consortium (task 3) is to find out whether this can in fact be achieved.* If that can be done, the possibility on the horizon is that contributions can be made not only to political economy but to development economics, by defining a set of principles by which export taxes can contribute both to equity and to a more competitive economy.

In the second proposed research territory, *reinforcing pro-poor coalitions*, the literature has profusely observed that poor people, not anywhere constituting a cohesive interest group with its own strategy for advancing the interests of the poor, risk being politically marginalized. The experience of the last twenty years suggests in fact that pro-poor coalitions do often form. But we have few systematic findings on what initial conditions cause such coalitions to form, and our first recommendation within this territory (task 4) is that *research of this kind, to explain the ways in which pro-poor coalitions form is needed as a precondition for good policy design*, probably involving a larger sample of study countries than simply the case-studies referred to here.

The next question is what (fiscal) incentives can be provided to encourage pro-poor coalitions to form? Here also we are on uncertain ground. However, one possible way forward is to focus on the *composition of public expenditure.* Our paper Hudson et al. (2011) argues that every variation in the composition of public expenditure changes the balance between those who gain and those who lose from the continuance of current policies—and thereby the likelihood of both conflict and poverty reduction. This yields the concept of the *social efficiency wage*—the rate of social wage, or public spending, which most effectively buys off the risk of conflict and political instability—and the related concept of *pro-poor expenditure*—the level and mix of public spending which maximize the poverty-reducing impact of public expenditure.[34]

---

[34] As the political leverage of the poor increases, so the level of the social efficiency wage converges on pro-poor expenditure.

This raises the issue of the mechanisms through which variations in the expenditure, or taxation, mix can be used to deliver changes in well-being and in state cohesion. To make a preliminary distinction, a change in the fiscal mix (say a shift from spending on military purposes to spending on agricultural research, or a change from taxation on the rich to taxation on the middle class) has an obvious economic impact, through its influence on demand, employment, and thence on well-being, and at the same time a political impact by altering the balance between interest groups. *We believe that the impact of expenditure and tax mixes, both through economic impacts (task 5) and through political and institutional signals (task 6), on state capacity represents an unexplored territory for development research, and would hope to investigate it further under the ESID (Effective States and Inclusive Development) research programme,* using not only standard qualitative and quantitative methods but also experimental methods. These have proved valuable in explaining the influence of conditional cash transfer programmes on trust and intracommunity relationships in Colombia (Attanasio et al. 2009). A particular way in which they add value is by showing that conventional incentives (providing more money) are often ineffective and may be counter-productive as fiscal incentives intended to change behaviour (Bowles 2008).

In the third research territory, *Escaping from the low-tax trap*, we build on ground broken for us by, in particular, the Centre for the Future State (CFS) and the Crisis States Research Centre (CSRC). More research is needed to build on this experience, and indeed use it for capacity-building purposes. *We propose (task 7) to examine the role of institutional changes (such as independent revenue authorities), sequencing of tax and expenditure reforms, equity-based reforms (such as closing of tax loopholes), and innovative new tax bases in escaping from the tax trap, using both case-study evidence from escapees and cross-country evidence.* This research strategy has not been used, in the form of comparative quantitative analysis, by either CFS or CSRC.

Finally, aid donors have been argued by some studies (including one from CFS) to contribute to the 'low-tax, weak-state' problem, by reducing the incentive to governments to build up tax revenue, because aid flows with lower political costs are always there as an alternative. Some commentators have expanded this approach into a broader critique of the 'institutional damage' done by aid flows to the recipient country state, arguing that aid increases corruption as well as weakening the tax base. This may connect with recent empirical work which suggests an insignificant correlation between aid and growth. *Our proposal (task 8) is to tackle these ideas head-on by examining the relationship between tax structure and level, expenditure composition and level, aid and ultimate development indicators (growth and poverty).* This brings together the fiscal work proposed on tax, expenditure, and aid.

4

Governing Natural Resources for Inclusive Development

Anthony Bebbington

Introduction: The Resource Curse as a Primarily Political Phenomenon

The extraction of minerals and hydrocarbons lies at the core of modern economic and social development. Coal mining was central to the industrial revolution, and the labour consciousness and organization which it inspired became, so Mitchell (2012) has argued, constitutive of modern democracy. More recently, mineral extraction has driven economic growth and social investment in countries as diverse as Canada, Chile, Botswana, and Australia. And in a general sense, oil is at the very centre of contemporary capitalism (Huber 2009). The consequences of extractive industry have not, however, always been felicitous. As Michael Ross (2012) has recently shown, performance across oil dependent polities and economies has been very uneven. A quick sampling of *The New York Times* or *The Economist* would similarly reveal cases where resource extraction comes coupled with lost opportunities, poor economic and social indicators, democratic failure, and civil strife: the so-called 'natural resource curse' (Auty 1993, 2001).

There is a cottage industry of scholarship that attempts to confirm, refute, or explain the existence of this ostensible resource curse. The purpose of this chapter is, however, different. It focuses on the institutional and political relationships that govern the interactions between resource extraction, economy, and society. More specifically, it outlines elements of a framework for analysing these relationships, the conditions under which they are likely to be reproduced or changed, and the ways in which they might mediate the relationships between extraction and inclusion. The chapter grounds this framework in two perspectives. The first of these draws on a more general literature dealing with the politics of institutional change. The second engages with the specific relationships of scale, space, and time that characterize the natural resource sector and give it its specificity. The implication will be that any effort to understand the governance of extraction and of its relationships to development *must* be spatially and historically explicit.

The framework is inspired by three claims. The first is Terry Karl's insistence (2007, p. 256) that 'the "resource curse" is primarily a political not an economic phenomenon', and that therefore the institutional and political distortions that characterize many extractive economies 'cannot be undone without a huge coordinated effort by all the stakeholders involved' (Karl 2007, p. 258). Second is the assertion that any political economy of extraction must deal explicitly with the materiality (and therefore spatiality) of the resource in question (see Bridge 2008; Bakker and Bridge 2006). Third is the argument of Mahoney and Thelen (2010) that path-dependency arguments should be combined with theories of institutional change that attend to both endogenous and exogenous sources of such change. Taken together, and applied to the particular case of natural resource governance, these claims point us towards the analytical centrality of politics, space, and time.

In the course of elaborating this framework, the chapter makes the following arguments. First, prior political settlements and coalitions structure the forms taken by an expanding extractive economy but are subsequently shaped by this expansion. Second, a critical factor determining how this subsequent shaping occurs is the extent to which social mobilization and shifting political coalitions drive institutional innovation *and* the extent to which institutional learning (in the private, public, and civic sectors) occurs such that social conflict can be turned into institutional change. Third, the actors involved in these processes operate at subnational, national, and transnational scales, and there are important interactions among these scales. Actors operating at transnational scales include companies, multilateral bodies, and civil society networks. These actors influence patterns of investment, social conflict, and institutional learning and make clear that a political-settlements and political-coalitions approach to natural resource governance cannot focus on the national level alone (e.g. Khan 2010; Acemoglu and Robinson 2012).

The chapter is organized as follows. Following a summary review of how resource curse debates have converged on the centrality of governance, I outline an approach to institutional continuity and change that draws on notions of political settlement and political coalition. I then link these insights to a discussion of the centrality of space, scale, and time for analysing the politics of natural resource governance. Finally, and in light of these concepts, I explore institutional arrangements through which resource extraction might foster inclusive development and the conditions under which these institutions might emerge.

Settlements, Coalitions, and the Politics of Governing Resource Extraction

The issues raised by large scale natural resource extraction go well beyond 'resource curse' arguments about the extent to which such extraction is, or is not, associated with disappointing levels of growth and human development performance (Collier and Venables 2011; Fahr-Weber 2002; ICMM 2006). The growth of investment in mining and hydrocarbons also fuels discussion of the implications this holds for human rights, environmental security, democracy, sovereignty, social conflict, and regionalism (e.g. Perreault 2013; Watts 2004; Dunning 2008; Mitchell 2012). However, the evolution of resource curse debates has been helpful in that it has debunked deterministic arguments regarding the necessarily adverse effects of resource extraction and has instead focused on the importance of institutions and governance in mediating the relationships between extraction and development (Bebbington et al. 2008; Humphreys et al. 2007). In particular, whether mineral expansion triggers the resource curse effect or instead fosters growth is deemed to depend on the quality of macroeconomic management, on whether a fiscal social contract exists or not, on degrees of transparency, and on the overall quality of governance (Fahr-Weber 2002, p. 14). This convergence on institutions, however, begs other questions: how can the institutional arrangements governing extraction at any one point in time be explained? In what contexts might exclusionary institutional arrangements change? And under what conditions, and through what processes do inclusive institutional arrangements emerge (or fail to emerge)?

One approach to the first of these questions is through the language of political settlements. Di John (2009, p. 290) defines political settlements as 'historically specific bargains over institutions' while for Khan (2010, p. 1) a 'political settlement emerges when the distribution of benefits supported by its institutions is consistent with the distribution of power in society, and the economic and political outcomes of these institutions are sustainable over time'. These definitions insist that societal institutions exist in a relationship of co-constitution with power relations in society. This claim is very similar to Acemoglu and Robinson's (2012) conceptualization of political equilibrium as a distribution of political power and political-economic institutions that can co-exist. These arrangements persist over time to the extent that: a) they deliver a level of economic growth that can satisfy the expectations of different groups across the distribution of political power; b) they are consistent with prevailing notions of what constitutes a politically legitimate—or at least acceptable—state of affairs; and c) relatively disadvantaged actors do not accumulate sufficient power that they become able to destabilize the settlement through force, electoral processes, or discursive shifts that introduce new ideological challenges to dominant settlements.

These conditions of existence draw attention to themes raised in other literatures on institutional change.[1] First, while institutions might be institutionalized, their stability and reproduction cannot be taken for granted and instead depend on factors that are both endogenous and exogenous to these institutional arrangements. Second, institutions do not 'self-reproduce' even when they reflect apparently consolidated asymmetries of power. Instead, the reproduction of institutions takes a great deal of work (Mahoney and Thelen 2010)—investment of resources, crafting of supporting ideologies, monitoring in order to pre-empt resistance, investment in means of violence, and so on. Third, if the maintenance of existing institutions reflects the power of particular coalitions, then shifts in coalitional politics may be one route towards institutional change (Hall 2010). In this approach, accounting for the natural resource governance institutions persisting at any one point in time would therefore require a characterization of the political settlement allowing for the continued existence of these institutions. The language of political settlements appears less helpful, however, when the analytical challenge is to explain how such governance institutions might change. Other literatures suggest that social mobilization, shifting political coalitions and policy networks might play important roles in this regard.

The role of social mobilization and contentious politics in institutional change is well documented. Tilly's work is especially important here in that it draws attention to this relationship over the long sweep of European history (Tilly 2004, 1998, 1990). Contention—though also war (cf. North et al. 2009)—emerges as playing an important role in the emergence of democracy (in Tilly's language) and open-access social orders (in North et al.'s terms). Mahoney and Thelen (2010) refer to a similar phenomenon in their discussion of 'insurrectionary' agents as one potential source of endogenous institutional change. While not all aspects of these authors' arguments are the same, they each draw attention to the role of contention in institutional change. In no instance, however, is the relation linear. This implies that analysis must also trace the intervening variables that mediate the effect of force on institutions, increasing, decreasing, and/or translating the ways in

---

[1] I am very grateful for Clark University graduate student participants in my seminar 'Governing Development' for helping think through the arguments in the following pages, as well as my collaborations with Rimisp, Latin American Centre for Rural Development where I have also worked on some of these ideas in the conceptualization of rural territorial dynamics (Berdegué et al. 2012).

which demands expressed through force become re-expressed as new institutional models.

Explanations of how such mobilization occurs vary in the literature, though three sets of factors are recurrently important: the role of changes in the political opportunity structure and how they create new possibilities for mobilized political expression; the role of changes in the resources (financial, informational, human, and so on) that actors are able to mobilize; and the role of discourse in framing identities through which people feel able to organize and express collective political demands (Crossley 2000). In any one instance, the relative role of each of these factors will vary, though adequate accounts must attend to each.

A variant on the mobilization theme is expressed in accounts that stress the role of social and political coalitions in institutional change. Analysing the Botswanan case, Poteete (2009) argues that key to the explanation of patterns of institutional emergence, change *and* stasis is the nature of the dominant political coalition—be this the actual political coalition controlling the state, or the modified coalition that those currently in control of the state need to re-engineer in order to sustain this control. Di John (2009) frames a similar argument for Venezuela, while Thorp et al.'s (2012a) multi-country discussion from Latin America argues that—in addition to questions of timing, sequencing, leadership, and the nature of the resource—the governance of extractives depends on elite politics and commitments. '[W]e see the role of competing elites as fundamental in shaping the state, from within and without. We see the state as gaining or losing degrees of autonomy from specific elite interests with time, and the role of the bureaucracy as important in this' (Thorp et al. 2012, p. 5).

These interpretations, however, beg further questions regarding the factors that might lead these coalitions and elite commitments to change. Bebbington (2012) brings together authors exploring the extent to which social conflict might explain such shifts in dominant coalitions and institutional forms (though again this demands explanation of the genesis of such social mobilization). Poteete (2009) suggests that changing coalitional politics might also drive change, and she relates these coalitional changes to the emergence of new economic activities and new social actors. Thorp et al. (2012) also place some weight on political leadership as an important factor in molding coalitional politics, as well as the effect of certain taken-for-granted ideas (or what might be called 'political cultures').

For Peter Hall (2010, p. 207) '[t]he [general] premise is that institutional change is best understood by integrating coalitional with institutional analysis'. Some foci of coalition analysis frame it, in practice, as a process of parallel institutional formation (Hall 2010) in the sense that, if existing institutions reflect the equilibrium results of the coordinated work of those interests that endorse these institutions, then new institutions would reflect the results of the coordinated work of a differing set of interests brought together in the coalition promoting institutional change. Other approaches would understand coalitions in more identity-based and discursive terms, emphasizing the extent to which discourse (a set of ideas, imaginaries, and aspirations) is a condition of existence of a coalition, giving it identity and vision and helping bring it into being by providing an axis around which various actors can come together, perceive alignment of their interests, and act collectively (Birner et al. 2011; Hajer 1995). Other approaches (Flora et al. 2006) are more instrumental and focus on how coalitions serve as advocates for change.

As Hall's (2010) observations imply, there is no necessary relationship between coalition formation and progressive changes in natural resource governance. Coalitions also emerge to advance already dominant and exclusionary interests. This is evident in the reading of the less-than-successful cases brought together in collections such as Collier and Venables (2011) and Thorp et al. (2012). Sometimes these coalitions pursue new opportunities and sometimes they defend dominant institutions and groups. However, in other instances emergent coalitions for progressive resource governance can displace those pursuing different visions. In yet other cases the process may involve processes of gradual learning and calculation within a coalition such that the coalition itself begins to see the need for institutional change and slowly shift its own discourses on the governance of the environment (cf. Acemoglu and Robinson 2006; and more generally the work on social learning—Social Learning Group et al. 2001). This learning might be led by particularly powerful actors in these coalitions who transmit this learning to others. Indeed, an argument can be made that some transnational extractive industry companies have learnt the need to engage local populations and environments in new, more open, ways and have sought to convey this learning to national elites in the private and public sector, albeit with greater and less success (Sagbien and Lindsay 2011). More generally the learning occurring within the industry group ICMM or through initiatives like the EITI might be seen as instances of transnational actors seeking to lead a range of national coalitions along paths towards behavioural and institutional change (however limited and unsatisfactory these may seem to activists and critical scholars: Benson and Kirsch 2010, 2009).

Any account of the role of coalitions in institutional change must also explain how they resolve collective action challenges. Indeed, many of the same concepts needed to explain social movement emergence in conflicts over resource extraction (Bebbington et al. 2008) are relevant to explaining coalition emergence. How do coalitions emerge if (as is almost always the case) incentive structures mean that the potential net gains of forming a coalition are greater for some actors than for others (in ways that will differ by gender, class, generation, ethnicity, and so forth)? How do coalitions mobilize the resources necessary to keep the coalition going? How do actors within coalitions negotiate the institutional change that they will demand collectively if (as also will almost always be the case) different alternatives imply different distributions of costs and benefits among actors (Hall 2010)? How, in the case of coalitions that bring together local and external actors, are collective commitments to particular forms of environmental regulations, social redistribution, and political recognition negotiated? And finally, if 'equity' or 'sustainability' are cultural rather than absolute constructs (Humphreys Bebbington and Bebbington 2010), how do actors within a coalition arrive at shared conceptions of equity and sustainability towards which the institutional change they demand will lead? These latter questions emerge as particularly significant—and thorny—in the negotiations that can occur among aboriginal peoples, NGO activists, and reformist government bureaucrats who at one level may be part of the same resource governance coalition, but at another level see the world in *very* distinct ways (Blaser 2010). The tensions that can arise from this, and the extent to which they can frustrate the emergence of new resource governance institutions, have been made palpably clear in the conflicts *within* the coalition seeking to pass new legislation in Peru on free prior and informed consultation/consent.

These questions imply that an adequate analysis of coalitional emergence must address incentives, issues of identity, ideas, and even world view (when involving aboriginal groups), and a detailed analysis of the diverse actors that make up the coalition. Indeed, to the extent that incentives are perceived in ways that depend on the ideas about fairness, rights, costs, and benefits, and given that these ideas may not be the same across members of a coalition, then identity, ideas, and intra-coalitional dynamics must bear more of the causal burden than do incentives: as Hall notes, 'the politics of ideas is intrinsic, rather than epiphenomenal, to the processes of coalition formation that underpin institutional change' (Hall 2010, p. 213).

The centrality of ideas brings us to the third social vehicle through which change in resource governance institutions may occur: the operation of epistemic communities. Epistemic communities are best understood as 'a network of professionals with recognized expertise and competence in a particular domain and an authoritative claim to policy relevant knowledge within that domain or issue-area' (Haas 1992, p. 3). These networks can be both national and transnational (Keck and Sikkink 1998), and while Haas's notion of epistemic communities focused especially on networks of professionals whose ideas help frame policy debates, this process of framing discourses and then ushering them into policy formation often includes actors with other identities—supportive politicians, movement and civic cadres, business people, bureaucrats, and so on (c.f. Fox 1996). Among other things, epistemic communities can play important roles in framing the 'viable models' of new institutions noted earlier, as well as in framing core ideas around which coalitions and mobilizations might emerge. They may also contribute to the identities that can derive from these ideas. A Latin American example of this might be that of the policy, intellectual, and technocratic networks that have worked for so many years on indigenous peoples' territories and have subsequently become involved in debates on extractive industry governance. It is also reasonable to argue that scholarly work on natural resource extraction and development has become part of such networks— Collier's work on the natural resource charter, or the interactions among Soros, Revenue Watch International, and scholars such as Joseph Stiglitz and Michael Ross would be examples here, as also would the links between Mines and Communities and scholars such as Stuart Kirsch. As with discussions on development, scholarly discussions on extraction need to be treated as endogenous to the very political processes which they are analysing.

Such epistemic communities can serve as agents of resource governance change themselves, as they 'subversively' (in Mahoney and Thelen's language) seed policy and public discussions with concepts and ideas that become sufficiently persuasive that they elicit institutional change (whether at national, subnational, or international levels). This in turn demands explanation of what might make ideas 'persuasive', especially given that the determination of dominant discourses on resource extraction generally happens in contexts characterized by asymmetries of power in which those more powerful have clear preferences for particular ideas. Such persuasiveness might derive from: palpable environmental changes that undermine the cogency of previously dominant ideas; the arrival of new information that adds credibility to new sets of ideas (cf. North 2006); or shifting calculations on the parts of elites as to forms of resource governance that might best suit their interests (Acemoglu and Robinson 2006; Boix 2008; Tilly 1992). More often, though, such ideas become influential when they are bundled with movements and coalitions.

Theoretically, these observations imply that an adequate account of changes in the institutions of natural resource governance must explain how such mobilizations, coalitions and policy networks emerge in the first instance, how they articulate with existing institutional arrangements, and how they are translated into the final effects that they ultimately have. At the core of this explanation must be an account of how incentives, ideas and identities influence the emergence of actors promoting change in extractive industry governance, and of the models for new regulations that will be the basis of such change. Such accounts must explain why mobilization, coalitions, or policy networks emerge to play this role in some contexts rather than others.

Visualizing the Framework

The foregoing arguments are summarized visually in Figure 4.1. At the core of the framework is the co-constitution of economic development, political settlements, and political coalitions as outlined by Khan (2010) and Acemoglu and Robinson (2012). Offsetting the tendency of settlements language to 'feel' static, the framework introduces two elements of dynamism. First, and following authors such as Boix (2008), is the argument that patterns of economic development ultimately modify class structures in ways that cannot be easily controlled by dominant coalitions. This modification can take a variety of forms—the creation of new marginalized and disenfranchised populations, the emergence of new capitalist classes, the emergence of modernizing middle classes (as per Boix 2008). Each of these forms serves to destabilize existing settlements. This destabilization can be both

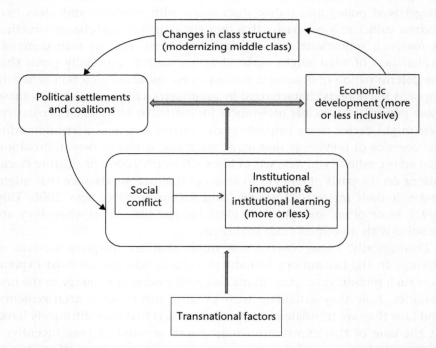

Figure 4.1. A schema for analysing political settlements, coalitions, and the politics of resource extraction
Source: Author.

incremental or abrupt (involving mobilizations) but either way it constitutes forms of conflict that put pressure on existing institutions and has
the potential to lead to institutional change. Such change itself contributes
to further modification of the forms of economic development occurring.
In the case of extractives this might be, say, because it involves new tax
regimes, new land-use planning guidelines, or new forms of ownership.

Thus far the framework treats institutional and governance change as
endogenous to the relationships among settlements, coalitions, and the
economy. However, the change process can also be affected by exogenous
factors and actors. This is especially the case for the political economy of
extraction which is characterized by an important presence of international
companies, multilateral agencies, international advocacy networks, and
transnational nongovernmental organizations, as well as by international
commodity price volatility which can also elicit domestic coalitional and
institutional change. One example of this would be the dramatic effects of
the collapse of tin prices on the power of miners' unions in Bolivia and their
political coalitions with the state and parties. Another example would be
the cumulative influence that transnational advocacy around free prior and
informed consent has had on domestic politics and regulations governing
consultation and participation.

A contemporary process of institutional contention in the politics of
mining governance in El Salvador illustrates some of the relationships
outlined in this framework. In response to policy reforms in the mid-
1990s, mining companies had begun to conduct geological exploration in
El Salvador. By 2005, the activities of several companies were beginning
to generate serious social conflict, such that by 2007/8 the conflict had
become so severe that even the pro-business government ARENA placed a
de facto moratorium on mining activity. When a social democratic FMLN
government came to power in 2008 they inherited this moratorium, along
with much pressure from movements to convert it into law. However, the
FMLN also inherited the fall-out of the moratorium. By 2009 two mining
companies whose projects had been put on hold were using the provisions
of the US-Central American Free Trade Agreement (CAFTA-DR) to sue the
government of El Salvador for recovery of all their expenditure to date, for
future lost profits and for losses due to falls in their share value (as well as
the costs of taking legal action). While one of these cases was dropped in
2011, the other is still being considered by the International Centre for the
Settlement of Investment Disputes (ICSID) albeit no-longer under the rules
of CAFTA-DR.[2]

---

[2] For more on this see Bebbington (2012).

In this context, the FMLN government has been caught between two pressures. Social movement organizations, along with parliamentarians and the political bases of the FMLN, are not happy that an ostensibly left-of-centre government would not ban hard rock mining once and for all given that it had committed to do so during the electoral campaign. They are pressuring the government to follow through on these electoral promises. Yet at the same time the government feels the pressure of fiscal imperative. On the one hand, some officials wonder whether mining might generate tax and royalty revenue for government programmes, while on the other hand these and others worry that ICSID will find against the government and impose fines on the scale of a hundred or more millions of dollars. The corollary fear is that this would open the door to a slew of legal suits from other companies, especially if the moratorium were converted into law. Meanwhile informal political pressure from the embassies of investor countries has also continued (personal communications from senior government officials).

The government's response was to buy time and conduct a Strategic Environment Assessment (SEA) of the mining sector, with a view to crafting a policy on the basis of that SEA—the calculation being that if a policy restricting mining were based on an independent SEA, it would offer more legal protection against future lawsuits from other companies with concessions and exploration projects. That SEA came to the view that environmental vulnerabilities (primarily related to water quantity and quality) were so severe, social risks (primarily related to conflict, violence, and divisions dating back to the civil war) so acute, and government capacities so limited, that prior to any promotion of mining it was imperative to build capacity within government to regulate mining investment, ensure environmental protection, establish and enforce no-go areas, create early warning systems for identifying conflict, establish tax and royalty systems, and so on. This was then translated by the government into a proposal for legislative change that would suspend all mining activities until a raft of other capacities and policies had been established. This proposal is currently (at the time of writing) under review in the Salvadoran congress.

Here, then, is an example of political coalitions in the 1990s supporting the rise of mining investment in a way that was largely unchecked. This invisibility of early mining investment in turn reflected the nature of the post-war political settlement in the country, dominated as it was by national economic and traditional political elites. However, as the changes triggered by this early mining activity became visible they were perceived as threatening certain groups in rural society. These groups—in coalition with other national and international actors—steadily organized in a process that generated levels of conflict that upset the existing settlement, leading to a distancing between parts of ARENA and the mining sector. The coalition between the subsequently elected FMLN government and movements, however, was in turn challenged by different transnational interventions (involving mining companies, foreign embassies and ICSID). This in turn has triggered another experiment at institutional change in the form of the SEA and proposed legislative change. The fate of that proposed law, however, will depend on ongoing coalitional dynamics within the Salvadoran Parliament.

Space and Time in the Governance of Extraction

The coalitional politics, social mobilization, and policy networking discussed in the previous section all occur some*where* and some*time*. The *where* of these political processes occurs within other geographies: the geographies of resources themselves (where they are located, where they are transported, and so on); the interactions between resource geographies and geographies of human settlement, water, economic activity, and so forth; and the uneven and politically symbolic geographies of cities and regions, of metropolitan areas and aboriginal territories, and of national, subnational, and international jurisdictions. Meanwhile the *now* of extraction is characterized by institutions and power relationships inherited from the past, as well as memories of that same past. Indeed, the literature on the extractive economy has become increasingly aware that *where* subsoil natural resources are located and *when* they are discovered and developed each matter a great deal for the quality of resource governance and in particular for the relationships between extraction and patterns of development (Thorp et al. 2012). This section discusses different ways in which space and time need to be addressed in any effort to understand the politics of, and the institutions that govern, natural resource extraction.

Space and the Politics of Resource Governance and Development

Flows, Scales, and Territories

The mining and hydrocarbon sectors can be understood as global production networks (Bridge 2008; see also Ferguson 2006) in which a range of actors come together to extract, transport, transform, and sell natural resources, and to channel the flows of capital (investment and profit), commodities, materials, information, and people that make the extraction and valorization of natural resources possible. Many of these flows reach beyond national jurisdictions, though some flows (e.g. of taxes and royalties, of labour, or of water) occur at a national and subnational scale.

Many of these flows have their own governance arrangements. Some of these are governmental or multilateral. Thus, international (e.g. World Bank, IFC) and bilateral (e.g. EXIM Bank, KfW) financial institutions govern concessionary loan and grant flows linked to extraction through decisions on loan conditions as well as through the conduct of public reviews such as the Extractive Industries Review. Global/international regulatory bodies (ILO, UNDRIP, NAFTA, free trade agreements, and so on) govern obligations and rights that are attached to these flows. For instance, ILO 169 attaches obligations regarding free, prior, and informed consent, and free trade agreements attach rights to seek redress against national decisions by presenting cases to multilateral bodies such as ICSID. Grant-giving by non-profits working on extractive industry can be subject to public regulations, as can their information work. Likewise when extractive industry raises capital (perhaps especially speculative capital) on specialized stock exchanges such as the TSX or AIM this can also be subject to public regulation.

Other arrangements are voluntary and private (Auld 2012; Cashore et al. 2004). In the commercial private sector, examples would include CSR, certification, and labelling of various sorts. In the civic private sector, examples would include decisions over grant-giving, strategies of information provision, and so on. The Extractive Industries Transparency Initiative (EITI) which attaches obligations related to transparency on tax payments, is a combination of voluntary, private, and public in that participation is voluntary, but many governments as well as companies and NGOs participate.

These different mechanisms for governing flows can themselves induce the emergence or attention of other private actors that seek to influence these arrangements. There are many examples of this: Revenue Watch International's work on transparency, Oxfam's work on corporate standards, Mining Watch's work on the flows associated with Canadian mining companies, and so on. In many instances these private responses combine the efforts (or at least names) of organizations that operate at subnational, national, and international levels. Such governance mechanisms also often induce (or can grow out of) the work of researchers or think tanks that seek to challenge and frame ideas so as to influence how extraction is governed. Some of these challenges can be contentious, as for instance in the arguments that occurred among public bodies, the World Bank, and civil society organizations over the Extractive Industries Review—all of which, ultimately, were arguments seeking to influence how the Bank would govern and attach conditions to multilateral capital flows for extractive industry. However, for the most part struggle over the design of institutions to govern flows tends to be less contentious and takes the form of negotiation, legal proceedings, coalition-building, and lobbying.

While institutional arrangements such as these are not a-spatial (meetings, arguments, negotiations, and so on, always occur somewhere, and that *where* is significant), they are generally not bound by territorial units. They govern flows, not spaces. However, extraction is also governed through spatially defined institutions which often (though not always) focus on the spatialized consequences and contexts of extraction: environmental impacts, infrastructure-building, the spending of geographically targeted royalty transfers, land-use ordinances, and so on. Many such territorialized mechanisms are public, defined by the jurisdictions of government. Others, though, are private (e.g. territorially defined social organizations, such as communities, that seek to exert control over the space they occupy) and more generally a range of territorially defined actors emerge to negotiate and contest this level of governance (e.g. geographically defined federations of water users, aboriginal peoples, peasants). These contestations are much more prone to contention, including violent contention (Bebbington and Bury 2013), though there is also plenty of coalitional politics at play (Poteete 2009).

Understanding the governance of natural resource extraction and the forms that it takes within particular countries and locales thus requires analysis of how both flows and spaces are governed and how these institutions of governance are stabilized and changed through combinations of contention, coalitional politics, and arguments over ideas. Such analysis also must consider the conditions under which one domain of governance might supplant or interact with another. For instance, countries' mining and hydrocarbon codes (which reflect a form of territorial governance at a national scale) can come to be defined by capital flows linked to international financial institutions (as when countries adopt World Bank recommendations for mining laws). In some instances, though, countries might seek to undo codes that were promoted by international institutions and replace them with domestic codes (as has happened, for instance, when resource nationalist positions come to power). In many instances (as Kaup 2010 notes for Bolivia) the resulting codes end up becoming some form of uneasy combination of these positions. In this sense, processes of institutional change often involve a politics of scales in which actors reach across scales at the same time as they seek to redefine the scale at which an extractive industry problem is defined (Bulkeley 2005).[3]

Space and Contention in the Governance of Extraction

The simple fact that natural resource extraction is a point-source activity, and that the geographies of extractive activities are relatively immutable, produces particular challenges for the governance of resource extraction and

---

[3] There are many examples of this. One simple example would be struggles to define whether a mine's approval is a local, regional, national, or global governance issue, and thus to define who should and should not be involved in decisions over the mine's fate.

not infrequently underlies much of the contention surrounding it. Space, therefore, has to be treated as endogenous to any analysis of the interactions between institutions and politics. We discuss how this is so in the following domains: the relationships between space, externalities, and contention; the relationships between space, rents, and contention; the awkward relationships between rents, national redistribution, and a spatialized politics of recognition; and the ways in which these spatialized politics of extraction mean that political settlements around its governance are inherently unstable as a result of tensions between different national and subnational actors.

Resource extraction, even when as 'clean' as technologically conceivable, produces significant *externalities*. In the 'clean' version these externalities are limited to dramatic landscape transformation, significant increase in the movement of heavy machinery and heavy loads, increases in noise pollution, the presence of large-scale installations on previously rural landscapes, and the arrival of new sources of 'risk' and 'uncertainty' in the landscape (in the form of large-scale tailings ponds that might breach, pipelines that might leak, waste-waters that might escape, and so on). In the 'dirty' version of extraction, the externalities can involve adverse impacts on water quality and quantity; careless management of tailings, waste rock, and waste waters with implications for pollution; and adverse social impacts (prostitution, night-life, new diseases) in human settlements near sites of extraction. In either version it is probably also the case that there are localized effects on the political economy—with inflation of land and labour costs (with typically adverse effects for local labour-intensive agriculture, as well as for general patterns of access to housing as it becomes more expensive) and increased opportunities for criminal activities. There is ample evidence of this latter effect, whether in the form of 'tapping' of oil pipelines in Nigeria (Watts 2004; Kashi and Watts 2008) or of mafia presence in the economy of service provision to sites of extraction (Arellano-Yanguas 2012). This localization of externalities typically induces new sources and forms of conflict motivated by perceptions and experiences of loss, by manoeuverings for compensation, or by efforts to gain access to employment and economic opportunities (Bebbington et al. 2013).

It also merits note that exposure to these externalities varies spatially *within* a locality. Some human settlements are more or less affected by noise, water, or landscape impacts; some economic agents are more adversely affected than others by increased labour costs; some benefit more than others from the increased circulation of cash in a local and micro-regional economy; and some fall within what companies define as their zone of direct influence while others do not (which means that potential access to compensation and CSR activities is unequally distributed, with some persons *included* and others not). These locally varied exposures to costs and benefits have implications for patterns of inclusion and exclusion, and also for the possibility that local coalitions for changes in resource governance might emerge (Bebbington et al. 2013; Humphreys Bebbington and Bebbington 2010).

At the same time, the localization of extraction inevitably produces tension over the socio-spatial distribution of *rents*. On the one hand, subsoil resources are more often than not vested in the nation with the state being responsible for the 'trusteeship' and management of these resources (which is why it is the central state that grants licenses and concessions and approves projects). Furthermore, this central state often sees in these minerals a source of revenue to finance national social and infrastructural programmes (or, in patrimonialist versions, private gain for governing elites). On the other hand, the resources are physically extracted *from* a particular region, and subnational groups typically make some claims on these resources because of their spatial origins. These claims may take various forms: an aboriginal population may claim that the resources are coming from their *territory* and that this territory is constituted by both the surface and subsurface, regardless of the formalities of national law; a regional government may claim that the resources are a subnational resource that should be a revenue base for regional development plans; municipal or customary authorities may argue much the same; and so forth. The socio-spatial distribution of revenues deriving from extraction is therefore inevitably a source of spatialized political tension in ways in which the geographical location of manufacturing or agriculture is not.

Which of these sources of tension—over the spatialization of externalities or over the spatial distribution of rent—is more significant likely varies across cases. Recent econometric work in Peru has concluded that the majority of contemporary social conflicts over extraction derive from struggles over the amounts, management, and distribution of fiscal transfers back to the regions of extraction (Arellano-Yanguas 2011, 2012). More important is to recognize that these different catalysts of conflict are generally all present, mobilize different interests, interact with each other, and are all inevitable consequences of the spatially uneven nature of extraction and the materialities of the resources involved. Furthermore, the attempt on the part of 'regions of extraction' to secure significant transfer of benefits pits them not only against central government but also against other subnational authorities who do not enjoy significant fiscal transfers and who also want access to resource rents.

The *national* ownership of subsoil resources, coupled with their *subnational* existence and the different spatial scales at which a *politics of recognition* are made manifest, present further axes of latent or open contention surrounding the governance of extraction. While all natural resources might have symbolic resonances, it is probably only the subsoil that has been powerful enough to lend itself to feelings of resource nationalism. While this 'nationalism' is usually supported by constitutional provisions that vest ownership of the subsoil in the nation, it is also fuelled by the sense that more than being 'owned' by the nation, the subsoil is actually *part of* a nation, and its control by any other than national government is cast as a problem of sovereignty and national integrity (Coronil 1997; Perreault 2013). The subsoil thus becomes the subject of intensities of protest and levels of nationalization that are not as apparent in other sectors. This national symbolism has also meant that the subsoil becomes bundled with languages of citizenship in ways that can lead populations to argue that they have the right to make very specific claims on the subsoil and the revenues that might derive from it (Perreault 2013). The generation of wealth from the subsoil often induces the emergence of national subjects ('the people', 'the poor') claiming that this wealth should be redistributed to them, as well as political movements offering such redistribution in return for political allegiance.

However, these resources exist in, and are extracted from particular territories, and this process can lead to conflicts between different uses of the land (traditional vs. extractive) and different modes of governing this land—for example, conflicts in which company governance of space becomes pitted against customary forms of governance associated with particular social and political identities ('indigenous', 'tribal', and so on). Consequently extraction also interacts with a different politics of recognition—not this time the recognition of rights of the national citizen deserving of redistribution, but instead of the subnational identity-based group deserving of substantial compensation or bearing particular governance rights. In the process, not only are these identity-based claims set against the claims of the extractive enterprise, but they also become set against the claims of the national subject demanding 'extraction for redistribution'. This situation complicates coalition-building and the consolidation of political settlements. Indeed, this has arguably been the case in the Andean countries.

These three considerations (*externalities, rents, recognition*) mean that the spatialized governance of extraction presents immense challenges and is itself also an axis of contention. From the perspective of extractive industry companies, the concentration of conflict in the spaces in which they operate, and the relative vulnerability of their physical operations to sabotage (precisely because of their spatial extensiveness, typically remote location and geographical fixity), means that they place a premium on *securing* these spaces. It is this idea that underlies Watts' (2003) notion of governable spaces, drawing on his own experience in the Niger Delta where companies seek to make the spaces of their operation governable (from their point of view), while other actors also seek to render them governable from *their* point of view. The same notion is present in Ferguson's (2006,

p. 204) characterization of the spaces of operation of extractive industry as 'enclaved mineral-rich patches efficiently exploited by flexible private firms, with security provided on an "as-needed" basis by specialized corporations', and more generally in his claim (2006) that contemporary development can be read as a set of 'transnational topographies of power' in which transnational networks link and govern non-contiguous spaces across the globe in ways that render the governance of some spaces categorically different from that of other spaces within the same nation state. Thus, in the case of extractive industry, spaces of company operation become governed in ways that are transnationalized and quite distinct from other subnational spaces. From Ferguson's viewpoint this difference inheres in the crafting of less-than-transparent deals between companies, security services, and state elites. Meanwhile national and transnational activists, as well as extra-legal interests in some instances, try to muscle in on and usurp these practices of governance.

As a consequence, national-subnational *settlements* around the governance of extractive activities and revenue transfers tend to be very unstable. Extreme versions of this instability are manifest in the sorts of armed conflicts and secessionist movements that Collier and Hoeffler (2005, 2004), Ross (2008), Le Billon (2001), and others have considered. Less extreme variants are the chronic tensions between national and subnational authorities and elites in countries such as Bolivia, Peru, or Nigeria. The few cases where this national–subnational relationship is less tense and unstable (e.g. Chile, Botswana) appear to be characterized by: a spatially circumscribed geography of extraction (e.g. Botswana); a geography in which extraction and human settlement do not overlap significantly (Botswana, Chile, Norway); and an early agreement that revenues should be controlled by central authorities and redistributed through national programmes rather than spatially earmarked transfers (Botswana and Chile). The reasons for such early agreements vary—in one instance appearing to be a result of strong and respected centralized bureaucracies (Chile), in the other a calculation on the part of subnational elites that this was in their favour (Botswana) (Poteete 2011; Thorp et al. 2012; Battistelli and Guichaoua 2012).

Given the extent of the rents in question, and the gravity of the conflicts to which they can give rise, these apparently subnational problems can spill over into national politics. Indeed, the point-source nature of the extractive economy can *produce* powerful actors because of the scale of rents *and* externalities at play as well as the potential resonance of the political discourses that can be mobilized in struggles over these rents and externalities. Some of these powerful actors can be of the warlord or armed insurgent variety, but more 'mundanely' they can and have been regional political and civil society leaders who on the backs of conflicts over extraction become national political figures. In this same process subnational narratives on extraction (regarding taxation, environment, territory, indigenous rights) can become parts of national debates over extraction. The politics of extraction and struggles for different types of inclusion can thus be vehicles through which the framing of national political debates and the composition of national political settlements are altered. This being so, national–subnational dynamics need to be central to any analysis of the ways in which extraction, governance, and inclusion relate to and co-constitute each other (Arellano-Yanguas 2011, 2012).

Time and the Politics of Resource Governance

History as Sequence

Historicized approaches to the relationships between resource extraction and development identify three primary senses in which 'history matters': the particular sequences in which institutions become 'layered' (Thorp et al. 2012); the nature of international commodity and credit markets at the time that resources begin to be exploited or governed in particular ways (Ross 2012; Paredes 2012); and the timing of when resources are discovered in relationship to the dynamics of political settlements within a country (Battistelli and Guichaoua, 2012). However, '[t]hat "history matters" does not equate to "original conditions rule"' (Thorp et al. 2012, p. 4) and so these reflections are not arguments for the existence of entrenched path-dependent effects. However, this emphasis on history does recognize path-dependent *tendencies* whose change requires particularly significant forms of agency (or serendipity)—or, in Karl's already quoted terms, 'a huge coordinated effort by all the stakeholders involved' (Karl 2007, p. 258).

One of the most deliberate attempts to engage such historical questions is that of Thorp et al. (2012) for whom 'the challenge is to take the analysis sufficiently far back in time to detect the key decisions and influences that shaped institutions and competences, and the role of resource abundance at these points' (p. 6). In this spirit, their comparative study of Botswana, Niger, Nigeria, Bolivia, Chile, and Peru frequently digs back into the late nineteenth century for the Latin American cases and the late colonial period for the African cases. Orihuela (2012) explains the success of Chile's governance of copper in terms of 'the way the layering of institution building allowed the country to resist later periods of great instability and boom' (Thorp et al. 2012, p. 214). The origins to this story, he argues, lie in the nitrates boom in the latter nineteenth century. Certain aspects of this boom reflected resource curse features—in particular while nitrates were taxed heavily, other forms of domestic taxation fell ('from 20% in the 1840s to almost nothing in the years 1895–1905' Orihuela 2012, p. 24). This nitrate revenue gave the executive considerable autonomy and power from society. However, other changes in Chilean society—the emerging strength of unions, a prior commitment to bureaucratic technocracy—meant that other checks on the state increased, limiting the extent to which the executive could use this rent in a way that was completely autonomous of society. They do not argue that the nitrates boom was a success story, but nor did it lead to a complete distortion of public institutions. Then, when the copper boom followed in the mid-twentieth century, it was managed technocratically. Indeed central to Orihuela's (2012) explanation of Chilean success is the existence of a long history of publicly motivated, competent bureaucracy and technocracy that served to keep the polity in check, but in some sense also infused the culture of dominant elites. If this is so, then it means that the instruments of the Chilean success are not easily copied—for Chile's success does not lie in the instruments it created (e.g. copper funds and the like for the countercyclical management of resource rents) but rather in the fact that these instruments grew out of a far longer historical commitment to technocracy that guaranteed the independence of these funds from political raiding (Collier and Venables 2011). This historical layering of institutions (understood both as organizations and routinized norms) is therefore important to understanding Chile. A similar layering—albeit of less historical depth—is, Thorp et al. argue, part of the Botswana success in diamond governance. In that instance, a commitment to central government institutions pre-dated the discovery of diamonds, reflecting instead a commitment to cattle-owning elites as well as the recognition that a strong, competent central state was essential in the face of potential South African interference. So here, a combination of layering and straight serendipity helped explain the good management of diamond revenues.

Different forms of layering can have converse effects. Nigeria's discovery of oil came right after the Biafra war in a context of acute social and political fragmentation and a collapse of any centralized political authority in the Niger Delta. Oil became a means of managing competition among regional elites in a context in which a post-war, chronically weakened civil society and public sphere negated any prospect of checks and balances and accountable government. The rest is history—or tragedy (Watts 2003, 2004; Kashi and Watts 2008). In an equally adverse 'layering', uranium had been discovered in Niger prior to independence, and so even though formal political authority passed to the post-colonial state, France was uninterested in ceding control over and access to Niger's mineral deposits—not least because France itself was developing a consolidated nuclear industry as part of a domestic energy policy, creating a further political imperative to secure access to this uranium (Guichaoua 2012). There is a clear parallel here (albeit on a smaller scale) with the relationship between domestic, hydrocarbon-based energy policy in the USA and the equal determination of the US to sustain control over oil supplies around the world regardless of the institutional distortions that this might create in supply countries (Mitchell 2012). In these analyses two sets of institutional layerings, one in the resource-consuming country, the other in the resource-supplying country, couple to co-constitute adverse relationships between extraction and development.

A different sense in which history matters is in the time periods used to identify the presence or absence of the 'resource curse'. Breaking down time-series data into particular segments, Michael Ross (2012) argues that the resource curse is actually a feature of a specific historical period, and moreover of a specific set of institutional contexts within that historical period. In his analysis, the oil-specific version of the resource curse (what he calls 'the oil curse') is a feature of the post-1970s period in those countries which nationalized their oil industries. He says:

> As a global phenomenon, the political ailments caused by oil and gas production seem to be limited to both a certain set of countries . . . and the post-1980 period. Before about 1980, there was little or no global association between oil wealth and either less democracy, less work for women or more frequent insurgencies, and the oil states had impressively faster economic growth. (Ross 2012, p. 227)

This is not to say—he notes—that things were rosy prior to this period: one only needs to read socio-environmental histories such as Santiago's (2006) brilliant *Ecology of Oil* on Mexico to recognize this. However, the political distortions that Ross associates with the oil curse (less democracy, more insurgency, gender inequity) have become more systematic over the last three decades. In an argument that begins to look similar to that of Thorp et al. Ross concludes that these distortions are especially apparent when oil is discovered in contexts of autocratic rule or weak democracies (i.e. democracies with poor 'pre-existing checks on the executive branch' and weaker civil societies (Ross 2012, p. 229).[4] In such circumstances, patrimonial management of oil revenue is much more likely as—consequently—is the emergence of regional armed secessionist movements contesting regional exclusion from the benefits of oil. Meanwhile transitions to democracy are less likely: 'No country with as much oil as Libya, Bahrain, Oman, Algeria, or Iraq has ever made a successful transition from authoritarian to democratic rule' (Ross 2012, p. 234).

[4] Echoing Orihuela's interpretation of Chile, Ross suggests that oil did *not* strengthen the hands of autocrats in Latin America nearly so much because of the region's 'prior experience with democracy and labor unions' (p. 229).

One problem with Ross's analysis is the question of why such autocratic leaders have no interest in introducing forms of oil wealth management that would allow more stable economic management or in building institutions for volatility management (also noted as a critical institutional capacity by Collier and Venables 2011). He argues that:

> To enact . . . countercyclical policies, politicians must be able to forgo the short-term political benefits of immediate spending for the long-term ones of sustainable growth. These trade-offs are easier to make when incumbents believe they or their party is likely to stay in office long enough to profit from future gains; when the government is more constrained by checks and balances; when citizens are both well-informed and have confidence in their government; and when they are not sharply divided into competing factions that seek to exclude each other from future benefits. (p. 230)

However, autocrats with weak civil societies are presumably likely to believe that they will stay in office for a long time. The weaker autocrats who have to play competing factions off against each other are those who do not necessarily have such certainty. This brings the analysis back to the question of political settlements, suggesting that fragile settlements orchestrated by non-democratic leaders in weak civil societies are the most likely to manage natural resource wealth in ways that do not elicit sustained (and diversifying) growth with inclusion.

History as Memory

Historical memory is also important in the governance of resource extraction. Indeed the ways in which history is recounted and remembered can itself constitute an important variant of how ideas matter in struggles over the governance of extraction. Memories and histories can be used to frame political debates over natural resources, as well as to articulate political coalitions seeking particular sorts of institutional change. At a national level, memories of extraction and of war have interacted with resource governance (and have been consciously mobilized by political actors *in order to make them* interact with resource governance). In Bolivia, for instance, memories of the war with Chile have been critical to mobilizations around the governance of gas in the last decade, leading directly to the demise of plans to export gas to, or through, Chile (Perreault 2008, 2006). More generally, historical memories of colonial control can favour the emergence of resource nationalisms: 'Postcolonial societies are likely to produce forms of resource nationalism and re-interpret collective memories around the issue of resource ownership and control' (Thorp et al. 2012, p. 7). The continuing resonance among activists of Galeano's *Open Veins of Latin America* (1979/1998) is a prosaic indicator of this more general claim.

At a subnational level, historical memories of marginalization and disadvantage have also affected politics surrounding extractive industry. This can take many forms, with regional, ethnic, and racial identities being variously mobilized in the process. Ross (2008) identifies a number of such examples that have spilt over into violence—such as Aceh, the Niger Delta (see also Watts 2003), or more recently Bagua in Peru (Bebbington and Humphreys Bebbington 2011). This is not to say that memory necessarily feeds into acute conflict. More often it is a point of reference, leading resident populations to associate extraction with prior moments of repressive dispossession and to therefore be both circumspect but also immensely pragmatic in how they negotiate the arrival of extractive industry (as Humphreys Bebbington 2010, has shown for the Chaco of Bolivia). And, of course, at times the memories can be ones of boom and employment, inspiring support for new rounds of investment in resource extraction.

Grappling with History

If these insights suggest that the politics of natural resource extraction *must* be understood historically and with much sensitivity to time, sequences, and memories, they also leave hanging a series of questions. How far does an analysis need to go back in time? Thorp et al. (2012) take some of their analyses back more than a century—and of course Putnam's famous study of Italian political and social institutions reached back many centuries to find the sources of uneven regional performance (Putnam 1993). Few studies can afford such luxuries, but perhaps a rule of thumb is to reach back at least to the last natural resource boom in order to understand how political coalitions and institutions were fashioned then and see how far and in what ways they trace through to contemporary governance arrangements. As Thorp et al.'s analysis makes clear, this does not imply falling into historical determinism. Instead the approach would involve working forward from that starting point and analysing, at subsequent critical junctures, the options that were open to actors and the reasons for the political decisions that they subsequently took (or did not take).

Ross's analysis also poses a methodological challenge—how to select the time periods into which one would break up the analysis of cycles in the governance of extractives. Ross opts for periods defined largely by international factors (e.g. significant price changes), though at a national level an equally salient argument could be made for breaking up periods by regime cycle on the grounds that regime changes suggest shifts in dominant political coalitions. While a general rule for analysis cannot easily be defined, the implication is that it is worth looking for significant sub-periods within longer-term processes of political and institutional change in the extractive sector, and to recognize that the politics of governing extraction may change significantly between these periods.

Finally, the issue of historical memory raises the question not only of what is remembered, but also what is *not* remembered about prior phases of resource extraction. Thus, while methodologically it is important to attend to the ways in which key ideas about the past are framed and mobilized in contemporary politics of extraction, it remains important to keep asking why other parts of extractive industry history are erased from political discourse.

Governing Resource Extraction for Inclusive Development

Bonnie Campbell, an expert on mining governance, has argued that the effects of mining on inclusion and poverty reduction in Africa have been so disappointing in part because policy has focused on designing codes for mining itself rather than on governing the interactions between mining and development (Campbell 2008a). Of course, the discussion in the preceding two sections would suggest that such bias itself would reflect the dominant political settlement and the absence of coalitions, social movements, and policy networks with the power to induce policies and institutions much more oriented toward the promotion of inclusion. This section discusses different ways in which extractive industry might foster inclusive development and the sorts of coalitions that might induce institutions promoting such inclusion.

Channels of Inclusion

The channels through which resource extraction might foster inclusive development can be separated very simply between those channels that are directly related to the ways in which the extractive enterprise governs and organizes itself (channels 1 to 4) and those that derive from the way extractive industry as a sector is regulated by third parties, above all the state (channels 5 to 8). Each of these is important. We note the following channels:

1. Employment: populations can be included in or excluded from the political economy of extraction depending on the direct and indirect employment effects of mining, oil, and gas investments.
2. Supply chain management: companies can manage their supply chains in ways that offer more, or less, opportunities for local and regional populations to be included in their activities.

3. Corporate social responsibility and transparency: company approaches to employee and community well-being, to redistribution of profits through company-sponsored social programmes, and to financial transparency are all additional influences on who is and is not included in the benefits of extraction.

4. Ownership: though this occurs *much* less frequently, companies can also include populations and the workforce in the ownership structure of the extractive enterprise, either as shareholders or joint owners.

5. Public ownership: a number of extractive enterprises, particularly in the hydrocarbons sector, are publicly owned and as such allow for some sort of social inclusion in their operations, even if in practice such operations generally run as enterprises owned and organized by government.

6. Planning and consultation: populations can be included or excluded depending on practices and rules governing how resource extraction is planned for, who is consulted and how, and how far the voice of those consulted can affect the unfolding of the extractive economy (and relatedly, how far consultation and participation is managed such that it does little more than legitimate decisions and project designs already made (Li 2009)).

7. Taxation and social expenditure: how far populations are included in access to the financial resources generated by extractive industry depends entirely on the ways in which the sector is taxed and the extent to, and means through which this fiscal revenue finds its ways into social investment and other development programmes.

8. Environment: the potential for adverse environmental effects is high in the extractive economy. To the extent that environmental damage is a mechanism through which contemporary and future generations are excluded from (net) benefits, then the governance of environmental impact is important for social inclusion.

These different channels make clear that inclusion can take different forms. While inclusion is often taken to refer to access to the benefit flows associated with resource extraction, 'inclusion' can also refer to the incorporation of particular ideas and valuations in the planning and regulatory processes surrounding extraction. In addition, inclusion might also occur through involvement in decision-making processes—whether these are land-use planning and zoning processes, or processes linked to the management of the actual extractive enterprise. Inclusion can, then, have economic, socio-cultural, and political components, and these are not necessarily co-present. In the following, and for reasons of space, we focus on inclusion in the material opportunities generated through employment and taxation.

Inclusion through Employment and Taxation

It is frequently argued that one of the least significant mechanisms through which resource extraction fosters inclusion is employment. This is because the capital-intensive nature of modern operations restricts job creation, and furthermore tends to skew job creation toward higher-skilled positions. There are two important caveats to this observation. First, extractive industry companies and their associations have argued that such claims understate the indirect employment effects of the mining, oil, and gas industries. Indeed, indirect employment effects *can* be significant when companies endeavour to make them so, as Langton has recently noted in her 2012 Boyer Lectures (Langton 2012). Second, the observation is relevant only to large-scale mining: artisanal and small-scale mining generates far more employment (and much less, or no, tax revenue) and so might be deemed to be very inclusive in immediate livelihood terms (Hilson and Bancharigah 2009; Maconachie and Hilson 2011).

There is more general agreement that the channel which has the greatest potential significance as a means of promoting inclusion is that which runs from taxes and royalties to social expenditure (Hujo 2012; Arellano-Yanguas 2012; Bebbington 2012). This claim underlies contemporary policies in countries such as Bolivia, Ecuador, and Venezuela that have sought to capture greater shares of revenue through increasing tax and royalty rates or through full or partial nationalizations, though it is also an argument used in more orthodox, neo-liberally inclined regimes as well as by extractive industry companies themselves as an argument to justify the expansion of resource extraction. The channels linking extraction and social inclusion in this model run as follows:

extraction → taxes and royalties → social spending (social policy, social protection: targeted and non-targeted).

This, however, can be a relatively short-term view of the potential role of fiscal resources generated by extractive industry insofar as it emphasizes tax take as a means of increasing financing for social spending in the here and now. Such short-termism can be driven by government concern to use social spending to elicit political support, offset unrest, or seek alliances with certain subnational (formal and non-formal) authorities. Likewise it can be driven by the pressure of popular demands for rapid evidence of redistribution. Tax and royalty revenue can, however, be linked to social spending and social inclusion in a medium- to long-term sense if this revenue is used to manage both the asset portfolio of a country (e.g. through strategic investment in certain forms of infrastructure or human capital) and the structure of production through mechanisms that seek to manage revenue in ways that do not damage other sectors of the economy (e.g. via Dutch Disease effects) and/or promote diversification beyond natural resources (Collier and Venables 2011; Thorp et al. 2012). Such potential effects on growth constitute a medium term pathway to social spending and inclusion insofar as growth generates future revenue for redistributive social investment. In this rendition the longer-term pathway from extraction to inclusion runs as follows:

> extraction → taxes and royalties → sovereign wealth funds/national development banks → economic development and diversification → employment and tax generation → taxes for social policy.

Inevitably there are trade-offs between the short-, medium-, and long-term channels between extraction and social spending (Ascher 2012). The more tax and royalty revenue that is committed to immediate social spending reduces that which is available for saving in sovereign wealth funds, or for use in national development banks, infrastructure investment, and so on. There are also complex relationships among policies that save revenue in order to avoid the Dutch Disease and the promotion of economic diversification. First, if efforts to avoid currency appreciation are only partially successful, then the opportunities for diversification are constrained due to the combined effects of cheaper imports and more expensive exports, as appears to have happened in Chile, notwithstanding its success in keeping resource wealth off-shore and spending it counter-cyclically (Fuentes 2011; Guajardo 2012). Second, even when exchange-rate appreciation is successfully managed, other domestic factors can still inhibit diversification, such as small domestic markets, environmental constraints, and so on (as perhaps is the case in Botswana: Battistelli and Guichaoua 2012). An interesting exception in this regard is that of Indonesia, and this may indeed be partly because its far larger internal market facilitated diversification. Also the proportionately smaller weight of oil in its economy meant that the potential exchange-rate effects were far smaller (see an interesting discussion of the Indonesia case by Ascher 2012).

While there may be trade-offs between shorter and longer channels between extraction and inclusion the more important question regards the determinants of these trade-offs. One current in the literature notes the importance of technocratic factors. For instance, oft commented in the Indonesian case was the important role that the technically strong and politically protected Ministry of Finance played in managing revenues for the long term, and of avoiding political pressures that would distort policy oriented to long-term growth (Hofman 2007; Ascher 2012). Indeed, in some sense the strength and proven independence of the Ministry provided the credible commitment (Sen 2012) that investors needed to see in order to invest in ways that had the effect of diversifying the economy. Ascher (2012) also makes the interesting observation that the commitment to technocratic independence was somehow (causally?) entangled with a particular approach to corruption in which the only corruption that was allowed in Indonesia was that which would not have systemic growth and diversification inhibiting effects (i.e. corruption that gave particular favours and market opportunities to members of the Suharto family). What was not allowed was corruption of the sort that would demand 'growth suppressing macroeconomic policies (protectionism, overvalued exchange rates, distorted interest rates)' (Ascher 2012, p. 250).

The mere existence of technocratic mechanisms that offer the prospect of strategic long-term management of resource extraction revenues is not, however, sufficient. Among the mechanisms for saving resource generated in the eight country cases presented in Collier and Venables (2011), only two of these (Malaysia and Chile) actually withstood political interference and raiding. Furthermore, they claim, the ostensibly best-designed fund (Cameroon's oil fund) was the one that succumbed most easily to raiding (2011, pp. 11–17).

Raiding of such revenues (whether in the form of sovereign funds or regular government finances) can occur for many reasons each of which relate to the dominant political settlement and its relative stability. Most obviously raiding occurs because of unchecked corruption and theft, for which there are many cases: Nigeria, Angola, Cameroon, and so on. That such raiding happens and that resource revenues can be managed with impunity and complete lack of transparency reflects the existence of narrow settlements that are sustained through the use or threat of force and tight networks of loyalty somewhat akin to mafias and more generally the structures to which the literature on the 'dark-side' of social capital has drawn attention (Putzel 1997). However, 'raiding' can also occur when the settlement is one that incorporates groups (or at least elites representing groups) with capacity to mobilize and/or withdraw critical political support when they conclude they are not receiving an appropriate share of benefits. Such raiding may not be of existing funds but more 'pre-emptive' in the sense that political claims are made on resource revenues even before they are transferred to central government. This circumstance is perhaps more characteristic of populist settlements—and populist forms of resource nationalism—in which a settlement is consolidated precisely because it is predicated on redistribution. This may characterize contemporary circumstances in countries such as Venezuela and Bolivia. (It would not characterize a situation such as that of Norway because, while the settlement there is also predicated on redistributive social spending, it is also predicated on an acceptance of high tax rates— that is, resource revenues do not replace income or sales tax.) In this sense the settlement determines the relative political feasibility of these different channels from extraction to social inclusion—and also by implication the relative sustainability of the social inclusion that accompanies extraction.

Coalitions for Inclusion

As noted earlier, the extent to which these different channels of inclusion are present at both local and national scales varies greatly. Some companies in some countries manage supply chains to foster employment, others do not; some countries have institutionalized mechanisms of consultation and participation, others do not; and so forth. In the language of earlier sections of the chapter, this variation would be understood in terms of differences among political settlements and political coalitions across space and time. This in turn raises the question as to what sorts of coalition and settlement might foster greater inclusion.

One hypothesis in this regard might be that company-level initiatives to enhance inclusion are more likely to constitute responses to narrow coalitions, while changes in government regulation of the sector might reflect responses to the demands of broader-based coalitions. Indeed, it *is* possible to find cases of companies operating more inclusively in some contexts than others and to explain this difference in terms of the varying degree of social protest and mobilization that the company encounters across these sites. Likewise it is possible to encounter some companies that are generally more inclusive than others within any given country, and to explain this difference in terms of their differing subjection to pressures from watchdogs, activist shareholders, and public debate in their home countries. In these instances, while change is induced it is explained by the existence of narrow coalitions: the absence of a broader coalition means that such change is not likely to scale up beyond the operation or company in question.

Conversely the emergence of public institutions fostering enhanced inclusion might be expected to derive from broader-based coalitions (the broader base being necessary to counter special interests that would otherwise favour less inclusive modes of governing the extractive economy). In some instances this broader base will not include the industry itself. The Salvadoran example discussed earlier would be one instance of this, while another would be the Bolivian experience in which the coalition embodied in the Movement Towards Socialism government of Evo Morales secured legislative change that increased state involvement in and taxation of the hydrocarbon sector. In other cases, such broader coalitions may well include at least some parts of the extractive sector itself. An example of the latter scenario would be the coalition that pushed for a change in tax distribution rules in Peru in the early 2000s. In this case, tax transfer rules were changed so that 50 per cent of the taxes paid by extractive enterprises would be returned to regions where extraction was occurring. In this case the coalition seeking this change included mining companies who believed that such transfers would reduce criticism of, and protest against, companies (Arellano-Yanguas 2012).

The dynamics of such coalitions are likely to be complicated by the fact that in many instances, moves towards one form of inclusion can involve the relative exclusion of other interests. The clearest instance of this is the scenario discussed in the second section of the chapter in which the expansion of the extractive frontier is a vehicle for increasing government revenues earmarked (at least rhetorically) for national-level social investment policies. In these instances, the inclusion of a large part of the citizenry (through social policy funded by revenue from resource extraction) requires the existence of institutions that would prevent populations living in areas of resource extraction from blocking expanded investment in the sector. A similar scenario is that where efforts to increase central government tax take from extraction in order to finance national policies would imply reducing regional governments' revenues from the same source. In instances such as these, whether the coalition is able to induce change or not depends on the extent to which these excluded blocks have the necessary 'holding power' to prevent such change.

While a range of other scenarios can be imagined, these hypothetical and actual examples reflect the importance of understanding the institutional relationships through which resource extraction is governed as endogenous to an existing political settlement, while also exploring the processes through which both endogenously and exogenously driven institutional change might occur. More specifically, focusing on cases where institutional change has fostered inclusion can serve as a basis for identifying the types of coalitional dynamic through which exclusionary settlements might be destabilized. This in turn would suggest the types of political process that might be supported with a view to increasing the likelihood that resource extraction might contribute to inclusive development.

Part III
The Politics of Social and Legal Citizenship: Promoting and Protecting the Rights of the Poor?

Part III

The Politics of Social and Legal
Citizenship: Promoting and Protecting
the Rights of the Poor?

5

The Politics of What Works in Service Delivery

Claire Mcloughlin

Introduction: The Debate on the Politics of Service Delivery

The pervasive failure of governments in developing countries to provide services that meet the basic needs of their population has been largely, though not exclusively, attributed to problems of weak capacity. At the same time, there is now resounding consensus in aid circles that politics matters, institutions 'rule', and development agencies need to understand (even if they are not fully able to engage with) the political aspects of reform (Leftwich and Wheeler 2011; Unsworth 2010). It is not that politics has been absent from the debate about the under-provision of vital public services, just that in practice it has rarely been systematically examined as the principal cause.

It is well understood, at the conceptual level at least, that politics often underlies or exacerbates capacity constraints (Booth 2011a). The idea of public services as an inherently political undertaking, intimately bound to the nature of the state and the genesis of the social contract, has enjoyed both a long tradition in scholarly enquiry and a recent revival alongside the rise of state-building in development discourse (OECD 2008). The central message from the seminal *World Development Report 2004*—that poor services are a measure of the failure of representative democracy to secure the 'long-route' of political accountability—remains deeply influential. Empirical studies likewise continue to document how political actors, based on calculations of political returns (attracting votes), often prefer to allocate goods and services to certain social groups rather than pursue inclusive, broad-based provision (Collier 2007).[1] In practice, aid interventions

---

[1] See, for example, Andre and Mesple-Somps (2009); Burgess et al. (2010).

designed to address so-called 'political market imperfections', typically through enhancing transparency or user participation, implicitly embody assumptions about how political actors' incentives are created, maintained, and ultimately can be altered in favour of inclusive provision (Keefer 2007; Gauthier and Reinikka 2007).[2]

At the point of implementation, where policies often encounter vested interests and falter, whether and how services are delivered may depend in particular on the structure of incentives facing providers and recipients (Pritchett and Woolcock 2004; Collier 2007). Specifically, service delivery is likely to face problems to do with the motivations of frontline staff, the heterogeneity of customer needs and demands, and the difficulty of measuring and monitoring performance (Collier 2007). The principal–agent problem has been a central framework for understanding why behaviour in service delivery organizations so often 'fails to correspond to the expected pattern' (Blundo and Olivier de Sardan 2006, p. 14).[3] As Pritchett and Woolcock (2004, p. 196) explain, because the provision of services is key, discretionary, and transaction intensive, with multiple principals and agents, delivering them through the public sector may well be 'the mother of all institutional and organizational design problems'. In developing countries, the bureaucratic arena is itself highly politicized, interconnected with societal interests, and often forms the basis of patronage (Batley 2004).

In spite of recent conceptual advancements in analysing the politics of service delivery, technical studies and evaluation reports seeking to explain how public services perform are often entirely disconnected from political economy questions about actors and their incentives. Moreover, where politics is considered in the diagnosis of performance, it is typically cast in a constraining rather than an enabling role or, worse, confined to unconvincing, unexplained categories like 'political will', or 'patrimonial politics', or 'weak incentives' (Hickey 2007). As Crook (2010) concluded in his review of the literature examining civil service reforms in Africa, 'lack of political commitment' is the favourite catch-all term for failure, and politics remains the 'poor cousin' among a group of better-understood, capacity-based explanations. In sum, the widespread consensus that politics matters has not been matched by rigorous research into how different *forms* of politics are likely to determine whether and how well services perform.

---

[2] Incentives are 'the rewards and punishments that are perceived by individuals to be related to their actions and those of others' and can be material or non-material (Ostrom et al. 2002, p. 36).

[3] The 'principal–agent' model draws attention to the difficulties that citizens (as 'principals') face in ensuring the actions of self-interested politicians (the 'agents') are aligned with their purpose, and the problem that governments (as 'principals') face in constraining the behaviour of their bureaucracies (as 'agents') (Batley 2004).

In seeking to address the need for more systematic, variegated analysis of the politics of service delivery, this chapter departs from the main thrust of recent studies in two ways. First, it focuses exclusively on the role of politics, broadly interpreted,[4] in accounting for service delivery performance. Second, it explores how politics has enabled, as opposed to constrained, that performance. To this end, the chapter traces the forms of politics that underpinned eight cases of relatively successful delivery, drawing on evidence from a range of country contexts and sectors (roads, agriculture, health, education) where independent evaluations demonstrate improved outcomes. In this way, the focus is explicitly on understanding the politics of what works. Specifically, the task is to identify the characteristics of the political environment in which these cases evolved: from the micro politics of implementation, to the politics of sector policymaking, to the macro political context. Piecing together these layers of politics is constrained by the fragmented nature of the literature, which often treats them as disconnected. Nevertheless, the findings illustrate that it is possible to trace the connections between performance at the point of delivery, and the main forms of politics operating at local, sector, and national levels.

The cases under scrutiny here, as Bebbington and McCourt (2007) observed in their own search for 'success', often emerge against the odds, and are never wholesale triumphs. As Grindle (2005) puts it, success, like development in general, is a moving target. Even policies that produce good results may over time 'go bad', ceasing to be effective or, worse, producing unintended consequences. Setbacks, missteps, and reversals are characteristic of any path of reform (Benequista and Gaventa 2011). While these constitute good reasons to be cautious about labelling cases as ones that 'work', there is nevertheless a general openness to the idea that tracing success, or progress at least, might be a useful learning exercise (ODI 2011). Accordingly, new research into the politics of service provision is turning its attention towards explaining variation and exception in the face of overwhelming poor performance (Booth 2011b), identifying institutional arrangements that are comparably better at dealing with some of the problems that arise in public service provision (Besley and Ghatak 2007), and understanding why some cases run against the general patterns of institutional failure or corruption (Leftwich 2010). Like these studies, the purpose here is not to provide a blueprint for success elsewhere, but rather, to understand how politics has enabled inclusive service delivery in particular cases.

---

[4] Politics is here understood to encompass 'all the activities of conflict, cooperation and negotiation over decisions about institutions and rules which shape how resources are used, produced and distributed' (Leftwich 2010, p. 10).

Case Studies of the Politics of What Works

Important conceptual advances in understanding the politics of basic service delivery have centred on the role of actors, incentives, and institutions in enabling or constraining reform. However, empirical research is lagging, offering little present scope for systematic learning or policy uptake. Comparative studies of the political factors that account for variation in service outcomes, either between sectors within a country, or across regions within a sector, remain rare. This review also revealed a paucity of cases subjected both to political analysis and technical impact evaluation. More critically, these two approaches rarely cross paths in the service delivery literature (as elsewhere). Political analysis is typically pitched at the macro level, or alternatively provides highly localized insights into specific blockages to reform at the sector level, with few connecting the two. Impact evaluations offer largely technical accounts that sometimes struggle to accommodate politics in a meaningful way.

The above limitations, partly a reflection of the broader dichotomy between the received wisdom that 'politics matters' and the reality that capacity is easier to document and measure, present a practical challenge to studying the politics of service delivery. The implication for this study is that the cases analysed in this chapter were pieced together retrospectively, connecting available, sometimes contradictory, technical material with academic research, grey literature, and political analysis. Because of the post hoc nature of this process, the cases should be read as indicative, rather than comprehensive or conclusive accounts of the political determinants of what worked.

In so far as the literature allows, the cases carefully unpick the macro, meso, and micro political conditions in which human development outcomes were improved through service delivery. The selection presents an opportunity to consider the influence of politics in both 'social' (health and education) and 'productive' (roads and agricultural marketing) sectors in diverse country settings: Bangladesh, Ethiopia, Ghana, Rwanda, Indonesia, Malawi, and Peru. In each case, independent impact evaluation verifies the progress made, and moreover that improvements have been sustained over the long term (minimum five years). The selection also aimed to show variation between different organizational arrangements for delivery—ranging broadly from direct state, to contracting out, to co-production, to state–NGO collaboration.[5] This variety is shown in Table 5.1.

---

[5] In practice, no case fits neatly into a single category, partly because the complexity of organizational arrangements is not often captured in the literature, and partly because a particular service may be provided through bundles of modes operating at different levels or points in the production and delivery process.

Table 5.1. Case studies of the politics of what works

Sector	Country	Main mode of delivery
Maternal and child health	Rwanda	*Performance-based financing*
	Bangladesh	*Decentralized state provision*
Basic education	Ghana	*Complementary (state–NGO collaboration)*
	Ethiopia	*Decentralized state provision*
Rural roads	Indonesia	*Decentralized state provision*
	Peru	*Contracting out*
Agricultural marketing	Malawi	*State-run*
	Ghana	*State-run*

Source: Author.

Maternal and Child Health in Rwanda

A number of sources have recently drawn attention to the progress made in the Rwandan health sector since 1994 (Pose and Samuels 2011a; Basinga et al. 2011; Brinkerhoff et al. 2009). Although the genocide virtually destroyed the country's health infrastructure, available data indicate nearly all health indicators have been restored to pre-genocide levels, and Rwanda is now on track to meet the child and maternal health MDGs. This follows a striking decrease in the maternal mortality ratio between 2000 and 2005 (30 per cent), and a sharp reduction in under-five and infant mortality between 2005 and 2007 (32 per cent and 28 per cent, respectively). Progress is expected to continue as the number of women giving birth in health facilities, and the number of births attended by skilled personnel, increases (Pose and Samuels 2011a, pp.11, 15–16).

The scale and timing of this progress is intimately connected to the exceptional context of the post-genocide period and the nature of the ensuing post-war political settlement. Pose and Samuels (2011a) trace the evolution of health sector reform in Rwanda along the same timeline as wider processes of stabilization and social reconciliation in the country. Planning was initially hampered by a period of stagnation in the late 1990s, during which time the country, governed by the interim Government of National Unity, was reliant on emergency humanitarian aid and characterized by sporadic conflict. Only when the period of political reconstruction began in the early 2000s could reforms begin to be designed and piloted, but still, national-level implementation could not fully get underway until after the first multi-party elections of 2003 (Pose and Samuels 2011a, p. 7).

Booth and Golooba-Mutebi (2011, p. 15) argue that the shock and challenge to national survival presented by the genocide helped install a leadership determined to pursue nation-building, noting that President Kagame is widely regarded as 'both visionary and determined to the point of ruthlessness'. They conclude that, in several respects, the regime since 2000 has been characterized by 'developmental patrimonialism': that is, the ruling elite has successfully centralized rents and deployed them with a view to the long term—as formally articulated in Rwanda's Vision 2020. Furthermore, because the regime has been free from the need to create rents to generate political support, policy has been driven almost exclusively by a genuine commitment to economic and social development as an antidote to a legacy of ethnic division (Booth and Golooba-Mutebi 2011). Morgan (2010) notes that the near-complete destruction of infrastructure and human capital appears to have enabled policy innovation free from the constraints of a historically entrenched system.

At the technical level, Rwanda's achievements in health are widely attributed to a package of health reforms that simultaneously address the supply and demand side (Kalk et al. 2010).[6] On the supply side, the Performance Based Financing (PBF) initiative—a form of 'contracting in' piloted in 2002 and rolled out nationally in 2006—is a prominent mode of provision.[7] The initiative provides financial incentives to public- and NGO-managed district hospitals to increase utilization and quality of care, based on performance against a set of indicators (Pose and Samuels 2011a). Supplementary funding is allocated by central government acting in a stewardship role, and the initiative receives financial and technical contributions from the World Bank, WHO, and a number of bilateral aid agencies.[8] High-level backing from the Rwandan government was cemented in 2006 after rigorous evaluations revealed positive impacts on the availability and utilization of services (Soeters et al. 2006). Notwithstanding ongoing academic debates regarding the effects of PBF on long-term worker incentives (Meessen et al. 2006; Kalk et al. 2010), a recent multi-donor impact evaluation of outcomes across 166 districts found improvements in both the use and quality of maternal and child health services (Basinga et al. 2011).

Echoing the wider observations about the role of determined leadership in Rwanda's broader developmental success, several authors note that strong political leadership, from the President down to village level, has been critical in providing the impetus for health reform in the post-genocide period (Pose and Samuels 2011a; Brinkerhoff et al. 2009). The effects of leadership style have also been notable in the implementation of PBF. Morgan (2010) analyses how the government's will and firm commitment to the

[6] This includes decentralization, community-based provision, and, on the demand side, the well-known community health insurance—the *Mutuelle de Santé*—a scheme providing a national subsidy for those too poor to pay for health.

[7] The approach is sometimes referred to as 'paying for performance' (P4P).

[8] Funding is coordinated through an *Inter-Agency Working Groups on Results Based Financing*, affiliated to the International Health Partnership (Kalk et al. 2010).

programme meant it was able to push the initiative forward in spite of an initial cool response from donors. Others similarly note government commitment was critical to steering a course through the diverging views of the multiple stakeholders at the implementation stage (Rusa and Fritsche 2007). Morgan (2010) cites the example of government champions being able to hold together a commitment from donors to not introduce PBF in the 'control areas' during the pilot evaluation stage of the programme. This capacity to assertively engage donors is indicative of the wider observation that, in spite of being heavily aid dependent, Rwanda has been able to pursue its own agenda, acting as a 'true partner' and encouraging the coordination of aid at central and local levels (Pose and Samuels 2011a).

Leadership is closely linked to strong top-down incentives, and this is another factor that features prominently in accounts of the success of performance-based financing in Rwanda. Booth and Golooba-Mutebi (2011, p. 16) argue that the Rwandan civil service scores highly on vertical coordination and technocratic integrity—essential instruments for regimes to effectively implement their policy vision. They further argue that the legitimacy and integrity of the Rwandan regime, evidenced in the complete absence of high-level political corruption, affords it considerable moral authority (Booth and Golooba-Mutebi 2011).

At the national level, as Pose and Samuels (2011a) describe, the administration has strategically revived the deeply embedded Rwandan cultural values of *imihigo* and *guhiga*, requiring mayors, village chiefs, local leaders, and civil servants to sign annual performance contracts on which they have to swear an oath. Some authors observe synergy between this wider emphasis on performance, which Brinkerhoff et al. (2009) describe as 'front and centre' in the Rwandan public sector, and the success of PBF. At the technical level, Meessen et al. (2006) note that deploying values and social norms of integrity and honesty lowers the transaction costs of command-and-control mechanisms like PBF. Pose and Samuels (2011a) conclude that Rwanda is an example of how formal standard-setting, evaluation, and feedback mechanisms can be successfully deployed alongside more traditional, culturally embedded means of enforcing contracts, accountability, and obligations.

Maternal and Child Health in Bangladesh

Bangladesh has achieved what the World Bank (2005b) has described as a 'spectacular rate of progress' on health indicators since its independence in 1971, most notably in reducing fertility, but also in increasing the use of antenatal and postnatal care. Pose and Samuels (2011b) similarly cite 'extraordinary improvements' in infant and maternal mortality in the country, including a 44 per cent decline in the maternal mortality rate between 1990 and 2001 (Mridha et al. 2009, p. 1). This progress has occurred alongside sustained growth in health infrastructure: from a very low base of virtually no health facilities at independence, to now substantial numbers of district hospitals and local community clinics (Mridha et al. 2009). The country has used successive five-year development plans to move from a narrow urban-based delivery system to a more broad-based rural programme capable of reaching vulnerable groups (Pose and Samuels 2011b). Much of the literature acknowledges that in spite of the impressive gains made in maternal and child health, inequalities remain between regions and between ethnic and socioeconomic groups in access to services (Mridha et al. 2009; World Bank 2005b; Hossain and Osman 2007).

Several observers note that success in Bangladesh is surprising, paradoxical even, given the country's poor record on governance and the prevalence of corruption (Mridha et al. 2009; Pose and Samuels 2011b). In explaining this paradox, some point to Bangladesh's consistent commitment to prioritizing maternal and child health in spite of a swathe of policy shifts made by successive regimes (Hossain and Osman 2007; World Bank 2005b; Pose and Samuels 2011b). The nature of the post-independence political settlement, as Parks and Cole (2010) argue, is relatively stable, and patterns of elite competition and cooperation remain predictable and consistent, though the actual coalition in power changes every few years. Some analysts have suggested electoral competition and the perceived political capital to be gained from service provision have played an important role in driving social sector reform in Bangladesh. Hossain and Osman (2007, p. 39) note strong party competition between 1991 and 2006 has driven health reform, as successive ruling parties have attempted to scale up their efforts in order to outperform their predecessor. This, they argue, is mirrored in the local politicization of services; characterized by increased party control over the distribution of resources. Mahmud et al. (2008) observe that since the 1980s, government has gradually withdrawn from the productive sectors to concentrate more on providing public services, partly because politicians perceive social spending as a political win-win that provides political credit alongside business opportunities.

It has also been suggested that electoral politics have determined the nature of the reforms undertaken, based on the type of popular support they have been able to attract. Hossain and Osman (2007) describe how achievements made during the 1990s were mainly limited to reforms to improve access—a type of reform that typically enjoys political support and is rarely administratively complex. They observe that 'the objectives of the reform were broadly aligned with the conditions of governance, which therefore did not present a major obstacle to their achievement'

(2007, p. 39). Further, reforms to increase access were popular with citizens and service-providers, specifically doctors, attracting the support of local and central political elites and the donor community. Similarly, Mahmud et al. (2008) argue that, broadly speaking, successive governments have pursued the path of least confrontation, adopting reforms that were relatively easy wins accomplished by 'a stroke of the pen'. Since the 2000s, much-needed quality reforms have yet to make it onto the policy table, reflecting the perceived difficulties of tackling the interests of the now well-organized professional public servants whose political clout was strengthened through the expansionary reforms of the 1990s (Hossain and Osman 2007).

At the local level, effective state-NGO collaboration has been important (Pose and Samuels 2011b), alongside the role of the decentralized public health system (Mridha et al. 2009). Public health in Bangladesh is delivered through a tiered structure of facilities at tertiary (division), secondary (district), and upazila (sub-district) levels. While there are no available country-wide evaluations of the decentralized mode of provision, Faguet and Ali's (2009) micro-level study of health outcomes across two upazilas—one successful, one unsuccessful—provides an insight into the local structural, political, and institutional factors that may account for the variation in indicators across localities. The study found that while the health 'hardware' (infrastructure, administration, staff) of the two upazilas was similar, the successful upazila was in closer proximity to the capital, had a history of sustained NGO involvement, and a relatively open, tolerant religious tradition.

Even more important than these structural factors, Faguet and Ali (2009) argue, was the ability of 'local leaders' to promote changes in health behaviours. This was made possible because they were embedded in a dense 'web of relationships' between citizens, legal authorities, and service providers that conferred on them local authority and legitimacy, making the local population more susceptible to their messages. This network of relationships also underpinned a higher degree of accountability by public servants in the successful upazila. The authors argue, therefore, that 'if services are to respond to a population's particular—and changing—needs, and be credible in the eyes of the population, the elected representatives of that population should be involved in their production (Faguet and Ali 2009, p. 216). They conclude that, in order to understand success and failure in public service delivery, we need to dig down beneath the 'rules of the game': that is, to look beyond the organizations, institutions, and informal rules and conventions that govern incentives, to examine the underlying beliefs, understandings, and dispositions that drive behaviour.

Complementary Education in Ghana

Ghana has made substantial progress in increasing access to basic education since the post-colonial period: the net enrolment ratio in primary school increased from 60 per cent to 77 per cent between 1999 and 2008 (UNESCO 2011, p. 117). In spite of this achievement, the 2011 Education Monitoring Report warns that based on current levels of public education expenditure, and in light of sharp cuts in the education budget in response to wider fiscal crisis, the country is unlikely to meet its MDG targets without a substantial increase in aid (UNESCO 2011). Little (2010, p. 44) is similarly cautious, noting that enrolments remain well below the Education for All (EFA) goals, and completion rates are problematic, with only 63 per cent of children making it to their fifth year of primary school. Furthermore, there are signs progress has levelled off since the early 2000s, partly because of the difficulties of reaching the last 20 per cent of primary-age children, particularly in the north of the country, where the great majority of children do not complete the compulsory nine years of primary education (Little 2010; Casely-Hayford and Hartwell 2010, p. 529).

A number of studies have analysed the relationship between Ghana's uneven progress on education over the past three decades, and the level of 'political will' exhibited by successive regimes (Little 2010; Pedley and Taylor 2009; Kosack 2009). These studies provide similar accounts of why the country invested relatively more in primary education in the periods before 1966 and after 1986, whereas the intervening period was characterized by structural decline. Little (2010) and Pedley and Taylor (2009) both observe that governments that prioritized access to education—namely, under the Convention People's Party (CPP) (1951–65) and the Provisional National Defence Council (PNDC) (1982–92)—were driven by a need to actively court the support of the masses. Kosack (2009) develops this further, arguing that the fluctuating levels of political will correlate with whether or not the two 'vital constituencies' in education reform—poor families and employers— were mobilized by a 'political entrepreneur'. In contrast, regimes under which access to education declined owed their power base to the urban middle classes and therefore tended to stress improving standards (Little 2010, p. 44). Pedley and Taylor (2009) note that, while governments in the democratic era since 1996 have committed to 'Education for All', elite and middle-class interests continue to influence a focus on secondary education.

Against this background of inconsistent progress, resource constraints, and the continuing challenge of reaching underserved populations, the important contribution of complementary education in Ghana is increasingly being recognized (Casely-Hayford and Hartwell 2010). The School for Life (SfL) programme, piloted and rolled out across the north of the country since 1995, is considered one of the few successful examples of complementary education (Rose 2009). The programme provides accelerated learning to underserved populations through a form of co-production whereby formal organizations and communities or service recipients both make resource contributions; for example, volunteer facilitators (teachers) are recruited from within the community, trained by the Ghana Education Service (GES), and paid by the community in food, small amounts of cash or household labour.[9] The programme is highly adapted to local preferences: schedules work around children's local work demands, the curriculum is simplified, and instruction is in the mother tongue.

A recently completed impact assessment found SfL had reached 85,000 children and over 4,000 rural communities across twelve districts, with close to 90 per cent of these children completing the programme and becoming functionally literate, and almost 70 per cent transitioning to the formal education system at upper primary levels. The integration of SfL students into the formal system was shown to have had a positive impact on the overall gross enrolment rate for public primary schools in the north.[10] The programme also improved gender equality (at least 40 per cent of those enrolled in SfL were female) and helped diffuse messages about the importance of good-quality education (Casely-Hayford and Hartwell 2010).

Much of the literature examining SfL points to the role of a supportive government–NGO relationship as an enabling factor in the overall success and sustainability of the programme. While the programme is exclusively donor-funded, with no public finance, government has been encouraging in its stewardship role, increasingly recognizing the contribution of complementary education at the policy level since 2003 (Casely-Hayford and Hartwell 2010). At the implementation level, SfL is managed through collaborative arrangements between donors, non-state actors, and government agencies. Central and local government, donors, and NGOs sit together on its Executive Board, providing policy advice and appointing senior staff (2010, p. 528). The legitimacy of SfL has been acknowledged at the lowest tiers of government, where several District Education Offices have signed Memorandums of Understanding (MOU) with SfL. Casely-Hayford and Hartwell (2010) argue that in turn SfL has influenced the state sector's notions of quality provision, and has begun training formal public sector teachers in its native language and community-based literacy approach. Batley and Mcloughlin (2010, pp. 144–5) argue that this type of informal mutual agreement, based on independent contributions by the partners and

---

[9] This definition of co-production is based on Joshi and Moore (2004).
[10] Specifically, the evaluation found that SfL increased access to primary education by 14% in the North; from a gross enrolment rate of 69%, to 83% (Casely-Hayford and Hartwell 2010).

non-hierarchic relationships between them, allows for joint learning, relies on the accumulation of human capital, and may extend through processes of imitation, example, and institutional replication.

Some of the literature examines more closely the actors and incentives behind the government–NGO relationship in the case of SfL. It is broadly accepted that donors have been instrumental in encouraging the government's collaborative stance towards complementary education in general, and SfL in particular. Rose (2009) observes that donors are often the ones promoting the inclusion of NGO provision within education plans. In the specific case of SfL, Casely-Hayford and Hartwell (2010) note that the programme gained public visibility, and increased government recognition, only after USAID included complementary education within its education strategy and began financing it in 2005. But as Kosack (2009) points out, aid has generally only been effective in Ghana where donor goals coincide with those of the government. There are indications that government incentives may be positively aligned with donors in this instance because of the particular dynamics and funding arrangements of SfL. Rose (2009, p. 230) notes that experience in Ghana is indicative of a wider pattern whereby governments are happy to include NGO provision in education plans provided the provision is supported by external resources rather than competing with formal government schooling.

Primary Education in Ethiopia

Despite being historically one of the most educationally disadvantaged countries in the world, having seen poor enrolment and educational attainment in the adult population in the early 1990s, Ethiopia has achieved a 'rapid and equitable' expansion of access to primary education since the end of the civil war in 1991 (Engel 2011). The 2011 Global Monitoring Report observes the country now has a real prospect of achieving Universal Primary Education by 2015, having reduced the number of children out of school from 6.5 million to 2.7 million from 1999 to 2008 (UNESCO 2011). Notwithstanding continuing concerns over quality, there is evidence that this rapid expansion has been accompanied by reductions in geographic and socioeconomic inequalities in access (in particular, a narrowing of the gender gap), alongside growing rates of primary school completion (Teshome 2008; Engel 2011). Accordingly, Ethiopia has recently been described as having 'the most pro-poor budget in Africa' (Engel 2011, p. 15).

The literature examining the progress made in education in Ethiopia draws attention to the strong ideological commitment to pro-poor reform and equality of access reform exhibited by the ruling political party, the Ethiopian Peoples' Revolutionary Democratic Front (EPRDF). Brown and

Teshome (2007) explain how this ideology is linked to the party's military history, its experience of mass mobilization in resistance to the Dergue, and the fact that the poor are its key political constituency. Likewise, Engel (2011) argues that the political legitimacy of the EPRDF rests on its identity as a 'vanguard movement of the poor', and that education has been regarded by the regime as a central pillar of the post-war nation-building project, as a means of addressing past sources of instability (2011, p. 14). This is illustrated by Teshome's (2008, p. 58) description of successive education policies as being 'loaded' with references to democratic values, human rights, and citizenship, and conveying explicit aims 'to produce good citizens who understand, respect and defend the constitution'.

Chanie (2007) and Engel (2011) argue that decentralization in Ethiopia has been central to the ruling party's political survival, and arose from an urgent need to resolve struggles for power and resources between ethnic political elites, and to accommodate the various ethnic groups' specific geographical features, economic activity, and social and cultural values. In the education sector, central government finances services through intergovernmental transfers, but retains control over curriculum and overall policymaking while other aspects of the stewardship role—namely, planning, standard-setting and accreditation, evaluation, monitoring, and allocating local discretionary budgets—are devolved to woreda education offices (Garcia and Rajkumar 2008).[11] A 2008 World Bank study found that in spite of sub-optimal arrangements for funding, planning, and role allocation, decentralization improved service delivery, and disproportionately favoured poorer, more remote, food insecure, and pastoral areas, narrowing the gap in attainment between disadvantaged and better-off woreda (Garcia and Rajkumar 2008, p. ix). While acknowledging the problems in attributing sector outcomes to decentralization, Dom et al. (2010, p. 51) support this finding, arguing that decentralization has had positive redistributive effects, and has coincided with steeper upward trends in a number of education indicators.

There are mixed signals about the relative roles of top-down versus bottom-up accountability and participation in the decentralized system of education in Ethiopia. On the one hand, Brown and Teshome (2007, p. 45) argue that the ruling party's Marxist roots which underlie its commitment to pro-poor policymaking have also engendered a top-down, command approach to implementation. At the formal level, and Dom et al. (2010) describe in detail how decentralization has been tempered by strong top-down influences and constraints on local government autonomy. At the

---

[11] Levels of government in Ethiopia are: zones, woredas (districts), and kebeles (community councils) (Garcia and Rajkumar 2008).

informal level, Chanie (2007) has argued that intergovernmental transfers in practice centre on informal, patron–client relations characterized by an imbalance of power between strong central and weaker regional political parties. These dynamics sustain upward accountability, central domination, and regional fiscal dependence (2007, p. 361).

On the other hand, some studies have suggested that decentralization in Ethiopia has generated positive social capital and collective action around services (Engel 2011). Dom et al. (2010, p. 46) find decentralization has allowed woredas to raise local awareness of national strategies and more effectively mobilize community participation and resources. Engel (2011) similarly notes increased community willingness to dedicate scarce resources to education, indicated by the fact that community contributions frequently make up between 10 and 20 per cent of the woreda budget (Garcia and Rajkumar 2008, cited in Engel 2011, p. 20). There is also some suggestion that the government's decision to allow teaching to be delivered in local languages, using locally relevant curricula, has contributed to more active participation in the teaching–learning process (Engel 2011, p. 18). Smith (2008), however, conveys a more mixed message, noting that while there may be gains in terms of increased local pride, self-identity, and social capital, the impact of the education policy on long-term national unity remains unknown.

Rural Roads in Indonesia

Indonesia has recently been lauded as a democratic success story, having in a relatively short time made the transition from a centralized authoritarian regime to a democratic state that has pursued what Harris and Foresti (2011) describe as an aggressive programme of 'big bang decentralization'. While problems of corruption and neo-patrimonialism remain pervasive, decentralization is considered to have enabled progress towards increased accountability, as well as allowing citizens to express their preferences in the delivery of public goods at the local level (Harris and Foresti 2011).

As part of its ongoing decentralization reforms, the Indonesian government has, since 1998, adopted what is considered to be an innovative approach to the provision of small-scale infrastructure and rural roads development under the national Kecamatan Development Program (KDP) (World Bank 2010).[12] In this community-driven development approach, central government devolves an annual block grant to sub-districts to fund infrastructure projects chosen by villages, of which roads are the most popular (Olken 2010). Projects are facilitated and managed by local NGOs, which

---

[12] The programme now comes under the remit of the National Program for Community Empowerment (PNPM).

are responsible for managing funds, sourcing materials from the private sector, and building the roads through local labour (Guggenheim et al. 2004). The World Bank funds the programme and government, NGOs, and donors collaborate in monitoring and oversight at local level. Available data indicate that by October 2009, the programme had built or rehabilitated over 62,000 km of roads, with wider positive impacts in reducing household vulnerability and decreasing unemployment (World Bank 2010). Evaluations have found the technical quality of the vast majority of the infrastructure to be 'good' to 'very good', the method of building more cost effective than equivalent government contracts, and the roads to be well maintained by communities (Olken 2010; Guggenheim et al. 2004).

There is some consensus that the incentives for the post-1998 democratic state to adopt a community-driven approach to development derived in part from the underlying socio-economic conditions in the country (World Bank 2010; Guggenheim et al. 2004; Chowdhury et al. 2009). In analysing the origins of the KDP in particular, the World Bank (2010) emphasize that the context of rural poverty, political upheaval, and financial crisis—namely, the East Asia crisis and the sudden downfall of President Suharto—provided an impetus for government to deliver programmes that could 'bypass the graft-prone top layers of government' in an effort to 'increase the people's trust'. Guggenheim et al. (2004) similarly argue that this 'major institutional transition' weakened the appeal of centralized, top-down development in favour of more populist approaches like the KDP. In spite of this, they contend the programme did not in fact represent a reactionary or wholesale shift of political will in response to socio-economic crisis. Rather, it was a continuation of Indonesia's long-standing political commitment to rural economic development that had its origins in President Suharto's personal quest to address food insecurity. They describe how in practice, therefore, the KDP was not an entirely new mode of delivery, but was able to build on pre-existing institutions for local participation (Guggenheim et al. 2004). Chowdhury et al. (2009) argue that the political appeal of direct transfers to the poor has been the same for Indonesia's authoritarian and democratic regimes alike; that is, they have an immediate and visible impact on recipients, and can be 'pitched' as confirmation of the government's commitment to poverty reduction.

Sources acknowledge that the success and sustainability of the KDP model of provision is at least partly attributable to its demand-led, participatory nature (World Bank 2010; Guggenheim et al. 2004; Chowdhury et al. 2009). Chowdhury et al.'s (2009) comparative study of local infrastructure before and after the introduction of KDP concluded that the programme did improve the overall availability of local public roads, as well as better reflecting local, and in particular women's preferences for roads as opposed to other types of infrastructure. The World Bank (2010) notes that the participation of women and poor people in the programme has been high (average 45 per cent and 60 per cent respectively). Olken's (2010) study of the effects of participation in the programme across forty-nine villages concluded that overall participation did help increase the programme's legitimacy, and that the process and mechanism of participation mattered more than the actual outcomes (i.e. the type of project selected). Where community decisions were taken through plebiscites (direct democracy), as opposed to a deliberative meeting, the community (particularly women) were more likely to be satisfied with the projects chosen, and more likely to perceive them as legitimate, regardless of whether the outcome matched their preference (Olken 2010). Gibson and Woolcock (2008) found that in the KDP's deliberative forums, rights-based claim-making was the preferred 'currency of exchange', and allowed marginalized groups to challenge elite dominance over decision-making.

The literature provides varying accounts of the relative merits of bottom-up versus top-down accountability in addressing corruption in the case of the KDP. Guggenheim et al. (2004) argue that strong top-down control and joint government–World Bank monitoring at local level helped curb the potential for elite capture, noting the collaborative local effort between the Ministry of Home Affairs and local community NGOs in exposing corrupt officials. Field experiments by Olken (2007) found that in practice, bottom-up and top-down controls over corruption were operating together, with different effects. Whereas citizen engagement was able to act as an effective check on the potential for shirking by community labourers, it was not an effective check on missing materials, and only increased government audits were able to reduce 'missing' expenditures. Olken's study concludes that grassroots participation in monitoring is only effective where there are limited free-rider problems and limited elite capture. These observations chime with the findings of studies of accountability systems across other sectors which indicate that success requires a combination of bottom-up and top-down pressure (Unsworth 2010).

Rural Roads in Peru

Peru has recently made significant progress in improving access to roads in rural and mountainous areas, where some of the country's most vulnerable populations live. Since 1995, the Peru Rural Roads Program (PCR)—a national programme run by government and jointly funded by the World Bank and Inter-American Development Bank—has rehabilitated and maintained some 15,000 km of rural roads and 7,000 km of paths (used primarily by women and children) (McSweeney and Remy 2008). A number of evaluations have demonstrated improvements in local economic productivity and increased investments in health and education as a result of the programme (Valdivia 2010). A 2005 study found the programme led to an 8 per cent increase in school enrolment, a 55 per cent increase in number of visits to health centres, a 16 per cent increase in use of agricultural land, and a 20 per cent increase in rural household income (Simatovic 2008, p. 7). The programme has also been noted as a promising approach to addressing gender in transport, with some sources highlighting how the programme has particularly increased women's access to markets and school enrolment (Bravo 2002).

Much of the literature attributes the success of the PCR to a number of 'innovative' institutional design characteristics that, as Valdivia (2010) argues, set the right incentives for the agents. Under the programme, local governments and communities that live adjacent to the roads identify priority projects according to the level of local demand. Women and men are consulted separately to enable women to fully make their voices heard. The local government then issues performance-based contracts to Routine Road Maintenance Microenterprises (MEMVRs), formed by local people, to carry out the required work.[13] The state requires that at least 30 per cent of the employees of the MEMVRs be women, reflecting a broader commitment to gender equality, as seen at national level in the gender quota for political candidates (Simatovic 2008). Several authors have argued that the PCR's inclusive mode of provision has enabled genuine local ownership, helped insulate it from local capture, and ultimately underlies its sustainability (Simatovic 2008; Valdivia 2010). Valdivia (2010) argues the programme has avoided corruption because outputs are highly observable, and because monitoring is carried out jointly by local government and community associations. McSweeney and Remy (2008) point out that the MEMVRs have incentives to be accountable and to perform well because they are formed from, and embedded in, local communities that live close to the road, and therefore have a direct stake in maintaining them. In this way, the case supports the point made elsewhere that accountability may work best when it is genuinely locally anchored.

Simatovic (2008) argues that the programme's participatory and inclusive design characteristics have in turn strengthened democracy and citizenship, and altered state–society relations, in rural areas. In her evaluation of the programme's effect on citizenship, she concluded that the decentralized model, the mainstreaming of citizen participation, and the engagement of local users in the maintenance of the roads, had increased political

---

[13] As of 2008, 650 MEMVRs had been created, generating 4,800 permanent jobs and some 35,000 temporary jobs (Simatovic 2008, p. 25).

participation, strengthened democracy and local civil society, strengthened new leaders, improved local management skills, and aided political inclusion (2008, p. 3). She also argues that participatory institutions increased the level of trust between local actors and the state, 'thereby breaking down the effective distance between the rural population and the state, altering a tradition of vertical relationships, little respect for social organizations, and the discretionary authority of personnel' (2008, p. 24).

In contrast to this, Wilson (2004) has provided an account of road-building in the Peruvian Andes that reveals more contested relationships. She argues that road–building in Peru has at times been characteristic of the state's 'territorialising project', that is, making claims to political/social space, and exerting control over people and resources at a distance, which often involve strategies of persuasion, force, and seduction, and transplanting local offices and administrative districts. She notes that roads may have different connotations to rural communities; in some instances, they may be seen as a path into the wider economy, polity, and society; in others, they might be considered a threat to autonomy, and communities might evade 'incorporation'. In some cases, roads in Peru have become a site of elite resistance to 'modernity', and been bogged down in acrimonious disputes between local elites over access to resources and local labour. In the Peruvian case, Wilson (2004, p. 535) concludes that, overall, while the Peruvian state has oscillated between prioritizing and neglecting road-building, the most successful cases have generally occurred where there was 'consensus reached between state and population that roads-building was the way forward to modernity and progress'.

Wilson's (2004) account adds thick description to the conceptualization of services as the point where the state becomes 'visible' to citizens and, reflecting Migdal (2001), one among other means through which the state establishes its own 'rules of the game' as dominant over other social norms. As a real and symbolic aspect of people's daily survival strategies, services can act as an effective means for the state to achieve social control and compliance. In this way, the Peru case supports the view that basic services can be understood as tools for state- and nation-building; whereby the state may use service provision to establish its control and authority over territory ('penetration'), to create a common culture ('standardization') and to resolve disputes, create political loyalty, and bind critical populations to the state ('accommodation') (Van de Walle and Scott 2011).

Cocoa Marketing in Ghana

For the past twenty-five years, Ghana has consistently achieved annual growth rates of above 5 per cent, making it one of the fastest growing agricultural economies in the world (Wiggins and Leturque 2011). In analysing this remarkable progress, Wiggins and Leturque (2011) note that the country's agriculture sector, and in particular its cocoa marketing system, has been particularly successful in connecting smallholder farmers with domestic and export markets. In this system, the government acts in a stewardship role through the state-run marketing board, Cocobod, which oversees the production of the crop and maintains a monopoly over its export. Farmers sell their cocoa beans to Licensed Buying Companies (LBCs), and the cocoa is moved to ports and exported by the government-owned Cocoa Marketing Company. Studies have shown that Cocobod has performed impressively over the past decade: produce is of premium quality, farmers receive a relatively large share of exports, and the system is surprisingly corruption-free (Williams 2009; Hubbard 2003). This success makes Cocobod somewhat exceptional when viewed in the context of its own history of corruption in the period prior to the 1980s (Williams 2009). Moreover, it goes against a wider pattern of poor performance in comparable systems across developing countries, many of which have been difficult to reform due to vested interests and rent extraction (Hubbard 2003; Williams 2009).

Several analysts have noted that strong leadership has been an important factor in ensuring that the Ghana cocoa marketing system has been effectively insulated from political interference (Williams 2009; Shepherd and Onumah 1997). As Williams (2009) argues, the charismatic and motivated political leadership of J. J. Rawlings was instrumental in pushing through a series of 'well-directed' reforms to the system during the 1980s and 1990s. Wiggins and Leturque (2011) note that agricultural growth took off after Rawlings came to power in 1981, and has since been sustained in part by the regime's consistent commitment to agricultural development during a period of relative political and economic stability. Williams (2009) argues that the authoritarian nature of the regime made it well positioned to be able to push through genuine economic reforms.

Others have observed that, although reforms to the cocoa marketing system were financed by donors under structural adjustment, the government has been able to retain a sense of local ownership over the system, and to resist donor pressure for full liberalization (Hubbard 2003; Wiggins and Leturque 2011). As Hubbard (2003) concludes, the nature of the reforms adopted by government balanced efficiency with national ownership, thereby satisfying the donors as well as Ghanaian nationalists. Some argue that the effects of this strong leadership, and in particular the government's commitment to quality, have trickled down to the organizational level. Williams (2009) argues that the system's relative insulation from corruption is partly explainable by the Cocoa Marketing Company's almost Weberian standards of organizational performance; with high levels of professionalism, merit-based appointments, and reliable salaries.

There is some indication that the incentives behind the government's long-term commitment to cocoa marketing are at least partly derived from a political impetus to court the support of cocoa farmers, and that this political imperative has transcended authoritarian and democratic regimes. Wiggins and Leturque (2011) describe how Rawlings built this constituency of support among cocoa farmers through a combination of personal charisma, authoritarianism, and the fragmented nature of the opposition. Remnants of the influence of cocoa farmers as a source of state legitimacy are still perceptible, and reforms to increase farmers' share of exports gained added momentum after democratization in 1992, in response to widespread dissatisfaction at the low price of cocoa. Williams (2009) argues that since democratization, the government of Ghana has faced political pressure to respond to the demands of cocoa producers, partly because of the scale of the cocoa industry and the noticeable weight of cocoa interests in democratic politics, and partly because producer prices are a frequent topic of discussion in the media.

Agricultural Input Subsidies in Malawi

Malawi has recently come to be regarded as a relatively successful case of economic progress, poverty reduction, and human development in sub-Saharan Africa. In acknowledging this, Vandemoortele and Bird (2011) note that, although questions remain regarding the sustainability of recent growth in the country, overall progress is undeniable. Between 2004 and 2009, the country achieved an above-average annual GDP growth of 7 per cent, much of which was driven by the agricultural sector, estimated to contribute around 39 per cent to the economy (2011, p. 11).

The introduction in 2005 of the Farm Input Subsidy Programme (FISP)—a government-funded programme that increases poor smallholder farmers' access to agricultural inputs—has been seen as key driving factor behind Malawi's recent economic progress (Chinsinga 2008; Dorward and Chirwa 2011; Vandemoortele and Bird 2011). Through this programme, the government provides vouchers (or coupons) for maize fertilizer to farmers who are considered to be 'productive but otherwise resource constrained' (Chinsinga 2008). Targeting and distribution is devolved to district and local levels, undertaken in consultation with traditional authorities, local government, and Village Development Committees (VDCs) (Vandemoortele and Bird 2011). Notwithstanding ongoing concerns and emerging evidence that the programme has been prone to local elite capture (Eggen 2011), several studies have recorded positive impacts. A recent evaluation concluded that it had 'substantially increased national maize production and productivity, contributing to increased food availability, higher real wages, wider economic growth and poverty reduction' (Dorward and Chirwa 2011, p. 232). Similarly, Chibwana et al. (2012) argue that dramatic increases in maize outputs have had wider positive effects on national and household food security.

In examining the political incentives behind the government's adoption of the FISP, much of the literature has emphasized that, for a number of reasons, food security is now a highly salient political issue in Malawi. Furthermore, agricultural inputs have over time accrued a large basis of popular support. Several authors attribute this at least partly to the sheer dominance of agriculture in Malawi's economy, and to the fact that an estimated 85 per cent of the workforce is employed by it (Chirwa et al. 2006). Others note the country's history of chronic food insecurity (Chinsinga 2007; Vandemoortele and Bird 2011). Devereux (2009) argues fertilizer subsidies were politicized under the patronage-based rule of President Muluzi (1994–2004), whose political power base was concentrated in the densely populated and food-insecure south of the country. Either way, Chinsinga (2007, pp. 10 and 15) concludes that food security has become intimately bound up with the very legitimacy and survival of regimes in Malawi. Underlying this, she argues, is an implicit social contract that government will provide citizens with agricultural inputs as a social safety net in times of need.

While there is some debate about whether the origins of the underlying political salience of agricultural input subsidies in Malawi derive from popular pressure or patronage politics, or both, there is consensus that elections played a catalytic role in the introduction of the FISP in 2005. As Chinsinga (2008) explains, these elections were preceded by two periods of severe hunger in the early 2000s that prompted both political parties to pledge to introduce universal subsidies if elected in 2005. Following the elections, opposition parties in parliament were able to put pressure on the ruling party to stick to its pledge to adopt a universal subsidy, in spite of the President's reservations about financing. Birner and Resnick (2010) note that the characteristics of fertilizer distribution—specifically, that it is visible, short-term, and targeted—make it particularly appealing to politicians, since it allows for greater political returns relative to other, longer-term agricultural investments (e.g. training, new crop research). In what appears to be a confirmation of this, Dorward and Chirwa (2011) have noted that the FISP was a high-profile aspect of the President's successful re-election in 2009.

Some of the literature analyses the relationship between donors and the government of Malawi in the case of the introduction of the FISP as being indicative of local ownership of the programme. Vandemoortele and Bird (2011) have argued that a key factor in Malawi's recent success has been increased government assertiveness towards donors, coupled with long-term vision and development planning. Many donors were initially sceptical of the FISP; others were in total opposition, based on concerns about market distortions, the risk of wiping out the private fertilizer sector, and concerns that the programme might not efficiently target the poor (Chinsinga 2008). Chinsinga (2008) argues that donors only changed their positions once it became clear that government had made a political decision that was closely linked to its legitimacy. She concludes that, where there is strong government leadership backed up by a democratic mandate, there must be a 'culture of pragmatism, negotiation and compromise among donors' (2008, p. 27). Birner and Resnick (2010) argue that it is important to understand these contestations in terms of broader ideological differences, which are often neglected in accounts of agricultural policymaking. Even in this case, where policy has been heavily driven by internal politics, the effects of the post-Washington Consensus can be seen, specifically with regard to the framing of the inputs as 'market-smart subsidies'.

Synthesis: The Recurring Politics of Success?

An important finding from the case studies is that the robustness of the evidence linking aspects of politics to outcomes should not be overstated. While progress in each case is validated by rigorous impact evaluation, the relationship between these outcomes and the pervasive forms of politics operating at different levels is more often implied than proven. Notwithstanding these caveats, a number of themes about the forms of politics that underpin success recur across the case studies, suggesting there is some merit in pursuing them as lines of enquiry in future research.

Periods of Crisis and Adjustment

Overall, the case studies support the theory that major sectoral reforms are often instigated and designed in the wake of periods of major crisis or political upheaval, during which time the normal rules of the game are thrown into flux (Batley 2004, p. 39). This finding is demonstrated most clearly in the case study on Indonesia, where the community-driven development mode of provision gained momentum after the economic crisis and the fall of Suharto, which weakened the appeal of a centralized state. In the aftermath of crisis, determined leaders may seize the opportunity to frame services as nation-building projects, as indicated in the case of Rwanda, where improvements in health were seen as an important pillar of reconstruction following the genocide. Similarly, in Ethiopia, commitment to education was envisaged and actively promoted as a means of generating good citizenship as part of a wider programme of nation-building. This supports the view that 'political junctures' (e.g. elections, moments of crisis, post-colonial settlements) can persuade regimes to renegotiate the social contract between state and citizens (Hickey 2006).

Political Settlements and Variation across Regime Type

While not often explicitly framed as such, there are examples in the case studies of how the nature of the political settlement influences the policy choices states make with regard to service provision. In Bangladesh, for example, a stable political settlement has been seen as a key factor in consolidating the state's credible and consistent commitment to health delivery in spite of periods of regime change. In a similar vein, Rwanda's long-term vision and remarkable achievements in health have been at least partly attributed to its particular form of 'developmental patrimonialism'. The cases also support the view that while elections may catalyse state responsiveness, the influence of formal political systems cannot be understood independently of the role of other institutions (Hickey 2007; Carbone 2009). The extent to which social contracts are articulated by an active civil society and through debate in the media may be key in this regard. In Malawi, for instance, while the political imperative to provide subsidies and the choices the state made were almost certainly catalysed by elections, the formative social contract that pitches food security as a key source of state legitimacy may have been a more important driver of the states responsiveness to its citizens. Likewise in Ethiopia, the ruling party's ideology and its particular identity as a movement of the poor has been seen as a more important underlying driver of commitment to pro-poor spending in education than elections per se.

Calculations of Political Returns

The cases also emphasize that political actors make policy choices that benefit poor people on the basis of calculations of high political returns. The (perception of) returns may be greatest not only where provision is a potential or existing source of state legitimacy, but also where the service is particularly politically salient, and/or is targeted towards the main constituency of support of the ruling party. Echoing studies from the wider literature, the cases illustrate that the imperative for broad-based provision may derive from political actors pursuing 'political entrepreneurship', that is, courting a mass constituency of the poor in the service of their political careers. Levels of 'political will' for primary education in Ghana, for example, have been shown to fluctuate over time according to the extent to which the ruling party has been dependent on the support of the poor, and the extent to which the interests of the poor were articulated by a political entrepreneur.

Similarly, agricultural policies gained particular political salience in Ghana and Malawi under regimes that courted the support of farmers, and continued to be a central source of state legitimacy where they subsequently attracted a large basis of citizen support. Overall, the cases advance the hypothesis that pro-poor provision is more likely where the state derives or seeks to enhance its legitimacy through the provision of a particular service (Di John and Putzel 2009).

Top-down Control and Embedded Accountability

There is some evidence in the case studies in support of recent thinking, by Leonard (2008) and Crook (2010), that organizations can be effective—even in clientelist settings—where they are insulated from political interference by strong, top-down authority and leadership carried through to the level of implementation. This is explicitly demonstrated in the corruption-free bureaucracy of Cocobod, and also in the bureaucratic arena in Rwanda, which is characterized by strong, top-down performance incentives. The Rwanda case indicates that top-down incentives and bureaucratic control may be reinforced where the state is perceived as legitimate and has moral authority, and where top-down control draws on culturally embedded norms of accountability. But while the role of top-down accountability comes out strongly in Rwanda and Ghana, in other cases there is evidence that a combination of top-down and bottom-up accountability can drive progress, as in Indonesia, where they worked in tandem but to different effect. The case studies therefore support the move in wider literature towards examining top-down and bottom-up accountability as complementary as opposed to being an 'either or' proposition (Joshi 2012).

The cases also illustrate findings made elsewhere that pro-poor service provision might occur where forms of social accountability draw on moral reciprocity, are locally grounded, and build on a culture of participation (Booth 2011a; Hickey 2006; Hossain 2010). For example, the accountability of local leaders in the health sector in Bangladesh depended on the extent to which those leaders were 'embedded' in local networks of relationships between local authorities, citizen groups, and service providers. In Peru, the fact that agencies contracted to build and maintain roads were formed from local communities increased local ownership and therefore generated incentives for good performance.

The Political Salience of Sectors

The cases demonstrate that the characteristics of a particular service affect its political salience and in turn the calculations of political returns made by political actors. Specifically, the findings reinforce the point made elsewhere that the extent to which a service is targetable, 'visible', measurable, and easily credited may determine the likelihood of state responsiveness (Mani and Mukand 2007; Mcloughlin and Batley 2012; Pritchett 2002). For example, direct transfers for roads in Indonesia were appealing because roads are highly visible and direct transfers are easily creditable. In Bangladesh, progress in health reform is at least partly attributable to the nature of the reforms—namely improving access rather than quality—which ultimately pursued the path of least resistance. This supports the theme raised earlier that anticipation of resistance by interest groups may explain why some reforms are pursued and others are not, and different types of reform attract different types of politics (Grindle 2005).

The Micro-politics of Modes of Provision

The cases also indicate that particular modes of provision may influence the extent to which citizens can engage in collective action. In both of the roads cases—Peru and Indonesia—the participatory approach was considered to have enabled services to be more adapted to local preferences, and particularly to women's preferences. In Peru, participatory institutions had effects (both positive and negative) on notions of citizenship and interactions between the state, society, and elites at a local level. Similarly, decentralization in Ethiopia—a mode of provision essential for accommodating diversity in the context of high ethnic fragmentation—has in turn generated positive social capital and enabled collective action. However, it is not possible to conclude on the relative success of modes from the evidence available. It seems likely that the performance of modes is very context specific. Moreover, the cases make it clear that modes are not simple categories (e.g. direct state versus contracted-out provision); most real-life cases are composites of more than one mode and include both formal and informal elements (Joshi and Moore 2004).

At the micro-level politics of implementation, the cases highlight that the terms of collaboration between the actors engaged in delivery may enable or constrain service outcomes. The Ghana School for Life study indicates that whether or not public services are delivered effectively depends on the extent to which there is mutual agreement and positive, reciprocal relationships between state and non-state actors. This supports the findings from the relatively small body of research suggesting that effective and enduring—less brittle—forms of collaboration between government and non-government service providers seem to arise where the relationship has evolved rather than been created, rests on mutual agreement, and preserves the financial autonomy of partners (Batley 2011; Rose 2011). Similarly, Olivier de Sardan (2010) has argued that whether or not public services are delivered effectively depends on the precise terms on which collaboration occurs, the co-ordination between actors, and the personal relationships between them.

Conclusion

The studies presented in this chapter support the prominence given in the wider literature to the nature of the political regime and the origins of elite incentives as important determinants of inclusive service delivery. They additionally illustrate that the state, or governing political party, may pursue inclusive provision where a particular service or good has historically been viewed as a key source of its legitimacy and an expression of the social contract. The chapter has also shown how calculations of political returns on the part of political actors, linked in some cases to the pursuit of political entrepreneurship, are an important source of credible political commitment. Moreover, this commitment is affected by and formative of the characteristics of different sectors, in particular their political salience. In some of the cases, strong, top-down accountability reinforced by an ostensibly legitimate state with some degree of moral authority has facilitated inclusive delivery, particularly where top-down control has 'insulated' delivery systems from negative political interference. However, other cases illustrate the positive effects of social accountability systems, where these are genuinely locally grounded in moral and cultural norms.

While there is convergence here and elsewhere around recurring themes on the politics of service delivery, significant gaps in understanding remain. Overall, there are very few documented cases of progress that combine an objective assessment of outcomes with systematic analysis of the political determinants of those outcomes. It is evident that resources alone do not determine outcomes on the ground: politics intervene (in either an enabling or constraining role) between policy intention and implementation. However, it is striking that there has been more focus on the politics of policymaking—specifically, the state's and elite actors' incentives to choose pro-poor policies, and how these choices are mediated through (in most cases distorted by) formal political institutions and interactions between voters and politicians. The point of implementation, where formal policies most often fail and where 'real' policies emerge from the interplay of interests and incentives, has been relatively neglected. Similarly, two key aspects of service delivery—the characteristics of sectors and their mode of delivery—have more often been treated as managerial rather than political concerns. More than just technical factors, these aspects influence the relative power of principals and agents, providers and consumers of services.

Future research might usefully incorporate a 'bottom-up' perspective—that is, a focus on those institutions, incentives, and actors that are effective at the point of delivery, rather than on those that in the formal scheme of things are supposed to set the institutional and policy framework governing implementation. This implies greater attention to the point of contact between citizens (as users) and the state, and adding meaning to the concept of the social contract, which is frequently described as central to the politics of services, but often left without explanation. To this end, modes of provision could usefully be examined as a theatre of politics—that is, the space where politics is 'realized' in decision-making structures and where the state is experienced by citizens. This approach would be particularly appropriate and timely given the growing recognition that, in practice, service delivery is often facilitated through informal, ad hoc arrangements that rely on relationships of reciprocity and alliances across blurred public–private boundaries.

6

Political Factors in the Growth of Social Assistance

Armando Barrientos and Sony Pellissery

A large expansion of social assistance programmes has taken place in developing countries in the first decade of the twenty-first century. Large-scale anti-poverty transfer programmes providing direct transfers to households in poverty have spread to a majority of middle-income countries in the South. In low-income countries, the growth of social assistance has been slower and more speculative, due in part to delivery capacity and financial constraints. Impact evaluation studies indicate that, taken as a whole and in combination with economic growth and basic service infrastructure, well-designed anti-poverty programmes can make an important contribution to the reduction of global poverty and vulnerability (Lopez-Calva and Lustig 2010).[1] Social assistance has become an important component of poverty reduction and development strategies in the South. There is a fast-growing literature on anti-poverty transfer programmes in developing countries (Fiszbein and Schady 2009; Grosh et al. 2008; Hanlon et al. 2010). To date, the focus of this literature has been on issues of design and impact. It is widely acknowledged that politics does matter for the adoption, design, and implementation of anti-poverty transfer programmes, but this remains a substantially under-researched topic (Hickey 2008b). The main objective of this chapter is to review and assess the scarce literature on the politics of social assistance, with a view to identifying relevant approaches, knowledge, and knowledge gaps.

---

[1] They can also make a marginal contribution to the reduction of inequality. A recent cross-country study on declining inequality trends in Latin America identifies two main explanations: (i) a fall in the premium to skilled labour; (ii) the impact of higher and more progressive government transfers. See (López-Calva and Lustig 2010).

There is a degree of uncertainty around terminology in the context of international development, thus we start with some definitions.[2] Social policy includes the provision of basic services—in the main, education and health care, but also water and sanitation in low-income countries—and social protection. Social protection includes three main components: social insurance, social assistance, and labour market interventions. Social insurance covers contributory programmes covering life-course and work-related contingencies. Social assistance comprises tax-financed programmes managed by public agencies and addressing poverty and deprivation. It has become commonplace to distinguish 'passive' from 'active' labour market policies, with 'passive' interventions aimed at securing basic rights in the workplace and 'active' interventions enhancing employability.

Our chapter focuses on social assistance or anti-poverty transfer programmes, that is, tax-financed programmes directed by public agencies with the objective of reducing, preventing, and eventually eradicating poverty (Barrientos 2007). Programmes in low-income countries are sometimes financed from international assistance. They are tax-financed but the taxes are collected in a different jurisdiction.

There is huge diversity in the design of social assistance in developed and developing countries. In high-income countries, social assistance has an income maintenance design, providing income transfers aimed at filling in the poverty gap. In developing countries (Barrientos et al. 2010), social assistance includes a variety of programme designs, including pure income transfers, as in non-contributory pensions or child grants and allowances; income transfers combined with asset accumulation and protection, as in human development conditional transfer programmes or guaranteed employment schemes; and integrated anti-poverty programmes covering a range of poverty dimensions and addressing social exclusion. There is also diversity in scale, scope, and institutionalization in social assistance across countries, and across programmes within countries.

This chapter conceptualizes the politics of social assistance in developing countries as a two-way process. On the one hand, social assistance is shaped by political processes. The extension of anti-poverty transfer in the South reflects growing attention to poverty reduction. In many countries in the South, social policy, but particularly social protection and assistance, has risen in importance in political and policy discourse and debate. Lula's re-election in 2006 is credited by many to the success of *Bolsa Família* (Zucco 2008). In India, the re-election of the United Progressive Alliance (UPA) in 2009 is largely credited to the introduction of the National Rural Employment

---

[2] Uncertainty over terminology and scope is greatest in international policy debates.

Guarantee Act (NREGA) in their first term (Yadav and Palshinkar 2009). The first important set of issues and questions revolve around the influence of politics on the shape of social assistance in the South. On the other hand, social assistance programmes feed back into politics at the national and local levels. Social assistance programmes have the potential to enhance the political participation of groups in poverty at the local level, align electoral support, and change policy priorities and the effectiveness of service delivery.[3] At the national level, social assistance programmes have the potential to lock in left-of-centre or populist coalitions, and perhaps generate wider changes in policy. A discussion of these feedback processes would throw light upon potential issues of dependency and political manipulation by elites. A second important set of questions and issues revolve around the significance and orientation of these feedback processes.

The existing literature on the politics of social assistance is scarce and country or programme specific. A full review of the literature will not be attempted here, but relevant studies will be referred to and integrated throughout the chapter. There is a fast-growing literature focusing on the micro-level interaction of social assistance and politics. This literature is country or programme specific (De La O 2006; Giovagnoli 2005; Pellissery 2008; Zucco 2008). There is a scarce literature examining the macro or structural political factors facilitating or restricting social assistance (Hickey 2008b, 2009). The most significant gap in the literature relates to conceptual frameworks capable of explaining the politics of poverty reduction programmes. The existing literature draws from the conceptual frameworks developed to study the politics of redistribution.[4] This framework provides interesting insights, but there are few gains in collapsing processes of poverty reduction into processes of redistribution. For high-income countries, Esping-Andersen has provided the most influential framework for examining the production of welfare in advanced capitalist countries,[5] but efforts to adapt the framework to the examination of developing countries have not paid sufficient attention to politics or social assistance. Particularly the challenges to develop an appropriate framework arise from the issues of incorporating different forms of democracy (since democracy has seen uneven development in the global South), identity politics that shapes participation

---

[3] A good case in point is NREGA introduction in India. With the introduction of the programme, poor people got the opportunity to interact at the sites of work location, and to organize themselves as 'NREGA workers'. Some state governments facilitated this potential opportunity to bring accountability in to the work systems and to improve governance by using the feedback from the NREGA workers (Pellissery and Jalan 2011).

[4] See, for a recent survey, Robinson (2010). The classic source is Meltzer and Scott (1981).

[5] Politics and social assistance played a larger part in his earlier work (see Esping-Andersen 1990). Attempts to adapt the framework to developing countries have focused on institutions, and ignored politics (see Gough and Wood 2004).

in political processes and limited accountability that many of the authoritarian states possess. Our attempt is to address these issues which are neglected in the literature on politics of social protection.

Given the vast ground to be covered and the absence of comprehensive approaches to the issue under investigation, it is important to set out the approach and methodology adopted in this chapter at the outset. It is beyond the scope of the chapter to try to cover all programmes, countries, and regions. It is necessary to be extremely selective on these. Our chapter will focus on three countries: Brazil, India, and South Africa. The justification for selecting these three countries is straightforward. They are three large middle-income countries with a rich experience of social assistance innovations. They are leading countries in their respective regions. Together they provide a range of approaches to the extension of social assistance and also demonstrate the diversity of political institutions. The country selection will inevitably influence the discussion in the chapter.[6] It can be argued that the three countries selected have conditions which have led to a rapid growth in social assistance, conditions which are hard to replicate elsewhere. The point of the country selection is to learn about the role of politics in social assistance, not necessarily to ensure representativeness of conditions in the South. The analysis in this chapter will provide insights and perspectives valuable to other developing countries, and the framework presented should enable one to assess the strength and weaknesses of the relevant institutions and to identify feedback effects from, and to, political processes in those contexts.

Our methodological approach will be twofold. A comparative study of the politics of social assistance in the three countries selected will help identify inductively key issues and questions. This will be preceded by a discussion of how best to model the interaction of politics and social assistance in developing countries. This discussion will help give shape to the main features of an appropriate deductive framework. A process of triangulation will help achieve the main objectives of the chapter: to identify key approaches, findings, and knowledge gaps.

---

[6] The selection of cases can also get complicated when we note that different programmes within a single country can show different levels of political support. Indonesia has introduced large-scale social protection programmes since the financial crisis in 1998 to help families cope with the effects from financial shocks. They include food subsidies (Raskin), Unconditional Cash Transfer (Bantuan Langsung Tunai), Conditional Cash Transfer (Program Keluarga Harapan), Cash for Work and School Assistance. Among these, unconditional cash transfer programmes have been the least politically acceptable both at local level and national level, primarily due to targeting errors (see Bambang Widianto 'The Political Economy of Social Protection in Indonesia', a paper presented during the international conference on 'Reforming Social Protection Systems in Developing Countries' held 20–1 October 2011 at the Institute of Development Research and Development Policy, Rurh Universitat Bochum, Germany).

The rest of the chapter is divided into three main sections. The second section introduces and discusses a framework for examining the politics of social assistance. The third section presents the main findings from the three country case studies and draws out the main differences and similarities. The final section goes back to the main research question and discusses whether politics matter for the growth and effectiveness of social assistance in developing countries, and draws out the main conclusions.

Approaches to the Politics of Social Assistance

As noted there is scarce literature on the politics of social assistance. By far the most widely used approach assumes a situation in which politicians compete for support among voters, and voters exercise preferences in line with their interests and advantage. Politics in this context has the function of aggregating voter preferences.[7] In conditions of an inclusive franchise and a single-issue policy, the preferences of the median voter signal the direction of policy. Applying this perspective to social assistance would suggest that highly unequal societies with high poverty incidence would opt for more generous forms of social assistance (Alesina 1999). In conditions where low-income groups are a minority, coalitions including the middle classes would be required to support greater expenditure on broad-based social assistance (Gelbach and Pritchett 1995). Social assistance would be weakest in conditions of greater equality and low poverty incidence. These predictions are at odds with the facts of the expansion of social assistance in developing countries, and fail to explain both its timing and scale.

An issue is that several features of political systems in developing countries differ from the assumptions of the median-voter model. Political competition is imperfect in situations where the franchise is restricted, or where patrimonial or identity politics filter the aggregation of preferences in favour of elites. In these contexts, politics reflects more directly the concentration of power and influence as opposed to the calculated preferences of the population. The greater the concentration of wealth and power, the weaker will be the policies addressing poverty. In situations where identity politics dominate, the design and implementation of social assistance is likely to be fragmented and unequal (Keefer and Khemani 2003a). Imperfect political competition gives greater autonomy to politicians representing powerful interests and elites.

---

[7] 'What institutions or policies a political system generates depends on the distribution of power in society and how political institutions and mobilized interests aggregate preferences' (Robinson 2010, p. 39).

The role of public agencies charged with implementing social programmes becomes more significant after programmes are legislated for and adopted. The degree of autonomy of civil servants, and the nature of their linkages to political elites, can have implications for the reach and effectiveness of social assistance programmes (Alesina and Tabellini 2004; Besley and Ghatak 2007; Mookherjee 2004). In particular, in countries with federal structures, the links between public agencies and local politicians is of some significance for the evolution and implementation of these programmes (Giovagnoli 2005).

Even this brief discussion highlights the complexity of the political influences over social assistance and the variety of potential approaches to studying these influences. Small variations in political structures can have large effects on the direction and relative weight of the predicted effects.

To address this complexity, the chapter develops a phased approach to this issue. Table 6.1 provides a summary. The framework presented in Table 6.1 should be approached as a means of separating out the different dimensions of social assistance to highlight the political influences specifically relevant to a specific dimension. The most productive way of approaching the framework as an analysis tool is to imagine the different columns as sections of a concertina. In practice it is hard to separate out the different political influences on social assistance, and their variation across countries and across time, but by extending the concertina, it is possible to highlight the political issues of greatest relevance in specific dimensions. Once that work is done, it becomes possible to bring all the influences together.

The first two rows define which political factors are included and excluded. The first column assumes *direct democracy*, voters exercise their preferences directly through the political process. Political representatives, government, and civil society are assumed to follow voter preferences. They have no influence over decision-making. The main function of the political process is to aggregate voter preferences. This simple account of the political process is relevant to the adoption of social assistance strategies and programmes. The clearest examples of direct democracy in shaping social assistance arise in contexts where social contracts are being renewed. The new 1988 Constitution in Brazil, for example, was the outcome of a popular decision at the end of twenty years of dictatorship from 1965 to 1985, to reconsider the basis for citizenship in the country. The Constituent Assembly discussions led to the inclusion of a right to social protection based on citizenship, as opposed to the contributory principle which had dominated the development of social insurance.[8] The right to social protection based on a

---

[8] For a discussion of the citizenship and contributory principles in the context of social protection and the social security reforms in the 1980s in the UK, see Plant (2003).

Table 6.1. An incremental framework for understanding the influence of politics on social assistance in developing countries

	Adding complexity incrementally			
	Direct democracy	Representative democracy	Representative democracy with a measure of government autonomy	Representative democracy with a measure of government autonomy and participation
What does the analysis abstract from?	Representatives Government Civil society	Government Civil society	Civil society	
What political influences are included?	Democratic process	Democratic process Representatives	Democratic process Representatives Government	Democratic process Representatives Government Civil society
Focus points/areas	Preference aggregation	Social assistance and electoral support Priority of antipoverty policy	(De)centralization (responsibility for poverty reduction) Agency competition/cooperation Horizontal and vertical integration	Accountability Public support Interest groups
Key social assistance dimension	Adoption	Design, incidence, and budget	Implementation	Accountability Dynamics/evolution over time Forms of accountability Participatory processes
Practical issues/findings relevant to social assistance	Principles and values (citizenship/contribution/dessert)	Design Reach/incidence Budgets Leading agency	Beneficiary selection Transfer level and type Coverage Agency coordination Monitoring and evaluation	
Feedback effects	Social pacts—social contracts—access order	Party dominance Coalition formation/stability Electoral support Pro-poorness	Local political support and power Autonomy of local bureaucracies	Sustainability of social assistance Priority of poverty reduction and equity policies in public dialogue Influence of civil society and NGOs Political sustainability
Critical issues	Social contract—which can be understood as the point at which direct democratic processes operate? Social pacts? Coalitions? Influence of donors in LICs	Building and maintaining coalitions Interests and values Basis for electoral advantage Credibility and trust Competitive versus identity politics Opportunities for reform/scale up	Federal/estate/district politics, respective roles, responsibilities, and gains Strengthening technical and political networks coalitions Public perceptions of effectiveness and sustainability of political support Elections and opportunities for change and reform Closed or open-source models as far as lower instances	Managing political change (changes in government, etc.) Coalition building Feedback into political processes

Source: Authors.

citizenship principle has become embedded in government policies aimed at securing a minimum guaranteed income for all residents in Brazil (Mesquita et al. 2010). This provided the basis for the expansion of social assistance in Brazil. In fact a procedural definition of a social contract can be described in terms of the intervention of direct democratic processes. In practice, single-event social contracts, like the Brazilian experience, are rare. Social pacts and dominant coalitions might lead to the same policy outcomes, but without the presence of direct democracy.[9]

The important point about direct democracy and the extension of social assistance is this: where political processes revert to the simple function of aggregating preferences, social assistance institutions are likely to emerge. Of course, social assistance can also emerge in conditions where direct democracy conditions are absent. It would be interesting to consider the implications from this point of departure, both in terms of design and scale.[10] This will involve collecting and evaluating single events leading to the expansion of social assistance. In the context of the development of social assistance in low-income developing countries, the role of international partners adds a complication to the aggregation of preferences with important implications for social assistance outcomes in these countries.

The second column in Table 6.1, entitled *representative democracy*, envisages preference aggregation through political representatives. This ensures a focus on attracting and sustaining electoral support. The priority given to anti-poverty policy then plays within the political processes selecting representatives and endowing their decisions with legitimacy. This level of abstraction is particularly relevant to issues around the design, reach and incidence, and budget-setting for social assistance programmes. The last two are intimately related. In most developing countries, parliamentarians set the budget for anti-poverty programmes with direct implications for the scale of the programmes.

There are specific features of political processes which have particular relevance at this level of abstraction. The need to build and sustain coalitions often influences the scale and location of anti-poverty transfer programmes, as well as the distribution of programme budgets (de Janvry et al. 2009; Giovagnoli 2005). Historically, rural interests and their representatives show a preference for broad-based, tax-financed programmes, while urban interest and their representatives have a preference for occupational

---

[9] The 'War on Poverty' in the USA in the 1970s or the building of welfare states in European countries in the post-Second World War period provide examples of an expansion of social assistance based on the emergence of a broad consensus across governing coalitions but without originating in a single event. Rawls's 'veil of ignorance' is an abstract construct which can be interpreted as a counterpart to direct democracy (see Rawls 1971).

[10] This applies to the distinction between Bismarckian and Beveridgean social security, for example.

employment-related social insurance plans.[11] A specific issue in this context is how to explain the fact that selective anti-poverty transfer programmes could secure a broad base of political support in some developing countries. Identity politics can help sustain and enlarge social assistance programmes in some countries like South Africa or India, but limit them in other contexts, as in ethnically divided low-income countries in sub-Saharan Africa. The issue of electoral advantage arising from the perceived effectiveness of social assistance is also an interesting issue at this level of abstraction.

The third column takes account of the degree of autonomy of public agencies.[12] This level is particularly relevant to issues of implementation and scaling up of anti-poverty transfer programmes. The degree of autonomy of public agencies is essential to understand the operation of social assistance in the context of decentralized political and programme structures. In many low-income countries, process deficits and fiduciary risks are very significant and strongly influence the scale and scope of anti-poverty transfer programmes. In the context of transfers which are combined with asset accumulation or protection or in the case of anti-poverty programmes, horizontal and vertical coordination is central to the effectiveness of the programmes. Monitoring and evaluation processes provide measures of effectiveness and impact.

The features of the political processes which are important at this level include the linkages between different levels of government and the distribution of political influence and power. In highly centralized countries, the responsibility and political gains for social assistance programmes are located at the federal or central government level; whereas in countries with a decentralized administrative and political structure, the distribution of responsibility and potential electoral gains are outcomes from interlinked processes. These imply the need to pay attention to public perceptions of the effectiveness of the programmes to a greater extent than where programmes are heavily centralized. The relative autonomy of public agencies grants a stronger influence on technocratic networks.

The final column incorporates civil society organizations and their political influence. In developing countries, civil society organizations have not had a strong influence on social assistance growth. Trade unions and employers, for example, have not been directly affected by the extension of the programmes.[13] Community and NGOs in some countries are mainly involved in ensuring the rights of potential beneficiaries and managing

---

[11] See, for example, the origins of the Swedish pension system.

[12] By autonomy we understand the extent to which public agencies can influence the shape of social assistance in line with their own particular preferences or interests.

[13] Private sector employers of agricultural labour in India are probably an exception. The National Rural Employment Guarantee in India has helped raise market wages in this sector.

processes of accountability of programme managers. Their engagement has some implications for the reform and extension of programmes.

As noted above, the most productive way to apply this framework as an analytical tool is to imagine the different columns as parts of a concertina. Extending the concertina enables an analysis of the different political influences on social assistance, which need to be brought together at a second stage. Two additional points on the framework are important. Firstly, the framework assumes that national politics are dominant in terms of their influence on anti-poverty programmes. This can be contentious because we find below that local politics sometimes overrides national politics in the context of social assistance. In Brazil, we find local-level dynamics more clearly. In India too, state-level primacy for the emergence of social assistance is clear. In India, separating out design and implementation gives local-level politics an overriding importance at the implementation stage. Local-level politics might need to be examined separately and then integrated within the national level. However, our approach to give primacy for national-level politics is important since we are attempting to find a workable model beyond the case countries presented here. Federal institutions have to be treated as context variables that will bring changes to the model presented. International political influences, for example, through the Millennium Development Goals or through regional commitment and policy diffusion, have not been fully incorporated into the model, except through their influence at the national level.[14,15] Secondly, the framework does not specifically address any potential political influences over the dynamics of social assistance, except through issues of scale. It will be important in this context to pay special attention to social assistance as a whole as opposed to particular programmes. The political influences on the institutionalization of social assistance programmes are an important research issue.

The revenue side of the framework is in many respects crucial, both to the shape and scale of social assistance, and to the quality of the political linkages. For example, there are good reasons to hypothesize that those governments able to rely on revenues from natural resources might have a greater degree of autonomy from voters in the design of policy than governments reliant on direct taxation. The extent to which revenues are centralized or dispersed in deferral political systems largely defines the relative influence on the different levels of government and politics. Including the revenue

---

[14] Global social policy approaches give international organizations a dominant role (see Deacon 1997).

[15] Regional influences might be significant in certain contexts, especially where clusters of specific types of programmes can be observed at the sub-regional level. In Southern Africa, pure transfers to groups considered to be acutely vulnerable are dominant, especially non-contributory pensions and child grants (see Devereux 2007). Human development transfer programmes are dominant in South America (see Cecchini and Martínez 2011).

side would require a significantly longer chapter, but perhaps not a great deal of change to the framework developed above. Whilst highlighting the importance of the revenue side, this is left out of the discussion here.

Comparative Analysis of the Politics of Social Assistance

This section focuses on case studies constructed to map out and analyse the political dimension of social assistance growth in India, Brazil, and South Africa. These are the main findings.

India

Introduction of social assistance in India can be traced back to British colonial legacy.[16] On the one hand formal social security was introduced for employees in the formal sector after the European model. In effect, this was divisive, as the well-off sections employed in regular jobs were able to gain the welfare benefits, and close to 90 per cent of the labour force (primarily in the agriculture sector) was excluded. On the other hand, in its low-growth period until the early 1990s, central government paid little attention to this issue and largely development, particularly rural development, was the focus. These anti-poverty programmes aimed to provide food and nutrition,[17] supply basic services like education, health care, and housing, generate employment through public works programmes,[18] and improve natural resources and rural people's assets through Integrated Rural Development Programmes.[19] Anti-poverty programmes, as emerging from the nation-building discourse, dominated the politics of social assistance.[20]

The Constitution of India had left the issue of social assistance as a 'desirable activity' under its directive principles. Therefore, federal states (formed

[16] For a long view, see Osmani (1991).

[17] The largest of the programmes, the Public Distribution System, which distributes essential food items and non-food items (e.g. kerosene) through a network of fair-price shops, incurred expenses close to 1% of GDP primarily as subsidy. This was largely untargeted until 1990s. Apart from this, specific nutritional programmes for children and pregnant women were in place under an umbrella programme of the Integrated Child Development Scheme (ICDS).

[18] Since the 1960s a large number of public works programmes which provided cash or kind in exchange for labour was a predominant mode of relief especially in times of drought in rural areas.

[19] These sets of programme were initiated in 1952 and the community was consulted while designing what kind of programme could bring developmental changes. Thus, intervention varied from providing assets such as milk animals, to improving dry land, to providing market linkage or finance for small business.

[20] There is considerable scholarship studying the advantages accruing to the political class from the introduction of such anti-poverty programmes. See for instance, among others, Kohli (1989); Harriss (2004).

according to the regional languages after independence in 1947) undertook initiatives to introduce social security measures. The state of Uttar Pradesh introduced the earliest programme of old-age pension in 1957.[21] Different states began to introduce different programmes such as pension for agricultural landless labourers, maternity benefit, disability benefit, relief for educated unemployed persons, and employment guarantee depending on the 'need' for the same in respective states. Thus, paternalistic and patrimonial principles dominated the origin of these programmes more so than right to welfare or justice principles (Jayal 2001). Very often, these programmes were also introduced as electoral instruments, with the title of the programme prefixed with a politician's name, which would signal who should be credited for such a programme. These state-level programmes were aimed at workers in the informal sector, primarily agricultural workers on whom the political class relied for votes. Thus, welfare regimes in India could be classified as 'clientelist' or 'populist'. A couple of exceptional states had the influence of left-leaning politics to demand social assistance (Harriss 2004).

In the last two decades, there was a reversal of the story. Central government enacted a number of social assistance measures by systematically expanding the fundamental rights (such as the right to life, the right to employment) enshrined in the constitution of India. From the social assistance viewpoint, three developments are important. First, in 1995 central government introduced the National Social Assistance Programme (NSAP), under which five different benefits were provided, which complemented what federal states were already providing. These benefits were the Old Age Pension Scheme (reaching 8.3 per cent of elderly households), the Widow Pension Scheme (6.2 per cent of widow households), the Disability Pension Scheme (14.1 per cent of disabled households), the Family Benefit Scheme (one-time relief for the families where the main breadwinner died in an accident), and Annapurna (food for elderly households).[22] What triggered this development is very closely tied to the story of liberalization that India followed since 1991. Social sector expenditure for the period 1991 to 1995 showed a distinct decline in state expenditure, primarily since the centre's aggregate transfer to states got reduced (Guhan 1994, 1995; Prabhu and Chatterjee 1993) in the process of state retrieval. This provided an opportunity for bureaucratic–civil society entrepreneurs to argue for direct transfer through initiating social assistance programmes. Introduction of the programme in proximity to the next general election and prefixing of the

---

[21] See Dev (1998) for a list of programmes showing the year they were introduced and the states in which they were introduced.

[22] The figures for reach are based on the World Bank (2011). General evaluation of these programmes concludes that though the benefits are small, it makes a big difference to the households (Dutta et al. 2010).

schemes with the name 'Indira Gandhi' are facts worth noting. These programmes were meant for poor households. The identification process for poor households took place every five years, which has been much politically contested both locally (Hirway 2003) and between the federal state and central government in determining the threshold of the number of poor people in a state, since that determines the quota of transfer from the centre to the state. The poor households identified through the survey, classified as 'Below Poverty Line' (BPL), are eligible for different NSAP programmes. Often, concentration of poverty in particular social categories helped to create a clientelist politics of its own through this targeted approach.

Both the second and third important developments took place in 2004 when the Congress Party government had been voted to power in a coalition with left-wing parties. A wider civil society movement that pressed for food security got a significant policy voice through civil society actors who were appointed as members of the National Advisory Council. This civil society activism was successful in getting the bill enacted by parliament in 2005 for the Employment Guarantee Act that ensures 100 days of employment for every rural household.[23] The programme reaches approximately 33 per cent of rural households. Unlike the NSAP of 1995, this was legislated as a right and parliamentary scrutiny was very high. Left parties, being in coalition, also had pressed for social security programmes for the vast majority of unorganized sector workers. Eventually, in 2009 a Social Security Board was legislated. The health insurance programme (Rashtriya Swasthya Bhima Yojana), designed particularly for the workforce in the unorganized sector, has already provided insurance against hospitalization for forty million households.

A key challenge faced when all social assistance programmes were introduced has been the assertion from right-wing advocates that social assistance expenditure is both ineffective and wasteful. The inequality discourse has been effective in countering such positions. The growth story of India has widened inequality rather than bridging the gap. Therefore, the introduction of social assistance would be helpful as an inclusive instrument for the poorer sections of the population. Socio-economic divisions within the country demanded programmes that could create support from across different sections. For instance, the NREGA programme has been devised to provide labour for wage-seeking households during the lean agricultural season, without harming the landlord–labourer relationship. However, when agricultural wages rose, landlords showed resistance to NREGA itself. At the

[23] It is important to note that the prefix of 'Mahatma Gandhi' was introduced to the programme after the government was voted to power without coalition forces, particularly left parties in 2009.

same time since the NREGA programme improves community infrastructure such as roads or irrigation facilities this acted as an incentive for landlords. Taxpayers in urban areas were allured by the promise that when rural households were provided with employment in the villages, they would refrain from migration, bringing ease to the already hugely pressured urban infrastructure (Ambasta et al. 2008; MacAuslan 2008).

Lower levels of administration such as district or village government, although elected bodies, enter into the politics of social protection when the programmes are being implemented. In the interpretation of eligibility criteria or selection of beneficiaries, local politics play a critical role (Raabe et al. 2010; Shankar et al. 2011). However, in designing the programme and finance, it is the politics at federal level and central government level which matters. Thus, implementation deficits and corruption in the programme indicate an absence of government autonomy from social forces. Introduction of the social assistance programmes hugely shapes local politics since local elites act as brokers to facilitate access for the target population.[24] This ability to satisfy local elites by the national- or state-level elites through the introduction of policies acts as a feedback mechanism.

Acting as a countervailing force to such a nexus between local elites and national elites is the role of NGOs and other civil society institutions. The politics of civil society organization is primarily about how these organizations are able to score a goal against local politicians and bureaucrats. Therefore, being able to provide access to a social assistance programme, which was denied by a politician or a bureaucrat, increases the credibility of an NGO. In the case of NREGA this has come to the fore when social audits conducted by NGOs reached contradictory conclusions to government agencies. In other words, accountability achieved is through the participation of citizens as mediated through civil society organizations.

Accountability at the central government level is diffused due to an absence of single-ministry or autonomous agency in India. There are over 300 different types of anti-poverty schemes spread over thirteen different ministries. There is hardly any coherence amongst these programmes. No attempt is made at integration at national level. Often, NGOs have been successful in achieving integration at local level, since they prioritize the needs of the local population and claim for complementary anti-poverty programmes for one particular locality. This has helped NGOs to remain a sustaining force. On many

---

[24] Since the elected body of panchayat (village-level government) has control over huge amounts of money allocated for NREGA works, panchayat elections in many northern states have become more contested (with more money spent by candidates during elections) since the introduction of NREGA. A study has shown that participants in the NREGA programme are more likely to be selected along caste lines when a member of their caste is elected as head of a panchayat. For the same effects on social pensions see Pellissery (2008, 2005).

occasions, the government has used the help of NGOs to carry out this role in a concerted manner throughout the state by creating NGO consortiums.[25]

To sum up, the expansion of social assistance in India through central government initiatives has to be seen as a process of change management due to economic liberalization and pressures from left parties for inclusive growth. A wider social contract is still elusive due to identity politics, and linguistic identities are further reinforced by the federal structure. When the same elected political party is in power at both central and state level, there is synergy for social assistance delivery for brief periods.

Brazil

Brazil provides one of the most important examples of effective delivery of social assistance in the developing world (Barrientos 2011). Not only has Brazil introduced important innovations in social assistance (*Bolsa Escola* is the precursor of human development transfer programmes in Latin America) and important technological innovations in programme implementation, like the Single Registry, it has also managed to make a large reduction in poverty over time and also to reduce inequality. More importantly, it has managed this in the context of, until recently, low growth performance. The policy process in Brazil has been intensely political, predominantly in a positive sense. The feedback effects from social assistance are also important, especially in the electoral success of Lula in 2006.

The starting point in tracing the rise of social assistance in Brazil is the 1988 Constitution, which followed a long period of right-wing dictatorship from 1965 to 1985. The Constitution was intended as a new social contract extending citizenship to all. The Constitution enshrined a right to social protection, and led to a rethink of the role and scope of social security and the role of government to provide it. Prior to 1988, the role of government was to support private organizations and NGOs in the provision of social assistance (Jaccoud et al. 2009, 2010). The Constitution recognized social assistance for the first time as an area of government responsibility. It also introduced the citizenship principle behind social assistance, access was a right for all Brazilians; in contrast to the dominant contributory principle behind the development of social insurance from the 1920s.[26]

---

[25] The experience of Andhra Pradesh, which leads in the implementation of NREGA, has a state-wide NGO consortium where regular monthly meetings are held between NGOs and government agencies at state level, district level, and sub-district level. This has been instrumental in coordinating natural resource management and NREGA in the state. On how this helped to improve food security in the state see Pellissery and Sanju (2011).

[26] 'What institutions or policies a political system generates depends on the distribution of power in society and how political institutions and mobilized interests aggregate preferences' (Robinson 2010, p. 39).

The Constitution emphasized assistance to vulnerable groups, in particular older people and people with disabilities living in households in poverty. The Constitutional right led to the reform and expansion of two non-contributory pension schemes, the *Previdencia Social Rural* and the *Beneficio de Prestacao Continuada*. They had been introduced in a different guise in the 1970s, but with very limited reach and effectiveness. These were re-shaped, expanded, and extended. A separate initiative developed from municipal activism, it was grounded on minimum-income guarantee proposals combined with education. In 1995 municipalities began to introduce *Bolsa Escola*, transfers with schooling conditions. Their origins are in proposals for a guaranteed minimum income, again following the lead established in the Constitution, addressing poverty. The Workers Party, and Senator Suplicy, the first elected political representative of that Party, campaigned for this policy after the fall of the dictatorship. The proposal was taken up in several municipalities run by Workers Party politicians, but with an important change in connecting direct income transfers with conditions relating to schooling. The view was that without the links to basic services, the transfers would have very little effect in the medium and longer run, and much less policy and political traction. *Bolsa Escola* is a hybrid minimum-income guarantee and human development instrument, which reflected thinking on the left and centre that income transfers were not sufficient in the context of persistent intergenerational poverty. *Bolsa Escola* spread to other municipalities and in 1997 the government provided counterpart funding. In 2001 *Bolsa Escola* became a federal programme. Scaling up during Cardoso's presidency was probably because its *Plan Real* to address hyperinflation had great short-term adverse effects, therefore it needed to be balanced by poverty activism in the short run. This led to scaling up *Bolsa Escola* and eventually making it into a federal programme.

During the Cardoso administrations in the late 1990s and early 2000s, addressing poverty through direct transfers became the new orthodoxy, in part through political competition within the government (e.g. Jose Serra creates the *Auxilio Gas* to compete with *Bolsa Escola*), but also competition with the Workers Party. This led to a proliferation of transfer programmes, with overlapping target populations. Together with other federal transfer programmes, it became *Bolsa Familia* in 2003.

In 2010, the two main non-contributory pension programmes reached about ten million households with a budget of around 1.5 per cent of GDP, while *Bolsa Familia* reaches over twelve million households with a budget of 0.4 per cent of GDP.

Parliamentary oversight and policy formulation has been a significant feature in Brazil (Britto and Soares 2010). Parliament's active role in defining policy initiatives in poverty reduction goes back to the 1991 proposal for a minimum guaranteed income by Senator Suplicy from the Workers Party; since that date several proposed bills and amendments have been presented and discussed in Congress every year. The proposals and amendments cover the spectrum, from right-of-centre politicians attempting to reduce the scope and reach of *Bolsa Familia* to left-of-centre parliamentarians aiming to expand the programme. Few bills successfully become law. Parliamentary activism reflects strong public opinion and interest in social assistance. There is much less parliamentary attention on the non-contributory pension programmes, in large part because their constitutional recognition implies that discretion over their implementation is very limited. Effectively the government is required to provide entitlements to all Brazilians who qualify for the benefits. Budgets simply reflect these entitlements. In the recent past parliamentary attention has made several attempts to change the target population, for example by redefining the scope of households for the purposes of defining entitlements, or restricting entitlements to the *Previdencia Social Rural* to residents in rural areas.

There are three levels of government in Brazil: federal, estate, and municipal. In Brazil municipalities are federal agencies with the same standing as the federal institutions. The estate level has not been active in social assistance. The federal government has influence over policy formulation, budgets, and implementation. Relationship between federal agencies and municipalities works through agreements and joint financing. An important federal tool to stimulate quality and performance is a Decentralization Index, which ranks municipalities according to their effectiveness and performance with implications for the federal financing streaming down. The Index is both a carrot and a stick (Lindert et al. 2007). It supports municipalities with deficient capacity and penalizes underperforming municipalities. The Index is a technocratic response to principal–agent issues, but increasingly modulates the partnership between federal and municipal levels. The Single Registry collects information on all households applying to any social assistance programme; the database enables the selection of beneficiaries and provides information on their progress through time. It also enables a stronger coordination among programme agencies, as it can be accessed by all agencies involved in the programmes.

The federal government allocates a fixed number of places for *Bolsa Familia* to municipalities. Local politicians and officials are responsible for registering potential beneficiaries. The information is assessed by the federal government and a score for each household determines eligibility. Local politicians and officials have some influence over the implementation of *Bolsa Familia*, through adding further interventions to *Bolsa Familia* or raising benefit levels, and also through ensuring the programme is implemented effectively (e.g. whether they have filled the federal government allocations). The implication is that feedback effects are significant at the local level too. Politicians who can demonstrate effectiveness in implementing *Bolsa Familia* receive electoral support and recognition. Civil society and NGOs have a limited role in ensuring accountability of the programme at the local level, but the direct political accountability is more significant.

It could be argued that the expansion of social assistance in Brazil, and particularly *Bolsa Familia*, has extended the life of centre-left (Cardoso) and left (Lula) ruling coalitions. They are a dominant political force. Importantly, the expansion of social assistance developments has been shown to be consistent with fiscal responsibility, and retains a large measure of political support. Perhaps the most significant feedback effect from social assistance to politics is the rise of social policy and social assistance to the top of the political agenda. Poverty reduction has a high profile, and delivers electoral support for pro-poor politicians.

South Africa

In South Africa, social assistance can be traced back to the 1920s, with the introduction of the non-contributory pension for poor whites. Social assistance followed the European model of developing income transfers for groups of deserving poor facing acute vulnerability, but with the filter of racial politics. Social pensions were restricted to whites initially, but later incorporated Indians and coloureds and then blacks. The conditions of entitlement and benefit levels were differentiated along racial lines, until the mid-1990s when discrimination was abolished (Barrientos 2008; Lund 2008; Seekings 2008; van der Berg 1997). Over time, the range of direct transfer programmes expanded to include disability and family grants. By the time the first ANC government came to power in 1994, social assistance was fragmented due to the homelands policy of apartheid, and acutely under-resourced (Lund 2008).

The fall of apartheid led to a new Constitution in 1996 which reaffirmed a commitment to social assistance. Section 27 states that 'everyone has the right to access . . . (i) social security, including, if they are unable to support themselves and their dependents appropriate social assistance' (Seekings 2008; Woolard and Leibbrandt 2010). The ANC government took steps to review and strengthen social assistance provision. It established the Lund Committee which led to proposals for a Child Support Grant (CSG) to replace the Family Maintenance Grant. In 1997 the government also published a White Paper on Social Welfare which stated the objective of replacing poverty relief with a developmental approach to welfare. The CSG was initially designed to address child malnutrition and was focused on children up to six years of age. Over time, it was extended to include children up to seventeen years of age. These measures led to a significant expansion of the reach of social assistance grants (Woolard and Leibbrandt 2010). By 2010, one in every two households had a social assistance beneficiary, and the budget has doubled since 1994 to over 3.5 per cent of GDP. Social assistance is the main policy instrument addressing poverty, vulnerability, and exclusion in South Africa. The grants are widely perceived to be effective in reducing poverty and vulnerability, to promote social inclusion and equity, and to have facilitated a difficult transition from apartheid rule.

The politics of the ANC have dominated the expansion of social assistance since 1994 (Nattrass and Seekings 2001). Initially, the challenge for the ANC government was to manage the transition from apartheid, while maintaining credible economic policies and fiscal responsibility. The government of national unity which directly followed the fall of apartheid in 1994 constituted more of a compromise than a new social contract.[27] However, several initiatives which strengthened social assistance like CSG, the constitutional recognition of the right to social assistance, and the White Paper on Welfare Policy developed within a context of wide-ranging support for transformation within the parameters of fiscal responsibility.

The next significant political debate around social assistance came with the discussions surrounding the Taylor Committee of Inquiry into a Comprehensive System of Social Security for South Africa in early 2000s.[28] A proposal for a basic income was receiving a substantial amount of attention from researchers and the trade unions. Intriguingly, the proposal for a basic income was supported by the National Party and the Communist Party (Matisonn and Seekings 2003). The arguments for a basic income in South Africa emphasized its advantages as a citizenship instrument, important in the context of racially segregated South Africa; as well as the more operational advantages of not requiring targeting and complex administrative implementation. The Taylor Committee supported the basic income proposal. The ANC rejected the basic income on three main grounds. Firstly, the White Paper on Social Welfare had argued for a change in the orientation of social assistance in South Africa, from poverty relief to a more developmental function. The basic income proposal was a step back from this objective. Secondly, there was no support within the ANC and outside for extending grants to the white population, especially given the large income differentials between them and the black population. Thirdly, maintaining fiscal

---

[27] The minister responsible for social assistance in the national unity government was in fact from the National Party (Lund 2008). The National Party and Inkatha left the Government of National Unity in 1996.

[28] Committee of Inquiry into a Comprehensive System of Social Security for South Africa (2002).

responsibility would have meant reducing the scope and generosity of social assistance in order to finance even a low level of the basic income.

Natrass and Seekings argue that while the ANC came to power committed to redistribution, and was/is expected to bring to effect significant redistribution, its capacity for redistribution has been limited by 'policies that keep the economy growing along an inegalitarian path, with a large section of the poor being shut out of income generating activities' (Nattrass and Seekings 2001, p. 495). There is debate among researchers on poverty trends in South Africa, but the general view is that poverty rates have remained broadly stagnant since 1994, while demographics has ensured that the numbers in poverty have risen (Leibbrandt et al. 2006; Leibbrandt et al. 2010). Social assistance has been extremely significant in preventing poverty from increasing. Overall, poverty and inequality outcomes remain problematic in South Africa, especially taking account of the fact that expenditure on social assistance has doubled as a proportion of GDP since 1994.

Right-of-centre politicians and business leaders are increasingly questioning the effectiveness of this large component of public expenditure and commonly voice concerns about potential dependency effects from the grants. Trade unions have pointed out the fact that unemployed groups constitute a gap in the social assistance grants system. On the left, some NGOs have explored the potential for judicial routes to expanding the grants (Seekings 2008). This has tested the position of the government on welfare policy. The equalization of the age of entitlement to the Old Age Grant to sixty for both men and women (it was previously sixty-five for men), for example, followed a challenge in the courts over possible gender discrimination associated with a differential age of entitlement. NGOs like the Black Sash play an important role in monitoring and facilitating the implementation of social assistance on the ground. They also perform a key role in ensuring welfare rights are fully exercised.

The potential for change and reform of social assistance is limited by the type of politics which sustain the ANC, and the ANC's support for the existing social assistance architecture. Nattrass and Seekings argue persuasively that voter loyalty to the ANC depends on partisan identification with its role in bringing about political change in South Africa. To date, opposition parties are treated with considerable suspicion because of their association with apartheid; and few breakaway ANC groups have prospered. As Natrass and Seekings (2001, p. 488) put it: 'Popular discontent over unemployment and job creation was partly offset by relatively more positive assessment with respect to other issues, including fiscal and social policy, even though the electorate regarded unemployment as the most important'. Political conditions therefore preclude any large-scale reform to social assistance, due to the strength of partisan support for the ANC. At the same time, social assistance is important in maintaining and strengthening this partisan support, particularly in rural areas of the country. The feedback effect of social assistance on politics is therefore significant.

It is important to round up this assessment with a brief discussion of fiscal space. The government of South Africa has benefited from a significant improvement in fiscal revenues over time, from a high base. This has enabled a large expansion of the grants without affecting other areas of government expenditure. There are concerns that further expansion of grants expenditure could place pressure on service provision, especially in the context of the impact of the financial crisis (Van Der Berg and Siebrits 2010). Social assistance appears to have hit a ceiling in this respect. On the other hand, the government has committed itself to the introduction of a Comprehensive Social Security System in South Africa, replacing the patchwork of occupational pension plans with a government-supported, national, social insurance scheme. This large-scale social investment will add to fiscal pressures and will have implications for social assistance. It is not surprising that support for a national social insurance scheme comes strongly from trade unions and urban groups.

Triangulating the Case Studies

Tables 6.2 and 6.3 provide respectively a summary of key differences and similarities across the case studies. The cells on top of the diagonal summarize similarities/differences in policymaking and feedback effects. The cells below the diagonal summarize similarities/differences in implementation and programme dynamics.

The expansion of social assistance from small privileged groups (whites in South Africa, organized sector employees in India, those able to afford contributory insurance in Brazil) to a broader target population, in line with universal principles, involved intense political process in all case countries. In India an active civil society movement through the 'right to food' campaign formed the medium through which this was articulated. The civil society representatives acting as advisors to a coalition government persuaded the government from within. In Brazil the fragmented opposition parties, such as the Workers Party, came together to campaign for the expansion of municipal initiatives to federal level, resulting in constitutional recognition of social rights for all Brazilians. In South Africa, the ANC, the party that spearheaded the transition from apartheid rule, immediately facilitated the right to social security to feature in the new constitution. In all these democracies, the parliament plays a critical role in steering the given fiscal capacity for expanding the social rights to all citizens. Since the right to social assistance is constitutionally guaranteed, the judiciary has become a

Table 6.2. Similarities in political apparatus of social assistance delivery in case countries

		Brazil	India	South Africa
		Policymaking and feedback effects		
Brazil	Policy implementation and programme dynamics	NA	Multiple political parties and fragmented opposition. Local/sub-national governments initially provide socia national governments extend them. Social assistance investment opposed since it is not a tool for economic growth. Direct evidence on political parties re-elected to power due to introduction of social assistance policies.	Debates around new constitution generated new set of common values and social contract. Coordination for different social assistance programmes achieved in progressive manner in both countries.
India		Constitutional recognition brings higher parliamentary scrutiny for *Bolsa Familia* and NREGA in Brazil and India respectively and non-contributory social assistance programmes do not receive such scrutiny. High level of autonomy for lower levels of administration.	NA	Segmented approach to social assistance (in SA for whites and in India for employees of organized sector) exists early on. Later poverty and inclusive growth become key arguments for introduction of social assistance. Concentration of poverty in social groups brings political mileage for policy intervention (identity politics). Social assistance instrumental for managing change: in SA transition from apartheid rule; in India raising inequality due to liberalization. Cooptation of academics in the process of knowledge creation on poverty-linked policies.
South Africa		Basic income debates form the basis against which social assistance programmes are weighed.	Cross support from different sections of socially divided voting population generates facilitative politics for social assistance. NGOs play significant role in assisting/acting as countervailing force to government programmes.	NA

Source: Authors.

Table 6.3. Differences in political apparatus of social assistance delivery in case countries

		Brazil	India	South Africa
		Policymaking and feedback effects		
Brazil	Policy implementation and programme dynamics	NA	Political party campaigning in Brazil, compared to India where civil society campaigns, which forces introduction of social assistance. Decentralization index brings credibility to politics as a feedback mechanism in Brazil compared to demand generation through identity politics in India.	Municipal initiatives translated as federal level policy in a consolidation process in Brazil. In South Africa, social assistance is introduced at the time of new constitution as a strategy to support the black population.
India		Autonomous disbursement agency in Brazil compared with India's decentralized governance system (which intensifies clientelist politics).	NA	High-level coordination under single ministry in South Africa compared to large number of anti-poverty programmes spread over numerous ministries in India.
South Africa		Joint financing by local government and central government is present in Brazil. In South Africa, social assistance is centrally funded and delivered by provincial governments.	Limited or no autonomy for local-level government in South Africa compared to high level of discretion for lower levels of administration and politicians in India.	NA

Source: Authors.

new stakeholder in all the case countries, and from time to time the government is challenged to stand up to the promises.[29]

At the level of programme implementation there are important lessons for each other. Unique features of ranking different municipalities for reaching the target population (holding the politicians accountable) and the establishment of an autonomous disbursement agency are powerful tools

[29] In South Africa the judiciary pressed the government to grant equal entitlement ages for the old-age grant to be from age sixty for men (from age sixty-five). The government of India has been challenged in the court to increase the wages of employment guarantee to take account of inflation. In Brazil, the government has been taken to court to make the threshold of social pensions one quarter of the minimum wage.

to create credibility politics in Brazil. In India, decentralized elected bodies are responsible for the delivery of social assistance, while financing is from central government. This has left too much room for manoeuvring policy at the implementation level. Thus, evidence on effectiveness is conflicting. Social audits conducted by NGOs and government agencies have reported conflicting outcomes. The South African system of implementation has a high level of coordination at central ministry level, leaving little discretion and autonomy to local governments. The NGO role in implementation is crucial in India and South Africa, compared to Brazil. In all three countries, the role of multilateral agencies is found to be extremely important, especially in providing technical support for implementation.

At the level of programme dynamics the unique features of case countries were more prominent than similarities across case countries. This is to be expected since the interaction of programmes with a unique socio-cultural context may produce incomparable dynamics. For instance, corruption that pervades other segments of life and business in India is also remarkably present in all its social assistance programmes. The corruption is politically steered and bureaucratically carried out. Corruption structures access to the programme. On the other hand, in South Africa, the history of apartheid rule and the emergence of ANC leaves limited space for political competition. The economic inequality prevailing between the white and black population has restricted support for basic-income grant proposals within the ANC ranks. In Brazil the political competition between the Workers Party and Cardoso's poverty activism led to the mushrooming of various schemes which were later consolidated into *Bolsa Familia* replacing erstwhile *Bolsa Escola*. Despite these differences, there is commonality on debates around the stabilization of social assistance programmes. In all three countries general revenue finances the programme. Thus, debate on providing a stable finance to social assistance is active.[30]

In all three cases, feedback politics is significantly high. Although there had been initial resistance to the grants (compared to development funds) in both South Africa and India, once the programme is introduced, they gained huge popular support. In Brazil and India the introduction of social assistance has served to overcome anti-incumbency trends in the 2006 and 2009 general elections. In South Africa, the partisan support for the ANC has been strengthened because of social assistance. However, depending on

[30] Comparable is the case of Thailand where significant attempts to introduce social protection programmes have taken place in recent times. Many have argued that populist policies are a structural element of inequality (for instance, see Jitsuchon 'How can Thailand Escape a Vicious Cycle of Populist Policies?', a paper presented during the World Economic Forum on East Asia 2012 during 30 May–1 June in Bangkok). Inequality forces political parties to focus on populist policies at the time of elections. In Thailand such loss of macroeconomic prudence has left the finances so weak that a comprehensive social welfare system could not be built.

the architecture of governance, the feedback effect is different on local-level politics. Absence of coordination at central level for different social assistance programmes (and anti-poverty programmes) along with local autonomy has resulted in huge expenditures without convergence attempts in India. This has allowed local elites to turn the resultant divergence into political mileage. At the other extreme, there is a high level of coordination in South Africa by bringing all social assistance programmes under one single ministry. This gives no room for any feedback effect on local politics. The Brazilian system allows feedback on local politics as long as politicians can earn credits for reaching the targeted groups.

Discussion: Does Politics Matter?

In this section we return to the main questions of the chapter, and draw out the main conclusions.

Does Politics Matter for the Delivery of Effective Social Assistance?

The conclusions from the analysis in the chapter are that politics has played a central role in the expansion of social assistance in the three countries selected for detailed examination. This is a two-way process. On the one hand, political factors are at the core of the adoption, design, and implementation of social assistance. On the other hand, social assistance feeds back into political processes, helping reshape them.

What is the influence of politics in shaping social assistance in the South? Our case studies suggest that the influence of politics is strong. At one level, this is an obvious finding. At its core, social assistance is a manifestation of solidarity values in particular countries and communities, values which are themselves political.[31] Social assistance represents institutions established with the objective of addressing poverty and vulnerability. Their scale and scope reflects shared understandings and the social priority attached to poverty. The main reason why this finding has purchase on current development discourses arises from the techno-managerial approach often employed by international organizations (Devarajan and Widlund 2007). This approach often ignores political influences on social protection institutions. The relevance of the politics for social assistance delivery is relatively under-researched. Explaining the rapid emergence of social assistance in developing countries has to address this knowledge gap.

---

[31] Rawls's (1971) 'political conception of justice' is a comprehensive statement on this point.

To achieve this, a stronger conceptual framework is needed. This framework will need to separate out, as we do in this chapter, the different dimensions in which politics matter, and the different dimensions of the influence of politics on social assistance delivery. The examination of three case countries in this study reveals that traditional approaches to this question focused mainly on investigating incentive structures as a motivation for elected politicians and non-elected bureaucrats (Alesina and Tabellini 2004). This is too limited as a tool for capturing the political dynamics around social assistance in Southern democracies. Social contracts and pacts, key events, ideology, and knowledge are important too. Unlike conventional wisdom, our case studies suggest several dimensions in which political influences need to be studied. A sole focus on elites or on full political competition are also limited as approaches to social assistance (Krishna 2006). These different dimensions need to be studied separately and then integrated to form a more comprehensive picture.

Social assistance institutions also help shape political processes. As noted in this chapter, these institutions feed back into political processes at different levels and in different ways. Many studies have discussed, and measured, the role of social assistance in aligning electoral support for incumbents. This dimension, if overemphasized, can reduce social assistance to a purely instrumental function (Hall 2008). Social assistance should also be considered as a legitimate form of aligning party coalitions and political support around pro-poor policies (Stokes 2004).

The growing institutionalization of social assistance as rights through intense political struggle is the story in all three case countries. This redefines groups in poverty as citizens (social citizens). A deepening of democracy follows. In India, for example, informal labourers had little to give and take from the state. Thus, the state's legitimacy itself was limited. Social assistance challenges this relationship and re-establishes legitimacy.

The case studies reveal a complex interaction between local and national politicians and the electorate, as in India and Brazil, but also point to the role of identity politics and filters, as in South Africa. At a higher level of abstraction, social assistance can embody, and therefore strengthen and develop, shared values and preferences. These institutions can firm up and develop social contracts and shared notions of social justice. In many countries, but especially in India, Brazil, and South Africa, social assistance is widely perceived as an instrument of inclusion. Just as in low-income countries with poorly developed social protection institutions, social assistance can be perceived as an instrument of exclusion. Feedback processes from social assistance and politics have not been studied sufficiently in the literature.

The delivery of social assistance cannot be de-linked from local dynamics and politics. Increasingly, political credibility requires procedural fairness.

At the implementation stage, efficiency gets redefined as egalitarianism once politics takes centre stage as a means to explain the delivery of social assistance. New centre–local relations are being created (e.g. joint financing, joint monitoring, joint issue-making, joint definition of targets) through the politics of social assistance. Leakages due to poor implementation are part and parcel of political resistance to redistribution by local elites.

In India there is a stark contrast between the politics of development (roads, drinking water, sanitation) and the politics of social assistance (pension, employment), indicating that politics of social assistance is better conceived as a *process* than as an *arena*.

On each component of this two-way process, further research is needed to provide deeper insights. Contrasting the autonomy exercised by Brazilian institutions for delivering social assistance with that of India and South Africa it is important to focus on how effective service delivery strengthens political credibility. It is also important to examine in more detail the influence of identity politics, as observed in South Africa and India, in reducing the role of service delivery in affecting credibility-based politics (Keefer and Khemani 2003b). Identity politics structures social assistance through stratified mechanisms. Identity politics could also prevent the expansion of social assistance. This is an important area for further research, the linkages existing between (in)effective delivery of social assistance and political credibility.

Decentralization of power to lower levels of administration could intensify politics around the delivery of social assistance. In India the highest impact of feedback processes is through local politics. In Brazil, though decentralization is significant, the influence of local politics is reduced through strong autonomous institutions at the national level that regulate the delivery of social assistance. In South Africa, high level of coordination of social assistance programmes under a single ministry creates an environment through which local politics gets distanced. In other words, decentralization has to work with other countervailing forces. If not, as in India, the main outcome is a situation in which authority diffusion is rampant allowing the capture of social assistance programmes by local elites.

Knowledge Gaps

We conclude this chapter by noting some glaring knowledge gaps. Conceptual frameworks developed to study redistribution in welfare states can provide important insights into the expansion of social assistance in developing countries; but they need to be adapted in at least two important respects: i) redistributive models, especially those relying on welfarist assumptions, are ill suited to the study of non-welfarist poverty reduction; and ii) neither 'ideal' conditions of political competition nor 'elite capture' models are appropriate to the study of the politics of the expansion of social assistance in developing countries.

- There is a literature providing country-specific or programme-specific information and discussion of social assistance. The main knowledge gap, and a key priority, is the need to develop comparative approaches and models.

- The feedback from social assistance to political processes has been studied to some extent in middle-income countries for specific countries/programmes. The knowledge gap is at the cross-country comparative level, and at the cross-state comparative level. Cross-country comparative studies can generate knowledge on the role of political institutions, democratization, left–right coalitions, and donors, inter alia, in the specific processes and outcomes as regards social assistance delivery. Cross-country studies, institutional/qualitative/quantitative, can support useful generalizations on the role of political institutions and processes on the expansion of social assistance. Infra-national comparisons can generate information on the relative influence of national–local politics and bureaucracies.

- There is scarce literature on the extent to which social assistance generates synergies and constraints in the delivery of other services and public goods in developing countries. In the context of human development conditional transfer programmes and employment guarantees, there is a prima facie case for examining these interactions. They have also been observed in pure transfer programmes, like South Africa's and Brazil's social pensions in the context of the bundling of services and transfers.

- There is a need to distinguish, analytically, social contracts and pacts, from scaling up and reform and evolution of social assistance, as was done in the framework above. Different forms of politics apply to these.

- Despite the usual 'development hubris', effective delivery of social assistance and the politics associated can be productively studied in high-income countries. Pace the significance of registration (Szreter 2007); the role of left parties in social assistance (Esping-Andersen 1990); the shift to 'active' labour market policies following persistent high unemployment in the 1980s (OECD 2003). It is much less productive to focus on welfare states, which at any rate are a post-Second World War phenomenon predicated on full employment and 'standard' family structures. It would be useful to take a hard-headed view (no nostalgia) on actual social assistance in high-income countries and see what can be learned from this by developing countries.

7

The Politics—and Process—of Rule of Law Systems in Developmental States

Deval Desai and Michael Woolcock

Introduction: The Rule of Law and Politics

That the rule of law matters to development is one of those rare ideas that has achieved global consensus across the ideological spectrum in both the global North and South (Chesterman 2008). Rarer still, this consensus exists despite continuing disagreement about what the rule of law is, its relationship to growth and political change, and even the evidence of its accomplishment over the last five decades (Carothers 2006). The turn to a political conception of the rule of law—a turn founded on a reappropriation of the vernacular of the rule of law as a form of political order (e.g. Fukuyama 2011)—is one of several approaches that are seeking to rearticulate the nature of the relationship between the rule of law and development (Trubek and Santos 2006)—*contra*, for example, the rule of law as secure property rights. We situate the move to articulate the rule of law in terms of political settlements as an example of this turn, and one which we support as it foregrounds the way in which law shapes and is shaped by existing distributions of power.[1] In this chapter, we develop an account of the role of the rule of law in securing inclusive development outcomes (with an emphasis on the poor and marginalized) in the context of an evolving political settlement.[2] We also offer a friendly critique

---

[1] The views expressed in this chapter are those of the authors alone, and should not be attributed to the World Bank, its executive directors, or the countries they represent. We are grateful for helpful feedback received from commentators and participants at the ESID review workshop in Delhi.

[2] We do not make claims about the rule of law in fragile states in this chapter; we have argued elsewhere that these are subject to different donor dynamics and imperatives (see Desai et al. 2012). Rather, we focus on states with a semi-functioning formal system and the ability to resolve disputes, enforce rules, enable political, economic, and social activity, and hold actors accountable (Olivier de Sardan 2009, p. 6).

of the analytical deployment of political settlements, suggesting that the rule of law must be understood not only instrumentally but also in terms of the legitimacy it derives from the processes in and through which it has emerged and, in turn, the value with which it imbues those processes.

The chapter proceeds in eight sections. Following this introduction, the next section provides a conceptual overview of debates around the rule of law and political settlements, and details our five-part conceptual framework that we derive from the literature. In the following five sections we go on to explore these five parts : institutional form, institutional function, policy frames, political organization and contingent factors. The final section concludes.

Conceptual Overview

It is axiomatic that the rule of law (hereafter 'ROL') shapes political, economic, and social activity (Dworkin 1986). But diverse meanings abound. It can be limited to the willingness of the state or sovereign to subject itself to the same rules as everyone else (Raz 1977; Tamanaha 2012). A Rawlsian view (Rawls 1999) would emphasize social process, while Dworkin (1986) highlights the normative value of outcomes. Trebilcock and Daniels (2008) suggest that ROL exists on a spectrum from 'thin' (i.e. judging law by the legal validity of the processes giving rise to it and governing its application) to 'thick' (i.e. judging law by the substantive outcomes it produces). The term has been used in many other ways besides: Tamanaha (2004) and Carothers (2006) note the plethora of definitions, many rooted outside the Western tradition. This leads to a proposition that ROL is an 'essentially contested concept' (Gallie 1956; applied to ROL by Waldron 2002), ontologically incapable of being definitively defined, taxonomized, and catalogued. Indeed, a substantial body of literature has arisen highlighting the constant debate and dissonance between conceptions of ROL, seeking to stress contest in definitions (Bergling et al. 2009).

Two key ideas flow from this. First, ROL is under-theorized in practice. Carothers (2009, p. 51) finds that 'a tendency exists toward uncritical and sometimes wishful thinking about [ROL; there are powerful] temptations, to believe certain things about the rule of law and its place on the international stage that are misleading and sometimes unhelpful'. As a result, development practitioners' use of ROL tends to be driven by institutional models and transplantable modes of doing business (raised as early as Trubek and Galanter (1974) and a feature of the literature ever since), with a general emphasis on securing property rights as a key institutional precondition to economic growth (Dam 2006b). For example, analyses of the justice sector generally focus on sets of written norms (including Coasean conceptions stressing strong property rights protection), organizational structures, and human capacity that affect the efficiency, quality, fairness, consistency, and accessibility of judicial processes (Reiling et al. 2007; World Bank 2002; Asian Development Bank 2004). This approach is compounded by the limited methodologies used to inform the evidence base. We do not seek to generalize: studies such as Owen and Portillo (2003) and Dale (2009) are robust both in their tools of data-gathering (from case-tracking to end-user surveys) and data analysis. Yet Hammergren (2002, 2003), taking an overview of analyses of ROL programming (with an emphasis on Latin America), sees several flaws: in the main, she argues, analyses are taken too early, have weak causality, are not sufficiently robust to alternative specifications and interpretations, and rarely operate at a level of local granularity. For example, an evaluation of Chilean criminal procedure reform did not gather comparable samples, making difference-in-difference impossible, and did not control the cases tracked for socio-economic, demographic and criminological conditions (Vera Institute 2004). As a result, Peerenboom (2002, p. 48) feels free to conclude, for example, that development institutions' policies in China towards ROL have been unsuccessful as they have not taken the time to understand its role: in that country context, ROL is neither an essential precondition for social order nor for economic growth.

Second, technical understandings of ROL mask political contestation around this 'essentially contested concept' and its role in shaping politics, society, and the economy. ROL plays a key role in the development of a political system, but one that is subject to political contest rather than technical intervention. Ginsburg (2010), for example, finds that independent courts can be anything from 'upstream triggers' for democratization to 'downstream guarantors of authoritarianism', depending on the nature of the politics surrounding them. Political contests around ROL also play a key role in social transformation: Levi and Epperly (2010) turn to the role of group politics in generating, transmitting, and (crucially) upholding social norms that shape ROL and economic change (summarized in Santos 2006). Importantly for our purposes, this story of contest suggests that ROL does not describe a pre-determined end-state of laws and institutions, but rather the role law plays in structuring the very politics of distribution, inclusion, and marginalization—in short, the development process itself.

Rule of Law and Political Settlements

Having arrayed the inchoate notion of ROL in this way, we can see the value of turning to political settlements as both explanans and explanandum. We do not attempt to provide an authoritative overview of the literature on political settlements. Rather, relying on Di John and Putzel (2009), Khan

(2010), and Leftwich and Sen (2010), we use it as a point of departure for our exploration of the relationship between poverty and marginalization on the one hand, and politics and process of ROL on the other.

A useful conceptual starting point is Kennedy's (2002) discussion of property rights. Following Hohfeld's (1917) seminal work, he argues that a property right is in fact a 'bundle[s] of rights' or rules, 'some of which authorize injury and others of which forbid it. Whenever there is a gap, conflict, or ambiguity in property law, one side can invoke all the rules in the "bundle" that suggest protection, and the other the rules in the bundle that suggest freedom of action' (p. 201). ROL in development, then, could be understood as the evolution of power enabling the more forceful invocation of one bundle over another (in stark contrast to de Soto 2000). An allied move might be to emphasize the relevance of ROL to development in the way that it structures the mobilization of such power by elite groups. In recent institutionalist literature, ROL emerges as key to equilibria between elite groups (North et al. 2009; Hilbink 2007). While North, Wallis, and Weingast see ROL as a precondition to modernity (and so take a static view of ROL), Berger (2008, pp. 38–46) argues that law needs elite political support to be effective, but that over time it must respond to broader-based norms as well. This understanding places an emphasis on the political *dynamics* of ROL: that is, how it is reconfigured over time so that the benefits of the evolving political settlement extend to the poor and marginalized.

The story of these dynamics is complex. Holston (1991, p. 1) sees law as a political tool mobilizable by elites. Olomola's (2010) study of linkages between formal and informal institutions in Nigeria's cotton industry found that Licensed Buying Agents—powerful actors in the middle of the cotton supply chain—'are fond of influencing the judicial process and bring[ing] any lawsuits against them to a deadlock' (p. 31), disempowering registered farmers. Yet others see law as levelling the political playing field (Trebilcock and Daniels 2008; Raz 1977). If we take the relationship between politics and ROL seriously in our analytic lens then contests over rules become contests over politics, and contests over politics become contests over rules. Law and politics become sites and vernaculars for the performance of each other. Thus Chabal and Daloz (1999, pp. 104, 136) find the threat to elites' patrimonial networks from rule enforcement (such as of anti-corruption laws) leads to an empty 'rhetoric' of ROL from elite groups.

This provides the starting point for a friendly critique of the political settlements literature, and shows what (and how) a politically rich understanding of ROL might contribute to a politically rich understanding of development. Khan (2010, p. 4) suggests that from a political-settlements perspective participation in institutions is instrumental: they must produce politically acceptable distributions of benefits, or elites will seek to change their processes and forms. This resonates with a 'thick' understanding of the rule of law. Yet, as we elaborate below, the strategic mobilization by actors of and around law and politics suggests that participation in the legal process can itself be transformative in a positive or negative sense, providing a platform for identity formation, group mobilization, and inclusion or exclusion (a concept that is uncontroversial across the political spectrum, from Foucault (1995) to North et al. (2009)). We do not mean by highlighting this to support a 'thin' understanding of the rule of law; indeed, we engage with the turn to politics in ROL because it is an important corrective to liberal formalist understandings of the rule of law that have been prominent in much development programming in recent decades. Rather, we raise it as we see ROL as simultaneously an instrument of the political order and structuring that order through rules and processes. As a result, we seek to rearticulate the value of process in the context of those politics.

Framework

In keeping with our emphasis on process and outcome, we begin with Maravall and Przeworski's (2003, p. 5) notion that ROL is a system that enables people to discern what they can reasonably expect from others. These expectations are often articulated in development terms as all people being equal and accountable before the law (Fukuyama 2011). However, this is ill borne out in practice: the literature on the role of ROL in supporting rapid growth in East Asia has suggested that the arrays of laws, regulations, and legal institutions were designed to allow for informal networks and for limited (or absent) checks on executive authority (Peerenboom 2004; Amsden 2001, pp. 251–83; noting that critics of this literature tend to find fault with the overemphasis on, rather than existence of, such difference: Nelson and Cabatingan 2010). Indeed, some states that have very limited or no legal scrutiny of the executive can sometimes drive forward inclusive or (nominally) pro-poor measures. In Malawi, Cammack and Kanyongolo (2010, p. 45) found that 'single-party, autocratic government provided the best environment for [an effective legal regime] to emerge, while the immediate transition years saw a breakdown in order, a weakening of state control and de-professionalizing of the public service coupled with rapid urbanization and a higher demand for public services, all of which resulted in less effective public goods delivery'.

We thus limit ourselves to a relational understanding of ROL, offering no preconceived end state for legal frameworks, norms, and their relationship to political organization. We explore the *dynamics of how elites and end users (particularly the poor and marginalized) contest within themselves and between each other the shape of legal and regulatory institutions, and are simultaneously shaped by these institutions.* We adopt multiple units of analysis: institutions, elites, and end users. As a result, we draw on a very broad range of disciplines or fields, offering synthetic insights without claiming exhaustiveness (e.g. we do not give full treatment to citizenship here). In general, the majority of the literature either takes an institutionalist perspective, focusing on the impacts of institutional change, or recounts a macro-level political narrative, with little analysis of how that feeds into legal institutional change (and how that, in turn, shapes political discourse). The literature does, however, offer *five* dimensions along which the politics of inclusion and marginalization shape and are shaped by ROL: institutional form; institutional function; policy frame; political organization; and contingent factors. We explore each in detail here.

Institutional Form: Hybridity and Contested Autonomy

We find an emerging trend in the conceptual literature around ROL arguing for function over form, or a move to discredit formalists as lacking an understanding of context (Tamanaha 2004; Desai et al. 2012). Similar arguments emerge from the recent push for 'best fit' rather than 'best practice' approaches to institutional reform more generally (Booth 2011a). Yet form remains important. For example, Coffee (2001, p. 80) argues that the form that a market regulator adopts (such as self-regulation, an independent body, a political committee) will, as the market develops, shape the evolving political consensus between elites. He studies pre-Great Depression market regulation and finds that it was state-based (a legacy of the original American political settlement); this drove significant unregulated and fraudulent cross-state securities transactions, contributing to the 1929 crash and leading to the creation of the Securities and Exchange Commission in 1934. Clearly in such a line of argument, form is closely linked to function: elites looking for certain functions may shape institutions to forms that, for the purposes of securing legitimacy for current and subsequent actions, appear likely to fulfil (on the basis of experiences elsewhere) those functions.

Hybridity

One way to engage with the politics of form is on the basis of the emerging literature on legal hybridity. There, we find two main and often-conflated types of hybridity. First, there is hybridity between established models of the state and economic activity, such as (neo)liberal versus developmentalist; democratic versus autocratic; modern versus pre-modern. In other words, developmental states move along their own developmental paths (Fukuyama

2010). Indeed, all ROL systems are by their nature hybrid and dynamic, as they draw upon a variety of models or sources of legitimacy as a response to the changing exigencies of circumstance and context (Adler and Woolcock 2010). Hybridity requires law to play many such roles, meaning ROL will look very context-specific. Cavarozzi (1992), Kurtz and Brooks (2008), and Weyland (1996), for example, explore the macro perspective of legal institutions supporting economic growth in South America, especially Brazil, and find that the role of law changed rapidly as the state reoriented its interventionist capacity to tighten political control but reduce state intervention in economic sectors (e.g. by introducing a new Competition Law and Innovation Law).

The second form of hybridity derives from the first: hybridity reflecting an institution or array that draws on multiple sources of political authority and legitimacy to support a hybrid model of the state. Trubek's (2008, pp. 22–3, 2009) studies of post-authoritarian Latin America after the 1990s financial crises emphasize the political complexity here: as these states emerge, elites need both flexibility and stability, arrayed in ways that reflect their existing claim on state assets. It would thus be a mistake to see ROL teleologically as a formal process of social formalization, although this may be normatively desirable. Dodson (2002, p. 219) and Foweraker and Krznaric (2002, pp. 46–7), in their studies of Latin America, find that elite domination can lead to hybrid orders such as 'institutionalized informality'. These are not rationalized in all dimensions of the state and some parts of these orders can be captured, often to the detriment of the poor and marginalized.

The formation of Township–Village Enterprises (TVEs) in rural or peripheral China in the late 1980s and early 1990s provides a useful case study for the emergence of pro-poor hybrid ROL institutional forms. A 'de facto alliance of local government and small collective enterprises' (Dam 2006a, p. 40), TVEs were used by local bourgeois entrepreneurs in an attempt to avoid a predatory state dynamic. As Peerenboom (2002, pp. 471, 479) puts it, 'if you can't beat them, join them'. Nevertheless, there was not insignificant local-level predation in impoverished villages or those had few other sources of revenue, and in which officials did not have the material means to serve either as patrons or as community benefactors (Unger and Chan 1999, pp. 71–2). Peerenboom (2002, p. 486) highlights the hybrid nature of this arrangement and the context of its rise and fall:

> TVEs reflect a host of context-specific factors, including the deepening of market reforms. As markets developed, TVEs faced increasing competition . . . The lack of clear property rights also hindered growth and development. Outside investors were reluctant to buy into TVEs given the lack of clear ownership rights and the influence of local government on management decisions. Seeking to

minimize unemployment, village leaders would take from the rich to support the poor, forcing strong companies to purchase or subsidize weaker ones.

This reflects the lesson from Adler and Woolcock's (2010) study of the Cambodian Arbitration Council that hybrid forms are by their nature dynamic over time. Similarly, Guthrie (1998, pp. 281–2) finds that the practice of *guanxi*—or personalized networks of influence—in China is declining in importance, especially in large-scale industry, as competitiveness becomes more important.

Legal Pluralism, Informal Norms and Institutions

Understanding the sources of legal hybridity requires an understanding of legal pluralism—'the fact that real social life is prodigal of sovereigns' (Gordon 1984, p. 69), each making their own brand of law that might overlap, cooperate, or compete. This emerges as a social fact (Tamanaha 2000), lived experiences of which often entail some engagement with 'informal' legal institutions.[3] The hybridity that often results from a multiplicity of informal institutions arises as a result of the interaction between different layers of institutional spaces (including formal and informal) (Merry 1988), and engenders corresponding dynamics of contestation over power and resources (Meagher 2010), connecting informal institutions and social networks to the politics of the mediation of power.

Thus, on the one hand, the literature portrays locally embedded institutions whose meaning can be contested by local actors; they are, in that sense, inclusive. In rural Karnataka, for example, Ananth Pur (2004) conducted a study of 'informal local governance institutions' (ILGIs) and found that all the ones surveyed were involved in dispensing justice:

> Villagers do not necessarily see dispute resolution by ILGIs as an end point, but rather as the first opportunity for justice because it is quick, affordable and accessible . . . In most villages, disputes brought before the ILGIs may be taken to the police station or to the formal legal system if not satisfactorily resolved there. The types of disputes that come before the ILGI are varied [and can range from petty theft to land disputes to sexual violence]. (p. 8)

---

[3] While we use 'informal' institutions and cognate terms throughout, we are mindful of and subscribe to the caution against overly stark dichotomies between state/non-state, formal/informal, modern/traditional etc. (Tamanaha 2000; Merry 1988, pp. 875–9). The importance of the idea of legal pluralism as social fact in the literature requires an understanding of the complex interplay of different institutional forms. We simply use the terminology of informality to indicate arrays of institutions that are not understood to be of the state in the orthodox liberal-democratic tradition.

Furthermore, the interaction between formal and informal institutions—the *hybrid dynamics*—has an impact on a broad range of development and local governance issues. A report from the Institute of Development Studies (2010, p. 52) finds that these councils are moving beyond traditional roles and are 'becoming more active in seeking access to public funds, influencing decisions about development projects, and raising matching contributions'.

On the other hand, informal institutions can also be exclusionary or simply embed a set of norms, values, and behaviours that are hard to dislodge. Ghana has a legacy of customary law whose embedded hierarchies were strengthened by British indirect rule, which established Native Courts and judicial recognition of custom. In the context of this history, Crook et al. (2010, pp. 24–7) find that customary land dispute panels are least attuned to popular ideas and expectations about how to settle land disputes, catering to a relatively narrow and elite set of clients using very formal traditional procedures. Panels are too embedded in the power relations of local land ownership and social hierarchies to offer adequate settlement. As a result, the politics of hybridity can also be exclusionary, relying on vertically integrated patronage networks.

The challenge posed by the literature, then, is to understand how effective hybrid arrays of formal and informal institutions come about in developmental states. In some cases, informal institutions may have more legitimacy than the state, and exercising state power to remove them may lead to political backlash or disengagement. This leads to complexities of the politics of state–non-state engagement. In others, the politics of non-state institutions may preclude or impede the state from pursuing inclusive or pro-poor objectives. Seeking to array this space of options, Fritz and colleagues (2009, p. 45) offer four possible relationships between formal and informal institutions: complementary; accommodating; substituting; and competing/subverting. Stephens (2009, p. 145) fleshes this out in the context of ROL systems, highlighting the politics of each move. Policymakers can expand state control of the justice system; attempt to enhance the cultural relevance of the formal system by aligning it with customary systems; attempt to 'improve' the quality of informal justice through state oversight and the insertion of legal or constitutional human rights standards; or attempt to subjugate informal processes in a structural hierarchy below the state.

Autonomy

The politics of hybridity in ROL systems play out in one key area of institutional form: the autonomy of justice institutions, or the ability of justice institutions to behave as autonomous political actors in order to carry out particular functions (Fukuyama 2011, p. 408). In China, for example,

Peerenboom (2002, p. 14) shows that judges are political appointees. However, Peerenboom (2008a, p. 5) suggests that putative reformers need to disaggregate the politics of the Chinese state in order to understand how reform might occur. Some low-hanging reforms are manageable, such as improving case processing times, but reforms really have to be understood as political, causing turf battles and conflicts between the component parts of the state, each of which have to be understood (at least analytically) as separate and distinct power-holders.

A complex understanding of autonomy that takes elite politics into account militates against the transplantation of independent 'forms'; rather, it suggests that we should understand autonomy as a contested concept that creates political winners and losers, requiring a more focused sociology of the actors within justice institutions. Garth (2002) explores the politics of expertise in guiding reform directed at autonomous justice institutions:

> The first law and development movement . . . left a legacy in Brazil of corporate lawyers with an expertise in U.S. corporate law and good connections to U.S. lawyers. The relatively scarce expertise they possessed became more valuable as the economy changed. If we trace the careers of this group, we find remarkable success in corporate law, the state, and the financial sector. These individuals led the movement to rewrite laws to conform to U.S. standards in, among other places, securities and intellectual property. The U.S. investment paid off both locally and for the United States. What did not happen, however, was substantial reform of the judiciary or reform of legal education. (p. 393)

Institutional Functions: Accountability and Basic Obligations

While the literature on the functions of legal institutions is vast, in providing a politically rich account of ROL we emphasize here its accountability role and support of the state in meeting its basic obligations. Both of these functions cut across other dimensions of state policymaking (Fukuyama 2011), for example enabling the delivery of basic services (Gauri 2011).

Legal Accountability

The literature on accountability refers to the legal ability to hold power-holders to account for their actions (Fukuyama 2011, pp. 582–4). The politics of movements towards greater accountability are contingent on political organization and the pragmatism of the political settlement: that is, a deep-seated understanding that moves to bolster elite legitimacy (including the ceding of some power) will need to occur as an economy grows

(Peerenboom 2008b, p. 5). However, the way in which those politics express themselves can differ significantly, from violent to non-violent revolution, through to incremental transition. This can be as much a result of historical contingency and accident as an outcome caused by an effective and evolving political settlement; to this end, Fukuyama (2011, pp. 589–606) contrasts the Glorious Revolution in Great Britain with the evolution of accountability in Denmark, indicating that the lack of violent conflict in Norway was a product of historical circumstance (such as the free flow of ideas into Norway) as much as design.

This caveat having been established, one message from Latin America is that accountability might counter-intuitively involve a *greater* politicization of justice actors—particularly the judiciary and legal profession. In the region, there has been a move from seeking to establish positivist, apolitical justice actors to a situation in which people have increasingly been able to bring cases of a political nature—to do with electoral law, or civil and political rights—as judges have taken political decisions to rule against the government. For example, in Pinochet's Chile, some Chilean judges made anti-government decisions, even though the Supreme Court justices leaned towards the government (Correa Sutil 1997). In Venezuela, 'the judges of the First Court for Administrative Contentious matters [*sic*] issued several important rulings against some policies enacted by President Chávez's government. After several incidents, the government's special police took over the court building and the judges were fired' (Pérez-Perdomo 2006, p. 187).

As the political settlement broadens, so the politics of legal accountability processes shifts. In Kenya, Benequista (2009) finds a combination of three factors to be key to understanding how the poor mobilized legal accountability institutions to stop evictions perceived as illegal: legal action (injunctions against evictions), media (to expose planned evictions), and local politics (strikes, blocking roads, use of District Commissioner). In India, a fourth factor—legal education—is highlighted from a campaign against evictions and compulsory purchases to support a private thermal power plant. Nevertheless, recalling Holston (1991), legal processes of accountability often remain limited in their utility to the poor. Newell and Wheeler (2006, pp. 15–16) argue that:

> Approaches to accountability that rely solely on legal reform are unlikely to appreciate the limits of the law, in terms of access and reach, for the majority of the world's poor. For example, constitutionally guaranteed rights (as with the right to water in South Africa and the right to health in Brazil) can create new possibilities for demanding accountability. Yet the difference in how these rights fit into legal traditions is critical. In Brazil, social mobilisation around constitutional provisions has provided an entry point for political struggles over accountability because the judiciary does not fill that space, while in South Africa court

cases . . . have had a more central role . . . By contrast, in India, despite the fact there is a strong tradition of using public interest litigation, there has also been resort to mock legal processes such as citizen hearings. And in Mexico, where there is little possibility of resolving accountability struggles through legal structures perceived to be convoluted and corrupt, social mobilisation around political objectives is key to increasing accountability. While law often allows for equity of treatment, it can also reinforce social inequities. In Bangladesh, the laws covering workers' rights date from the colonial period and heavily favour educated men. Women, who work almost entirely in the informal sector, do not fall under the auspices of these laws in practice. In Kenya and India the colonial Land Acquisition Act has been invoked to remove people from their land, often without compensation or redress . . . An apolitical view of promoting accountability through law reform, capacity building, training judges and the like is unlikely to yield improved access for the poor unless structural barriers and social hierarchies that inhibit meaningful use of the law by the poor are also addressed.

Basic Obligations

Basic obligations can be expressed in terms of the ability of civic and commercial actors to exercise state power to enable political, social, and economic activity (Fukuyama 2011, p. 601). Such activity is contingent on the formation of a political constituency that sees the state as having certain basic obligations; this can be due to material impacts on people's lives, implying a need for grass-roots mobilization and action. For example, Berger (2008) examines the use of the courts to compel the state to provide antiretroviral drugs to combat AIDS in South Africa in line with the constitutional provisions upholding economic and social rights, seeing the law of basic obligations as shaping a contest between the poor and the state. However, basic obligations can also bear relevance to intra-elite settlements: for example, Coffee's (2001) history of the development of securities markets in the US and UK found that a new political constituency developed that desired legal rules capable of filling in the inevitable enforcement gaps that self-regulation had created.

The ability to participate in the political determination of what constitutes a basic obligation can have important impacts on the poor and marginalized. For example, protective laws on the surface appear to provide protection for women against harmful and dangerous occupational environments. However, they can also subvert women's ability to make choices and operate to restrict their access to a wider range of employment opportunities. These laws might include total or partial restrictions on women to work at night, to accept employment abroad, or to engage in what are considered dangerous occupations, such as mining, deep-water fishing, those involving chemicals, among others (World Bank 2011b, pp. 234–5).

Policy Frames: Pragmatism and Equity

Pragmatism

ROL reforms are often framed as pragmatic or bold in the context of their political valence. Examining the pace of reform is an instructive example. The ROL literature offers a contrast between incrementalism (particularly in China: Dam 2006a) and a 'big bang' (e.g. in post-Soviet countries: Ford 2001), with the current trend—albeit not the abiding structures and incentives of large development agencies—favouring incremental reform, not least because building political constituencies for ROL reform takes time; Pritchett and de Weijer (2010) suggest several decades, even in the *fastest* reforming countries. Godoy and Stiglitz (2006) consider the lessons from legal retrenchment in post-Soviet states and their subsequent experience with asset-stripping. If a 'big bang' opens opportunities for the capture of economic resources and political and business elites are closely tied, politics may favour the rapid removal of assets even though it will lead to inequality and lack of inclusiveness, along with a ROL system that allows assets to be exported and competition to be minimized.

There is significant literature in praise of incrementalism, especially with regard to the experiences of China and countries in South East Asia (Peerenboom 2002; Dam 2006b; Przeworski et al. 2000; Friedman and Gilley 2005). However, incremental reform can also enable elites to sequence reform in ways that suit them, and reject reform that might undermine their interests even though it might be beneficial to the poor or marginalized. Take, for example, forest reform in Andhra Pradesh, in which wealthy lobbies worked to undercut reform that would increase regulation and oversight and which threatened their economic and political interests (Reddy et al. 2010, p. 5; Sarin and Springate-Baginski 2010, p. 32).

Finally, the role of international actors in a political settlement affects the pace of reform. If they play a key role, the pace of reform may be distorted owing to their institutional imperatives. For example, Dam (2006a, pp. 39–40) argues that China may have benefited from a continuation of leadership and an ability to resist the international, while post-Soviet states lacked the former and so international actors stepped in to fill the gap.

Equity

Adopting equity as a policy frame for ROL entails helping meet the material needs of the poor to shore up political support (Newell and Wheeler 2006), alternatively narrated as using ROL to buy off the disenfranchised (Peerenboom 2002). Gauri and Brinks's (2008) edited collection contrasts

South Africa (Berger 2008) and India's (Shankar and Mehta 2008) approaches to economic and social rights. Both allow litigation for economic and social rights and thus some judicialization of the policy space. South Africa restricts judicial powers of review of government actions to standards of judicial review, stopping the judiciary from making specific policy prescriptions: for example, in the *Treatment Action Campaign* case of 2002, the Constitutional Court held that the government had to make available free antiretroviral drugs to reduce the risk of mother-to-child transmission of HIV, but did not tell the government how to achieve this aim nor what any relevant thresholds (e.g. of severity) should be. This standard of review limits the judicialization of the political space. By contrast, India has generated its own standards of review, allowing judges to conduct direct data gathering, to appoint investigative commissions, and make specific policy prescriptions to the legislature; for example, in the *People's Union for Civil Liberties* case, the Supreme Court held in 2001 that the government must improve children's nutrition, and must do it through the provision of a hot meal for every child at school. Upon frequent delays in implementation, the Court appointed a commission in 2003 to investigate bottlenecks and make remedial suggestions to the government (Desai 2010).

As a result, an equitable policy frame for ROL—that is, one that broadens the political settlement through the equitable provision of goods and services to the poor and promotion of social mobility (Fukuyama 2011, pp. 599–600)—may turn on the politics of the justice actors within the system. One consequence of this, at least in India, is the emergence of the judiciary as a political class, which is required for the system to continue to work in an aggressively pro-poor fashion, but which may cause backlogs and reduce faith in impartiality (Dennis and Stewart 2004; Hirschl 2004).

Political Organization: Coalitions and Communication

Coalitions

The nature of coalitions intersects with a range of different tools that have influenced the broadening of the political settlement through law and justice. For example, public interest litigation, often aimed at changing the existing political settlement by altering 'structured inequalities and power relations in society' (Gloppen 2008, p. 344), has opened a judicial space in which groups can form and mobilize around specific issues, particularly socio-economic claims (which have tended to link the urban and rural poor with middle-class activist networks: Gauri and Brinks 2008). Access to information laws have opened spaces for new coalitions around specific issues such as rural corruption (linking activists and the rural poor: Jenkins and Goetz 1999) and more general issues such as press freedom and government accountability (in Mexico, this was driven by coalitions of urban middle-class activists and intellectuals: Gill and Hughes 2005). Legal empowerment tools ('the use of legal services and related development activities to increase disadvantaged populations' control over their lives' Golub 2003, pp. 3, 5, 25) entail interventions often driven by civil society actors such as legal education, legal coalition-building and community paralegal programmes.

The nature of political organization is common across these interventions as a factor determinative of the nature of outcomes. Gloppen (2008, p. 348), for example, talks about 'associative capacity' and Gill and Hughes (2005, pp. 126–9) about the 'formation of a pragmatic and adaptive coalition of . . . advocates'. The organization of political groupings plays an important role in shaping ROL in two ways: *first*, direct political support to contests surrounding the use of and changes to a particular set of rules and institutions; and *second*, indirectly shaping and being shaped by ROL institutions through the (re)generation, contestation, and consumption of shared understandings (see Gauri et al. 2013). As a result, it is important to recognize that legal tools that rest on or which are designed to form coalitions cannot be considered neutral tools to be wielded by the poor; they must be understood as modes of reconfiguring power requiring politics and ideology (contrasting Golub 2003 with Baxi 1982 and Rajagopal 2003).

First, forging direct political support for changes to ROL often entails calling upon a combination of foreign support and domestic coalitions, with different sources of legitimacy and different political aims (Daniels and Trebilcock 2004). At the domestic level, it also requires some group cohesion without mass cooptation (Fukuyama 2011, pp. 562, 598)—thus, in Tanzania, Mahdi (2010, p. 4) highlights the importance of organizing representation for small coffee growers who operate independently from large cooperatives who could otherwise capture regulatory reform. However, this analysis is contested by Peerenboom (2008b, pp. 10–12) who juxtaposes India with the 'East Asian Model' (EAM). He argues that India remains democratic, which (in this view) has resulted in lower growth; the EAM has followed a path of authoritarianism-growth-democratic reform, and indeed Latin America has shifted from authoritarianism to patronage through patronage democracy to democracy (Daniels and Trebilcock 2004). By contrast, Lele and Quadir (2004, p. 3) argue that India remains democratic, as law protects the interests of the entrenched and dominant classes who hold 'economic, political and ideological sway over the subaltern classes', benefiting from vertically integrated political parties coupled to low human development.

As a result, it is important to understand not just the cohesion of groups contesting rules, but the broad base and cohesion of possible beneficiaries from rule contests. For example, creating justiciable socio-economic rights moves particular social and economic contests to the courts. Gauri and Brinks (2008, pp. 335–40) argue that there is a well-documented concern about beneficiary inequality (i.e. that only the rich can litigate). However, the group of potential beneficiaries from a particular successful challenge is vast—for example, in the *Treatment Action Campaign* case, all maternal HIV sufferers in South Africa. Gauri and Brinks go on to argue that ensuring the broadest base of potential beneficiaries requires significant civil society or state support to participate in such contests. There is thus a strong link in the literature between direct political support and indirect shaping—coalitions are relevant to broadening a political settlement through ROL inasmuch as they deal with the creation of a cohesive group who share a common understanding of the role of the courts in solving *their* problems. Joshi (2010), in a study of recent employment guarantee schemes in India, explores essential preconditions for this to happen, which echo the preconditions for broad-based legal accountability discussed above. He finds that:

> For the law to work for poor people, at least initially a significant amount of energy, time, and resources have to be devoted to pursuing rights through the courts. Without a strong membership organization or support from an NGO, access to justice for the poor is difficult. Second, a strategy of pursuing litigation has to be adopted by activist organizations prior to any actual dispute, so that robust cases with detailed documentation can be built up for litigation. Third, such a formal confrontational strategy can be costly in terms of everyday organizational functioning and interactions with the local authorities. Finally, although the anticipated material benefits of successful court cases (in the form of increased wages) can be a powerful force for mobilizing rural workers, a litigation strategy may not deliver relief to the aggrieved—the poorest—because of the long time the judgments take. (p. 626)

As a result, the internal and external politics of third party participation in rule systems clearly have a strong impact on pro-poor outcomes, including the legitimacy of their claims to represent the poor. Maiti (2009, pp. 29–33) explores this in the context of comparative labour relations in Gujarat and West Bengal. In Gujarat, in order to meet significant demand, labour contractors (non-political actors) hire a large number of migrant workers from out-of state based on informal networks, and most are at-will employees. Contractors are comfortably able to bribe labour inspectors if caught. Employees thus remain part of their informal network that brought them to work. In West Bengal, however, labour unions play this role in a context where alternative employment options are very low. As political actors, they retain clear constituencies, and employees form part of their union as a political unit. As a result, union representatives risk action against them in the public domain if such bribery were to occur, and thus engage in bribery or similar activity to a lesser degree.

Third-party participation is complicated by the politics of justice actors themselves—the judiciary, lawyers, academics, ombudspersons, and similar institutional actors—their links to elite-led coalitions, their relationship with the balance of power, and their investment in the status quo. In Andhra Pradesh, for example, enforcement of forest regulation through the courts has been stymied by the forest regulator itself appearing as an interested party in cases (Reddy et al. 2010, p. 6). The complex politics of judicial independence in China shows the importance of seeing justice actors as part of a political process. Reforms to the (Party-appointed) judiciary are highly political, causing turf battles and conflicts between component parts of the state. The Party is able to adjudicate between these component parts; as a result, there is a tension between the proposition that strengthening ROL will weaken the Party's discretion (a 'good'), and the ability to do so in a way that significantly changes the existing power dynamic and creates an independent political actor in the judiciary, given that the Party is needed to mediate tensions (Peerenboom 2008a, p. 7).

Direct political support for ROL reform also depends on the relative power of elites (Fukuyama 2011, pp. 779–80). Following Kennedy's (2002) and Hohfeld's (1917) understandings of property rights, we understand from Holston (1991, pp. 721–3) that the power has to be used to quash competing property claims from non-elite groups, or groups not partaking of the political settlement (through litigation, legislation, influencing adjudicators, patrimonial networks, etc). As a result, legal education, legal empowerment strategies, and mobilization become important—not just for group formation and cohesion, but to provide the capabilities to non-elite groups to exploit this political tool—as does driving down barriers to access to justice from both the supply and demand side (e.g. the provision of legal services or lowering barriers to achieving standing in court). For example, Adler, Porter, and Woolcock (2008), in a study of Cambodian land titling, find that:

> Absent formal institutions which are able to deal with major conflict in a way which is perceived as fair, the poor use a variety of advocacy strategies to gain extra leverage in their negotiations with wealthier or more powerful parties. In the most successful cases the poor act collectively to approach powerful administrative officials, often district and provincial governors, to intervene on their behalf. Appeals to the media, local human rights NGOs and national level institutions have also proven useful. When formal law is drawn upon in these cases it is to legitimate multi-faceted bargaining strategies rather than with any expectation that the state could be relied upon to enforce the law in an equitable fashion. Such strategies clearly have the potential to shift decisions in favour of the poor in individual cases. There is, however, little in the way of institutional structure for this sort of bargaining. As such, collective action around

land issues tends to be local, ephemeral and targeted at powerful individuals within the administration. (p. 3)

Again, civil society is extremely important in framing the effective exploitation of law (Scott 1998, p. 5), but such claims are difficult to make and manage, relying on significant presumptions about the public sphere (and its legal framing through speech laws, and so on), vernaculars, social relations, and identity (Wayne et al. 2002; Avritzer 2002; Fung 2003). Thus, Hoffman and Bentes (2008) highlight low levels of knowledge about their rights among the poor in Brazil, while Berger (2008, pp. 47–8) discusses elite action to hoard information and legislate against CSOs in South Africa.

The second dimension of coalition-building around ROL—the shaping and contesting of institutions—is achieved through discursive limits imposed by ROL that frame the intersubjective meaning of issues—that is, the socially generated shared understandings of what ROL is and what it should do, and the comprehensible limits of what it might be. These facilitate or hinder the formation of groups: for example, Gauri et al. (2013) analyse the World Bank's justice reform project in Afghanistan and show that the Bank is trying to shift popular understandings of the citizen-formal justice system relationships in Afghanistan from a dynamic founded on tribal (lack of) engagement with the state to a 'state service/end user' dynamic. Hyden (2010, p. 8) extends this idea to the self-image held by parliamentarians in Ghana as 'delegates and guardians of their constituents'. He argues that this overshadows the role of parliament as a deliberative democratic forum, as parliamentary cohesiveness gives way to locally embedded politics.

We draw two main lessons from this. First, we cannot take a static view of political settlements and the concomitant ROL system: a constant reproduction of meaning and shifts in who shares a particular meaning system means that constituencies who can participate (e.g. who can litigate, who considers themselves to be an 'employee' and thus participate in an employment tribunal) are constantly shifting. This will have important implications for analysis, data collection, and monitoring methodologies, project design, and so on. Second, there is a similar problematization to be undertaken of the internal administrative dynamics of a justice system: analysts need to understand the politics of justice actors and how they construct themselves (Dezalay and Garth 1996, 2002).

Communication

Communication is an important corollary of coalitions: the meaning they ascribe to rules requires an appreciation of communicative spaces as areas of political contestation about rules and the roles of actors. Thus, Fukuyama

(2011, pp. 600–1) argues that a broadly communicated faith in the common law of England provides a foundation for high levels of trust in the judiciary, while Peerenboom (2008b, p. 7) shows that surveys about the Indian Supreme Court show high levels of faith in the institution despite low levels of faith in its ability to execute its function, displaying a colonial legacy akin to that found by Fukuyama in England. The literature on communication also displays a sensitivity to vernaculars that will allow the poor to engage with and contest rules and roles (Barron et al. 2011). Benequista (2009) studies programmes that used theatre to reach out to the poor, while Stefanova et al. (2010) explore the use of theatre to build awareness of legal issues relating to customary law and land-leasing in Vanuatu. Cornwall and Coelho (2007, pp. 22–3) nuance the importance of communication. They argue that context and political culture matter: again, law shapes communicative spaces as well as being shaped by them, from regulating the ability to speak (such as speech rights for women) to providing physical spaces for such expression. When there is divergence and dissonance between elite and local narratives and no space to allow for contest between the two, this can lead to low inclusiveness and poor access to justice. Scott (2009, pp. 334–7) brings to light a strong belief in the effectiveness of state judicial officers at the national level in China in the mid-nineteenth century, and the predatory realities of local magistrates at the sub-national level.

Contingent Factors

A final, overarching message from this political exploration of ROL is its contingency, especially on historical and colonial legacies (an issue raised in detail by Bayly et al. 2011; see also Benton 2002 and Harris 2010). Olivier de Sardan (2009, p. 12), in a study of local governance in West Africa, addresses the history of clientelism in West Africa and the resultant 'venality of justice' in a chief's judicial/administrative role. Harris (2010, p. 169) finds in his comparative study of the Dutch and British East India Companies' impact on ROL that the pervasiveness of contingent factors is so strong that 'it is wise to recognize that conditions are different and that preferences in trade-offs are different in different localities, and accordingly there should be plurality in policy recommendations'.

Rather than legacies, Lachmann (2002, pp. 174–5) highlights *unexpected impacts* from large-scale historical change in early-modern England. As the ecclesiastical establishment in the seventeenth century was weakened by the monarch in a political process of rewriting the elite balance of power, so the authority of clerical courts was undermined. The gentry were for the first time able to turn to common law courts to claim enclosure over manorial land, regarding which clerical courts had previously supported peasant claims.

Cornwall and Coelho (2007) and Roque and Shankland (2007) see similar mutations on a smaller scale and over a much shorter period of time as part of specific development projects. In Luanda, Associations of Water Committees (ACAs) were formed as representative associations to participate in the management of water standposts, which entailed organizing water distribution, collecting payment for water from residents, keeping the area clean, and carrying out maintenance of the standpost. ACAs decided to federate to increase their negotiating power with the provincial water company. This required them to delocalize—to become independent from their membership base, breaking the chain of accountability initially established to support their representative function and placing in question the legitimacy of their supervisory function. The scope for this mutation derived from the wider lack of clarity on organizational models and political/institutional rules of the game around water in Angola.

Conclusions

There remains a sizeable and enduring gap between the near-universal consensus regarding the general importance of ROL and its conspicuously thin record of actual policy accomplishment. Explaining the persistence of this gap, and devising effective strategies for narrowing it, must of necessity begin with revisiting core theoretical assumptions and the operational frameworks to which they give rise, even as such frameworks need to be informed by—and remain in active dialogue with—more detailed, context-specific evidence on whether and how prevailing justice systems 'work' from the perspective of actual and potential users of these systems, especially the poor. This requires a highly critical interrogation of knowledge and method from the perspective of societal contingency and a concomitant adjustment of the sorts of claims that can and cannot be supported, particularly with respect to the teleological (Tamanaha 2011). Having followed here the political turn in analyses of ROL, we have had to reach across several disciplines and country cases to establish an adequate account of the dynamic relationship between ROL and the political settlement in theory and practice, one which displays the importance of both outcomes and participation in—or mobilization through—legal process.

Beyond the familiar (and somewhat self-serving) academic conclusion that 'more research' is needed, we argue that 'justice' and 'the rule of law' are both 'essentially contested concepts' whose primary work is done through the productive debates to which they give rise in a given political space;

which is to say, 'more research' as conventionally understood will only yield marginal improvements in conceptual clarity and add only incrementally to our cumulative knowledge—the political salience, legitimacy, and action-ability of such concepts must be negotiated anew in each setting, between different epistemic groups (professions) and across divides of gender, ideology, and class. Such negotiation and deliberation is inherently a contested, dynamic process, likely to yield an idiosyncratic outcome that is a unique hybrid of local and external inputs mediated through political spaces of varying capability, legitimacy and robustness.

Even on the basis of this preliminary assay, however, some clear implications emerge for policy and practice. First, scholars and practitioners alike need to invest in richer data-gathering exercises, in empirical tasks that de-homogenize people based on conceptual as well as material differences; this will entail taking history, sociology, and anthropology (especially of justice actors) seriously. Second, we need to invest more substantial (and substantive) resource in the monitoring and *real-time* evaluation of ROL interventions; there needs to be constant reassessment, clear articulation of goals, with space for practical innovation, combined with modesty about timelines, trajectories, and a realistic appreciation of the value of pragmatism. Third, greater effort needs to be extended to invigorating communication programmes or programmes supporting construction of spaces for public engagement and discursive participation. This means not just indicating goals or imparting knowledge, but allowing groups (especially women, the poor, and marginalized groups) to participate, contest meaning, understand benefits, and form coalitions; it means recognizing that ROL reform is inherently a site of contestation, for which enhancing access to it is not just a matter of the removal of factors that stop an individual from bringing a case (e.g. geography, cost), but removal of obstructions to effective and sustained participation (communication, education, awareness). As a result, it requires development practitioners and agencies to develop a highly reflexive sensibility—and allied set of epistemological and methodological tools—on the ways in which they construct the spaces for and themselves participate in these contests.

Part IV
The Politics of Recognition

8

The Gendered Politics of Securing Inclusive Development

Sohela Nazneen and Simeen Mahmud

Introduction: Why Gender Matters in Securing Inclusive Development

Gender is at the core of securing inclusive development. Women's right to equality with men is accepted and promoted by many states and development agencies in development planning and policies. Yet enabling women's representation, participation, and voice in politics and policy processes and achieving gender equitable outcomes for women has proven difficult (Goetz and Nyamu-Musembi 2008; Mukhopadhyay and Singh 2007; UN/UNRISD 2005). This chapter explores the gendered politics of securing inclusive development through a synthesized review of available evidence[1] on the gendered nature of politics[2] and how this promotes or constrains women's participation and inclusion in decision-making and affects policy outcomes in selected case-study countries. By exploring the gendered nature of politics using feminist political analysis, we examine the different elements of political settlement[3] through a gender lens and draw conclusions on how a gender perspective deepens our understanding of political settlements. This is challenging since political settlement frameworks are gender blind

[1] We review different bodies of literature, such as feminist analysis of representative democracy, feminist analysis of the state, women in politics literature, gender and development literature, literature on women's/feminist movement's engagement with state/ international actors, feminist organizational analysis, etc.

[2] Largely refers to formal politics; we also investigate women's movement and collective actions.

[3] Political settlements refer to a balance of power between contending social groups and classes upon which the state is based (Di John and Putzel 2009); and it includes intra elite bargaining, contention between elite and non-elite groups, inter-group contentions (gender, caste, race, religious, ethnic, and so on).

and feminist scholars so far, have not developed a gendered analysis of this approach.

Understanding how women's 'political effectiveness'[4] ensures gender-inclusive development requires a deeper analysis of: a) what enhances women's individual/collective political agency; and b) the influence of structural factors that enhance/constrain women's agency, such as the nature of the state, political competition, relationship between women's movements and civil society. We argue that the following influences women's inclusion in politics and promotion of gender-equitable policies:[5] a) the divergent interests and incentives political and state actors have in promoting/obstructing women's participation and the gender equity agenda in politics and policy processes; b) the local, national, and international contexts that create opportunity structures for promotion of gender equity by these actors (including women policymakers and women's groups); c) how these actors negotiate gender equity concerns; d) the competing discourses on gender equity that creates opportunities for, or limit promotion of, gender equity in different forums. An analysis of the gendered nature of politics in different contexts unpacks: a) how states and elites in different political contexts perceive women as a development/political constituency, interpret women's needs and gender equity concerns, and how their interpretations influence policy outcomes; b) how the above interpretations are challenged and at times expanded by the women (and their allies) in formal politics and through movements and organized activism for securing inclusive outcomes.

This chapter has five sections. For contextualizing the discussion in this chapter, we provide a brief discussion on limitations of gender-mainstreaming processes and of gender-biased assumptions on representation that exist in liberal political theory. We present country case-study selection matrix and the analytical framework in the third section. The fourth section is on the gendered politics of securing inclusive development. In the final section we draw conclusions on how gender analysis of political settlements can expand political settlement frameworks and the current feminist analysis of women in politics.

Context: Limitations of Gender Mainstreaming and Gender Bias in Liberal Political Theory

The Politics of the Discourse around Gender and Development Policy

The gender and development arena has always been politically contentious because it confronts the basis of social organization in any society, that of

---

[4] See second section, this chapter.
[5] Gender equity takes into account that men and women have different needs, interests, and preferences and may require difference in treatments for equal outcomes.

the relationship between women and men. It has evolved through a difficult relationship between the international development agencies and feminist scholars and activists. The story of this evolution is well documented but worth reviewing for the general development establishment.

Although under certain political contexts women's inclusion in political institutions came about from their active participation in fairly large numbers in anti-colonial, anti-authoritarian, and anti-apartheid struggles, their 'political entitlements' (Agarwal 2011) led to mixed outcomes with respect to women's inclusion into policy processes. In India (1930s) this entitlement was confined to reserved membership in the local government and party membership; in Chile (1990s), despite the establishment of an effective national gender machinery, SERNAM, it failed to enable women's greater inclusion into public policy spaces; in South Africa (1990s) women who entered policy spaces included gender equity concerns in the policy agenda but there were huge accountability failures in implementation.

Within the development community, women first emerged as a distinct constituency in the 1970s. Boserup's (1970) path-breaking book *Women's Role in Economic Development* demonstrated how conventional development activities had bypassed women and the 'fruits of development were not trickling down to women'. Boserup's critique and the subsequent efforts of early women in development (WID) advocates exposed the hitherto unacknowledged but powerful assumption of development planners and policymakers about women's family responsibilities and tasks and the subsequent promotion of their domestic roles in development policy. This was instrumental in shifting the earlier view of women as dependents on men and passive recipients of welfare[6] to the view of women as economic producers who contribute to household and country economies.

Within official development agencies, however, the new focus on women soon became linked with poverty reduction and basic needs in which women were cast as 'managers of low income households and providers of family basic needs' (Kabeer 1994, p. 7). This approach failed to define women's problems in terms of unequal access to resources. In the late 1970s, some feminists distanced themselves from this approach, and problematized social and gender relations in developing countries and questioned the positivist models of development interventions: education and training, employment, agricultural technological change, and so on (Jackson and Pearson 1998, p. 3). They rejected the portrayal of women as a separate but homogenous category in development literature and emphasized that relations between men and women are social and therefore not

---

[6] Development resources are directed to market-oriented economic growth and the residual is welfare assistance for the dependent and vulnerable groups (Kabeer 1994, p. 6).

immutable. In any historical situation, the form taken by gender relations is specific to that context and needs to be constructed inductively (Jackson and Pearson 1998).

During the 1980s the efficiency argument of WID policy was reinforced by emphasizing women as economic agents in their own rights and that women's exclusion would have an adverse impact on development. But such recognition coincided with the shift in the approach of the international financial institutions (IFI) (World Bank, IMF) to development itself, in which the role of the government as a development agency was required to be curtailed to meet the objectives of fiscal austerity, and reduce balance of payments deficits and domestic government deficits. The many activities previously carried out by governments (transport, communications, tertiary health care, higher education) were to be privatized and social services (most closely connected to reproductive activities) would be reorganized and not-for-profit non-governmental organizations (NGO) would take on many of those functions.

The dominant development models also assumed that improvement in human well-being including women's well-being would not be possible without economic growth; in fact economic growth was seen as synonymous with development. Kabeer (1994) and others diagnosed this as confusing means and ends but with a political agenda that postponed redistributive measures and policies to redress inequality, with serious implications for gender equality. At the same time the tendency to frame gender equity concerns at national levels on instrumental arguments (in terms of social and economic gains for development) ran the risk of overlooking concerns with gender justice and women's citizenship entitlements. Feminists pointed out the hidden 'gender trap' (Kabeer 1994, p. 26) within the market solution: increased monetary costs of welfare services and of health and education services, increased reliance on women's unpaid care work, women's entrance into informal unprotected low-paid casual labour to supplement dwindling household incomes (Goetz 1995; Molyneux and Razavi 2005).

On the other hand, this new scenario opened up space for women's organizations and particularly the creation of women's NGOs, which were believed to be more responsive to the needs of people at the grassroots level (Jackson and Pearson 1998). Around this time Third World feminists raised concerns that economic growth-oriented development overlooked the needs and aspirations of poor women. Southern feminists also countered the WID assumption that it was the prejudice of planners that was primarily responsible for women's marginalization from the development process, and critiqued the absence of a deeper examination of structural factors that caused women's subordination in the development process (Razavi 1997). They claimed that the clearest lens for understanding the problems of development processes was the lived experience of poor Third World women in their struggles for basic survival, arguing that alternative development strategies were needed and that women should be targeted as beneficiaries of these new organizations in order to gain access to international development funding (Sen and Grown 1988). They also criticized the official language of gender mainstreaming that was adopted by the Beijing Platform For Action, first because of its preoccupation with procedures rather than outcomes, and second because despite its roots in social feminism, gender had become a technocratic term failing to address issues of power relations. More significantly, the lack of accountability of international development agencies (UN bodies included) to the Southern women in whose interests they claim to be acting is not commonly seen as part of the gendered politics of development (see Baden and Goetz 1998, p. 24).

By 2000 there was growing realization about the fragility of an international order based on unregulated financial flows. There was a 'new moment' (Molyneux 2002, cited in Molyneux and Razavi 2005) in the development policy agenda of the IFIs: a greater willingness to focus on social policy and poverty reduction, good governance through democracy, participation, and decentralization, but maintaining the core elements of trade and financial liberalization and tight monetary/fiscal policies (Molyneux and Razavi 2005). The trade-off between growth and equity was less clear-cut, but did not disappear, highlighting the need for greater attention to structures of global and local power and the evolution of gender injustices. The feminist critique that poverty analyses of policy are not necessarily adequate for addressing gender issues since women's subordination is not caused by poverty (Kabeer 1994; Jackson 1999), was validated by assessments of the poverty reduction strategy (PRS) process since the late 1990s. Women's groups and rights activists were energetic on gaining recognition for the need to bring gender perspectives in forums discussing macro-economic policies and forging political alliances with governments, NGOs, and social movements (Molyneux and Razavi 2005).

Clearly, feminist critiques and activists have been in the forefront of the discourse on gender and development, and the selective uptake of gender concerns by the IFIs present useful insights into the politics of this discursive context. One such group were women active within international financial and development bureaucracies (like the World Bank, ILO, UNDP) in getting women's interests and gender equality included into the development agendas of these agencies. Just as gender and development policy discourse has evolved over time, feminist advocates have used diverse strategies to mobilize and influence development agendas within their respective organizations. Razavi (1997) concludes that even in the face of persistent criticism from feminist scholars, the basic strategy of these transnational actors was to 'make a range of instrumental arguments that link gender equality to more "legitimate" policy concerns, market efficiency, growth and human resource development' to convince hardened bureaucrats (Razavi 1997, p. 1111). These efforts culminated in a range of high visibility policy documents of the World Bank and UN bodies where gender mainstreaming was projected as a dominant theme in development policy.[7] Later, with the advent of the anti-poverty approach feminist policy advocates took advantage of the paradigm shift and resorted to puting emphasis on poor women, and poor men, to present the gender equality agenda as less threatening to male bureaucrats and programme implementers. In the wake of structural adjustment another genre of feminist advocates engaged with mainstream economists in the development establishment using neoclassical efficiency argument: gender was introduced sometimes as a means for understanding the complexities of the adjustment process (i.e. intra-household allocations and inequalities and bargaining), and sometimes politically to demonstrate how gender biases and rigidities can frustrate adjustment policies (Razavi 1997, p. 1115). These accounts highlight the institutional constraints within which feminist advocates operate. They also point to the significance of those working outside the institutional contexts, namely citizen groups, feminist scholars, NGOs, who can take advantage of strategic entry points and more transformative discourse to influence the policy agenda.

Bringing 'Gender' Back into Development Policy

The 1995 UN Conference on Women in Beijing was seen as a landmark in setting a global policy framework to advance gender equality, but post-Beijing achievements in gender equality were 'more ambivalent and the causal influences more diverse and less unidirectional' (Molyneux and Razavi 2005, p. iv). Dominant development paradigms continued to equate development with economic growth and to assume that reductions in gender inequality in well-being have a linear relationship with development.[8] While some stark gender inequalities were reduced over time, others remain resistant to change or have even taken new forms. There is also considerable variation amongst countries with respect to reduction in gender inequality and no clear relationship is evident with the pace and level of human development. Structural adjustment of the 1980s and 1990s, left gender-specific impacts and put the burden of economic reforms relatively more upon women in the

---

[7] For example, World Bank (1995b) 'Towards Gender Equality: The Role of Public Policy'; the UNDP *Human Development Report* (1995).

[8] The World Bank claimed that countries with higher GDP had greater gender equality, implying that promotion of economic growth through liberalization was an important tool for closing gender gaps in well-being (World Bank 2001a).

poorest households. In fact, three decades of development policy focused on economic growth and gender mainstreaming has not delivered secure live-lihoods and an 'enabling economic environment', which were considered preconditions for attaining gender equality and women's rights.

While the term 'gender' has permeated through to national govern-ments and policymaking institutions, southern feminists at Beijing asserted that the focus on gender rather than women had become counterproduc-tive as it shifted discussion from 'a focus on women, to women and men, and finally back to men'[9] (Baden and Goetz 1998, p. 21). By 2000 there was a 'wave of reassessment of gender mainstreaming which demonstrated that the mere narrowing of gender gaps and equality in numbers were not enough to remove inequality in access to economic and political resources nor dismantle gender asymmetries'. Gender mainstreaming as the primary strategy for pursuing gender equity in and through development lost cred-ibility since concerns with 'gender equality' were not enough to 'redress' on-going gender injustices (Mukhopadhyay and Singh 2007). Gender analysis was reduced to technocratic discourse and gender mainstreaming via WID units had become a technical project, difficult to fit with the political pro-ject of challenging inequality and promoting women's rights (Baden and Goetz 1998; Mukhopadhyay and Singh 2007). Feminist phrases and con-cepts for understanding women's position in the development process were co-opted by international development agencies and national governments and became filled with new meanings to suit institutional needs. Within international and national institutions gender-mainstreaming practice faced continued bureaucratic resistance. A review[10] of gender-mainstreaming pol-icy implemented by the World Bank, UNDP, and the ILO found inadequate budgeting for the gender component of projects, insufficient development of analytical skills, and a general lack of political commitment, both within the organization, and at country level (Charlesworth 2005, p. 11). Clearly, as Staudt pointed out, there was need 'to know more about men who dominate decision-making in the bureaucracy and how they vary in diverse institu-tional settings' (Staudt 1997, p. 4).

On the positive side, however, the fact that social policy, good governance, participation, and decentralization are now high on the development policy agenda provides a critical moment to bring gender back into the discourse and practice in transformative ways. This moment has opened up the possi-bility of bringing to the foreground gender justice, rights, and citizenship in the process of development; created entry points for action to address gender injustices. It may also lead to the creation of new spaces for participation

[9] Nighat Khan, Director, Applied Socio Economic Research, Pakistan.
[10] See Razavi and Miller (1995).

by poor people and by women to claim rights, and to raise voices against gender specific capacity and accountability failures on the part of the state and private sector. But the risk remains that claims of 'participation' and 'empowerment' are driven by gendered interests leaving the least powerful without voice or choice, and of poor accountability to women's groups and constituencies (Cornwall et al. 2005).

Gender Bias in Liberal Political Theory on Participation and Representation

Feminist literature extensively discusses how women have been excluded from formal politics and decision-making processes in liberal theory, based on assumptions that women lack the rationality required for democratic deliberation (Pateman 1988; Okin 1979). Consequently, women's exclusion had been linked to an absence of public deliberation on and from political agendas issues such as, child welfare, reproductive health, and domestic violence, and so on. Analysis of women's exclusion in liberal theory led to an intuitive conclusion that the inclusion of women in electoral or decision-making bodies would make a significant difference in drawing attention to these neglected issues (Dovi 2006). Increased women's presence in public office was identified as a major pathway for promotion of gender equity concerns in policymaking. This led to the emphasis on gender quotas, the creation of national gender machineries in gender and development discourse (Tadros 2011). However, this linear connection made in development discourse between women's access (consultation in various citizen's/ policy forums and spaces) and presence (representation) in electoral/ decision-making bodies leading to influence has been critiqued by many feminists (see Goetz and Nyamu-Musembi 2008 for details). While women's representation and participation in political parties and policy places are necessary conditions for gender equitable outcomes, they alone are not sufficient.

Analytical Framework and Case-study Selection Method

Analytical Framework

The concept of women's 'political effectiveness'—access, presence, and influence (Goetz and Hassim 2003)—is useful for exploring whether women's inclusion in politics and policy spaces leads to gender equitable policy outcomes. For analysing women's access (ability to enter), presence (visibility and quality of participation), and influence (ability to present one's case and influence outcomes) in politics, we use the framework developed by Goetz and Hassim (2003). This framework allows us to explore these three aspects of 'political effectiveness' in three different spheres: the civil society arena, the formal political arena, and the state. It allows us to focus on women's political agency and also the nature of the mechanisms and processes through which women participate and represent.

We use this framework as a common analytical lens for examining selected country cases. The framework provides the same sets of indicators for examining political effectiveness in each of these spheres. Women's movements' political effectiveness in civil society is examined using specific indicators, such as, the depth of the movement, style of leadership, size and resources. Women's access, present, and influence in formal political systems is analysed using indicators such as the nature of the electoral system, party types, reservations for women, nature of political competition. Indicators such as the number of different forums that have quotas for women; nature of national women's machineries, and the constitutional framework are used for analysing women's relations to the state. A focus on these three institutional spheres unpacks women's participation as actors and inclusion in institutional spaces. This also helps to develop a general picture of the gendered nature of political settlement in a country by identifying which actors and institutional spaces are open to the promotion of a gender equity agenda.

The main constraint of using this framework is that how informal/clientelist power relations influence women's inclusion and participation or traditional elites influence the way state and political parties promote gender equity or not, and bottom-up mobilization by women and other groups for challenging existing settlements around gender equity, are not made explicit within this framework. The role played by gender ideologies and ideas in shaping actor's perceptions (other than party ideology) is also not explicit. We extend this framework and include women's participation and inclusion in citizen's forums, role of women in bottom-up mobilizations and policy spaces, and the role played by gender ideologies in shaping actor's perceptions.

Ten case-study countries are picked from South Asia, sub-Saharan Africa, and Latin America (see Table 8.1). Our analysis largely focuses on the first

Table 8.1. Case-study selection matrix

	Geographical regions		
Political context	South Asia	sub-Saharan Africa	Other regions
Post conflict/revolution	Nepal	Rwanda	Egypt
Stable	Bangladesh, India	Uganda, South Africa	Brazil, Chile, Mexico

Source: Authors.

two regions and we use the Latin American countries to highlight the points we make about the gendered politics of securing inclusive development.

Exploring the Gendered Politics of Securing Inclusive Development

This section explores women's representations and participation in political processes, institutions, and policy spaces. This responds to the Goetz and Hassim framework and tries to identify first, the overall levels of access, presence, and influence that women have in civil society, in the formal political arena and the state, and then the underlying reasons for this.

Gendered Politics: Women's Participation and Representation in Political Institutions and Processes

Women's participation and representation in politics are formally endorsed by the selected countries. Many of these countries have taken various measures to ensure women's access to the formal political arena. Compared to Latin America and sub-Saharan Africa, South Asia performs badly as a region when it comes to women's representation in national parliament,[11] local government, executive positions,[12] and the state administration (UNIFEM 2008).

The increase in women's presence in national legislature and local government in Latin America, sub-Saharan Africa, and South Asia is a result of the following: various affirmative action measures such as quotas and party lists, that make women's inclusion mandatory; support for women's representation among senior party leadership; strong women's wing and internal party advocates to lobby for women's political representation; and party ideology promoting gender equity. An increase in women's representation in elected bodies does not automatically enable women representatives to be politically effective. The support for and various other measures taken to increase women's presence in these elected bodies are largely a result of negotiations between different social and political actors. What influences the action taken by these actors are: the actual and perceived interests these

[11] The average value in Latin America is 18% and sub-Saharan Africa is 16% and the highest for both is 40% in some countries; in South Asia the average value is 15% and the highest is 34% in some countries (UNIFEM 2008).

[12] The average value of women in ministerial position in sub-Saharan Africa is 19% and the highest value is 45%; the average value of women in ministerial positions in South Asia is 18% and the highest value is 20%, the average value for Latin America is 23% and the highest value is 50% (UNIFEM 2008).

actors have in promoting women's representation; the context within which opportunities for promoting women's representation arises; the strength of these actors to negotiate and influence other actors; and the gender discourses that influence actions of these actors.

What Explains an Increase in Women's Inclusion and Presence in Politics?

Various structural factors influence whether a critical mass of women representatives will be present in elected bodies and political parties. The type of electoral system influences the willingness of the political parties to nominate female candidates for elections and the probabilities that women candidates may win elections. First-past-the-post systems and single member constituencies that we see in India, Nepal, and Bangladesh create difficulties for women to be nominated for general seats since most political parties fear that they may lose these seats (Tamang 2004; Rai 1997; Chowdhury 1994). This unwillingness of political parties results from women's lack of political *experience*, and the male party members' reluctance to lose their constituencies to women members. Research shows that proportional representation and party lists[13] lead to a larger number of women being elected as demonstrated in the cases of Nepal, Peru, Argentina, Costa Rica, Bolivia, and South Africa (Araujo 2010; UNIFEM 2008).

In contexts where the parties may be unwilling to nominate women, affirmative actions such as quotas, party lists for women, placement mandates, and legal sanctions for not implementing these actions ensure that a critical mass of women is elected to the parliament and local government bodies. All our case-study countries implemented quotas and these measures have increased the visibility of women representatives in elected bodies. The abolishment of gender quotas in the elections held after the revolution reduced the number of women in parliament in Egypt. In Nepal, Rwanda, Peru, Argentina, Costa Rica, Bolivia, and Paraguay legal sanctions for not implementing women's quotas in party lists and the pressure on political parties to implement these led to a large number of women being nominated by political parties. These measures also signalled the commitment of the state towards ensuring women's representation (Araujo 2010; UNIFEM 2008). Absence of legal sanctions on parties for not fielding women candidates and lack of effective support for women candidates may translate into female

---

[13] In the proportional representation system several candidates are elected in a district. Voters choose between parties rather than individuals in most cases and political parties receive a share of the seats based on the overall share of the vote. Most systems have closed lists where the party determines the rank of the candidates, in open lists the voters may influence the order.

candidates hitting a 'ceiling of competition', that is, an increase in women candidates nominated as candidates does not lead to an increase in the numbers being elected, as demonstrated in the case of Brazil (Araujo 2010).[14]

Quotas[15] are one of the preferred pathways for ensuring women's representation in formal politics but they have been critiqued by feminist scholars as a 'quick fix' for addressing the endocentric nature of politics (Tadros 2011; Phillips 1991) and by others as 'undemocratic' (Goetz and Nyamu Musembi 2008). Whether quotas are able to create legitimacy for women's representatives and whether they are able to 'act for' (Phillips 1991) women is partly influenced by how quotas are introduced and whether a clear gender equity mandate exists for these women to act upon. At times, quotas are introduced in ways that expand the number of existing seats and women are included as 'add-ons' so that women's seats do not disturb existing competition for electoral wards or constituencies (e.g. Uganda's local government; Bangladesh's local government and parliament). This in effect leads to women representing larger constituencies that are also meant to be represented by 'regular' ward representatives or MPs, and women are often sidelined. In Bangladesh, where women MPs are nominated by the parties to represent these add-on seats, women MPs have their legitimacy as 'real' representatives questioned by the people. This add-on approach to gender quotas indicates the following: a) reluctance on the part of the political elite to disturb the existing organization of political power; b) an opportunity to use the add-on seats as patronage for loyal supporters; c) increasing credentials as a gender-sensitive regime through making superficial changes. At times, quotas may reach a plateau, especially if these are open party lists on potential candidates instead of actual candidates, after increasing the number of women representatives in the initial stages; and with numbers stabilizing requires reform (Araujo 2010). In fact, the Brazilian experience shows that quota laws need to be drafted carefully. There also need to be clear guidelines for implementing these. For example, in Mexico, the quota laws do not technically apply in districts where candidates are selected through primary election (Htun 2005). A strong presence of the women's movement monitoring compliance with the laws and rules of affirmative action and gender quotas ensured implementation of the gender quota in Costa Rica (Htun 2005).

A direct link to a constituency can be effective in increasing women's legitimacy and presence as representatives. In Bangladesh, at the lowest tier of

[14] There was an initial increase in the number of women in office after party lists were introduced but it reached a plateau (Araujo 2010).

[15] Quotas include: candidate quotas where women are required to be nominated to run for office; and reserved seats implies women hold a certain number of seats in the parliament or local government. In reserved seats women can be directly elected or nominated by others.

local government, research shows that after the direct elections were introduced in 1997 in the reserved seats for women, women members' expectations and how the general public viewed their role underwent a qualitative shift (Nazneen and Tasneem 2010). However, being directly elected by a constituency does not automatically lead to women representatives acting to promote women's interests. In Uganda, where women have a significant presence in District Assemblies, the fact that they do not have a clear gender mandate limits their effectiveness. The youth, army, and all other groups that have reserved seats are elected by their national organizations which create legitimacy and provide a direct mandate to represent the group's interests. The gender quotas in Uganda were introduced to ensure numerical representation of women; women representatives running in reserved seats have to appeal to a narrow male district elite and professing a commitment to gender equity may not appeal to the electoral college which elects them (Goetz and Hassim 2003; Tripp 2003). In South Africa, coming in on a strong gender equity mandate created space for women representatives to raise issues, although the system of party lists created difficulties when at times women had to tow the party line instead of promoting gender equity (Tripp 2001; Hassim 2003; Fester 2014).

Aside from these affirmative action measures, other factors also influence whether women are able to participate in electoral and party politics. Political parties' views on gender equity and women's participation, recruiting and mentoring strategies, internal democracy and mobility within the parties and the strength of the women's wing, all effect whether party policy debates are accessible to women's inputs and participation. The Latin American experience reveals that though women are present in large numbers among party rank and file there are relatively fewer women in leadership positions within these political parties, which limits their ability to negotiate demands in party policy debates in leadership spaces (UNIFEM 2008; Htun 2005).[16] A strong women's wing, such as the African National Congress (ANC) women's league, played a central role in pushing for quotas on party lists and also on the party's position on gender equity during the transitional period in South Africa. The strong link the ANC women's league had with other parties' women's wings and the women's organizations allowed them to create pressure within the ANC and parliament to promote gender equity issues (Kemp et al. 1995; Fester 2014). If gender equity is formally endorsed by the senior party leadership and the party ideology, as in the case of the ANC in South Africa, then pushing for women's representation

---

[16] A 2008 study reveals that there is systematic discrepancy between member numbers and leadership positions in Latin America. For example, Mexico has an average of 50% women in both major parties but they hold only 30% of the executive posts (UNIFEM 2008).

in formal politics and the promotion of gender equity policies become relatively easier. In Rwanda, endorsement by Kagame and the ruling party has somewhat eased the promotion of women's representation and gender equity policies (Burnet 2008).

Whether formal endorsement of gender equity by a party's senior leadership translates into increasing women's influence as a group depends on the level of institutionalization and the level of command and control (centralized or localized) of the party. If the party organization has an 'informal-centralized' model then promotion of gender equity interests (including women's representation) will largely rely on patronage systems and dominant individual leaders than on transparent rules-based systems (Goetz and Hassim 2003; Tripp 2003). All our case-study countries in South Asia and sub-Saharan Africa have political parties that fit this model. These types of parties can promote women's interests quickly and allow for the inclusion of a large number of women in politics, since the centralized party leadership is able to overcome resistance from a conservative opposition. The influence of women representatives in these parties will depend on their relationship with the top leadership and their patronage. Both Rwanda's Rwandan Patriotic Front (RPF) and Uganda's National Resistance Movement (NRM) had leaderships who were willing to promote women's representation and gender equitable policies, which led to measures being taken to increase women's representation at various levels and various policy measures for promoting gender equity. In Uganda, NRM leadership was interested in women's representation mainly for the following reasons: a) establishing a vote bank through the creation of a new constituency; and b) appearing to address a 'progressive' agenda that enhanced NRM's legitimacy (Goetz 2003a; Tripp 2003). The disadvantage of an informal-centralized model is that once patronage is withdrawn, women's influence inside the party and in policymaking can erode quickly, as can be seen in the Ugandan case in the last decade (Tripp 2003; Goetz 2003b).

Besides party type, the nature and culture of political competition influence women's participation in politics. Campaign financing systems and the levels of violence and intimidation in political campaigns influence women's participation in politics (Tripp 2003). Women have a weaker resource base. In Brazil, where funds are collected by the parties and distributed according to priorities, women face significant difficulties (Araujo 2010). Where substantial finances are required to run for office and campaign-financing is inadequately monitored by the state, women tend to lose out. Rising levels of violence and criminal elements in campaigns, as in the case of Bangladesh, masculinize political spaces which exclude women. The culture of aggressive political debates in parliaments and in local government bodies (and other political spaces) may also reduce the political effectiveness of women who are newcomers in politics, particularly those who are the first generation to come in through quotas. The lack of knowledge on government or parliamentary procedures and expertise on technical matters also contribute to women's silence. Research on South African local women councillors and MPs, and on Bangladeshi women MPs show otherwise active and vocal women being rendered silent in formal meetings (Fester 2014; Mbatha 2003; Chowdhury 1994).

What Explains Women Representatives' Influence in Promoting Gender Equity?

Undoubtedly, quotas, party lists, and other forms of affirmative action have increased women's descriptive representation. This form of representation has value since it changes social perceptions about women being in political spaces and creates possibilities for the articulation of women's needs and gender equity concerns (Mansbridge 1999). Beaman et al.'s (2008) study on *panchayats* in India reveals that as they are exposed to female leadership, men's prejudice against women's performance reduces overtime, though their preference for male representatives may not change. But does inclusion in politics lead to political influence?

The empirical evidence on whether descriptive representation leads to substantial representation remains inconclusive (Childs and Krook 2009).[17] Many studies show that the presence of women can lead to changes in legislation and policies, while there are others that show little or no difference between styles and behaviours of male and female leaders. It is argued that if a critical mass of women were present in politics and policy spaces, they would have a significant impact. Studies show that a critical mass[18] of women in local-level forest management committees (Agarwal 2011) or in parliament, such as in the Nordic countries, have led to women being able to influence positive programme and policy outcomes (UNIFEM 2008). Studies conducted in the Western democracies reveal that the presence of a critical mass of women allows them to raise matters of concern, especially issues such as reproductive health, violence against women, policing, and labour rights (see Cueva 2004; Weldon 2002). Both Weldon's (2002) and Htun and Weldon's (2010) research on parliaments using large data sets indicate that a critical mass of women in parliament is more effective when there are strong links with women's movements and where an effective national gender machinery exists. The findings of these two studies indicate that there

[17] See Childs and Krook (2009) for a detailed discussion on critical mass theory and how this issue has been researched.
[18] The popular notion is that one third of the representatives are women.

is a need to move beyond critical mass theory and focus on *how* the substantive representation of women occurs instead of just focusing on *when* women act for women.

The critical mass theory assumes that there is a linear relationship between numbers and outcomes and a (yet unknown) tipping point at which there is substantive representation (Childs and Krook 2009). This linear assumption does not always hold. How women (or male) representatives may choose to act depends on: a) contexts and opportunities for raising women's needs and gender equity concerns; b) the identity and interests of the individual representatives; c) how representatives and others perceive 'women's issues'; and d) the gendered nature of the policy-making processes. John's (2007) study on women representatives in urban municipalities in India indicates that the presence of a critical mass of women may not *automatically* lead to the promotion of gender equity concerns. The female councillors in these reserved seats acted as individuals who were linked to their parties and did not want to be identified as representatives of women's interests or gender equity which put them at a disadvantage. They only made exceptions during times of crisis. For example, women councillors in Bangalore were active when it came to women's welfare issues, such as widows' pensions.

In fact, feminist scholars point out that affirmative action measures do not *automatically* reproduce substantial representation (Phillips 1991; Htun 2004), as the impact of women's inclusion is mediated by different factors. Women ushered in through the gender quota by different affirmative action measures may not necessarily focus on negotiating gender equitable programme and policy outcomes for women, or have policy leverage. Feminist scholars also argue the underlying principle of quotas is essentialist as it homogenizes women assuming that all women have the same values and that men are unable to represent gender equity concerns (Goetz and Nyamu-Musembi 2008).

Some studies conducted in India show that quotas work well for social groups that are geographically concentrated with clear group interests, particularly for groups based on caste rather than gender (Htun 2004). As gender interests are shaped by multiple factors and women in an electoral constituency have diverse interests as a social group, representation of these through gender quotas taking 'women as an independent category' is difficult (Menon 2000). Research also shows that quotas in many contexts, such as in Rwanda, Uganda, Bangladesh, and Egypt (before the revolution) have largely benefited educated and politically elite women in accessing political office. However, their social legitimacy to represent gender equity concerns or their understanding of women's group interests may be constrained (Tadros 2010; Burnet 2008; Tamale 1999; Chowdhury 1994).

Though the connection between women's presence in politics and the inclusion of issues in public debate that are *perceived* as 'women's issues' is inconclusive; women representatives do tend to express more concern over domestic violence, reproductive health, and women's welfare compared to men (Tripp 2003; Goetz and Nyamu-Musembi 2008). Rai's (1997) study on women parliamentarians in India shows that although women's issues were not high-priority issues for women MPs, most felt the compulsion to take up matters of women's welfare and violence against women, and these issues tended to unite women MPs across party lines. In all of the case-study countries during the transitional period, women representatives have focused their energies on reforming or introducing new laws on domestic violence, reproductive health, and property rights. In Uganda, Rwanda, and South Africa women representatives were part of constitutional commissions and were able to include gender equality clauses in the constitution despite opposition by traditional elites (Goetz and Hassim 2003; Tripp 2003; Burnet 2008).

Women parliamentarians in Rwanda, Uganda, South Africa, and Brazil have also created cross-party caucuses on gender equality, and in South Africa they have created a standing committee in the parliament on women's rights. These caucuses have had mixed success in promoting gender equality in parliamentary debates. The Rwandan women's caucus was instrumental in drafting and lobbying for the Inheritance Act in 1999, which allowed women to register property and open bank accounts under their own name for the first time (Burnet 2008). In Uganda, the women's caucus was able to use the principle of non-discrimination to push through affirmative action for women's representation. However, they were not effective in promoting the co-ownership clause in the Land Act 1998 as they could not create a common platform as the NRM party leadership was not in agreement with this demand (Goetz 2003a; Tripp 2003). In South Africa, the ANC women's caucus created effective links with the male parliamentarians and lobbied for change in the Constitution and other gender equitable policies (Kemp et al. 1995; Hassim 2003). The women's caucus in the Brazilian Congress, along with feminist lobbying groups, have managed to secure the approval of laws against domestic violence and sexual harassment, legislation on women's health and maternity benefits (Sardenberg and Acosta 2014). These findings indicate that a closer analysis of the contextual factors within which gender quotas are being introduced is required for understanding the political effectiveness of women representatives.

Unsurprisingly, given the entrenched nature of patriarchy combined with other class, caste, and racial interests at the local level, women representatives have difficulties in promoting gender equitable programmes and policies in the case-study countries. Studies on India, Bangladesh, and Uganda show that women representatives face male resistance in accessing development budgets, centrally allocated resources, and in chairing important committees (Hossain and Akhter 2011; Mohanty 2007; Goetz 2003a). Countries such as Bangladesh have provisions that stipulate that women should be chairs of at least one third of all project development committees and members of one third of all project implementation committees and distribute 30 per cent of the resources allocated by the centre. Though these provisions have ensured women's inclusion into committees, their capacity to represent gender equity concerns remains debatable and women members have been used by chairs to implement their own projects (Nazneen and Tasneem 2010).

Despite these difficulties faced by women representatives in local government, both quantitative and qualitative studies show that women representatives have tried to address complaints filed by women, and the needs of women, such as access to water and other common resources and women's employment in government schemes. Comparative research on *panchayats* in West Bengal and Rajasthan provinces in India show that there is a systematic difference in the complaints and requests filed based on the sex of the person filing the complaint. More women than men filed complaints on water resource management. The number of drinking water projects were 60 per cent higher in councils with female heads compared to councils which had male *sarpanchs*. In West Bengal, female-led councils undertook road-building projects at a higher rate than male-led councils, where jobs were likely to go to females. The authors of the study claim that there was no difference in the type of requests that were made to male- and female-headed councils but the difference was in the nature of the response to women's requests (Chattopadhay and Duflo 2004). Admittedly, just because female *sarpanchs* prioritized water or roads does not necessarily imply that these are perceived as women's needs, even if more women have complained about these. In fact, Agarwal (2011) points out that many of the female *sarpanchs* perceive these as general issues that are important for both men and women in their constituency. Actually, what are considered as women's needs at times may adversely influence what is taken up in the local councils. Female representatives may be reluctant to push issues that are perceived as 'women's issues' or being identified as the women's representative since this may put them at a disadvantage electorally.

There are considerable research gaps in understanding the links between women's inclusion in politics through quotas and other measures and their ability to exercise influence and promote gender equity. Systematic and comparative research on women representatives is required to explore: what type of women enter politics through quotas and other means; what type of gender agenda is espoused by them; how do women become critical actors promoting gender equity; what strategies do women use to negotiate gender equity interests with their parties and other social actors; when and why do other actors facilitate the promotion of gender equity agenda; and so on.

Women's Representation, Participation, and Influence in Bureaucracy and Invited Spaces

The difficulties women representatives face in the formal political sphere led women's movement activists and also the state to focus on ensuring the representation of women in other institutional forums. These include various government machineries, women's ministries, gender commissions, and so on. We also focus on women's inclusion and participation in the invited spaces (semi-formal) created by the state for engaging citizens at the community/local levels such as health-watch committees, and policy consultation processes, such as those for the Poverty Reduction Strategy (PRS).

National Gender Machineries

All of the case-study countries have created national gender machineries for 'bureaucratized representation' (Goetz 2003b) to promote gender equity in state programmes and policy. In Chile, Servicio Nacional de la Mujer (SERNAM), the national women's machinery, played a key role in advocating for legislation against domestic violence, sexual harassment, and gender discrimination, including laws on day care for seasonal workers and maternity leave for domestic employees (Waylen 1997). In Rwanda, the Women and Gender Ministry played a key role in creating a clear gender focus within the bureaucracy and in disseminating women's demands that emerge through the Women's Councils at the village level and their national secretariat (Burnet 2008). In Uganda, the Women's Ministry, which had strong links with women's organizations and associations, acted to promote their demands (Goetz 2003a).

For Bangladesh, Uganda, Rwanda, and Nepal, the discussion in international UN women's conferences on state gender machineries facilitated the establishment of national gender machineries. In the sub-Saharan context—for example, Rwanda and South Africa—these national gender machineries, such as the Gender Equality Commission (South Africa) and the Ministry of Women and Gender (Rwanda), were also products of negotiations between the women's movement and the transitional government, where the latter wanted to signal its commitment to gender equity. In Chile, the democratic transition and women's participation in the democratic movement, and pressure by the women's movement on the state and political parties created space for the creation of SERNAM (Frohman and Valdez 1995).

The effectiveness of 'bureaucratized representation' by these gender machineries depends on their: expertise, budgets, ability to review policies formulated by other departments, ability to co-ordinate different policies on gender, and ability to sanction other departments if they fail to promote gender equity in their policies. In Bangladesh, though the Ministry of Women and Children's Affairs (MOWCA) co-ordinates the affairs of other ministries using gender focal points, it has limited influence since it cannot sanction any government body for not addressing gender equity in their policies or programmes (UNIFEM 2008). Resource constraint is a major drawback; in South Africa the Gender Equality Commission's work was stretched in terms of time, staff, and money, which created difficulties for fulfilling its mandate (Fester 2014). In Chile, SERNAM's activities have been constrained by lack of finance, lack of autonomy, close ties with political parties, and an absence of institutional power to influence other ministries. At times SERNAM's goals that threaten gender relations have been overtly opposed by other ministries and government bodies (Waylen 1997).

The political and international contexts may also affect these national machineries' ability to perform. The work of the Commission on the Status of Women in India (CSWI) attracted attention during the UN women's decade (1975–85), which led to a concerted effort to study the impact of various development measures on poor and rural women in India. CSWI's work also gained importance in the 1970s because the emergency period imposed by the Congress Party created a context where work on women's issues was not considered as politically dangerous as other subjects (Kumar 1995). Many of the national gender machineries had gained momentum and support from the state around the time of the Beijing conference (UNIFEM 2008), which points to the role played by international discourses for creating space.

Women in Bureaucracy

Bureaucracy is a gendered hierarchy where women occupy the lower ranks; and inclusion of women in higher positions creates the possibility for change (Randall and Waylen 1998). Uganda and Rwanda have taken affirmative action for including women in the cabinet and also in high-level bureaucratic positions. Whether women's inclusion in bureaucracy through quotas and in higher positions changes how it addresses gender equity depends on *which* women are incorporated through affirmative action and *whether* they have interests in promoting gender equity. Goetz (2003b) point out that women in the cabinet or chief executives are less likely to be feminists promoting gender equity. Even if they had strong links with the women's movement, as Goetz's study (2003a) on Uganda shows, feminist women in Museveni's cabinet were unable to speak for incorporation of the co-ownership clause since they had to adhere to the collective responsibility of the cabinet.

Top bureaucratic officials may act as 'femocrats' (i.e. feminist bureaucrat) to advance gender equitable policies (Kardam 1997) through skilful mobilization of facts, accurate identification and cultivation of allies within the bureaucracy, and ensuring fit between the suggested policy changes and the goals of the specific bureaucratic organization.

Women's representation in public bureaucracies can be increased through affirmative action. For example, Bangladesh has a 15 per cent quota for women in bureaucracy. These quotas can help women to overcome barriers to entry but they may also stall further recruitment (as in the case of Bangladesh) and undermine the perceived merit of women who were hired to fill quotas. In Bangladesh, women bureaucrats are also concentrated in higher numbers in 'softer' sectors such as education and health, which then reduces the possibilities of women's representation in important sectors such as finance, infrastructure, and agriculture (Sultan, n.d.). Studies conducted in the US show that bureaucratic officials, irrespective of gender, are willing to promote gender equity concerns when: a) there is room for manoeuvre within the organization to raise gender concerns; and b) when addressing gender concerns would not lead to sanctions and would advance their careers (UNIFEM 2008). These indicate the importance of the design of the institutional systems that incentivizes promoting gender equity concerns.

The presence of women in larger numbers in specific sectors may create scope for increased responsiveness to women's needs at the front-line level. Studies are inconclusive about whether the gender of the staff influences how front-line workers address women's needs. Goetz's (1997) study on state microfinance institutions show that women clients are more comfortable in raising issues with the female front-line workers given the gendered hierarchical nature of the relationship between the worker and the client. In fact, women workers were more willing to use their discretionary powers to address these concerns raised by their clients. Although these understandings did not translate into systematic action on behalf of the front-line workers since the incentive, monitoring, and performance measurement systems did not include addressing gender equity concerns as a performance measurement indicator.

Women's Participation in Invited Spaces and Citizen's Forums

Contemporary measures for enhancing responsiveness of the state include the creation of gender-sensitive local government processes, the inclusion of women in local citizen's councils, the establishment of new spaces for consultation on service delivery and policy processes. However, implementation of citizen's councils or state-created consultative forums are conducted in a ritualistic manner, which limits their effectiveness. For example, Kerala and Madhya Pradesh provinces in India require one third of the participants in village meetings to be female to reach quorum. Kerala also requires local councils to earmark 10 per cent of the development funds they receive from the state for 'women's development projects' and all female subgroups of the village assembly are in charge of planning for and spending this fund. However, there are cases reported in Kerala where women have been coerced into diverting these funds for other purposes. Local councillors have tried to influence which type of women are present in village assemblies to make the 30 per cent quorum (Goetz 2003b).

Studies show that the extent to which women's needs and gender equity concerns are represented in citizen's forums and invited spaces depends on the following: a) who (including which women) enters these spaces and their ability to voice demands; b) how representation of women's needs and gender equity is facilitated in these spaces; c) if these spaces have authority to influence the way service is delivered; and d) whether women and other actors willing to act on behalf of women are able to establish horizontal and vertical links with other groups and state actors (Cornwall and Coleho 2007). Mohanty's (2007) research on watershed project committees in Rajasthan, India illustrates these points. She found elite men (based on caste and class) decided which women were included in these committees and the men controlled the agenda. Interestingly in the same area the women's participation in the Integrated Child Development Scheme (ICDS) was high and effective. Women participating in these schemes were recruited from the community by government officials, which rendered a form of 'professional' status on women. This demonstrates that the institutional design of these forums and local gender ideologies have strong influences on whether women are able to participate effectively.

The lack of an institutionalized place in policy/service delivery discussions and formal rights to redress may constrain the quality of women's participation in these invited spaces. Goetz's (2003b) analysis of joint monitoring of the Public Distribution Scheme (PDS) in Mumbai, India illustrates these points. The Regional Controller of Rationing had invited civil society groups, including women's groups, to participate in official monitoring and preventing corrupt practices, but women had no formal rights. However, upon his departure, women lost access to this official space.

Interests of traditional and ethnically defined local elites may constrain how women's participation and gender equity is addressed within local citizen's forums. For example, traditional authorities objected to the introduction of democratic councils and women's representation in councils in South Africa (Mbatha 2003).

Community gendered norms and power relations at the local level may limit how much space women have for voicing their demands and the role they play. Agarwal's (2011) comparative research on Joint Forest Management (JFM) groups in India and Nepal found that communities were resistant to women's representation in these spaces created by the state. In community forest groups where external actors, such as gender-sensitive state officials and NGOs, have stipulated conditions on women's inclusion in committees and focused on distributional equity issues, women's participation in the Community Forest Groups (CFGs) changed. Effective links with women's movement organizations or social movement oriented organizations with a strong focus on gender brings women's interests to the forefront in these spaces.

Most of the research discussed above has focused on: how various structural factors limit women's participation; specific programme or case analysis of where women have successfully negotiated for change in delivery of services; and how women's sense of citizenship emerged from being engaged in 'invited' forums (Agarwal 2011; Cornwall and Coleho 2007). A political-settlement perspective may allow us to trace in a context-specific, historical manner how these different methods used for women's inclusion into these state-created forums, lead from development of a sense of citizenship towards a redrawing of social contracts with the state by women as a collective group?

Women's Movements Representing and Influencing Gender Inclusive Development

Women's movements in developing countries have a long history; women's groups and associations have been a part of anti-colonial movements, independence struggles, anti-authoritarian movements (Basu 1995; Waylen 1996; Molyneux 2001). Women's participation in these independence or anti-colonial struggles, revolutions, or wider political movements have allowed women during critical moments of state formation to make claims over being included in political institutions and policy.

Despite being vibrant and innovative, the women's movement has had fewer successes in terms of engendering political processes and institutions (even taking into consideration the introduction of quotas) in the last century (Basu 2010).[19] The movement has been successful in pursuing legal

[19] This does not imply that women's representation in politics was not highlighted in the feminist agenda. By the time the second wave of the feminist movement started in the 1960s in most Western democracies, women had the right to vote and other formal political rights, though the gender bias within political institutions remained. Given this context, when agendas were drawn up for action, they were influenced by the context within which women's issues were being debated.

reforms and bringing about changes in state policies in particular areas such as reproductive health, education for women, child welfare, and labour rights. Feminists also point out that these policy changes were facilitated by the instrumental needs of the state, such as controlling population growth and increasing productivity. In fact, feminists have been more successful in bringing discursive changes in how women are thought about as a development category compared to tangible policy gains (Mukhopadhyay and Singh 2007).

At the national level, mobilization around policy processes in particular has been led by women's groups which are largely composed of professional middle-class and elite women. The elite and middle-class composition of women's/feminist groups and their leadership in mobilization around policies have led to debates about the elite bias/focus in women's/feminist movements. It has also raised questions about whether women's groups effectively represent the interests of grassroots members and about their accountability to this constituency (Basu 2010). For example, in Bangladesh, women's movements have been successful in mobilizing around violence against women and legal reforms but have failed to mobilize around issues that are pertinent to poor rural women, such as migration or equal wage in the informal sector. In Brazil, Chile, and Mexico, feminism took the form of 'popular feminism' only when the movement was able to bring into the fold concerns of urban and rural working-class women (Lamas et al. 1995; Frohman and Valdez 1995; Soares et al. 1995). The elite and middle-class bias in the women's movement and whether it is able to represent the interests of poor women or create strong alliances with grassroots and working-women's groups is a debate that is pertinent for unpacking political settlement around gender from a feminist perspective.

At the local level, grassroots women's groups have usually mobilized around women's needs, such as the quality of service delivery by the state with the focus on holding the state to account (Macpherson 2008; Molyneux 2001). These movements focusing on local concerns have allowed women to contextualize their concerns within the wider social/political context and also integrate a gender analysis. While some of these movements are focused on specific or singular issues, such as women's protests against price hikes in India or Kenya; or protests against the dismantling of state services as in Peru or Chile (Basu 1995; Waylen 1997), but some of these local movements also addressed gender inequity. For example, the anti-alcohol movement in Andhra Pradesh, India by local women's groups, not only focused on banning alcohol and violence against women and created space for raising different issues, it also instilled a sense of citizenship among women and demands for wider participation (Goetz and Nyamu-Musembi 2008). Grassroots membership organizations, such as Self-Employed Women's Association (SEWA) in India, which aimed at organizing informal women workers, have been successful in creating structures and strategies that allow them to negotiate workers' wages and working conditions at the local level and also in national policy spaces (Kabeer 1994). The domestic women workers' association in Brazil (Sardenberg and Acosta 2014) and the membership-based migrant women workers' association in Bangladesh started off as small associations (Nazneen and Sultan 2014) and later evolved into larger organizations advocating national strategies and policies that would serve the interests of their members.

Women's groups use diverse strategies for mobilizing and negotiating around gender equity concerns at different political and social forums. Analysis of women's movements in our case-study countries shows that these movements by grassroots, policy advocates, and other organizations use the following common strategies: a) build coalitions within the movement on particular issues; b) form alliances with other civil society organizations (CSOs) and the media; c) target selective parts of the state bureaucracy, including local government, concerned ministries, the national gender machinery; d) cultivate allies among women representatives and also among male politicians; e) use international women's rights discourse/human rights discourse to package their demands; and f) establish and highlight their expertise and experience on the particular gender equity issue around which they are mobilizing (Nazneen and Sultan 2014; Randall 1998).

These strategies have produced mixed results in legitimizing women's demands and generating responsiveness from the state and political actors. The issue-based coalitions and alliances have raised the visibility of women's activism within the civil society arena, and also helped to project the strength of their demands. For example, the Ugandan Land Alliance was crucial in raising women's demands for co-ownership (Tripp 2004; Kawamara-Mishambi and Ovonji-Odida 2003). However, these coalitions suffer from internal power struggles. Usually the well-resourced, national groups tend to dominate how agendas are set and the activities of the coalitions, and marginalize the grassroots organizations. This has implications for whether coalitions are seen as being representative of a wider constituency around a particular issue. The Convention on Elimination of All Forms of Discrimination (CEDAW) ratification coalition in Bangladesh is a good example of this particular legitimacy problem (Nazneen and Sultan 2014). Discussions in previous sections on Uganda and South Africa show that allies within the state bureaucracy and political parties, particularly men, and the strong links between women's movements and women representatives created scope for the movements to raise their issues in various forums (Goetz 2003a; Mbatha 2003; Hassim 2003; Htun and Weldon 2010). These coalitions and alliances also demonstrated a clear constituency for which the 'femocrats' and sympathetic representatives were working.

Targeting by women's movements of selective parts of the state which are responsive to women's rights has produced results in representing women's rights issues in different state forums. In the case-study countries women's movements have targeted particular ministries or different levels of the government depending on the nature of the demand and the context within which issues are being raised. This indicates that there are plural entry points in dealing with the state and that opportunities for women may vary across different state institutions (Randall 1998). Comparative studies of how these entry points vary and in-country analysis of when and how women's movements have been able to access different state institutions need to be conducted.

The space available to women's groups to promote a gender equity agenda in politics may vary depending on political opportunity structure context. States that are going through a transitional phase, where the stability of elite alignments is in flux, may create opportunities for women's movements to participate in the negotiation processes and promote gender equity concerns (Castellijo 2011). Immediately after independence or in the post-revolutionary period there is a high level of interest in women's position and condition among the political elite. These issues are closely tied to the modernizing/nation-building agenda which lends them legitimacy (Waylen 1996). Women's movements are able to establish effective links with the political leadership and state during this period, but this interest in improving women's status among state and political actors wanes as time passes (Molyneux 1985; Goetz 2003b).

These observations hold true for some of our case-study countries. The state and the political leadership took a keen interest in women's representation and gender equity in Rwanda and Uganda immediately after the transitional period and women's movements in these countries were able to access the party leadership, voice their demands, create a new discourse around women's rights, and resist traditional authorities (Tripp 2003; Goetz 2003a; Burnet 2008). The inclusion of women in politics through use of quotas, women's active engagement in incorporating the gender equality clause in the constitution in Uganda and South Africa, and changes in inheritance law in Rwanda, all happened during this period. In South Africa, during the period of transition from the apartheid regime, women had the greatest voice and influence on the political leadership and the state machineries (Hassim 2003). In Bangladesh, the women's movement exerted the most influence during the decade of the 1990s when transition from an authoritarian phase took place. Women were able to gender mainstream the national five-year development plans, ensure direct elections for women in local government, and secure legal/policy changes on violence against women (Nazneen and Sultan 2010). In Chile, Brazil, and Mexico, the anti-authoritarian movement created scope for large-scale activism by women, particularly when they mobilized to demand answers for those who had disappeared under the authoritarian regimes (Kemp et al. 1995; Lamas et al. 1995; Soares et al. 1995). This created 'political entitlement' which women's groups claimed during the transitional phase to democracy, however, the space became fragmented as these countries entered a more stable phase and women formally entered policy spaces (Molyneux 2001; Basu 2010).

The international discourses on women's rights and gender equity have played an important role in creating space for women's movement groups to access the state and be consulted on various issues (Tripp 2012). In the case-study countries, for example, in Bangladesh and Rwanda, the UN international conferences and CEDAW shadow reporting processes have created the need for the state to consult women's movements on these issues/processes so that they are able to legitimize states' positions (Burnet 2008; Nazneen and Sultan 2010). In fact, discourses are important features of women's political opportunity framework. Competing ideologies and discourses may influence openings for women's participation in political processes and institutions or place limits on the representation of women's claims (Rai 1996). A key gap in using political-settlement literature for understanding the politics of securing gender-inclusive development is that the political-settlement framework does not include how different ideologies and discourses on gender influence political and social actors.

What Can We Say about the Gendered Politics of Securing Inclusive Development?

The analysis presented above using the extended Goetz and Hassim (2003) framework shows that there are different reasons why women's participation and representation in politics is supported by different actors. For women's rights activists, some women representatives, and male political leaders, the support of women's representation and participation is ideological. However, most of the actors, particularly political party leaders and the state, have instrumental/pragmatic reasons for including women in political processes and institutions. It is important to unpack these interests and incentives and how these interests are negotiated for understanding whether women's inclusion in politics translates into electoral and policy leverage.

The nature of political opportunity structures, that is, the openness of the political institutions to women's demands, the presence of elite allies in different state and political arenas, and whether states represses women's demands, all have implications for women's effective participation in political processes. Our analysis shows that coalitions and alliances and strong links between women's representatives and the women's movement may have different degrees of influence in promoting women's interests in politics depending on the nature of the political opportunity structures.

Also the discussion in the previous sections of this chapter show that during critical moments of state formation, women were able to claim political inclusion because of their participation in independence or anti-colonial or anti-authoritarian struggles and armed conflicts. Women's roles in these struggles created 'legitimized' entitlements for their inclusion into politics and representative institutions. For India and South Africa, women's active participation and role in sustaining the national struggles influenced how women came to demand inclusion in electoral bodies or political institutions when both these nation states were reforming political structures (Agarwal 2011). In Rwanda and Nepal, women's participation in armed conflict provided legitimacy for claiming equal constitutional rights and also for quotas in the system in the post-conflict scenario (Burnet 2008; Tamang 2004). In Bangladesh, Chile, Uganda, Brazil, and Mexico transition to democracy and women's participation in anti-authoritarian struggles created scope for women to demand inclusion in political institutions (Nazneen and Sultan 2014; Goetz and Hassim 2003; Waylen 1997; Basu 1995).

These findings are summed up in Table 8.2.

Conclusions

Based on our post hoc analysis of the nature of gendered political and state institutions in different country contexts, the following factors play important roles in determining how gender equity concerns are represented and decided upon in politics and policymaking:

1. The interests and incentives of the political and social elites in promoting/obstructing gender equity concerns in political and policymaking processes.
2. The relationship and negotiations that take place between the feminist constituency and these actors on gender equity.
3. The political opportunity structures that create or limit space for making claims around gender equity.
4. The discourses around gender which influence the gender ideologies of these different actors.

Table 8.2. Factors that enabled women's participation and representation in political processes and institutions in case-study countries

Countries	Factors that enable women's participation and inclusion						
	Support among top party leadership.	Coalition within women's movement/and alliances with other civil society organizations including grassroots.	Strong links between women's movement and women representatives/presence of male allies.	Women's movement's ability to resist traditional elites.	International discourse creates legitimacy for women's participation and representation.	Transitional context creates space for women's inclusion (democratic transition; post-revolutionary; post-independence).	Support among bureaucrats.
Nepal	Strong rhetoric within the Maoist party for women's participation.	Broad coalition among women's groups, however ethnic/caste/class interests are not effectively addressed in terms of the electoral system envisaged.	The links between mainstream women's movement groups and the Maoists not strong.	Women's participation in Maoist movement strengthened their position and ensured their legitimacy to make demands for change, which allowed them to contest traditional elites.	Well established in Nepal, which created scope for debating women's inclusion in politics.	Post-conflict; new constitution being formulated, which created scope for debating gender power relations at home/also also in other institutions. Women's participation in the armed struggle created a sense that the new state owed women.	Some support but influenced by class/caste/ethnic interests.
Bangladesh	Women's seats created to strengthen party position and gain legitimacy with international actors.	Strong coalitions within the women's groups and alliances but plagued by internal struggle.	Ineffective links with political parties, very little influence.	Women's participation in politics was not resisted by traditional elite; male resistance to direct elections and other forms of affirmative action exists.	UN decade created scope; CEDAW used to create an alternative discourse to promote women's participation in politics.	Democratic transitions/state repression on other political activities, and women's participation in the struggle for democracy created space for raising women's concerns in the post-authoritarian period.	Existence of femocrats to promote women's participation.
India	Some political leaders have strong commitment to gender equity.	Strong coalitions within women's movement.	Not very effective links with mainstream political parties, although post-independence women's movement had strong claims over Congress for their role in national	Women's representation in the national parliament debated as class/caste and how it translates into gains for these identity-based groups became a key issue.	UN decade and the work of CSWI created a strong focus on women.	Post-independence period—impetus for modernization created scope for promoting women's interests. Women's participation in the independence struggle created political	Existence of femocrats.

(continued)

Table 8.2. (continued)

Countries	Factors that enable women's participation and inclusion						
	Support among top party leadership.	Coalition within women's movement/and alliances with other civil society organizations including grassroots.	Strong links between women's movement and women representatives/presence of male allies.	Women's movement's ability to resist traditional elites.	International discourse creates legitimacy for women's participation and representation.	Transitional context creates space for women's inclusion (democratic transition; post-revolutionary; post-independence)	Support among bureaucrats.
			struggle. Some of the right political parties have strong links with women's wings, however their gender ideology does not focus on promoting gender equity.			entitlements for women. Political repression during emergency period created scope for focus on women.	
Uganda	Support among NRM; NRM had incentives to have women as vote banks.	Strong coalitions within the movement and alliances with other CSOs. However women did not focus on institutionalizing the electoral gains. Cross party caucus became weak.	Fragile links now; initially NRM was supportive later NRM patronage created difficulties for women's movement groups.	Resisted by traditional elites; especially about women's participation in parliament and local government—which dilutes power of the traditional elite.	International discourses and donor funding for gender equity create incentive. Also increase legitimacy.	Transition from dictatorship created scope for renegotiation around gender.	Existence of femocrats.
Rwanda	Support from Kagame and RPF; strong rhetoric on gender equity. Women not	Cross-party caucus existed during transition.	Strong links between women's movement and RPF women's representatives.	Women's inclusion resisted by traditional elites. Women's participation in the RPF and the resistance created scope for women to push for inclusion; created credentials.	The international discourses, especially Beijing and Platform for Action (PFA) had a significant influence in reshaping the gender equity agenda. Also created incentive for the state to address these	Post-conflict situation created scope for negotiating women's inclusion in politics. Large number of war widows and also women's involvement in RPF translated into the need to change existing gender power structures. constitution.	Existence of femocrats, and also inclusion of women in large numbers in bureaucracy. Women were willing to promote gender equity.

	perceived as a threat to RPF.			issues. Rwanda wanted to show that it had moved past the tragedy. Donor assistance and the UN also helped in reshaping institutions. International discourse used to increase profile of women's demands.		Existence of femocrats.
South Africa	ANC strongly endorsed gender equity concerns and women's representation.	Women's National Council played a key role; later cross-party caucus played key role. Alliances with other social movements.	Strong links with political parties, particularly the ANC. Also male allies within political parties.	Resisted by traditional elite; espcially devolution at the local level.	Transition from apartheid created scope for raising gender issues and changes in institutional arrangements for women's representation. Women's participation in the anti-apartheid struggle gave scope for women to claim political entitlements.	

Source: Authors.

Undeniably, our analysis is limited both methodologically[20] and empirically. But it shows how different elements of political settlements[21] could be used for understanding the link between women's inclusion in political processes and gender-inclusive outcomes. But does exploring the gendered politics of securing inclusive development using a political-settlement lens adds value to what we know from feminist political analysis? Are there synergies that exist between the two bodies of literature?

Possibilities of Political Settlement Perspective: What Are the Gaps in Gender/Feminist Analysis and New Questions Emerging?

The political-settlement perspective focuses on structure, agency, and their interaction. This makes political settlement a useful perspective for understanding how women as actors are included and women's needs and gender equity concerns are negotiated in politics and policymaking and the subsequent outcomes. Different elements of political settlement, such as focus on political and social elites (including traditional elites) and their interests and incentives for addressing/hindering gender equitable policies and development outcome and how different political/institutional arrangements facilitate their power to do so, may help in unpacking the opportunities and limits of women's participation in politics and the possibilities for securing gender-inclusive development. The framework also allows us to identify the challengers who negotiate and redraw the boundaries. It allows us to develop a template identifying incentives, interests, institutional nature, and where centres of power lie in negotiating gender equity concerns.

Using this lens to analyse the gendered politics of securing inclusive development in developing countries may contribute to furthering our understanding about gender in Third World politics and development in the following ways.

First, research into women's political representation and policy effectiveness in developing countries has important gaps (Goetz and Hassim 2003). Research on gender analysis of policies focuses on outcomes of policies on women; for example, the impact of health or education policies. These analyses rarely take into account the particular relationships that exist between the state and political and social elites that lead to certain forms of policies. A political-settlement perspective may be helpful in unpacking these relationships and why certain forms of policy measures are undertaken.

---

[20] We did not conduct a rigorous comparative study. We used a common framework to explore the gendered nature of women's inclusion in formal politics and their policy influence in the selected case-study countries based on existing literature.

[21] For example, various actors, interests, and institutions; see Di John and Putzel (2009) for a detailed discussion of various elements.

Second, feminist research on women's representation extensively debates how women are not a homogenous social group and the difficulties this poses in representative democracies. There is less focus on how, when, and why electoral and policy elites consider women an important constituency. When and how can women (including women's groups), who in many cases are excluded by elite or non-elite actors, through collective mobilization challenge existing political settlements on gender? These issues can be explored through this political-settlement perspective.

Third, the gender and development research has focused on the impact of quotas on the promotion of gender equity interests. There is less focus on who (which women) come in through quotas and how that influences policy choices. Little research exists on women in formal political parties and how they negotiate with different political or social constituencies on gender equity concerns. A political-settlement perspective may allow for a more nuanced link between the politics of inclusion and the politics of influence, particularly focusing on how women (and men) become critical actors promoting gender equity concerns.

Fourth, much of the development research on gender and women's inclusion in politics does not use a context-specific and historical analysis of how women as a collective group were able to secure 'political entitlement', especially during moments of state formation and how this interpretation of entitlements affects women's collective ability to secure inclusive development. A political-settlement perspective may be effective in analysing policy areas by focusing on how women initially gain inclusion and trace the effect of these political entitlements on women's ability to influence and secure inclusive development.

Fifth, while feminists acknowledge that patronage and clientelist politics limits women's political effectiveness and the state's accountability to women (and for promoting gender equity concerns, Goetz and Jenkins 2005), there are very few studies that unpack the gender impact of clientelist and patronage-based politics, exploring women's representation in politics, policymaking, and the outcome that results in these contexts.

How Does a Gender Lens Strengthen the Political Settlement Perspective?

A gender lens brings in dimensions that may strengthen the political-settlement framework. The political-settlement framework focuses on incentives and interests and is based on a rational choice analysis that leaves out the role played by ideologies. Gender ideologies play a key role in motivating the behaviour of the actors, both of political and social elites, excluded elites, oppositional non-elites, and women who may want to contest these ideologies. In fact, competing ideologies and discourses around these ideologies influence the nature of the political opportunity structure within which women's interests and gender equity concerns are negotiated. But can political-settlement frameworks accommodate this discursive element around gender ideologies?

This question has relevance for other marginalized groups and non-elite groups if the political-settlement perspective is used for capturing bottom-up negotiations around inclusive development. How we think about inclusive development and interpret the needs of marginalized groups and are challenged by the alternative interpretations forwarded by the marginalized groups (or those actors who promote their interests) and these alternative interpretations *do* influence the way policies are framed; though these discursive changes may not necessarily lead to a tangible change in policy outcomes.

Second, analysis of how gender-inclusive development is secured allows for deepening our understanding of the following factors in achieving and sustaining a political settlement, such as actions by non-elite groups, use of bottom-up strategies by marginalized/excluded groups, and how participation at the local level may create scope for influencing the actors/discourses at the national policy level. It also creates the possibilities for expanding political settlement's focus on the role played by policy coalitions and transnational actors (generally ignored in political settlement), the significance of informal relations between different actors (intra-elite negotiations, negotiations with excluded elite/oppositional non-elite) in negotiating an outcome, (generally ignored in PS frameworks) and in influencing the inclusive nature of political settlements.

Where Are We Now?

In sum, both a political-settlement approach and feminist political analysis stand to gain from closing the gap between these two bodies of literature. Given that there are no studies that analyse political settlements from a gender perspective in the developing world, research in this area embodies possibilities for generating new knowledge. In this chapter we went about addressing this issue in a roundabout manner focusing on different bodies of literature that may provide information on different elements of political settlement. Our discussion on gendered politics and existing feminist political analysis show that there are knowledge gaps in understanding gendered politics of inclusive development. In order to move forward we need to focus on addressing the dilemmas that arise from what the political-settlement framework excludes (ideology, discourse, bottom-up strategies) and expand the parameters.

9

Ethnicity, State Capacity, and Development: Reconsidering Causal Connections

Prerna Singh and Matthias vom Hau

The relationship between identity, and more specifically ethnicity, and state capacity has received increasing attention in the social sciences.[1] Scholars have developed sophisticated arguments about how variations in the quality and reach of state infrastructure and services have shaped ethnic-based identification and mobilization (Fearon and Laitin 2003; Lieberman and Singh 2012; Loveman 2005; Wimmer 2002). Similarly, there is a growing literature on how ethnic identities influence state capacity outcomes. Most prominently, a large and influential body of scholarship in political economy argues that ethnic diversity impedes public goods provision. Cross-national studies in this tradition, most prominently the seminal article by William Easterly and Ross Levine (1997), suggest that ethnically heterogeneous countries usually suffer from inadequate public goods such low-quality schools, poor roads, and insufficient electricity grids (see also Rafael La Porta et al. 1999). Sub-national studies come to comparable conclusions, whether in developed or developing contexts.[2] The much-cited article by Alberto

[1] The order of authorship is alphabetical. The chapter is part of a larger research initiative on ethnicity and state capacity. We are grateful to the Ministerio de Ciencia e Innovación (MICINN) in Spain, the Weatherhead Center for International Affairs (WCFIA) at Harvard University, and the Effective States and Inclusive Development (ESID) Research Centre at the University of Manchester for their generous funding of this endeavour. We would like to especially thank Fulya Apaydin, Jorge Dominguez, Sam Hickey, Steve Levitsky, Kunal Sen, Hillel Soifer, and all the participants of the 2013 workshop on ethnicity and state capacity in Cambridge, MA, for their helpful comments on the argument developed so far. All errors are our own.
[2] Ken Jackson (2013), for example, identifies ethnic diversity as leading to inferior public goods provision in sub-Saharan Africa.

Alesina, Reza Baqir, and William Easterly (1999) is just one of a large litera-ture arguing that more ethnically diverse cities and counties in the United States are less invested in core public goods.[3] Broadly similar findings have been reported for developing countries. For example, Abhijit Banerjee and his co-authors (2005, 2007) find support for the ethnic diversity and public goods provision hypothesis in India, while Edward Miguel and Mary Kay Gugerty (2005) show how local ethnic diversity in Kenya is associated with lower-quality public goods.

This chapter pursues a critical reassessment of the ethnic diversity and public goods provision scholarship. Our main line of critique concerns the causal mechanism supported by this literature. Most of the works in this research tradition focus on inter-ethnic cooperation. Specifically, they hypothesize that ethnic fractionalization leads to conflicting preferences, which in turn prevent inter-ethnic cooperation, either to generate desired goods or to pressure the state to provide them. Yet, an exclusive focus on inter-ethnic cooperation ignores a wider range of other plausible causal pathways through which ethnicity might influence public goods provision. The main thrust of this chapter builds towards filling this gap. We review a broader literature that does explore, or at least gives us some useful implicit insights about, the effects of ethnicity on state capacity. Against this back-drop we identify and develop distinct theoretical mechanisms through which ethnicity shapes the ability of states to provide public goods.[4] The chapter thus uses various bodies of work as a springboard to distil a larger set of possible causal pathways that move beyond the idea that collective action across different ethnic groups has a direct impact on state capacity. Those mechanisms include the mobilizing efforts by a particular ethnic group, the behaviour of other collective actors, and institutional change.

In particular, our first broad set of mechanisms focuses on the ways in which the actions of ethnic groups directly affect state capacity. Within this set, an initial batch of mechanisms emphasizes the link between inter-ethnic cooperation and the ability of states to provide public goods. Another batch highlights the link between mobilization by a particular ethnic group and state capacity. Here the focus is on how the level of ethnic inclusion can affect ethnic mobilization, which can have positive or negative effects on state capacity, depending on, most importantly, the type of ethnic-based collective action.

---

[3] Other major studies on ethnic diversity and public goods provision in the context of the United States include Goldin and Katz (1997), Lieberman (1993), Luttmer (2001), and Poterba (1997). See Costa and Khan (2003) for an overview of this literature.

[4] Tilly (2001), McAdam et al. (2001), and Rueschemeyer (2009) are important inspirations for treating the development of causal mechanisms as key to theoretical advancement.

A second set of mechanisms puts the analytical spotlight on the ways in which ethnicity shapes state capacity by affecting the interests and behaviour of other collective actors. One group of mechanisms in this line of reasoning focuses on the alliance strategies of societal elites. In particular, they hypothesize that distinct forms of ethnic exclusion or ethnic mobilization entail different types of coalitions between these elites and subordinate sectors and/or the state, which in turn shape the extractive capacity of states. Another batch of mechanisms in this line of reasoning emphasizes that the effects of ethnic exclusion or ethnic mobilization on state capacity are mediated by state elite preferences, whether derived from political survival considerations or informed by broader cultural understandings of ethnic groups, official nationalist narratives, and collective memories of prior ethnic conflict.

Our chapter further suggests that institutional change—through both formal and informal institutional arrangements—constitutes a third major causal pathway by which ethnicity shapes state capacity. Within formal institutional arrangements, we explore how ethnic mobilization can result in the inclusion of ethnic groups through existing representative institutions (e.g. in the form of quotas or power-sharing arrangements) and how this influences state capacity through feedback effects on ethnic-based collective action. We also examine how ethnic mobilization can prompt the creation of new formal institutional arrangements, which can in turn affect the territorial reach of a state and its capacity to provide public goods. In addition, we also analyse how the inclusion of mobilized ethnic groups through informal institutional arrangements is likely to entail the biased distribution of state resources.

Taken together, and summarized in Table 9.1, this chapter identifies three broad sets of mechanisms through which ethnicity might influence state capacity. The next section provides a conceptual background discussion of the key concepts. The subsequent sections develop in more detail how inter-ethnic cooperation, the mobilization of ethnic groups,

Table 9.1. How ethnicity affects state capacity: causal mechanisms

	Causal mechanism set
(A)	Actions by ethnic groups • Inter-ethnic cooperation • Mobilization by particular group
(B)	Actions by other collective actors • Alliance strategies of societal elites • Strategic actions by state actors
(C)	Institutional change • Ethnic inclusion via formal institutions • Ethnic inclusion via informal institutions

Source: Authors.

the alliance strategies of societal elites, the interests and perceptions of state officials, and formal/informal institutional change operate as causal mechanisms that link ethnicity to state capacity. In the concluding discussion we try to foreshadow possible implications of this chapter for an alternative approach to the influential ethnic diversity and public goods provision hypothesis.

Conceptualization and Measurement Strategies

Both ethnicity and state capacity are much-debated concepts that have generated a large and often controversial literature on how to conceptualize and measure them.[5] In this review chapter we flag major differences and similarities in the conceptualization and measurement of these two concepts, which allows us to situate political economy works on the ethnic diversity and public goods provision hypothesis within the broader literature and put different bodies of scholarship into dialogue.

Ethnicity

At the most basic level, ethnicity refers to relations of membership structured around a belief in a shared culture and common ancestry. These relations are considered significant by members and outsiders, and are constituted through processes of self-identification and external ascription (Barth 1969; Jenkins 1997).[6] Yet there exist a variety of different approaches on how to disaggregate this conceptualization of ethnicity and make it operational for empirical research (Lieberman and Singh 2012; Wimmer 2012a).[7]

The majority of studies that examine the ethnic diversity and public goods provision hypothesis approach ethnicity in demographic terms. This research tradition is primarily concerned with the relative size and number of distinct ethnic groups within a unit of analysis (a country, or a sub-national unit, whether metropolitan areas or municipalities). Accordingly, its

---

[5] See, for example, Chandra and Wilkinson (2008) and Lieberman and Singh (2012) for distinct approaches to the conceptualization and measurement of ethnicity. Hendrix (2010), Soifer (2012), and Saylor (2013) are recent methodological discussions on the measurement of state capacity.

[6] This conceptualization avoids compartmentalization by treating 'race' and nationhood as subtypes of ethnicity, and not as analytically distinct phenomena (Wimmer 2008, 2012). The fusion of beliefs in a common culture and shared ancestry with claims for national sovereignty and the control of a state is characteristic of nations, while the association of phenotype with common descent delimitates racial groups and categories.

[7] Here we follow Adcock and Collier's (2001) distinction between root concept and fully specified conceptualization.

measurement strategies seek to identify the extent of ethnic fragmentation or heterogeneity. In so doing, studies usually rely on an ethnic fragmentation index, which measures the probability that two randomly selected individuals in a given country, city, or county belong to different ethnic groups. Specifically, cross-national analyses in this line of work tend to focus on ethnolinguistic fragmentation (ELF) and employ various data sets, most importantly the *Atlas Narodov Mira* (Atlas of the Peoples of the World), an ethnolinguistic fractionalization index first developed by researchers in the Soviet Union during the 1960s, which increases its value with the number of different language groups and the relatively equal size of these groups (Easterly and Levine 1997, pp. 1218–23; La Porta et al. 1999, p. 238). Other studies construct an ethnic fractionalization index based on self-identified racial identity from census data (Alesina et al. 1999, pp. 1254–5) or surveys (Luttmer 2001, pp. 502–5). Sub-national studies of ethnic diversity in developing countries equally replicate the ELF-based approach and build ethnic fractionalization indices based on their own survey data (Miguel and Gugerty 2005, pp. 2341, 2364) or on existing census data (Banerjee et al. 2005, pp. 641–3).

Yet, this is not the only way to operationalize ethnicity. A comprehensive look at the literature reveals that there are at least two other major approaches to conceptualization and measurement. One of them combines ethnic demography with a focus on relative group power. This perspective compares ethnic groups in terms of their control over economic and socio-political resources (Baldwin and Huber 2010; Cederman et al. 2010; Cederman and Girardin 2007; Chandra and Wilkinson 2008; Lieberman 2003; Østby 2008) and differentiates between the extent of ethnic exclusion that prevails in a given social arrangement. Another body of scholarship focuses on ethnic mobilization, which broadly refers to collective action that draws on a sense of shared origins and identification with a joint way of life as the basis for political claims-making (McAdam et al. 2001; Olzak 1983; Yashar 2005). Ethnic mobilization manifests itself in a variety of institutional and organizational vehicles, including political parties, social movements, civic associations, and the like. Meaningful variation at the aggregate level can be traced to different intensities in the collective action of ethnic groups, distinct strategies (e.g. violent and non-violent tactics), but also differences in the nature of demands and geographical location (e.g. rural vs. urban) of ethnic mobilization.

Taken together, there are at least three contrasting approaches to move from root concept to a more specified conceptualization of ethnicity. As we will show below, each of these approaches tends to lead to distinct causal mechanism hypotheses about how ethnicity affects state capacity.

State Capacity

There is also a general consensus about the basic definition of state capacity. Most of the relevant literature refers to state capacity as the ability of states to penetrate society and implement their decisions (Saylor 2013; see also Besley and Persson 2009; Mann 1984; Migdal 1988; Stepan 1978; Soifer and vom Hau 2008). Scholars further agree that the concept is multidimensional and needs to be further unpacked (vom Hau 2012; Soifer 2008, 2012).

We identify two broad approaches to the disaggregation of state capacity. One perspective centres on the *outputs* of state activities in order to detect variations (e.g. Alesina et al. 1999; Algan et al. 2011; Baldwin and Huber 2010; Miguel and Gugerty 2005). Specifically, the focus is on the aggregate level, distribution and geographic coverage of public services and goods, whether those are policing, education, health care, or transport infrastructure. This conceptual approach characterizes most of the political economy scholarship on ethnic diversity and public goods provision. These works usually combine some measure(s) of education with other measures of public goods. For instance, Easterly and Levine (1997, pp. 1211–12) focus on educational attainment, together with a measure of telephones per worker.[8] Alesina et al. (1999, pp. 1256–7) trace public goods provision by examining the share of spending on education, roads, and sewage and trash collection in different cities and metropolitan areas of the United States. Banerjee et al. (2005, pp. 644–5) concentrate on the extent to which similar kinds of public goods are available in Indian villages, while Miguel and Gugerty's (2005, pp. 2341–7) measurement strategy is equally concerned with education and examines local school funding collected per student and maintenance fees for water wells. Taken together, this brief sketch illustrates that schooling (in combination with indicators of infrastructure) is the most prominent measurement strategy in an output-centred approach to state capacity.

Another body of work, however, puts the emphasis on *inputs*, or the particular organizational characteristics that underpin the ability of states to pursue their projects (Soifer and vom 2008; vom Hau 2012; Giraudy 2012). Works in this line of research usually highlight (one or more of) the following features as distinctive of high-capacity states. One is administrative competence, which is indicated by an effective bureaucracy associated with meritocratic recruitment, standardized procedures, predictable careers, and a strong esprit de corps among state officials.[9] A second feature is territorial reach, or the spatial spread

---

[8] The telephone indicator is cross-checked against other indicators, for which there is less systematic evidence available: the percentage of paved roads, and percentage of power losses in the electricity system (Easterly and Levine 1997, pp. 211–12).

[9] Works establishing this position include Carpenter (2001), Evans and Rauch (1999), Gorski (1995), and Weber (1978).

(or unevenness) of state infrastructure across national territory.[10] A third one is extraction, or the ability of states to extract resources from society, which has long been at the forefront of the study of state capacity.[11] Combining input- and output-centred perspectives on state capacity enables us to bring these distinct literatures into dialogue and identify a range of causal mechanisms by which ethnicity influences the ability of states to implement their policy choices.

Causal Mechanism Set (A): Actions by Ethnic Groups

How does ethnicity then affect state capacity? Different bodies of scholarship identify a number of possible causal pathways. This chapter groups them into three broad sets. As shown in Table 9.2, the defining characteristic of the first set is that those mechanisms hypothesize a direct effect of the actions by ethnic groups on state capacity.

(A1) Ethnic Diversity and Inter-ethnic Cooperation

Within the first mechanism set, one batch focuses on inter-ethnic cooperation. Most of the political economy scholarship on the topic squarely fits there. Specifically, this literature argues that ethnicity, conceptualized as ethnic diversity, impedes public goods provision.

The starting point is the idea that the provision of public services such as roads, schools, or health clinics requires ethnic groups to cooperate with each other. In order to obtain public goods, individuals from different ethnic backgrounds must act together, whether they generate these goods themselves or lobby the state to provide them. Yet, collective action for public goods cannot be taken for granted, especially not in ethnically diverse settings. This is for at least two reasons. One, as suggested by Alesina et al. (1999, p. 1244), is that because of their culture or their socio-economic position, ethnic groups differ in their preferences for particular public goods. Another is that members of an ethnic group prefer the benefits of a particular public good to remain among their co-ethnics and therefore undervalue it if members of other ethnic groups can also access it.

In fleshing out this mechanism, many works in this research tradition focus on the way in which ethnic diversity impedes the capacity of *communities* to engage in collective action to provide public goods (Khwaja 2008; Miguel

---

[10] Important theoretical contributions to this perspective on state capacity are Mann (1984, 1986), O'Donnell (1993), and Herbst (2000). See also Soifer and vom Hau (2008).
[11] Major contributions to this literature are Bräutigam et al. (2008), Levi (1988), Lieberman (2003), Tilly (1992), and Slater (2010). For an excellent overview see Lieberman (2002); for a critical stance on taxation as an indicator of state capacity see Fukuyama (2004).

Table 9.2. Causal mechanism set (A): actions by ethnic groups

	Conceptual approach to ethnicity	Causal mechanism	Affected dimension(s) of state capacity
(A1)	Ethnic diversity	Inter-ethnic cooperation (–) (lobbying for public goods)	Public goods provision (–)
(A2)	Ethnic exclusion	Inter-ethnic cooperation (–) (lobbying for public goods)	Public goods provision (–)
(A3)	Ethnic exclusion	Ethnic mobilization (+) (violent tactics by ethnic group)	Public goods provision (–) Administrative competence (–) Extractive capacity (–)
(A4)	Ethnic exclusion	Ethnic mobilization (+) (non-violent tactics by ethnic group)	Public goods provision (+/–) Administrative competence (+/–) Distribution of public goods (+/–)

Source: Authors.

and Gugerty 2005; Algan et al. 2011; Fearon and Laitin 1996). The capacity of communities to act together, for example, to raise funds for schools, collect garbage, repair roads, clear drains, and maintain other public infrastructure projects, is clearly a very important channel for the provision of essential social services. Across most parts of the world the provision of public goods is, however, perceived as, and remains primarily, a state responsibility. Contrary to the assumptions of many of these political economy models, the provision of public goods is more a product of *state interventions* rather than collective action on the part of communities. Access to public goods, as emphasized by Banerjee et al. 'seem(s) to have nothing to do with "bottom-up" forces . . . and instead reflect(s) more "top-down" interventions' (2007, p. 3117).

This said, within this research tradition there are studies that implicitly focus on the 'top-down' dynamic of state provision of social services. The main argument here is that ethnic divisions generate conflicting preferences, which leads governments, for example, in US cities, to devote a lower share of expenditure to public goods (Goldin and Katz 1999; Poterba 1997; Alesina et al. 1999). While these studies do not specify this clearly, the way in which this 'preferences in common' (Habyarimana et al. 2009, p. 8) mechanism might be inferred to work is that conflicting preferences on the part of different ethnic groups leads to difficulties in coordinating collective action to pressure the state for the provision of public goods.[12] Describing this mechanism, Habyarimana et al. (2009, p. 8), for example, write that:

---

[12] In their experiments in Kampala, Habyarimana et al. (2009) do not find that individuals from different ethnic groups have different preferences, but studies by Trounstine (2013) in the US and by Lieberman and McClendon (2013) in sub-Saharan Africa find evidence of substantial preference divergence across ethnic groups.

If residents . . . can lobby together for funding . . . then the likelihood of a positive response from the local government increases. But if community members are unable to coordinate their lobbying—if, for example, some residents want better policing but others prefer that the government allocate its resources to improve local schools or transport infrastructure—then the likelihood that the government will increase its support for local defense units diminishes.

A similar mechanism is proposed by Algan et al. (2011) who argue that more diverse communities are likely to face more trouble in coordinating collective action to demand better social services from the government.[13] In sum, then, this body of scholarship hypothesizes that the extent of ethnic diversity undermines public goods provision by affecting the ability of a community to act collectively either to provide the goods themselves or lobby the state for the provision of the services.

It remains unclear, however, under what conditions a 'bottom-up' or 'top-down' path is chosen. We can imagine that whether a community decides to provide the public goods by itself or petition the state to provide these services is a deliberate decision that is contingent on various factors including the perceived effectiveness of the ethnic groups' ability to provide services, which are in turn likely to depend on the strength and structure of leadership and/or the organizational framework of ethnic groups;[14] whether they have a tradition of service provision[15] as well as expectations of the state's willingness and ability to provide public goods, which are in turn influenced by the prevailing 'political culture',[16] world historical time,[17] and previous legacies of state development.[18]

Another issue with the political economy literature on diversity and public goods provision is the following: the hypothesized positive relationship

[13] Algan et al. go a step further to suggest that this result may be supported in equilibrium through recognition by the government, in their case, the housing directorate in French cities, that 'in ethnically or religiously heterogeneous apartments, it can permit the decline of facilities, knowing that it will not face collective action from its residents demanding better services' (2011, p. 4).

[14] For example, Ann Swidler (2006) emphasizes the crucial role of ethnic/tribal leaders in encouraging or discouraging the provision of HIV/AIDS-related health services in sub-Saharan Africa.

[15] For example, Brokerhoff and Hewett (2000) point to significant differences in how different ethnic groups in sub-Saharan Africa deal with child health care, while Ben Ansell and Johannes Lindvall's (2013) cross-national study observes substantial variations in how different religious groups provide education.

[16] For example, whether the state is characterized as individualistic or liberal when compared to corporatist or social democratic ideological orientations (Esping-Andersen 1990; Hall and Soskice 2001).

[17] Most prominently, the period after the Second World War was characterized by heightened global expectations of service provision by the state (Meyer et al. 1997).

[18] Based on a comparative historical analysis of Chile, Mexico, Peru, and Colombia, Hillel Soifer (2013) shows that in relatively more effective states, the population subsequently expects more from the state and pressures it to do more, while in comparatively weaker states, the population relies more on self-help mechanisms for public goods provision.

between ethnic homogeneity and public goods provision ignores the possibility that the majority ethnic group could have preferences for, and mobilize in support of public goods provision that benefits their ethnic group but is detrimental to the welfare of the minority groups, for example, by opening schools that do not have provisions for minority language education. In this case, ethnic homogeneity might not in fact be supportive of state capacity, especially if conceptualized not in terms of public goods provision in the aggregate, but instead in terms of equal access to public goods.

An additional more broadly shared concern about this body of scholarship is its conceptualization and measurement of ethnicity in terms of fractionalization indices. This methodological approach violates key constructivist findings about the fluid, multidimensional, and socio-politically manufactured nature of ethnic identity (Chandra and Wilkinson 2008; Laitin and Posner 2001). It also makes the problematic assumption that *demographic* diversity necessarily leads to *political* divisions between ethnic groups (Singh 2011).

(A2) Ethnic Exclusion and Inter-ethnic Cooperation

In order to address this issue a recent body of scholarship starts off, very self-consciously, from a different conceptualization of ethnicity not just as ethnic diversity but as relative group power. As such, this literature has made an important move beyond purely demographic fractionalization indices to instead develop group-based measures that focus on the degree to which ethnic groups are disadvantaged in terms of access to economic resources (Østby 2008; Baldwin and Huber 2010; Cederman et al. 2011) and political power (Cederman and Girardin 2007; Chandra and Wilkinson 2008; Cederman et al. 2010). This shift, based on the general premise that ethnic diversity is more likely to have adverse political effects when demographic divides align with deficiencies in economic or political power, is clearly a significant advance in the study of ethnic politics.

The mechanism by which ethnic exclusion is posited to impact state capacity is, however, virtually the same as the one described earlier, through which ethnic diversity is hypothesized to work. Baldwin and Huber (2010), for example, explicitly draw on Alesina et al. (1999) and other studies to suggest that economic disparities between ethnic groups will lead to different preferences for public goods, which will make it more difficult for the ethnic groups to reach agreement on and mobilize for public goods and that this will affect 'governance', in particular, government provision of public health, education, public infrastructure and even a government's taxing capacity.[19]

[19] It is interesting that Baldwin and Huber (2010, p. 645) also suggest that 'under such circumstances politicians may try to win reelection by providing private goods for each group,

More generally, we believe that both the scholarship on ethnic diversity and ethnic exclusion leave unaddressed a major question about their implicit causal logic. The core claim underlying studies that conceptualize ethnicity either in demographic terms or in access to economic-political power is that this influences the likelihood that individuals across different ethnic groups will cooperate and mobilize collectively for state provision of public goods. If we reverse the logic, however, while the heterogeneity or economic-political inequality of ethnic groups reduces the chances of inter-ethnic collective action, it increases the likelihood of mobilization on the part of particular ethnic groups. As already noted, according to the ethnic diversity and public goods provision literature, common traits facilitate the formation of shared preferences and thus the propensity for collective action—an argument that applies not just to mobilization across distinct ethnicities but also among members of a specific ethnic group. Similarly, the experience of economic-political inequality might lead to a sense of relative deprivation (Gurr 1970) and ethnic opportunity hoarding, that is, attempts to concentrate status and wealth within a group's network boundaries (Tilly 1998),[20] thereby increasing the likelihood of ethnic-based collective action. In turn, such mobilization by specific ethnic groups could either enhance or impede state capacity, and therefore, requires further exploration in its own right.

(A3) Ethnic Exclusion and Violent Mobilization by Ethnic Groups

The mechanisms that follow are therefore less concerned with inter-ethnic cooperation and instead focus on ethnic mobilization, which broadly refers to collective action that employs a belief in a shared culture and common ancestry as the basis for group membership and political claims.[21] In turn, the impact of ethnic mobilization is traced across different dimensions of state capacity, including public goods provision, but also bureaucratic professionalism and extraction.

For identifying the specific effects of ethnic-based collective action, we draw on a major distinction made in the literature in ethnic politics and

---

especially when the number of groups is not too large'. We discuss this distinct mechanism of how ethnicity might affect state capacity through the informal institution of patron–client relations later in the chapter.

[20] Opportunity hoarding occurs 'when members of a categorically bounded network acquire access to a resource that is valuable, renewable, subject to monopoly, supportive of network activities, and enhanced by the network's modus operandi' (Tilly 1998, p. 91).

[21] See McAdam et al. (2001) and Olzak (1983). Ethnic mobilization can manifest itself in a variety of organizational forms. Most importantly, social movements, political parties, and civic associations constitute important 'carriers' of ethnicity and provide a crucial platform for the articulation of ethnic-based demands.

differentiate between *violent* and *non-violent* forms of ethnic mobilization.[22] Whether or not ethnic-based collective action takes on a violent form is contingent on a whole host of factors, an analysis of which is beyond the scope of this chapter. For our purposes it is sufficient to highlight two important findings. First, recent studies of ethnic violence have largely discredited the view that ethnic diversity is associated with violent ethnic mobilization. There is little or no evidence that ethnic factionalization directly affects ethnic violence (Fearon and Laitin 2003; Collier and Hoeffler 2004). Second, a number of recent studies have, however, demonstrated an association between the exclusion of, especially demographically large, ethnic groups from state power and the incidence of civil war (Cederman and Girardin 2007; Cederman et al. 2010). The causal mechanism suggested by this body of work moves from political exclusion to grievances to collective action. More excluded groups are more likely to perceive their situation as directly contradicting the nationalist principle of political legitimacy (i.e. ethnic likes should rule ethnic likes), and the resulting sense of injustice and resentment constitutes a crucial mobilization resource for organized violence against the state.[23]

There is a long tradition in comparative politics and political sociology that links the rise of high-capacity states to organized violence.[24] The arguments of this 'bellicist approach' (Centeno 2002) have, however, been primarily made for inter-state conflict. Different kinds of organized violence have different, sometimes even contrasting, consequences for state capacity. Another literature shows that civil war, and intra-state conflict, has a devastating impact on the competencies of states to extract resources and provide public goods (Kalyvas 2006; Thies 2005). This form of organized violence often pits civilians against civilians and usually does not involve

[22] In the next mechanism set (B), we also disaggregate ethnic mobilization in terms of its geographical location and the nature of demands. For our current purposes the distinction between violent and non-violent forms of ethnic-based collective action suffices. Organized ethnic violence includes systematic threats, harassment, anti-group demonstrations, the deliberate destruction of property, physical attacks on people, and communal rioting, and might even turn into guerrilla warfare and civil war. Non-violent forms of collective actions pursued by ethnic groups and their political representatives include electoral campaigns, lobbying, but also public demonstrations and rallies, vigils, pickets, and boycotts, strikes, road blocks, and other forms of symbolic confrontations. For a social-movements perspective on different protest strategies, see Diani and Bison (2004).

[23] Obviously the motivation of excluded ethnic groups to engage in violent collective action against the state needs to be complemented by the organizational capacity to do so. Past patterns of ethnic conflict also contribute to the propensity for violent ethnic mobilization (Cederman et al. 2010).

[24] According to this perspective, war (or the threat of war) induced economic elites to pay taxes and accept other controls on their behaviour (Levi 1988; Tilly 1975). Similarly, war pushed rulers to build an administrative machinery capable of mobilizing the resources necessary for the deployment of armies and the acquisition of military technology (Downing 1992; Ertman 1997). Finally, with the imposition of conscription state leaders became more responsive to citizen-soldiers and their demands for social provision (Hobsbawm 1990; Skocpol 1992).

mass military conscription and the coordination of large armies—the main causal processes highlighted by the bellicist approach as driving the positive relationship between violent conflict and state capacity. Seen in this light then, ethnic violence is almost certain to undermine the administrative and extractive competencies of states.

(A4) Ethnic Exclusion and Non-violent Mobilization by Ethnic Groups

The picture is less clear-cut for non-violent forms of ethnic mobilization. On the one hand, collective action of ethnic groups, in particular, minorities and/or excluded ethnic groups, for access to public goods or official recognition of historic injustices may place new issues on the political agenda and generate more targeted state policies (Banting and Kymlicka 2007, p. 17). For example, one of the major achievements of indigenous movements and ethnic parties in Latin America has been to bring previously marginalized ethnic groups into the political arena and turn their demands for recognition and inclusion into legitimate political issues, thereby changing the policy priorities of state leaders (Van Cott 2005). In turn, more targeted state policies could further the welfare of these groups and by doing so, promote the provision of public goods. A related argument emphasizes that ethnic mobilization can also help to establish new 'information linkages' (Tendler 1997) between the state and (previously) excluded groups that provide officials with more accurate knowledge about local needs and what kinds of public services work, thereby enhancing state administrative competence.

By the same token, however, non-violent ethnic mobilization could also prove to be detrimental for state capacity. Ethnic-based collective action may also focus on gaining control over state personnel and placing 'their own' within the state apparatus. If successful, this 'ethnicization of state bureaucracy' (Wimmer 1997, 2002) impacts state capacity through at least two major channels. One is administrative competence, or the extent of bureaucratic professionalism found among state agents. The recruitment of potentially less qualified co-ethnics might compromise the formation of a bureaucratic esprit de corps. The other concerns public goods provision. As illustrated by post-conflict Lebanon (Cammett 2011), ethnicization of the bureaucracy can also involve the biased and discriminatory use of public services. Under these circumstances, welfare provision can turn into a premium for political support, which in turn impedes universal access to these collective goods.

In sum, our discussion so far has shown that the impact of ethnic diversity or ethnic exclusion on public goods provision is not limited to the undermining of inter-ethnic cooperation. Ethnic mobilization, or the collective action by a particular ethnic group, constitutes another crucial causal pathway through which ethnicity shapes state capacity. We have further demonstrated that the effects of ethnic mobilization—whether violent or non-violent—are not limited to public goods provision and also impact on other dimensions of state capacity, most prominently administrative competence and extraction.

The primary causal link in all the mechanisms discussed so far are the actions of ethnic groups, whether in the form of inter-ethnic cooperation or mobilization by a particular ethnic group. It is useful, however, at this point to move beyond the notion of a direct causal pathway between ethnic-based collective action and state capacity and broaden our analytical lens.

Causal Mechanism Set (B): Actions by Other Actors

A plausible alternative is to consider how the dynamics of ethnicity influence state capacity through the (re)actions of other collectivities. Our starting point is the observation that distinct patterns of ethnic exclusion or ethnic-based collective action are likely to elicit distinct responses from other collective actors. In this section we therefore focus on ways in which ethnicity transforms state capacity by shaping the behaviour of other actors. Building on the recent emphasis on elites as a major determinant of state capacity[25] we concentrate on two sets of elite actors—societal elites and state officials.

(B1) Ethnic Exclusion and Alliance Strategies by Societal Elites

As shown in Table 9.3, the first batch of mechanisms in this set focuses on the interests and behaviour of the upper classes of the dominant ethnic group.[26] In the subsequent paragraphs we show that—whether instigated by the salience of ethnic exclusion or ethnic mobilization—the alliance strategies of these societal elites constitute another major causal pathway linking ethnicity to state capacity.

One mechanism variant puts the analytical spotlight on cross-class alliances. In this perspective ethnic exclusion influences the propensity of upper groups from the dominant ethnic group to form a coalition with lower-class co-ethnics, with different types of these alliances then shaping the ability of states to pursue their projects. More specifically, stark ethnic boundaries might lead the economically privileged to ally with subordinate sectors of the

[25] Amsden et al. (2012) and North et al. (2009) are prominent examples for this trend. See vom Hau (2012) for an overview.
[26] Those elites include, most importantly, the economically privileged sectors, but also civil society leaders.

Table 9.3. Causal mechanism set (B): actions by other collective actors

	Conceptual approach to ethnicity	Causal mechanism	Affected dimension(s) of state capacity
(B1)	Ethnic exclusion	Alliance strategies by societal elites (upper classes of dominant ethnic group ally with lower-class co-ethnics)	Extractive capacities (+) Administrative competence (−)
(B2)	Ethnic mobilization	Alliance strategies by societal elites (upper classes of dominant ethnic group ally with state)	Extractive capacities (+)
(B3)	Ethnic mobilization	Alliance strategies by societal elites (upper classes of dominant ethnic group withdraw from state)	Extractive capacities (−) Territorial reach (−)
(B4)	Ethnic exclusion	Political survival considerations of state elites (state caters to included ethnic groups)	Territorial reach (−) Distribution of public goods (−)
(B5)	Ethnic mobilization	Political survival considerations of state elites (state accommodates most powerful ethnic groups)	Public goods provision (+) Territorial reach (+) Distribution of public goods (−)
(B6)	Ethnic mobilization	Ideas held by state elites (state response shaped by perceived level of cultural difference or ethnic threat)	Public goods provision (−) Territorial reach (−)

Source: Authors.

same ethnic group and support the state's extractive efforts. Put differently, the exclusion of a common ethnic 'out-group' promotes a greater sense of solidarity on the part of economic elites towards members of their 'in-group' and induces them to form a cross-class coalition with lower sectors, leading to greater elite willingness to make economic concessions and pay taxes. In contexts of less explicit forms of ethnic political exclusion, however, economic elites are less likely to pay taxes on the grounds that these payments benefit their co-ethnics. The rise of distinct tax states in South Africa and Brazil illustrates this mechanism variant. In apartheid South Africa, the political exclusion of blacks led to the emergence of a cross-class coalition among whites and a 'politics of collective sacrifice' (Lieberman 2003, p. 254) among the economically privileged, while in Brazil, with a relatively less institutionalized racial order, white upper groups were less inclined to form a cross-class alliance, because they perceived both poor blacks and poor whites as distinct from themselves. The consequence was comparatively less tax compliance with the state (Lieberman 2003; see also Marx 1998).

Another version of this argument is equally concerned with cross-class alliances between elites and lower sectors of the same ethnic group. It equally suggests that the explicit exclusion of an ethnic out-group motivates economic elites to ally with their poor brethren from the ethnic in-group. Yet, in this perspective cross-class alliances induce elites to pressure the state to accommodate their new alliance partners. And a likely underpinning of these broad coalitional arrangements is the distribution of side payments to new ethnic constituencies (Waldner 1999, pp. 37–49), especially in the form of patronage-based recruitment into the state bureaucracy, which often has a negative impact on the administrative competence of states. The bottom line is thus a proposed negative relationship between explicit ethnic exclusion and state capacity. Inspiration for this mechanism variant comes from arguments about coalition dynamics and state capacity found in recent writings on the developmental state, a literature that is not directly concerned with ethnicity. Most prominently, the studies by Atul Kohli (2004) and David Waldner (1999) suggest that 'narrow coalitions' of states with capital-owning groups, such as in mid-twentieth-century South Korea, are generally more effective in promoting industrialization, while states with 'broad coalitions', such as in mid-twentieth-century Turkey, need to accommodate a variety of often contradictory citizen demands, and are therefore more likely to exhibit a politicized bureaucracy.

(B2/B3) Ethnic Mobilization and Alliance Strategies by Societal Elites

A second batch of mechanisms in this set centres on state–elite alliances, that is, on coalitions between societal elites and the state. Our starting point is ethnic mobilization and we analyse how differences in the demands and location of mobilized ethnic groups can affect the alliance strategies of societal elites vis-à-vis the state. Specifically, when ethnic mobilization involves redistributive claims and unfolds close to urban centres, which is where economic elites are more likely to be concentrated, then these upper classes are likely to see it as especially threatening to established property relations and to their economic status. These concerns about the potential loss of their privileged position make it more likely that economic elites will seek an alliance with the state against ethnic contenders. Upper groups are willing to pay higher taxes in exchange for the provision of security and the repression of popular threats. The alliance with the state thus helps societal elites to maintain their economic and political privileges, while enhancing the state's extractive capacity. On the other hand, when ethnic mobilization does not make class-based demands and occurs in relatively distant rural areas it poses much less of a threat for the established elites and they are less likely to seek an alliance and cooperate with the extractive efforts of the state.

Dan Slater (2010) develops and tests this mechanism for the context of South East Asia. In mid-twentieth-century Indonesia, ethnic mobilization was class based and took place in cities prompting societal elites to form encompassing 'protection pacts' with the state, which greatly enhanced the state's extractive capacities. Ethnic rebellions in the Philippines, by contrast, unfolded in remote provinces and were not redistributive in their demands, societal elites felt less threatened and formed flimsy elite pacts with the state, ultimately resulting in a state with relatively poor extractive capacities.

The effect of ethnic mobilization on elite–state alliances might also, however, be the reverse, with ultimately negative implications for state capacity. Economic elites who find their positions threatened by ethnic mobilization that advances demands for redistribution and the reordering of political power structures might be more inclined to withdraw their support from the state, reduce their tax payments, and instead focus their efforts on retaining their elite status by establishing private security measures and/or promoting the territorial reorganization of the state. Kent Eaton's (2007, p. 2011) study of Bolivia and Ecuador provides a particularly stark example of this mechanism variant. In these two countries, characterized by sharp geographical divisions between the centres of economic activity and the political capital, economic elites are greatly concerned about the recent rise of indigenous politics. In response, elites push for greater territorial autonomy among the economically most prosperous regions and the devolution of tax authority to these sub-national units, thereby undermining the extractive competence of the central state.

Taken together, the mechanisms developed in this section so far link ethnicity to state capacity outcomes via the alliance strategies of societal elites. Distinct patterns of ethnic exclusion or ethnic mobilization result in different cross-class alliances (i.e. coalitions between upper and lower strata of the same ethnic group) and/or elite–state coalitions (i.e. pacts between powerful economic forces and the state), which in turn shape the extractive capacity of states. The next section continues the focus on how ethnicity influences state capacity through its impact on collective actors but shifts the focus away from societal elites to state elites.

(B4) Ethnic Exclusion and Political Survival Considerations by State Elites

Our discussion so far has treated the state as a 'black box'. When analysing the causal impact of ethnicity on state capacity, the previous mechanisms all assumed that different social pressures on the state translate into distinct forms of public goods provision, administrative competence, or extractive capacities. This perspective remains incomplete, however, without taking another plausible causal mechanism into account. In this section we argue that ethnic exclusion or ethnic mobilization might affect state capacity by shaping the preferences and perceptions, and consequently the strategic actions of state elites. This emphasis on the agency of state leaders and high-level bureaucrats builds on a substantial literature that treats states as potentially autonomous actors with a self-directed agenda independent of civil society pressures or dominant economic interests.[27]

The first batch of mechanisms within this perspective focus on how ethnicity influences the fundamental interests of executive authorities and high-level bureaucrats: the maximization of state resources[28] and staying in power. Specifically, we trace how political-survival considerations of state officials shape the geographical coverage of the state and access to public services across state territory.

Explicit forms of ethno-political exclusion, especially from executive positions in government, might reduce the motivation of state elites to expand territorial reach and establish public services across national territory. When ethnic groups lack political representation and consequently, political voice, state authorities are less inclined to provide universal services, and can instead focus their efforts on providing public services to their preferred ethnic group(s) (Wimmer et al. 2009). As powerfully illustrated by the case of Iraq before 2003, the systematic political exclusion of an ethnic group (e.g. Shia Arabs) may give way to the territorial and social concentration of state infrastructure with the ethnic group(s) that has political representation in the ranks for the state (e.g. Sunni Arabs), coming to enjoy most of the public benefits provided (Wimmer 2002). By contrast, in instances of greater ethno-political inclusion, state elites might be more inclined to expand the state's territorial reach and provide public goods to the whole population, largely because their political survival is more likely to depend on support across ethnic boundaries.

(B5) Ethnic Mobilization and Political Survival Considerations by State Elites

State elites' preferences for political survival and resource maximization are influenced equally by patterns of ethnic mobilization. In this perspective, the decision of state leaders and high-level bureaucrats to expand the territorial reach of the state and provide public goods depends on the political and economic strength of mobilized ethnic groups. When an ethnic group is in control of desirable economic resources and is able to powerfully advance its collective demands, state officials might be more inclined to establish state infrastructure and invest in public services, largely because they feel threatened

[27] Evans et al. (1985) represents the classic appraisal of a statist approach. For recent overviews of this research perspective see Vu (2010).
[28] Whether these resources are used for their direct personal benefits or the 'sake of the people' is another question and of less importance for our current purposes.

by the mobilization and want to keep it under control. We extrapolate this argument from Catherine Boone's (2003) work on state capacity in Western Africa. Boone suggests that state elites are more likely to expand the territorial reach of the state and invest in the construction of local infrastructure (such as building roads, hospitals, or schools) when they feel challenged by an economically and politically powerful rural society (Boone 2003, p. 30–1).

Both of the mechanism variants discussed so far posit an impact of ethnic exclusion or ethnic mobilization on state capacity via the political survival and resource maximization strategies of state elites. State responses to ethno-political inequalities and ethnic collective action might also, however, depend on the preconceived ideas state officials hold about a particular ethnic group. In this line of reasoning, cultural representations, official national narratives, and collective memories mediate the effects of ethnicity on state capacity by shaping how executive authorities and higher-level bureaucrats perceive an ethnic group, and based on that what kind of reactions to ethnic-based mobilization they consider appropriate.

(B6) Ethnic Mobilization and Ideas about Ethnic Groups Held by State Elites

Cultural representations of an ethnic group play a notable role in the response of state elites to ethnic mobilization. Of particular importance appears to be the perceived level of cultural difference. When state officials view a particular ethnic group as amenable to assimilation into the larger society, they might be more compelled to channel public resources to expand the territorial reach of the state and provide public goods. This decision is primarily motivated by the expected returns following assimilation, in the form of political loyalty and/or economic contributions as new taxpayers. By contrast, perceptions of stark cultural differences might discourage state leaders and higher-level bureaucrats from investing extensively in state infrastructure or fiscal efforts. This mechanism expands on George Steinmetz's (2007) study of distinct types of German colonial state-building during the late nineteenth and early twentieth century. German officials, inspired by dominant ethnographic representations, deemed the indigenous populations of South West Africa as having the potential for entering their 'civilization', and therefore responded to ethnic mobilization (i.e. local revolts) by combining severe repression with the expansion of territorial reach and the provision of public goods.[29] By

---

[29] Other examples for a state expanding both its repressive apparatus and public goods provision (e.g. roads, health clinics) are Nazi Germany before the Second World War (1933–9) or Chile under Pinochet (1973–90).

contrast, ethnographic representations that portrayed Samoans as noble and endangered savages whose cultural survival was at stake, led colonial state officials to respond more mildly to local revolts and refrain from extensive infrastructure-building and public goods provision. For our purposes, Steinmetz's analysis reveals that dominant cultural representations of ethnic groups shape possible state responses to ethnic-based mobilization, with major implications for state capacity.

A similar argument can be made for official national narratives. In this perspective, state responses to ethnic collective action are influenced by the role state-sponsored nationalist discourses assign to a particular ethnic group. When state leaders and high-level bureaucrats see an ethnic group as a major security threat to state sovereignty and stability (and, by extension, their own political survival), they might be less likely to accommodate the demands of this group. In these instances, state infrastructure and public goods provision are not extended to parts of the state territory inhabited by the supposed threat-posers. A powerful example for this mechanism comes from Turkey. Official narratives that identify the Kurds as an imminent threat to the territorial integrity of the Turkish nation has led to a deliberate limitation of territorial reach and public goods provision in areas predominantly populated by ethnic Kurds (Yeğen 2006).

Another variant of this mechanism emphasizes the central role of collective memory in shaping state elite perceptions of mobilized ethnic groups. How state leaders and high-level bureaucrats remember past patterns of ethnic mobilization has major ramifications for their interpretations of contemporary ethnic collective action. Often, elite threat perceptions are coloured by historical experiences of ethnic conflict. When state authorities maintain a historical memory of a group as a threat to their political survival, they might be less likely to accommodate (or even acknowledge) demands from this group. As Paul Brass (1994) illustrates for postcolonial India, state leaders such as Nehru were more likely to positively consider demands made by distinct linguistic groups. By contrast, ethno-religious mobilization was treated with suspicion, to a large extent because of the looming history of the partition of India. This line of argument thus stresses that state elite perceptions of particular ethnic groups are tinted by the memory of past interactions and conflicts, and that these memories influence state elite responses to ethnic mobilization.

In sum, this batch of causal mechanisms helps to open the black box of the state. In this perspective, ethnicity influences state capacity by shaping the actions of state elites. Whether directly driven by concerns about political survival and state resources, or mediated by cultural representations, official national narratives, or collective memories of past ethnic conflict, it is via the preferences and perceptions, and consequently behaviour, of state officials that ethnic exclusion or ethnic mobilization impact on state capacity.

Causal Mechanisms (C): Institutional Change

The focus on the alliance strategies of societal elites and the strategic actions of state officials in the previous section provides an important corrective to the idea that ethnic-based collective action, whether in the form of inter-group cooperation or ethnic mobilization, automatically affects state capacity. As we have shown, there are many instances in which collective ethnic demands influence state capacity through less direct means. As summarized in Table 9.4, in the remainder of the chapter we turn to institutional change as another major indirect causal pathway. Institutions have long been treated as crucial to account for state capacity (Acemoglu and Robinson 2006; Mahoney 2010; North et al. 2009). Specifically, a growing literature treats institutions as both the means and end of political struggle, because they ultimately routinize power asymmetries (Mahoney and Thelen 2010; Wimmer 2012b). Building on this 'power-institutional' approach, we first turn to the nexus between ethnic collective action and formal institutions. We explore how mobilized ethnic groups might challenge and even change formal state institutions and how, in turn, these transformed institutions can influence state capacity.

(C1) Feedback Effects between Formal Representative Institutions and Ethnic Mobilization

A first batch of mechanisms identifies an iterative relationship between ethnic mobilization and existing formal representative institutions as a major driver of state capacity. In this perspective, ethnic groups are centrally concerned with formal recognition and inclusion. In order to change existing institutional arrangements ethnic groups frequently push for new legislation that establishes or advances their representation (see Amenta et al. 2010). Their demands include, but are not limited to, federalism, asymmetrical federal structures, consociationalism, but also affirmative action, quotas, and other special group rights in education, employment, health, and electoral systems. While the debate about what forms of ethnic mobilization are particularly influential in shaping representative institutions remains inconclusive,[30] there appears to be a consensus that, once introduced, these

---

[30] The literature on political parties points to a variety of factors that determine electoral success and, by extension, impact on institutional change. Scholars emphasize party appeals (e.g. exclusionary vs. populist-inclusive) (Chandra 2007; Madrid 2012), party organization (e.g. Levitsky 2003), ties to ethnic movements (Van Cott 2005), and political context, most

Table 9.4. Causal mechanism set (C): institutional change

	Conceptual approach to ethnicity	Causal mechanism	Affected dimension(s) of state capacity
(C1)	Ethnic mobilization	Feedback effects between formal representative institutions and ethnic mobilization (+)	Public goods provision (+/–) Administrative competence (+/–) Extractive capacity (+/–)
(C2)	Ethnic mobilization	Introduction of new formal representative institutions (+)	Public goods provision (+/–) Administrative competence (+/–) Territorial reach (+/–)
(C3)	Ethnic mobilization	Informal control over (parts of) state apparatus (+)	Distribution of public goods (–) Administrative competence (–)

Source: Authors.

institutions have major feedback effects on ethnic collective action. There are at least two rival models that map out the relationship.

On the one hand are those who argue that the expansion of formal representative platforms to incorporate ethnic groups has negative implications for state capacity. Drawing on case studies from eleven Southern African countries, Evan Lieberman and Prerna Singh (2012) find that the institutionalization of ethnic representation deepens ethnic cleavages and ultimately leads to an increased proclivity for ethnic violence, thereby undermining the administrative competence and fiscal capacity of the state. On the other hand, the literature on ethno-political exclusion (Cederman et al. 2010; Cederman and Girardin 2007; Chandra and Wilkinson 2008) suggests almost the opposite. In this perspective, the institutionalization of formal ethnic representation can potentially overcome power differentials among rival ethnic groups. This, in turn, leads to lower instances of mobilization and, potentially reduces the likelihood of ethnic violence.

(C2) Ethnic Mobilization and the Introduction of New Formal Representative Institutions

Another institutional mechanism variant also suggests that, *ceteris paribus*, mobilized ethnic groups push for recognition and inclusion via formal

prominently party-systems (Kitschelt 1988) and other institutional factors (Horowitz 1985). Echoing the literature on political parties, the main debates on ethnic movements centre on the conditions under which movements influence policy (Amenta et al. 2010). Some researchers stress that mobilization in itself is sufficient to induce policy change (McCarthy and Zald 1977), others point to particular forms of movement organization (e.g. Andrews 2004), movement strategies (e.g. Cress and Snow 2000), and the broader political context, particularly the support of powerful allies (Kitschelt 1986; Amenta 2006). Similar arguments have been made in the literature on civic associations (e.g. Skocpol 2003; Varshney 2003).

institutions. Yet, in contrast to the emphasis on feedback effects, the focus is on how new representative institutions transform the state apparatus. The implementation of these institutions usually entails novel bureaucratic procedures and structures, with varying effects on state capacity. Existing approaches are again divided about the expected benefits of these rearrangements.

On the positive end, recent studies of affirmative action in the United States and Brazil (Htu 2004; Sowell 2004) suggest that the construction of new state agencies facilitate the provision of services and infrastructure across wider segments of the society. Similarly, the decentralization of political authority via federalist or consociationalist arrangements might lead to new bureaucratic structures and competencies, with largely beneficial effects on the administrative competence and territorial reach of the state apparatus. On the other hand, the same representative institutions might also generate unexpected problems for state public goods provision. For example, affirmative action or federalist arrangements often introduce new veto points into the policymaking process, thereby impeding the effective provision of public services (Gerring et al. 2005; Huber and Stephens 2001).

(C3) Ethnic Mobilization and Informal Control Over (Parts of) the State Apparatus

Another mechanism in the institutional tradition focuses on informal institutions and puts the analytical spotlight on patron–client relations to explore how ethnic mobilization exerts influence on state capacity.[31] The emphasis here is on the inclusion of ethnic groups within the state via personalistic ties and tolerance for graft, and the effects of these arrangements on bureaucratic professionalism and the reach of public services.

Even though recent revisionist scholarship contends that state bureaucracies characterized by clientelism may still manage to ignite substantial economic growth (e.g. Kelsall et al. 2010; Darden 2008), a rather large literature remains sceptical. In this dominant view informal ethnic favouritism and patronage politics ultimately undermine state capacity (e.g. Knack and Keefer 2003; Kuhonta 2011; Lange et al. 2006; Lange 2009; Mahoney 2010; Sacks and Levi 2010). We therefore suggest that when mobilized ethnic groups gain control over (certain parts of) the state apparatus, they might

---

[31] The agenda-setting work on informal institutions is Helmke and Levitsky (2006). Works on the nexus between informal institutions and state capacity are not limited to patron–client relations, but also explore the role of customary law and norms of communal reciprocity and solidarity in shaping the administrative competence and territorial reach of states. See MacLean (2010), Tsai (2007), and Van Cott (2005, 2008).

exploit their newly acquired powers and use their position to systematically favour co-ethnics, with negative consequences for public goods provision and state territorial reach. For example, in the cases of post-conflict Lebanon or Uttar Pradesh in India, highly mobilized sectarian parties and movements employ welfare provision as premium for political support. The result is a highly unbalanced geography of public goods provision (Cammett 2011; Singh 2010). Similarly, the prevalence of informal ethnic favouritism among state elites generates strong disincentives for excluded groups to pay taxes and share resources (Wimmer 2002; Wolfe and Klausen 1997).

In sum, mobilized ethnic groups seek to achieve recognition and inclusion through the transformation of established institutional arrangements. Once implemented, formal representative institutions transform state capacity by providing opportunities for subsequent rounds of ethnic mobilization, and introducing new bureaucratic arrangements, while informal patron–client relationships usually entail a biased distribution of state resources.

Conclusion

This chapter has situated the political economy literature on ethnic diversity and public goods provision within a larger body of scholarship on the effects of ethnicity on state capacity. In its almost exclusive focus on inter-ethnic cooperation, or collective action across different ethnic groups, this literature neglects other plausible causal pathways. In response, we have identified a broader range of causal mechanisms through which ethnicity might impact on state capacity. Specifically, we have developed three sets of mechanisms and have shown how collective action by ethnic groups (whether in the form of inter-ethnic cooperation or ethnic mobilization), the actions and perceptions of other collective actors (whether societal elites or state officials), and institutional change (whether of formal or informal institutions) shape the ability of states to provide public goods.

Our critique points to the need of revisiting and nuancing the political economy scholarship. As a matter of fact, the chapter highlights the need for an alternative approach when exploring the effects of ethnicity on state capacity. Such a framework would: (a) start from the political salience of ethnicity rather than ethnic diversity per se, and connect public goods provision to the concept of state capacity; (b) develop a novel set of causal mechanisms that focus on state responses and institutional change rather than the actions by ethnic groups when tracing how ethnic mobilization impacts on state capacity outcomes; and (c) take a historical approach that would incorporate the crucial role of states as identity-shapers into explanations of ethnic-based collective action rather than treating ethnic divisions as a given demographic fact.

Such a novel framework would also explore interactions among mechanisms. It is likely that the presence of one mechanism has major implications for the effect of another, resulting in complementary, or sometimes contradictory effects on state capacity.[32] For example, strong urban-based ethnic movements are expected to engender broad alliances between societal elites and the state, and, as a result, lead to a greater tax base, while the same movements might also foster ethnic favouritism among state officials. The framework would also accommodate the context-dependency of causal mechanisms.[33] Ethnic diversity, exclusion, or mobilization only affect state capacity in certain social and political environments. It is therefore crucial to explore how specific contexts activate, intensify, or otherwise shape the directions of causal mechanisms. Particular important scope conditions include the historical legacies of ethnic exclusion (Lange et al. 2006; Mahoney 2010; Tilly 1998), the density of civil society (Varshney 2003; Wimmer 2002), and political regime forms.

More research is also required to revisit the empirical foundations of the ethnic diversity and public goods provision hypothesis and further develop a plausible alternative that addresses its major conceptual and theoretical shortcomings. What this chapter already indicates, however, is that ethnicity should be taken seriously when analysing state capacity. Ethnicity, and identity more generally, is not just the outcome, but also a possible determinant of the ability of states to implement policy choices, with major implications for development.

---

[32] On mechanism complementarity and scope conditions see, for example, Matthew Lange's (2012) study of the impact of education on ethnic violence.

[33] See Rueschemeyer (2009); Elster (1985).

Part V
The Transnational Politics of Development

10

The Politics of Aid Revisited: A Review of Evidence on State Capacity and Elite Commitment

Arjan de Haan and Ward Warmerdam

Introduction: The Impact of Aid in Political Perspective

There is little analysis of how donors, even where they do start adopting a political perspective, influence local institutions and the people they work with. This chapter, the result of a systematic review of the impacts of aid, or international development cooperation, on state capacity for and elite commitment to sustainable development, highlights that a better understanding of—and indeed reconceptualization of—the 'impact of aid' has the potential to directly inform practices of international development. This requires, inter alia, better empirical insight into the way donors interact with formal and informal institutions in the countries where they work. This is particularly relevant in aid-dependent countries, but knowledge about interaction between national and international institutions from other countries may prove relevant too. Moreover, it is critical to see aid as part of a spectrum of international exchange, rather than in isolation.

The chapter is structured as follows. The first section provides a birds' eye view of the existing literature and field of study, including of recent large research programmes. The literature on the impact of aid tends to be polarized, and fragmented, and hence the second section shows the different strands, and how the fragmentation of perspectives potentially impacts research and findings on the impact of aid. The third section refers to the de-politicization of aid, and its analysis, and discusses the role of political (or political–economy) analysis on the practices of donors. The fourth section discusses the more technocratic literature on aid, including on conditionalities, which we argue can be conceptualized in the form of implicit contracts, different aid modalities, and donors' efforts to support revenue generation and taxation. The conclusion pulls together the emerging findings, and argues the need to go beyond a conceptualization of 'the impact of aid', and integrate the continued presence of donors in the analysis of local politics.

Scanning the Field

The existing literature tells us relatively little about how aid impacts state capacity for and elites' commitment to sustainable development, despite oft-repeated assertions of the importance of these attributes. Particularly the question of how aid affects elite commitment, is not well researched. A word search of our one-hundred-page annotated bibliography (Warmerdam and de Haan 2011) does not give a single score on 'elite commitment'. The word commitment appears sixteen times, but only in three cases does this have analytical content (as opposed to reference to, say, morally inspired calls) (Nelson 1984; Killick 1997; Savun and Tirone 2011).[1] Given the investment in research on governance over the last decade or more, this is surprising (OECD 2010; World Bank 2007, 2008),[2] and it is important to discuss the emphasis in this research.

Following the growing attention to governance during the 1990s, DFID made significant investments in research to better understand ways in which improving governance can contribute to better development outcomes.[3] It funded three major research initiatives for a period of ten years: the Crisis States Research Centre (at LSE), the Centre for Future States, and the Citizenship, Accountability and Participation programme.[4] The Oxford-based Centre for Research on Inequality and Ethnicity was less squarely focused on governance, but its focus on structural inequalities is of relevance for this review (Brown and Stewart 2006).[5] This set of programmes was followed by the Africa Power and Politics Programme, which focuses on identifying diverse sets of governance that promote development (Booth 2011a) and which emphasizes 'working with the grain' as a step beyond the good governance agenda.[6] The studies present casual observations regarding donors'

---

[1] Nelson (1984), Killick (1997), and Savun and Tirone (2011).

[2] OECD (2010), World Bank (2007, 2008).

[3] Main findings that emerged from this are summarized in the DFID (2010) synthesis paper 'The Politics of Poverty: Elites, Citizens and States'.

[4] See Gaventa and Barrett (2010) for a meta-case study on the ten-year research programme, analysing effects of citizen participation.

[5] This argues that the reduction of inequalities (between culturally defined groups), should inform aid policy.

[6] Booth (2009, 2011a) and Kelsall (2011a); the APPP work by Olivier de Sardan is even more averse to generalizations, focusing on practical norms governing behaviour (quoted in Booth 2009, p. 12).

barriers to seriously engage with politics, but the impact of aid on politics was not a major topic of research.

This research, in DFID's Research and Evidence Division Staff's summary, generally reaffirmed the primacy of politics, and political settlements for all development (including for economic growth), as 'driver of change'. It emphasizes the importance of informal institutions, and donors' misplaced emphasis on formal institutions alone—a further shift towards understanding informal institutions is desirable, including for the understanding of the impact of aid. Citizens' engagement with the state was shown to be instrumentally relevant for development. It concluded that taxation is central in building effective states,[7] as this provides the legitimacy of states vis-à-vis its citizens and reduces aid dependency.

Research at the University of Oxford Global Economic Governance Programme focuses on the politics of donor–recipient interaction, particularly the issue of 'ownership', how this is negotiated, and the effect the constant discussions with external players regarding development policy have on recipient state institutions, democracy, and politics (Whitfield 2008). This argues that 'ownership' remains weak in many aid dependent countries, and policy decision-making processes dominated by donors, not only due to supply-side politics of aid, but also demand-side politics, especially where recipients are dependent on aid inflows to supply public services and any reduction in aid inflows could reduce the political legitimacy of the government (de Renzio et al. 2008). This is particularly problematic when policies are more in line with domestic demands, but are not supported by donors, resulting in aid reductions. A number of studies of the GEG Programme elaborate on differing political dynamics have allowed donors to either embed themselves in government, such as in Ghana (Whitfield 2006), or not, as in Ethiopia (Furtado and Smith 2007), and how this and other factors such as recipient ideology, size, and history have an influence on the negotiating abilities and strategies of recipient governments.[8]

There is more knowledgement about the role of aid on state capacity than on elite commitment. However, this is insufficiently understood, partly because the literature stresses the negative impact of aid and failures of capacity-building, paying too little attention to how decades of aid relationship have become ingrained in the day-to-day politics in some countries.[9] There is no consensus about the links between governance and development: these are of course

---

[7] See also the discussion by Mick Moore at <http://www.ids.ac.uk/news/what-s-so-exciting-about-tax-and-development-a-new-global-focus-on-tax-policy-aid-and-good-governance> accessed 29 May 2014.

[8] Also de Renzio and Hanlon (2007) on Mozambique, Fraser (2007) on Zambia, Harrison and Mulley (2007) on Tanzania, Hayman (2007) on Rwanda, and Bergamaschi (2008) on Mali.

[9] Arguably, the literature also tends to under-emphasize the cases where aid has contributed to enhanced capacity, such as in China (World Bank, 2007; the common view that there has been no donor engagement in these areas appears mistaken), Taiwan and Botswana (Bräutigam, 2000).

context dependent, and recent experience suggests that the link is more contingent than may have been assumed earlier (Andrews 2008; Leftwich and Sen 2010).[10] The contested field of capacity-building, discussed below, similarly highlights that many questions remain regarding the impact of aid, and that it may be necessary to rethink the way the question—particularly that of 'aid effectiveness'—is approached.[11]

Quantitative cross-country studies have looked at the impact of aid on growth,[12] despite doubts about data (Anderson et al. 2005), and some of these include a variable on governance. Bräutigam and Knack (2004) found a robust statistical relationship between high aid levels and *deteriorations* in governance, as well as a relationship between higher aid levels and a lower tax share of GDP, while increases in GDP per capita correlate with improvements in governance. The analysis does not allow us to discern the reasons for these correlations, but the authors suggest that institutional weakening and perverse incentives do play a role, and note the high transaction costs that accompany aid programmes.[13] Rajan and Subramaniam (2007) are pessimistic about the impact aid can have on *growth* because it may constrain the growth of the manufacturing sector due the effect of aid on exchange rates. The study concludes that aid *may* weaken governance, 'because aid inflows reduce the need for governments to tax the governed or enlist their cooperation'.

There is thus a significant gap in terms of empirical research on the impact of aid on capacity and, particularly, commitment. This absence may be unsurprising, given what we know about the depoliticization of aid, and the fact that the politics of aid has only recently entered into the mainstream of studies, following a period where 'good governance' research surged, but remained by and large technocratic.[14] On the other hand, the absence is puzzling, as there are very strong views on whether aid works or not, as we discuss next.

Half a Dozen Views on Aid

Hugely differing perspectives on aid exist, with at least half a dozen positions. To start, there are many who claim that not enough aid is given. Calls

---

[10] Andrews (2008), Leftwich and Sen (2010).

[11] Lancaster (2007) notes that the effectiveness of aid is measured as if human motives were the only objectives, thus ignoring in its assessment that there are various political and historical drivers of aid.

[12] Recent studies and overviews include Killick and Foster (2011), Arndt et al. (2009), Roodman (2007), McGillivray et al. (2006), and Doucouliagos and Paldam (2005).

[13] Collier (2002) builds on quantitative analysis (Collier and Dollar 1999) to develop measures to make aid smarter.

[14] Leftwich (1994); de Haan and Everest-Phillips (2010). Hughes and Hutchinson (2012) argue that aid interventions have failed to shift modalities, as they have an inadequate conception of politics.

for increased aid have been common at least since the Second World War, and there have been various waves of attention since. The immediate post-war period witnessed large-scale funding through the Marshall Plan, and growing aid to developing countries, focusing on technical assistance and cooperation. In 1951 a UN commission recommended an increase of aid, to about $5 billion a year, to help countries increase economic growth to 2 per cent (Riddell 2007, p. 27). The report 'Partners in Development' was one of the first and subsequently most-commonly quoted official reports arguing for an increase in aid (Pearson 1969), calling for rich countries to devote 0.7 per cent of their Gross National Income (GNI) to international development by 1975, but also to increase the efficiency of aid.

The optimism around 1970 was followed by 'structural adjustment' and stabilization of economies, and 'aid fatigue', even though throughout the 1980s there were calls for increasing aid. The 1990s, with the end of the Cold War, and economic and budgetary constraints in donor countries like the US and Japan, witnessed sharp reductions in ODA. The amounts of aid to allied countries declined, and donors may have reduced their attention to (potential) conflicts and violence in developing countries, which changed sharply with 9/11. More attention started to be paid to the use of aid for governance reforms in the former USSR, and for democratization in Africa.

From the late 1990s onwards, calls for increasing aid again became stronger, accompanied by a sharpened focus on poverty reduction as the over-arching goal for development,[15] illustrated, for example, in UN and World Bank publications. The Monterrey Conference became a symbol of reversal in views on aid, including the surprise announcement by the US President.[16] The UN Millennium Development project calculated the amount of aid that would be required to achieve the MDGs, showing a great deal of trust in the impact of aid.[17] Commitment to reach agreed levels of aid were reconfirmed after the financial crisis, but the political change particularly in Europe and the continued economic crisis since suggest we have once again entered a phase of aid fatigue, which is accompanied by the emergence of new donors and potentially a new aid paradigm.[18]

[15] An important OECD report in 1995 signalled a turnaround of the pessimism. The change of government in the UK in 1997 led to the formation of a new and separate ministry, and contributed to greater political interest.
[16] Monterrey Consensus Report of the International Conference on Financing for Development Monterrey, Mexico, 18–22 March 2002: <http://www.un.org/esa/ffd/monterrey/MonterreyConsensus.pdf> accessed 1 September 2014.
[17] UN Millennium Project 2005; Sachs 2005.
[18] So far, the attention to new donors seems to have developed as a separate field, and not entered 'mainstream' research programmes. For example, the 'Africa, Power and Politics' did

Three issues emerging from this body of literature are important for understanding the impact of aid on politics. First, views on aid remain informed by a moral commitment to help, and by the international politics that drives leaders to be (seen to be) responsible global actors. Second, these commitments have never been binding,[19] and arguably therefore the aid relationships remain couched in a charitable form, rather than strong (enforceable) international commitment. Thirdly, the way the commitments emerge—supply-driven, by and large (and combined with continued and increased donor fragmentation) continue to feed the problem of disbursement pressure.[20]

A second set of views, at the opposite end of the spectrum, stresses that too much aid is given. Public opinion often holds that too much money goes to foreign aid, and that very little positive effects are achieved, often because of corruption of the rulers of poor countries. Moyo (2009), who has received global attention, including from leaders like Rwandan President Paul Kagame, is particularly critical of the dependency that aid has created.[21] Easterly phrases the position in polemic style: Jeffrey Sachs 'thinks aid can end poverty and I think it cannot . . . The end of poverty comes about for home-grown reasons, as domestic reformers grope their way towards more democracy, cleaner and more accountable government, and free markets' (in Harman 2007), and the 'tragedy in which the West spent $2.3 trillion on foreign aid over the last five decades and still had not managed to get twelve-cent medicines to prevent half of all malaria deaths' (Easterly 2006, p. 4). According to him, the main problem of aid has been the emphasis on grand plans and the domination of 'planners', and the limited ability to motivate people to carry out such plans; increased commitments would again be dominated by these planners, and fail to learn from past mistakes.

Among the fiercest critique of aid derives from the idea that aid fuels corruption.[22] However, corruption has been looked at very closely by donor agencies over the last decades—for some perhaps even too closely as there is

not include collaboration with Chinese researchers or explicitly look at the impact of China. The role of new donors is analysed in Chapter 11 by Mohan, this volume.

[19] The UK's International Development (Reporting and Transparency) Act 2006 provides an exception. This commits the Secretary of State to report annually on expenditure on international aid, and progress towards the UN ODA target. The commitment to increased aid is combined with commitments to enhance effectiveness and transparency.

[20] Interviews at Sida found two-thirds of staff felt that disbursement rates were actively monitored in the day-to-day business (Ostrom et al. 2002); this study documents the agency's internal incentives and how this affects aid effectiveness and particularly sustainability. Also Ebrahim and Herz (2007, p. 6).

[21] Fischer and Kappel (2005), for example, describe how despite rent-seeking—which was the main obstacle to reform rather than low capacity—in Tanzania, donors continued to provide aid.

[22] Cooksey (2002) reviews corruption within donor agencies and among recipients, with a pessimistic but only partially substantiated review of reforms and attempts to address corruption.

recognition of the role this plays as an 'informal institution'. Conventional wisdom notes that aid is more effective in less corrupt states, which can be considered a variant of the notion put forward by Alesina and Dollar (2000) and others that aid is more likely to be effective in better-governed states. Tavares (2003) showed through cross-country regression that foreign aid is associated with lower corruption (which he highlights does not imply a causal effect), and this may have been because of the rules and conditions associated with aid, and the ability to pay salaries may reduce the corruption of officials. But there is increasing research that modifies generalizing statements (Dietrich 2010).

A third set of views represents a middle position between these opposites, focusing on the ways in which aid is provided, and on the need for better assessment (Riddell 2007; Manor 2005). Advocacy for more aid often goes together with calls for improving the quality of the aid system. Former Dutch development minister Jan Pronk (2001), reviewing the earlier aid literature and more recent analysis of aid–growth relationships, argues that aid should and can work as 'catalyst', rewarding for good development governance.

A number of arguments are put forward in this context. There is debate on what institutions to work with: for example Eyben and Ladbury (2006) argue that too much support has worked directly with the state, whereas in their view there is evidence that working with non-state actors has been effective. Another argument emphasizes that aid could be better targeted, that too much money is spent in countries that are not the poorest. There are powerful historical, political, and strategic reasons why aid is given to countries that are not poor. Many bilateral organizations have tried to focus their aid on the poorest countries, but the pull of other political considerations remains large (notably, since 9/11).[23] Burnside and Dollar (2000) showed that aid is effective, *if* its recipient governments have the right policies, particularly good fiscal, monetary, and trade policies.[24] Collier and Dollar (1999) combined an argument about the need to move aid to the countries with the largest numbers of poor people, with an emphasis on ability to use aid effectively.

Concerns about and analysis of aid dependency are relevant here (Fraser and Whitfiield 2008). Particularly in Africa, donor-funding formed half of some government budgets, often for extended periods of time. Donor-funding can undermine local accountability (Uvin 2004). New funding often leads to the setting up of new agencies, and this can detract from solving, and even

---

[23] A former USAID administrator criticized the European aid programmes for failure to align their aid to foreign policy concerns (Natsios 2006). See also Woods (2007). Kurlantzick (2007, p. 202) describes the recent Chinese aid programme as the core element of China's global 'charm offensive'.

[24] See further Dollar and Levin (2006) and Knack et al. (2010) who rank thirty donors on four indices, including aid selectivity.

worsen problems of existing public policy institutions.[25] A similar argument against increasing aid refers to what is commonly called 'absorptive capacity'. It is argued that recipient governments lack the administrative or policy capacity to effectively use increased aid flows, particularly when these are disbursed in a short period of time. Economists warn for the implications of large financial inflows on the economy, and the possibility that this may cause 'Dutch Disease', an appreciation of the exchange rate and resulting decline in competitiveness of national industries.[26]

A related argument stresses donors' habits, the patterns of behaviour and incentives that limit aid effectiveness.[27] Current aid is commonly compared with the Marshall Plan, which disbursed large sums of money in a short period of time; current aid is much more long-term with relatively small sums of money. Studies show that donor procedures tend to be cumbersome and time-consuming,[28] aid flows are often unpredictable, they often follow financial cycles on the side of the donors rather than demand by recipients, and donors' priorities change frequently. Many studies highlight that there are too many donor agencies, working in uncoordinated ways.[29] Some argue that donors' attitudes may have the potential to undermine progress, and aid has the potential to contribute to rather than reduce conflict (Browne 2007, p. 32). Tied aid, the use of foreign aid for commercial purposes, is generally thought to restrict its efficiency. While there has been widespread commitment to untie aid,[30] many donor countries continue to make collaboration with or purchase from their national companies a condition for the provision of aid.[31]

A fourth strand of literature focuses on the inner workings of aid agencies, often from a critical perspective. In an 'ethnography of aid and agencies', Mosse and Lewis (2006, p. 8) state that development policy is characterized by an incongruence between a seductive mix of 'development buzzwords' and a 'striking lack of progress in relation to a wide range of development

[25] Morss (1984) discusses the impact of donor and project proliferation on recipient government institutions.

[26] There is some agreement among economists that a foreign aid contribution of about 20% to the national budget does not have negative effects, and the economic impact can remain positive.

[27] Birdsall (2004) describes seven 'deadly sins'.

[28] This is strikingly described for USAID by Andrew Natsios as 'the clash of the counter-bureaucracy and development' (2010).

[29] See Acharya et al. (2006) and Morss (1984) who provided an early warning that was apparently not heeded. Booth (2011b) identifies piled-up donor initiatives as one of the causes for poor outcomes of service provision.

[30] In May 2008 OECD expanded the list of countries by eight to thirty-nine Highly Indebted Countries that will receive aid in untied form. <http://www.oecd.org/document/24/0,3343,en_2649_201185_40660248_1_1_1_1,00.html> accessed 29 May 2014.

[31] The OECD DAC statistics provide information about status of tying aid (table 23 and table 24 of the Statistical Annex of the Development Cooperation Report; <http://www.oecd.org/general/searchresults/?q=development%20cooperation%20report> accessed 1 September 2014).

indicators'.[32] Curtis (2004), building on cultural theory and stressing the various ways of thinking within donor agencies, highlights discrepancies between donor objectives and recipient needs or priorities in donor-funded programmes of civil service training. Eyben (2008) stresses the importance of personal relations within aid agencies, against the increasingly strong drives to focus on outputs. Hilhorst and Jansen (2010) emphasize how 'humanitarian space' separates aid practices (in this case, humanitarian operations) from its political environment. Much of the literature in this genre of critical analysis emphasizes and critiques donor practices, but does not extend to an analysis of the impact the projects did have on its trainees or institutions they supported.

Fifthly, another set of critical perspectives focus on the role that aid plays in maintaining global power relations. Much of the popular critique, particularly against the World Bank and in support of the agendas of subalterns and social groups in the South, obtains these forms of expression, but UN organizations like IFAD do not escape criticisms that aid institutions cause development problems. The Poverty Reduction Strategies Papers (PRSPs) processes have been interpreted as a means to maintain neo-liberalism (Porter and Craig 2004; Craig and Porter 2006).[33] Support to democracy and governance reforms is seen, by some authors, as consistent with this paradigm, for example with respect to the spread of a specific (neo-liberal) form of governance practices.

Finally, there is a set of arguments that puts aid in perspective, emphasizing that other policies and interests are more significant. As reflected strongly in writings originating in the US, aid is an instrument of foreign policy or diplomatic purposes.[34] Aid has been provided as a tool in Cold War competition, French aid has been instrumental in maintaining a sphere of influence, and Japanese aid was strongly motivated by commercial considerations (Hook 1995). The recent re-emergence of Chinese aid can similarly be interpreted as one of its diplomatic tools used to fulfil domestic commercial and economic development considerations, as well as global political and geo-strategic goals (see discussion in Chapter 11). Also, aid flows of the 'old' donors are rapidly becoming a smaller part of total financial flows: private capital flows have multiplied while official aid flows have stagnated (private charities have become important, too), and the financial contributions

---

[32] Mosse and Lewis (2006, p. 8). The reference to buzzwords in development practices is from an article by Cornwall and Brock (2005), also Cornwall (2007).

[33] Porter and Craig (2004) and Craig and Porter (2006).

[34] Alesina and Dollar (2000) based on quantitative analysis of bilateral aid confirm that foreign policy and strategic considerations (alongside economic needs and historical links) have a big influence on which countries receive aid. See further Berthélemy (2005), Dollar and Levin (2006), Hout (2007), Neumayer (2003), and Younas (2008).

of migrants from the South outstrip development aid (recent estimates put remittances at about US$ 300 billion or more, about triple that of official aid flows). The conclusion that aid isn't really all that important is critically important: it implies we may need to revise and broaden the question of the 'impact' of aid, or at least see aid as part of a continuum within broader international exchange.

The variety of views on aid are accompanied by little evidence-based conclusions about either the success or failure of aid. For example, Browne's (2007) conclusion that donors appeared 'at the wrong times and with the wrong attitudes' is only weakly substantiated with reference to three very different cases of 'fragile states': Burma (with boycott as the main question, coupled with the emergence of non-DAC donors), Rwanda (with the well-recognized failure to intervene before the genocide), and Zambia (where the question of Washington-Consensus prescriptions is key). How donors undermined development progress is not clear (except of course in cases where aid was grossly misused for Cold War purposes), at least not in the two cases where failure to engage may be the most important consideration. Moreover, there appears to be a disconnect between research and practice. For example, the overview of the last five years of the Centre for the Future State (IDS 2010) directly address development practitioners, arguing that they 'need to close off their mental models about governance and development that are rooted in OECD experience' (Unsworth 2010, Executive Summary). However, a political analysis of donors' actions seems to be lacking.[35]

Thus, the diversity of perspectives on aid, which are often left implicit, and particularly the polarization, is likely to influence our understanding on the impact of donor agencies. Moreover, simplification about agency staff ability to apply political analysis may be creating additional barriers. In fact, officials within donor agencies often do recognize that they are political agents as part of broader international politics, and they do position themselves in the local politics—even emphasizing a technical role is taking a political position. Future research can make an important contribution in closing a gap in the knowledge of the impact of aid, which has the potential to inform both the academic literature and development practice. This could entail a conscious reflection on and articulation of the perspective through which 'aid' is conceptualized, based in local narratives of the role of aid/donors—in their diversity—in local politics. This in turn would require 'internalizing' the role of donors as a 'permanent' feature of these local politics.

---

[35] See also Booth (2011c) on donors' recent emphasis on research uptake, and the barriers that continue to exist, in the case of public service provision in Africa.

Depoliticization of Aid: What Does the Literature Tell Us?

Political analysis remains poorly represented in international development debates. For example, in the writings of Jan Pronk on aid as catalyst, where one would expect an analysis of policies (and political change), much of the analysis draws on cross-country aid–growth regressions, and his conclusion that 'what is required is a special focus in aid policy on social harmony, political stability and peace' (Pronk 2001, p. 628) remained unsubstantiated.[36] At the same time, a lot of the political analysis has remained a safe distance from much of the international development debate, and certainly from international development practices; this perennially leads to calls to bring politics back into development.

Authors like Escobar, Ferguson, Ignacy, and Sachs have argued that the development discourse is Western created, imbued with dichotomies of Western superiority, justifying an interventionist and disempowering bureaucracy.[37] An oft-cited work is Ferguson's (1990) *The Anti-Politics Machine*, an ethnography of the aid industry in Lesotho (a highly aid-dependent country) that constructed the idea of Lesotho as a peasant society, in an attempt to justify the development agencies' own existence.[38] Chang's (2002) critique of international collaboration, more broadly, is that promotion of good governance implies pushing poor countries into adopting institutions that were non-existent in their own countries at similar stages of development.

Over the last ten years the role of politics in development has received increasing attention. This is demonstrated in the sequence of a perceived failure of the technocratic approach to adjustment in the 1980s, to the rise of an ambitious governance agenda,[39] of good governance, and of good enough governance, which opened up the space and need for better understanding of the role of institutions and politics within development. Booth and Golooba-Mutebi (2009) distinguish three types of political economy analyses, illustrating the diversity of perspectives that have emerged over time. First, Drivers of Change and similar analyses emphasize the constraints

[36] This was raised in a comment in the same journal *Development and Change* by Petras and Veltmeyer, for a realist political perspective, to which Pronk (2003) responded; in our reading again failing to provide evidence of aid impact on politics or the ability to influence policymaking. James Boyce, in response to Pronk, argued for the need to unpack both sides of the aid relationship (Pronk 2003, p. 387).

[37] Uvin (2004, p. 32). A related, anthropological, approach focuses on describing 'the interaction of ideas and relationships in development arena' (Mosse and Lewis 2006, p. 5).

[38] See Tania Li (2007) on the establishment of a national park in Central Sulawesi criticizes donors for analysing livelihood challenges as only technical problems; also Chhotray (2011).

[39] In the broader literature, this is reflected in the growing emphasis on institution in the work of North (1990). Cross-country regressions by Acemoglu et al. (2001), and the work of Mustaq Khan (2006) received much attention in the development debate.

that countries' histories and institutions impose on changes supported by donors.[40] Second, internal World Bank political economy approaches use stakeholder analysis and a range of public-choice and game-theory approaches. A third conceptual approach focuses on the room for manoeuvre, and 'change against the odds' as pioneered by Grindle in social sector reform in Latin America. In their own view, a ('layered') political economy approach to an explicit problem may be more likely to influence action than more generic forms of analysis, and they highlight the potential for donors to support third-party facilitation in reform processes. Additionally, as referred to earlier, their work emphasizes different forms of neo-patrimonialism, and the need for 'working with the grain'.[41]

Another politicized development practice is aid to promote democracy, which has been the subject of a fair number of studies, including as a variable in regression analysis. Kosack (2003) concluded that aid does not show a positive impact on quality of life, but it does show a positive sign if combined with a variable of democracy, and is ineffective in the case of autocracies—thus providing an argument for (though not ways in which) donors to enhance aid effectiveness while promoting democratization. Kalyvitis and Vlachiki (2010) use data for fifty-nine aid recipients during 1972 to 2004, using three categories of political regimes, and show a positive impact on democratization. Quantitative analysis has been used to assess the role of 'democracy aid' (Savun and Tirone 2011).

There is a recent growing interest in the role of elites in (economic) development.[42] Birdsall believes that Africa's institutional trap is related to the small share of income of its independent middle-income population, and that 'a robust middle-income group contributes critically to the creation and sustenance of healthy institutions, particularly healthy institutions of the state' (2007, p. 2).[43] Therefore, it is important to be more aware of the risks that (increasing) aid poses for this middle class (still poor, by international standards), through, for example, the labour market for skilled workers, interest rates, domestic investor confidence, and taxes. However, except in analysis of community-based development, the role of aid does not appear as a critical theme (e.g. Robinson's 2010 analysis of transnational elites). It does feature in the analysis of Mozambique's elite by Hanlon (2010), including

---

[40] For example, Duncan et al. (2002) with reference to Bangladesh.

[41] Kaminski and Serra (2011); this stresses that the nature of reforms went against a Washington Consensus, but does not explore the interaction with donors. Booth and Golooba-Mutebi (2011) analyse Rwanda's ruling party's relationship with Tri-Star investment and highlighting this has been controversial with donors.

[42] See, for example, <http://www.wider.unu.edu/research/projects-by-theme/development-and-finance/en_GB/Elites-and-Economic-Dev-Conf/> accessed 29 May 2014.

[43] See also the article on middle classes in the edited volume that describes declining inequality in parts of Latin America (López-Calva and Lustig 2010).

how structural adjustment led to reduced incomes of public services workers, and how aid money was used in privatization that benefited elites,[44] but this remains rather superficial and pays little attention to the different positions taken by different donors, and contradictions that presumably existed within donors' prescriptions.[45]

Naomi Hossain's (2005) work on elite perceptions of poverty in Bangladesh has been one of the few that directly touches on the question posed here, but this too was generally not linked to aid. She concluded that poverty was not a high priority for the Bangladeshi elite, not because they were ignorant or callous about poverty, nor because they failed to see a self-interest in tackling poverty, but simply because it did not have priority: poverty is not perceived as a threat, the elite thought much action was already undertaken, and their distrust of the state reduced appetite for further state-led action. The edited book by Reis and Moore (2005) *Elite Perceptions of Poverty and Inequality*, similarly concludes that many countries lack the kind of commitment that was behind the growth of welfare states in the nineteenth century.

Thus, there is an increasing body of political analysis in the field of development studies, and particularly in the area of commissioned research, that is required to have direct policy relevance. But calls for political analysis continue to increase, ever since the disappointment with reforms during the 1980s. Our observations confirm that of Unsworth that there continue to be barriers for more informed political analysis to inform practice. She concluded that for political economy analysis to endure, donors have to change the way they operate:

> The impact has been quite fragmented within agencies, and what [the Political Economy Analysis] hasn't done is induce any kind of fundamental rethink about how development happens and what the role of external players might be . . . [and] isn't affecting key decisions agencies make about how they recruit and deploy staff and train and use them. [46]

There is little empirical analysis of how donors, even where they do start adopting a political perspective, do influence local institutions and the people they work with.

---

[44] Hanlon (2010), building on earlier work (Hanlon 2004), shows how donors promoted corruption through their choice of elites to work with. Hanlon (2010) ends his analysis of Mozambique with reference to the possibility that Mozambique is now becoming a developmental state, which includes resistance to donors' prescriptions.

[45] World Bank, Social Development Department (2006) highlights and defines the need for analysis of political context to inform development planning, but with very little evidence of what the impact of these are on the ground.

[46] See <http://capacity4dev.ec.europa.eu/eu-working-group-land-issues/article/understanding-politics-development> accessed 29 May 2014; see further Unsworth (undated, 2009).

Of Aid Modalities and Conditionalities

Aid is provided in many different ways, in different 'aid modalities', a term used in particular to highlight differences between the project-mode of development that had become increasingly unpopular and sector-wide and national approaches like PRSPs.[47] The impact and how this is measured is substantially different for each of the modalities, and the choices between modalities also are critically important. The literature in each of these areas is large; this section discusses the lessons of each for the way we can understand the impacts of donors.

Project mode of aid delivery, road-building, livelihoods projects, and so on have generally been the most apolitical, and heavily criticized, including because of the 'islands of excellence' that resulted, the lack of scaling up of good practices, the proliferation of projects and possible drain on local administrative capacity.[48] At least implicit in this critique has been a notion that projects tend to be immaterial to broader politics and commitments (with the use of LogFrames as an illustration of this), and could possibly unintentionally reinforce power differences.

Technical cooperation, and capacity-building, is an example of project mode of approaches, and has a large body of technical literature of itself, and a body of critique.[49] Kühl (2009) argues that the concept of capacity development functions to meet the legitimacy requirements of aid organizations. Land et al. (2009) argues capacity development is (still) premised on planned technocratic interventions, without due attention to the political (and social–cultural) dimensions of change needed for sustainable outcomes. Similarly, Bergström (2005) highlights two critical conditions for successful (institutional development) projects: 'real' determination to achieve change on the part of the partner, and understanding of local context; neither of these were facilitated by Sida procedures.[50]

Project and technical cooperation can happen in a non-political or unreflective manner, but it can also be placed at the heart of political interventions, such as training of police, financial management, strengthening media, and electoral reform.[51] Project reviews and evaluations tend to look at

---

[47] Foster and Leavey (2001) discuss choices between aid instruments; also Irish Aid (2008) research report on good governance and aid modalities.

[48] The majority of aid is still delivered as projects (Riddell 2007, p. 180; see de Haan 2009, chapter 4).

[49] See for example Aron (2003) for post-conflict situations.

[50] James and Wrigley (2007) describe the 'mystery' of capacity building, which needs methods that strengthen ownership; are people-centred, engage with peoples' values and emotions, and adapt to context.

[51] The multi-donor support to Ethiopia may be an interesting case study of explicit and strongly worded attempts to improve governance and accountability.

'impacts', without much reflection—as far as we have seen—on the impacts on people and attitudes of the long-term international exchange people have become part of (and that would include scholarships).

A popular form of projects, because they provide benefits to poor people directly and immediately, are community-driven projects. There is a body of knowledge that has looked at the impact of community-driven models of aid delivery. Golooba-Mutebi and Hickey (2009), for example, analyse the Northern Uganda Social Action Fund, highlighting problems of intra-group conflict, lack of capacity to manage resources, and bad practices of group facilitators. They argue that community-driven models fail to engage seriously with predominant power and political relations, an issue that has been acknowledged by World Bank analysts as well.[52] They also suggest that (parallel) funding mechanisms like this may actually 'undermine the role and accountability of the state' (Gooloba-Mutebi and Hickey 2009, p. 33),[53] a question that runs through much of the literature and review of social funds (De Silva and Sum 2008).

The project modalities described above are distinct from the donor engagement at a more macro level, which have become important in the donor and academic literature since the adjustment approaches emerged. Public sector reform became the dominant mantra of the aid community, as a second step after the stabilization programmes that followed financial and economic crisis. The literature on this is large and often critical, while practices of reforms have continued and may be under-studied. Hirschmann (1993), for example, argued that the first generation of structural reforms led to 'collateral damage', emphasizing 'the complex inter-relationship between weak capability, task enormity, conditionality, aid fatigue, absorptive capacity and sustainability . . . the very people who were threatened by these policy reforms were the ones who were expected to carry them out' (quoted in Boesen 2004, p. 4). Public sector reform that has focused on formal arrangements is seen to have failed to produce real changes in behaviour, even though reforms sometimes succeed against the odds.[54]

The field of public sector reform is broad, and it is unlikely that general conclusions will emerge. Even individual and respected experts—deeply

---

[52] Mansuri and Rao (2004); Gaspart and Platteau (2006) explicitly warned against the 'perverse effect if cheap aid money' in the context of community-driven development. Wong (2010) describes two different models and paradox of engaging elites in projects in Bangladesh and Ghana.

[53] See also Hickey (2010) 'The Government of Chronic Poverty' (Hickey 2010) in the special issue of *The Journal of Development Studies*, on new potentials in moves to emphasize citizenship, but not much evidence on impacts of aid.

[54] Booth and Golooba-Mutebi (2009); Harrison (2004) discusses the emergence of 'governance states', and the role of the World Bank in shaping governance in Mozambique, Tanzania, and Uganda.

involved in donor-'driven' reforms in context over an extended period of time—may be very critical of donor approaches, their tendencies to pre-scribe templates, and increasingly unrealistic reporting requirements (Schiavo-Campo 2008), but would also be able to narrate stories of success, in difficult circumstances. Public financial management has received much donor (but less academic) attention, and is regarded as a key element of governance required for economic growth, and for absorbing donor funding (Hedger et al. 2007). Andrews (2010) reviews public finance management assessments of thirty-one African countries, and finds that much change has taken place, but that (de jure) budget preparation has been stronger than (de facto) budget implementation. Civil society engagement was generally well developed. Success in reforms tended to be larger when there were fewer actors involved. There were predictably substantial differences across countries, with growing and stable countries having stronger processes, and 'fiscal states' have better systems than 'rentier states'. Country characteris-tics matter a great deal, emphasizing the need for support to be based in local realities, and to create 'reform space'; but the review does not analyse whether donor organizations have practised this.[55]

While tax reforms have been part of many public sector reform pro-grammes, donor support to revenue generation through improvements in tax collection have not generated much analysis. There is common reference to the lack of attention to revenue generation, and possible disincentives that aid programmes lead to.[56] A critical question is whether taxation would con-tribute to stronger state–citizen relations, and the channels through which this would occur. McDonald and Jumu (2008) support the argument that taxation is better, in that respect, than both aid and natural resources[57]— which makes them conclude both that aid should be made more like tax, and that tax systems should be strengthened. Systems of taxation are diverse, and often follow colonial histories. There are various options for reform, the most common probably being the shift from indirect to more direct taxes. Forms of revenue generation or taxation are also central to relations between central governments and their local authorities, and donors can play a role in this, as Fjeldstad (2001) demonstrates for Tanzania. Sources of revenue also can impact types of expenditure: Hoffman and Gibson's

[55] A recent overview paper commissioned by the African Capacity Building Foundation (Hove and Wynne 2010), providing a 'balance sheet' of Medium Term Expenditure Framework (MTEF) and an Integrated Financial Management Information System (IFMIS) by and large confirms this.

[56] Important exceptions are Bräutigam et al. (2008), Moore (2007), Di John (2010a, 2010b, 2006), and Moss et al. 2006. Chapter 3, this volume, by Paul Mosley is much more detailed on the subject and can usefully be read in conjunction with this one.

[57] However, the literature indicates that natural resources are not necessarily a curse, and national institutions mediate the way resources are managed and redistributed.

(2005) comparison of Tanzania and Zambia concludes that a government's *sources* of revenue strongly affect its public expenditures. Local governments started to produce more public services as their budget's share of local taxes increased, while the revenue that local governments receive from sources outside their boundaries was spent more on employee benefits and administrative costs.

Another approach that arose explicitly out of the critique of projects as well as perceived need for public sector reform was that of sector-wide approaches, particularly in health and education. These imply that 'all significant funding for the sector supports a single sector policy and expenditure programme, under government leadership, adopting common approaches across the sector and progressing towards relying on Government procedures for all funds' (Foster 2000, p. 9). This approach was a response to three issues that are relevant for this review: the fact that conditionalities did not work, the need for institutional change, and the need to overcome fragmentation of budgeting. Closely linked to sector-wide approaches are donor approaches to general budget support, which were popular for some time as cutting edge to enhance aid effectiveness but more recently have given away (again) to project modes, partly because of donors' needs to see results and partly because the conditions for governance were found lacking. Budget support involves financial transfers to recipient countries' treasuries, combined with 'policy dialogue' and various forms of capacity-building. Molenaers et al. (2010) analyses the type of policy and political dialogue in the context of budget support, in the case of two political crises, illustrating the ambitiousness of this agenda (evaluation of UK budget support to Uganda had highlighted questions regarding assumed political commitment).

There is perhaps no area of donor intervention which generated more analysis than the Poverty Reduction Strategies Papers (PRSPs), which brought together international NGOs, the 'like-minded' donors, and the IFIs. There was a great deal of optimism—driven by very different constituencies—that PRSPs would imply a substantial change in aid relationships. While criticized from the start by various people, particularly regarding whether this implied at all a change from the Washington Consensus, from the middle of the 2000s critiques also started to appear from circles closer to the aid practitioners. The literature has become generally critical of the question whether PRSPS have really changed aid relationships (e.g. Booth and Piron 2004; Booth 2010). Booth et al. (2006) conclude PRSPs were unsuccessful in generating political buy-in for poverty reduction, similar to many of the findings on budget support. Moreover, the PRSP approach required a change in donor practices, and harmonization and alignment have come to the centre of attention under the Paris Declaration/Consensus, giving rise to a substantial amount of donor-focused literature. The conclusion of dissonance between donors' insistence on ownership, and the ways this is interpreted by recipients,[58] is relevant to understanding the dynamics of donor impacts.

The question of conditionalities is central to many of the questions about and choices for different aid modalities. We refer to modalities not in terms of the policy prescriptions that have obtained a highly charged reputation under the Washington Consensus, but in terms of the technical prescriptions regarding improvement of governance, including reducing corruption. The question of conditionalities had become a much-debated issue in the 1990s, after a decade of experience with structural reforms. Montinola (2010), using data from sixty-eight countries during the 1980s and 1990s, argues that conditional aid (the impact of IMF and World Bank aid on fiscal reform) can be effective depending on recipients' levels of democracy. The author suggests that aid can help democratic governments stay in power. Killick's analysis of the role of conditionalities, or 'pre-commitments' in aid relationships,[59] confirms the common wisdom that conditionalities do not work, but with an important emphasis: he argues that donors are 'often unable to put in place a system of rewards and punishments sufficient to overcome the frequent perceived conflicts of interest between themselves and recipient governments' (Killick 1997, Abstract). Instead, he argues, 'donors should recognize that their main contribution to policy reform in developing countries has been through influence on the contemporary intellectual climate, and persuasion of governments through regular contacts' (1997, Abstract).[60]

Again, general conclusions and cross-country quantitative studies are unlikely to tell the full story. We believe, and experience indicates, that agreed 'conditionalities' can work, but they arguably are no longer conditionalities according to the definition of Killick that emphasizes that they are a commitment that would not be made in the absence of aid. For instance, in China, the 'conditionalities' of aid on the one hand were resisted, but on the other hand the type of conditionalities that suited policymakers' reform agendas were actively embraced.

The debate on conditionalities is deeply politically charged, and may form a core part of the national poverty politics.[61] Further, the practice of

---

[58] Booth (2010) highlights that debates on country ownership remain technocratic, and provide no answers to what donors should do if governments do not take the necessary leadership. See further Browne (2007), Kanbur (2000), and Uvin (2004).

[59] Killick (1997) may be the most systematic exploration of the issue, based on evidence from twenty-one countries that had undergone structural adjustment. See also Dijkstra (quoted in Pronk 2003, pp. 396–8) emphasizing limited effectiveness.

[60] Killick's (1999) assessment of the impact of adjustment on poverty is relevant in this respect; in his view the link between the two is less strong than is commonly asserted. See also Buira (2003) on IMF conditionality, and Hayman (2011) on freezing budget support.

[61] Opposition parties in Orissa in the early 2000s organized a 'Quit Orissa' demonstration, against World Bank and DFID prescribing budget and staff cuts (which in the donors' views were in line with Finance Ministry prescriptions).

conditionalities is now challenged by the 'cash-on-delivery' ideas that have emerged, particularly from the US. Finally, debates on conditionalities are increasingly shaped by the emergence of China and other 'new' donors; their insistence on non-conditionality and fear of wanting to be seen to engage in internal politics is particularly and increasingly important for understanding the impact of aid on capacity and elites (see Chapter 11). Therefore, a political analysis of conditionalities appears significant, and conditionalities could usefully be conceptualized as an implicit contract between recipients and donors (who are among the first to realize when their conditionalities are working or not).[62]

Conclusion

This chapter is the result of a literature survey that was designed to provide insight into the relationship between aid and recipients' state capacity and elite commitment. While it is impossible to cover all the literature, including because of the emergence of 'new' donors and because aid practices are once again being rethought, we did establish that there is relatively little literature that directly addresses the question of how aid impacts state capacity for, and (particularly) elite commitment to, sustainable development.

Answering the questions on the impact of aid is complicated by four factors. First, aid is only one part of broader international policy, including bilateral relations, and 'other' objectives can significantly influence the implementation of aid commitments. This poses questions on assessing the success of aid, but also whether looking at the impact of aid alone limits or even distorts a perspective on local 'aid relationships'.

Second, views on aid are very diverse, fuelled by theoretical but also strong moral considerations, and often poorly substantiated critiques of aid—this makes interpretation of the findings of the impact of aid problematic—future research thus should build in a critical reflection of these differences, and integrate this into understanding aid relationships at local level.

Third, the governance–development link is disputed, for example, illustrated by moving academic emphasis of 'good governance' to 'good-enough governance' (Grindle 2004), and from a more state-centric focus to an emphasis on the interaction between state and non-state actors, between formal and informal institutions (IDS 2010; Hyden 2008), from drivers of change to 'politics of development' (Leftwich 2007), and finally a focus on

---

[62] To conceptualize this contract, we can draw on texts on aid negotiations, including those using game theory, principal–agent models, new institutionalism, and a political economy (Fraser and Whitfield 2008).

the neo-patrimonial state (Kelsall et al. 2010). This chapter has not directly covered the growing governance literature, nor has it addressed the question of aid to deliver services more broadly. We assume the importance of governance—in its broadest and dynamic sense[63]—for sustainable development, and note the diversity of governance–development links, and have looked primarily at the impact of aid on aspects of governance. Developing local narratives of aid relationships are essential to inform this ongoing debate, including regarding how the differing views and approaches within and across donors lead to unexpected outcomes.

Fourth, the practices of emerging donors are still under-researched. Evidence is needed on how the new players are influencing the aid dynamics, and the impact aid has on capacity and commitment. There are many ways in which this can be approached, but it is critical to link this to an enhanced understanding of the dynamics of the internal transformations of these emerging economies and their concomitant foreign policy objectives.

Further, there are questions about the interaction between research and development policy that are relevant here, contributing to complicating answering the questions for this review. The literature suggests the existence of barriers for more informed political analysis to inform practice; in any case, there is little analysis of how donors, even where they do start adopting a political perspective, do influence local institutions and the people they work with. Much of the literature provides a critique of aid practices, but it does: a) not seem to be based on in-depth understanding of what donors do; b) lack political analysis of why donors do—and present—what they do (for example, choices between aid modalities); and c) arguably miss a main point about how interaction with donors have structured practices, politics, and attitudes in the countries that donors work in.

The review thus confirmed our initial hypothesis that there is (even before the emergence of new donors) insufficient evidence regarding the role of aid, and regarding the specific impact on specific elements of governance (law, bureaucracy, elections, business regulation), and on the possible trade-offs (e.g. strengthening teachers while weakening PTAs). We conclude that in the specific contexts where aid has played a significant role, even if negative, a better understanding of aid dynamics is necessary. Future research can make a conceptual contribution by moving beyond questions of the 'impact' of aid, to a consideration of the role of international exchange in the articulation of local political economy.

---

[63] See Everest-Phillips (2007) for an emphasis on the need to move beyond technocratic approaches. Bräutigam, now the best-informed observer of Chinese aid, in a 2000 report highlighted the role of strong institutions in the successes of Taiwan and Botswana, and obstacles within aid systems to promote governance reform.

11

China in Africa: Impacts and Prospects for Accountable Development

Giles Mohan

Introduction: Asian Drivers and Effective States

Development cooperation is changing as rising power donors (re)enter the fray. While a growing body of evidence explores some of the economic trends (e.g. UNCTAD 2007), we know little about the impacts of new (and predominantly Asian) drivers of development on state capacity-building and elite commitment to development in poor countries, especially in sub-Saharan Africa. Africa is a key site given existing problems of economic development and governance, but crucially it is emerging as a strategic region in terms of resource access, trade, investment, aid, and migration (Alden 2007). Of the rising Asian countries China remains the largest player in Africa, and for this reason is the main focus of this chapter (Brautigam 2009). This chapter reviews the existing evidence on China's engagement with Africa and maps out a future research agenda in this area.

Over the past decade Africa has gained in international importance and the Chinese are among a number of rapidly industrializing nations that see the continent in strategic terms (Carmody 2011). Moyo (2009, p. 120) argued that the emergence of China is a 'golden opportunity' for Africa offering the continent a 'win-win' alternative to the scenario of an 'aid-dependent economy' by focusing instead on trade and investment and by providing the infrastructure that will enable Africa to 'move up the development curve' (Moyo 2009, p. 122). This ideal of 'help for self help' is underpinned by an accompanying discourse of development 'cooperation' rather than aid and donor–recipient relations (Rampa and Bilal 2011).

While Moyo (2009) is one of the optimists, the pessimists focus on the aid–governance nexus where the Chinese are accused by some of unscrupulous behaviour that undermines good governance (Manning 2006; Phillips 2006; Tull 2006; Naim 2007). Others (Marks 2006; Trofimov 2007) have taken this focus on aid further to argue that China is essentially a neo-colonial power, where African resources are 'plundered' by Beijing which cements the long-standing uneven division of labour between Africa and the rest of the world. In some ways the 'China threat' in Africa reflects a more general concern about China's challenge to US hegemony (Campbell 2008b).

The Political Effects of China in Africa

While we noted that most analysis of China in Africa has focused on the economic ties, and where studies have dealt with politics (e.g. Broadman 2007) it is a normative analysis about how to smooth flows of trade and investment. Recently there have been more critical attempts to analyse the politics of these relationships. Tull (2006) concludes his piece by arguing that 'China's massive return to Africa presents a negative political development' (p. 476) and his thesis usefully examines this in broad political economy terms—something I return to below.

The tendency of China to exacerbate African governance problems is seen by some as an extension of China's own lack of concern for human rights and accountability at home—the Chinese export the capitalism they know best (Henderson 2008). In terms of putting Chinese aid in the wider context of 'older' donors, Dreher et al. (2010, p. 18) point out that new donors 'do not generally exhibit a stronger bias against better governed countries', the corollary being that older donors, despite their criticisms of China, have also been willing to support corrupt and authoritarian states.

Although there have been useful contributions over the past few years as better data has emerged (e.g. Brautigam 2009), they still tend to attribute the power to China at the expense of Africa. For example, the 'Asian Drivers' agenda (Kaplinsky and Messner 2008), which we adapt later, is premised on a conflation of all Asian countries as sharing some essential characteristics and that they do the 'driving', which denies African agency. This is echoed in Carmody et al.'s (2011) analysis of Chinese 'geo-governance' in Zambia which argues that the Chinese state projects its power into Africa as part of a broader goal of shaping globalization, although they are among the few analysts to factor in African political agency (see also Large 2009; Haglund 2009).

Structure and Argument

The chapter starts by setting out an analytical framework, which identifies the channels through which China engages with African development. To avoid seeing these channels as dominated by Chinese agendas I use work around the African state to produce an analytical grid that factors in domestic politics. The chapter then looks at the actual impacts on governance by applying this framework to three case studies, although other cases are mentioned. The cases are selected as emblematic of the African state types identified in the framework and are not intended to be an exhaustive review of all African cases. I conclude with an outline of emerging trends and future research themes for the short to medium term.

The argument is that China impacts on African development in multiple ways that go well beyond the Western focus on aid. On one hand we have to be much more aware of the multiple interests and actors on the Chinese side combined with an awareness of African agency on the other. However, a common trait of this engagement is inter-elite brokerage, which has tended to bypass domestic channels of debate and accountability and so tends to undermine good governance. That said, in most cases it delivers much needed infrastructure which benefits wider society and so could kick start economic growth that in turn might spread benefits. Crucially, as civil society and political processes in Africa have started to contest this elitism and Chinese practices we are seeing slightly more transparent attempts to negotiate the relationship though these are relatively ad hoc and nascent. Moreover, China's entry to Africa is also through independent businesses who lie outside of Chinese state direction and whose impacts on local development could be significant in terms of job creation, although their political involvement will be limited in the short term.

Analytical Framework

In this section I elaborate an analytical schema for assessing the political impacts of China's development cooperation. It has two basic elements—the channels through which China impacts on domestic political processes based on an amended version of the framework developed by Kaplinsky and colleagues (e.g. Kaplinsky and Morris 2009; Kaplinsky 2008). As noted in the Introduction the emphasis on Asian actors 'driving' relationships tends to downplay African political agency and in practice this framework was used to examine economic linkages rather than political aspects. To address this we use the work of Alden (2007) and Tull (2006) who have developed classificatory schema of African regime types to hypothesize the possible impacts of China on African politics.

Asian Drivers

The first element is identifying the channels of interaction and impact. The framework distinguishes different channels of impact transmission, the distinction between complementary and competitive impacts, and between direct and indirect impacts. These channels are contingent and change over time, and vary in significance depending on such things as location, resource endowment, trade links, and geo-strategic significance. Six key channels stand out in importance: trade links, investment flows (Foreign Direct Investment (FDI) and portfolio investments), aid, governance, flows of migrants, and environmental spillovers (see Table 11.1). I will elaborate on each of these later in the chapter. As a heuristic it is also important to stress that these channels are clearly not discrete.

In each of these channels of interaction, there will be a mixture of complementary and competitive impacts. For example, with regard to trade, China may both provide cheap inputs and consumer goods to sub-Saharan Africa and be a market for African exports. On the other hand, imports from China can displace local producers. In relation to FDI, China can be a direct source of inward FDI into sub-Saharan Africa and perhaps crowd-in FDI into Africa from third countries as parts of extended global value chains. These are complementary impacts. But China may also compete with other economies for global FDI.

In terms of thinking through the developmental and political impacts, the key aspect of these interactions is the 'for whom' component. Countries may be affected differentially—in some cases, for example, the export of fabrics from China to Africa may feed productively into a vibrant clothing and textile value chain; in other cases, it may displace a country's exports and production for the domestic market. However, these effects are not just felt at the national level, but affect groups within countries differentially. For example, cheap clothing imports from China may displace clothing and textile workers, but cheapen wage goods and hence reduce wage costs for producers in other sectors. These impacts on a complementary–competitive axis may also change over time, and most importantly, they will vary for different classes, regions, and groups within economies.

Table 11.1. A framework for assessing the impact of China on sub-Saharan Africa

Channel	Impacts			
	Complementary		Competitive	
	Direct	Indirect	Direct	Indirect
Trade				
Investment				
Aid				
Governance				
Migrants				
Environment				

Source: Kaplinsky 2008.

The complementary–competitive axis of impacts is generally quite well recognized and understood. Less widely acknowledged is the distinction between direct and indirect impacts, partly because indirect impacts are difficult to measure. Indirect impacts occur in third-country markets and institutions. For example, China's trade with the US may open or foreclose the opportunities for African economies to export into that market. Similarly, China's high savings rate has had the effect of lowering global interest rates, indirectly facilitating investment in Africa. As in the case of the complementary/competitive access, the impact of the direct and indirect impacts can be gauged either at the country level, or at intra-national levels. Yet impacts are not just conditioned by the needs of the Chinese actors 'driving' this process, but are realized relationally through the ways in which these channels interact with African states and societies.

Making Sense of the African State

The second element is the nature of the political system with which these channels interact, which is largely but not exclusively a state-centred issue given the bilateral and elite nature of the way China engages with Africa (Taylor 2006, 2007). Carmody and Taylor (2010) use the term 'flexigemony' to capture the more dynamic interactions between China and a differentiated landscape of African politics. For them flexigemony denotes how 'Chinese actors adapt their strategies to suit the particular histories and geographies of the African states with which they engage' (p. 497). From an African perspective, the 'emerging' powers give recipient countries some leverage, what has been termed the 'revival of triangulation' (Large 2008). On the face of it China's interests do not radically alter the role Africa plays in the global division of labour (Tull 2006) but what is interesting to analyse is whether individual African states are able to harness this hegemonic rivalry for their own ends. How can we conceptualize African state agency?

In order to systematically analyse the relationships between Chinese channels of engagement and African polities we can use the typologies generated by Alden (2007). Alden sets out a broad typology of states—pariah states, illiberal regimes and weak democracies, and democratic countries with diversified economies. Tull (2006) also focuses on three groups of states—democratizing, mineral-rich, and post-conflict—which cover some of Alden's concerns. Alden's schema has an implicit scaling of democratization and his first two groups are essentially resource-rich states. Moreover, post-conflict tells us little about the underlying political economy and rarely covers whether China has a peacekeeping role.

With *pariah partnerships* China is seen as a source of stability and provider of FDI and development assistance which is denied by other avenues.

Examples are Chad, Sudan, and Zimbabwe, with Angola dropping in and out. The details will be explored below, but these cases show that while the Chinese will pursue interests in the face of glaring governance and rights abuses there are times when they draw the line for pragmatic reasons or through international pressure. So, it is wrong to characterize the Chinese as endlessly cynical in such cases.

The *illiberal regimes with weak democracy* cover much of the rest of SSA, but notably include Nigeria, Senegal, Tanzania, and Zambia. The relationships with the Chinese are brokered at elite levels to access strategic resources. But at the same time Chinese investments are more diverse and so bring much needed FDI and development aid, but this can compete with indigenous firms which can cause conflict. There are also strong ties between political elites and leading local firms so that foreign investments can proceed relatively quickly compared to states with stronger and more accountable institutions. In these states the Chinese are willing to secure leverage via self-aggrandizing symbolic infrastructure projects which impact on regime legitimacy.

The *democracies with diversified economies* are few and far between, but South Africa is the notable (and powerful) example. Alden includes Namibia, Botswana, and Ghana, though these are more debatable cases in terms of the diversification of their economies. In these states the relationship is complex and varies according to the local business interests and policy coherence of the state. There may be competition with local firms but the possibility exists for strategic guidance that could create more local benefits. Here local CSOs are more likely to exist and be able to voice dissent in policy arenas, which could affect the direction and nature of Chinese investment and aid.

As illustrated in Table 11.2 combining the two frameworks produces an analytical grid to track the political effects.

Before analysing specific exemplar case studies I will flesh out the six channels in more detail and assess aggregate trends at a continental scale.

Trade

Chinese trade with Africa stood at US$817 million in 1977 just before the major reforms that liberalized the Chinese economy, but from 2000 to 2009 bilateral trade rose from US$10.6 billion to US$91.07 billion (CAITEC 2010). In the first half of 2011, China–Africa imports and exports totalled US$79.01 billion, an increase of 29.1 per cent year-on-year (Chinese Custom 2011). African states have benefited from commodity exports such as oil, minerals, cotton, and logs; building of infrastructure, for example, transport and construction of public buildings which are a means of assuring social gains such as education and health care in the future; imports of machinery and auto-parts; and welfare gains from consumer imports from China. However,

Table 11.2. Political impacts framework

Channel	Impacts by state type					
	Pariah states		Illiberal regimes and weak democracies		Democratic countries with diversified economies	
	Direct	Indirect	Direct	Indirect	Direct	Indirect
Trade						
Investment						
Aid						
Governance						
Migrants						
Environment						

Source: Author.

competition with local industries resulted in some closures of local enterprises and job losses, especially around clothing and textiles (Amankwah 2005). This in turn contributed to losses in export to third-country markets and further capacity losses in terms of labour and management deskilling (Kaplinsky and Messner 2008).

As a means of stimulating trade and facilitating inward investment the Chinese have recently initiated a series of Special Economic Zones (SEZs) across Africa (Brautigam and Tang 2011). It is expected that these proposed SEZs will focus on value-added industries and provide liberalized investment environments for investors (*China Economic Review* 2011). According to Davies (2010, p. 26), the zones will create employment opportunities and generate foreign exchange reserves through more diversified sources of income. Although these zones are largely invested in and built by Chinese state-owned enterprises (SOEs), their main occupants are small and medium-sized enterprises (SMEs), amounting to 85 per cent of the businesses (Tang and Zhang 2011).

FDI

China's direct investment in African countries reached $1.44 billion in 2009 (Han 2011), in which non-financial direct investment soared by 55.4 per cent from the previous year (*China Daily* 2010). In 2008, nearly 1,600 Chinese enterprises had started business in African countries (Wen 2009). Some 180 of these companies were spearheaded by the 'going out' policy and have been designated by the Chinese state to benefit from preferential finance, tax concessions, and political backing in order to become true multinationals.

In terms of China and Africa one of the important differentiating factors is the scale and type of Chinese enterprise (Gu 2009). While we talk about packages of aid and investment it largely relates to the ties between key Chinese ministries, development banks, and large SOEs (Hubbard 2008). These projects are often spatially enclaved with relatively few multipliers in the local economy or 'deep' linkages to local society. By contrast we see Chinese private transnational corporations (TNCs) entering under 'open' commercial contracts, where they lack any of the protection afforded by the tying of loans to investment. And finally there are the myriad small Chinese private firms that date back, in some cases, to the colonial period (Mohan and Tan-Mullins 2009). Each type of firm has different levels of engagement with local capital, the state, and society and we will explore these differences through our case studies.

A recent policy vehicle for enhancing FDI in Africa is the China–Africa Development Fund (CADFund) established under the 2006 Africa Policy. The CADFund is the first equity investment fund in China focusing on Africa (Tradeinvest Africa 2009). Other than providing funds for companies, CADFund provides various consultancy services and information-sharing for investment in Africa, partner-sourcing, finance-structuring, and environmental and social issues (CADFund 2014). By the end of 2009, the CADFund had earmarked US$700 million for over thirty-five projects (CAITEC 2010).

Aid

One of the problems of assessing Chinese aid is that it is not measured in the same way as DAC aid (Glosny 2006; Lancaster 2007; Jacoby 2007; Kragelund 2008) and a lack of domestic transparency compounds the uncertainties, although the publication of an aid White Paper in April 2011 went some way to clarify these issues (Xinhua 2011). China does not separate Official Development Assistance from economic cooperation or investment as long as the intent is to expand local capacity. This is much more about mutual benefit than a discourse of charity or of 'catching up' (King 2010).

Many of the features of China's contemporary aid-giving were laid down during the Cold War period. Today, much of the aid is bilateral and delivered through three modes of grant aid, interest-free loans, and concessional loans (Davies et al. 2008). Aid is also project based (often turnkey) rather than sectoral or programme aid as encouraged by the Paris Declaration on Aid Effectiveness (Glosny 2006). One of the contentious elements is that much of China's aid and concessional lending is tied (Kragelund 2008). Hubbard (2008, p. 225) asserts that the Chinese insist that the Chinese contractor appointed by the Ministry of Commerce (MOFCOM) should 'purchase and import from China as much equipment, technology and services as possible', which is similar to the earlier Japanese model. This goes against the OECD's efforts to untie aid, although despite these efforts many DAC donors still have significant proportions of tied aid (Brautigam 2009). A similar issue is raised around export credits which are the preferred currency used by ExIm bank and potentially allow for more tying (Manning 2006), but Reisen and Ndoye's (2008) study for the OECD suggests that China's lending is not 'imprudent'. As Dreher et al. (2011) conclude 'we find little reason to blame new donors for using aid as a means to promote commercial self-interest' (p. 1961).

Governance

As already noted, China's engagement with Africa has often been reduced to a question of exacerbating governance issues. Yet China's impacts on governance and politics are multi-layered. Given its insistence on 'non-interference' and a respect for sovereignty the Chinese would argue that they do not have a direct impact on African politics, yet even if this were true, China can impact through multilateral institutions and, importantly, at the ideational level. These various channels will be discussed in turn.

First, the reason why China exercises some commentators and activists is that it seemingly attaches no conditions to its loans and therefore undermines the work of Western donors around governance (Naim 2007). Yet Dreher et al. (2011) found relatively little difference between 'old' and 'new' donors in terms of their aid-allocating behaviour despite ideological differences alluded to by analysts. While China publicly distances itself from internal political issues, the backlash against its role in Sudan saw a weakening of its 'non-interference' line (Large 2008). Holslag (2011) found that China is flexible and pragmatic in its political engagements with Africa. Additionally Glosny (2006) argues that the Chinese are aware they need to understand local institutional cultures to maximize the benefits from their interventions, something analysed in Eisenman's (2008) study of the Communist Party of China's International Department (CPC-ID). While this is not the same as direct influence it suggests that the Chinese have a series of 'quieter' foreign policy mechanisms (Shambaugh 2007).

Secondly, China's influence in Africa is also felt through its roles in multilateral organizations. Gu et al. (2008) note that China's role as an international actor has grown as a result of its economic rise. This occurs through a range of channels: its imports of energy and resources have shifted prices and ushered in a renewed period of geopolitical anxieties around security of supply; its currency reserves impact on other countries' financial markets, notably—but not exclusively—the US; it is a significant player in the WTO and other trade and investment forums; and as a polluter it impacts on climate change. In essence these are economic drivers with political effects but China also plays an increasing role in purposive political processes and institutions. While China still engages in bilateral diplomacy, it is leading the way towards what some have argued is a multipolar world (Wade 2011) that will reduce the influence of the US-dominated order of the past seventy years (Ikenberry 2008).

A third important political influence of China is at an ideational level. This revolves around, first, a post-colonial solidarity based on shared histories of colonization and, second, the potentially powerful demonstration effect of the 'China model'. Six (2009) argues that a key difference that China and India bring to the aid and development agenda is they occupy a 'dual position' (p. 1110) being both of the developing world but also key drivers of growth in the global economy. This means they do not need to fall back on teleologies of emancipation bound up in Western development discourse but are freer to be honest about their interest-based engagements with African countries. Six's insistence on the transparency of China's interests is fair although questions of 'solidarity' that are the watchwords of China's discourse of development cooperation also need to be empirically tested rather than taken at face value.

Obiorah (2007) argued that China provides a powerful development model, which has a number of possible effects on African development debates. First, he argued, African leaders can use this model to deny political rights to their people. Second, China exports its model via growth-oriented aid and overlooks the social impacts of its actions under the banner of non-interference. Ultimately so Obiorah feels it is the duty of African civil society to debate and discuss China's role, because rentier regimes will not engender such debate. While Obiorah is rightfully circumspect about the political (ab)use of the 'China model', problems arise in exactly what we mean by the 'China model' since arguably there are multiple models in different provinces, something acknowledged by both non-Chinese (e.g. Mittelman 2006) and Chinese analysts alike (Junbo 2011).

Migration

While most observers accept that China has sent an increased number of workers to Africa in the past decade, a major problem is that data are speculative (see Mohan and Tan-Mullins 2009). To assess the impacts on Africa of this migration requires what Mung terms a 'triangular' perspective in which 'the Chinese diaspora does not only relate to China, but also interacts with the society where it has settled' (p. 105–6). One upshot of increased trade and migration with Africa has been a rise in political responses to it, largely within civil society (Alden 2007; Davies 2007; Campbell 2008). A number of Africa trade unions and business associations have led the critique of China's role in national economies (Baah and Jauch 2009; Human Rights Watch 2011).

Moreover, there is some evidence of Chinese migration becoming politicized. Despite the tangible evidence of modernization that Chinese projects bring there are growing signs of disaffection with the Chinese among Africans (Trofimov 2007) though this has often been whipped up by Western media and varies between countries (see Sautman and Yan 2009; Gadzala and Hanusch 2010). Overall surveys that exist suggest a relatively high approval rating for the Chinese (e.g. Ngome 2009), but exceptional cases exist where the Chinese presence is used to fire nationalist sentiment.

Environment

As noted, much of the use of the Asian Drivers framework has been to analyse economic interactions to the relative exclusion of other development channels. A more complete approach to studying China's development footprint might draw on the insights of 'political ecology' (Peet and Watts 2004; Bryant and Bailey 1997). For a study of China and Africa relations natural resources and the environment are key for a number of reasons. First, given the resource focus of much Chinese activity, what are the implications for ecosystem sustainability in areas where new exploitation is taking place under conditions of lax regulation (Haglund 2009)? And are the Chinese any better or worse than other multinationals in this regard (Chan-Fishel 2007)? Second, China and other rising powers are moving into agriculture, which has huge implications for access to land, and thereby impacts upon the livelihoods of the poor (Mahmoud 2010). Third, China is a major producer of greenhouse gases which indirectly impact on low-income economies through climate change so that export production in China for Western markets has impacts on the poor in the developing world (Watts 2010). In turn this creates complex global governance problems where the relatively powerless developing-country governments have little say.

Analysis of Existing Engagements

The preceding analysis has identified the channels through which China engages with Africa and the nature of the states that in turn mediate these engagements and ultimately determine the developmental impacts. These two dimensions were captured in an analytical framework and in this section we use that framework to analyse the impacts across the three types of African state.

Table 11.3 provides an overview of the findings and the subsequent section gives detail of each case. Gaps in the table below indicate either a lack of knowledge (Unknown) or a weak relationship (Limited impact).

Angola

As an illiberal regime with weak democracy, Angola's post-war economy required huge amounts of social and infrastructural investment and so sought external financing. It was in this context that China, in need of energy resources, sought to offer Angola a series of oil-backed credit lines with little conditionality (Corkin 2011a). China's ExIm Bank provided the first funding for infrastructure development in 2002 and a 'framework agreement' for new economic cooperation was signed by the Angolan Ministry of Finance and the Chinese Ministry of Trade in 2003, whilst in March 2004 the first US$2 billion financing package for public investment projects was approved.

Two additional ExIm Bank loans of US$500 million and US$2 billion were made in 2007 with the repayment terms increased to fifteen years with a revised interest rate of Libor plus 1.25 per cent (Campos and Vines 2008). A further $1 billion loan from the China Development Bank was granted in March 2009 (rising to US$1.5 billion in 2010) with a view to supporting the development of Angolan agriculture. In the first official estimate of Chinese credit to Angola, the Chinese Ambassador said in early 2011 that an estimated US$14.5 billion in credit had been provided since the end of the war from the three Chinese state banks (Power et al. 2012). These credit lines have opened up well over a hundred projects in the areas of energy, agriculture, water, health, education, telecommunications, fisheries, and public works including key elements in the government's post-war National Reconstruction Programme. Project proposals identified as priorities by the respective Angolan ministries are put forward to the *Grupo de Trabalho Conjunto,* a joint committee of the Ministry of Finance and the MOFCOM (China). For each project put to tender, the Chinese government proposes three to four Chinese companies and all projects are inspected by third parties not funded by the credit line while sectoral ministries are in charge of managing these public works and making sure that sufficient staff are trained.

Additionally, oil-backed loans amounting to as much as US$10 billion have been provided by a private equity firm based in Hong Kong called the China International Fund. Further, some Chinese businesses based in Hong Kong have been a key feature of China's push into African markets. Levkowitz et al. (2009) have shown many of the Chinese companies currently operating in Angola have the same Hong Kong address at which a handful of individuals control over thirty firms. Key personnel involved in CIF have ties to Chinese state-owned enterprises and state agencies including China International Trust and Investment Corporation, Sinopec and possibly China's intelligence apparatus. By posing as a private firm, the Group

Table 11.3. Political impacts framework with indicative case studies

Channel	Impacts by state type					
	Pariah states (e.g. Sudan)		Illiberal regimes and weak democracies (e.g. Angola)		Democratic countries with diversified economies (e.g. Ghana)	
	Direct	Indirect	Direct	Indirect	Direct	Indirect
Trade	Cheaper manufactures; oil revenue.	Unknown	Cheaper manufactures; oil revenue.	Unknown	Cheaper manufactures; mineral revenue; textile and construction firms feeling competition.	Dutch Disease effects from recent oil discovery.
Investment	Infrastructure investment.	Possibly crowding in other Asian FDI.	Infrastructure investment; limited local employment.	Unknown	Infrastructure investment (e.g. Bui, Kpone); significant local employment.	International donors using Chinese firms.
Aid	Social and economic infrastructure; some vanity projects.	'Buys' support for China in multilateral forums.	Social and economic infrastructure; some vanity projects.	'Buys' support for China in multilateral forums.	Social and economic infrastructure; some vanity projects.	'Buys' support for China in multilateral forums; DAC donors concerned about lack of Chinese engagement. INGOs and (Bretton Woods Institutions) BWIs concerned about resource curse. Limited impact.
Governance	Elite brokerage. Involvement in internal conflicts.	International backlash over Darfur.	Elite brokerage exacerbates lack of transparency.	China supportive of EITI.	Elite brokerage Civil society accommodating rather than confrontational.	
Migrants	Employment creation; some politicization and targeting of migrants.	Limited impact.	Employment creation; some politicization of migrant presence.	Limited impact.	Employment creation; no major social tensions.	
Environment	Investment in hydropower; abuses of local populations; weak local regulation.	International condemnation and INGO activity (e.g. IRN).	Investment in resource extraction; weak local regulation.	Unknown	Investment in hydropower; weak local regulation.	Unknown

Source: Author.

creates numerous companies within a complicated organizational structure to invest globally, thereby enabling the Group to acquire assets 'unnoticed'. This credit facility has been managed by Angola's Reconstruction Office, the *Gabinete de Reconstrução Nacional* (GRN), which has been exclusively accountable to the Angolan presidency and originally managed most of the major infrastructure projects. In the major government reshuffle of March 2010 (in which the President called for a crackdown on corruption) a replacement was sought for the GRN in what was widely seen as a vote of no confidence in the agency and later in the same year the President announced that a company called Sonangol Imobiliária [Sonangol Real Estate] would be taking over responsibility from the GRN for implementing various projects relating to construction and the rehabilitation of infrastructure (Power 2011).

The Angola case points to the 'China–Africa' relationship being organized through hybrid and enclaved yet spatially diffuse institutions which are detached from national democratic processes. Agency on the part of selected Chinese and Angolan actors has produced in the CIF–GRN an institutional assemblage that sits within the state apparatus but is only connected to selected and clandestine elements within the state. As Corkin (2011a) argues this might be a response on the part of the Chinese to Angola's rampant corruption in which direct ties are seen as better than diffuse budget support. The creation of unaccountable enclaves within states echoes the Structural Adjustment era when 'parallel governments' (Hutchful 1989) were set up, mainly in finance ministries, by appointed technocrats. However, in contrast to the adjustment era there is no obvious political conditionality, rather a diffuse form of authority based on a small number of powerful actors.

Given that such a small part of the state is actively acting in this relationship is it meaningful to talk about 'the state' at all? Social collectivities–like states–that are driven by a small number of actors can have agency if they are given the authority to act by wider society. It is debatable if the Dos Santos regime has such a social contract yet the delivery of much-needed infrastructure not only deepens (or seeks to deepen) the regime's legitimacy but might benefit wider Angola society. In Dos Santos we see an active and single-minded leader who exercised his agency to create institutions to channel inward investment in particular directions.

Ghana

While I use Ghana as an example of a democratic country with a diversified economy it is noted that the economy is not hugely diverse. The presence and intensity of Chinese involvement is less evident in Ghana compared to Angola, largely due to the lack of strategic minerals although this has changed with the discovery of offshore oilfields in late 2007. Although China has had a long-standing relationship with Ghana since the 1960s, it is only in recent years that the relationship has been taken to a higher level.

Over the years, Chinese aid has been used to build physical infrastructure like roads (e.g. the Ofankor-Nsawam section of the Accra-Kumasi road) and buildings (the National Theatre). It was in 2004/2005 when relations improved and Ghana began to receive grants and interest-free loans directly from China such as a US$24 million debt relief on interest free loans (Interview with Xi, counsellor, 2008). In the 2006 FOCAC, Ghana and China signed six agreements, including a US$66 million loan for the expansion of Ghana's telecommunication infrastructure and a US$30 million concessionary loan for the first phase of the National Fibre-optic and E-government project. The project was executed by the Chinese telecom giant Huawei and aimed at linking all the ten regional capitals and thirty-six townships on fibre routes (*Daily Graphic*, 15 August 2007).

In general the process is similar to Angola in which the Chinese sign a framework document for construction and then engage their own contractor from China and procure the materials from the mainland. Upon completion, the Chinese effectively donate the building to the Ghanaian government (Interview with Xi, counsellor, Ghana). There is a perception amongst ministers and think tanks in Ghana that the Chinese are serving genuine infrastructure needs. As one think-tank told us, the 'Chinese also got it right from the beginning as countries must get infrastructure in place before any development can take place' (Interview, Private Enterprise Foundation 2008).

Undoubtedly the most significant Chinese engagement with Ghana is the Bui Hydroelectric Dam. Like many Chinese-funded infrastructure projects the majority of the money comes from ExIm Bank. The Bui Dam will cost US$622 million of which US$288 million is from buyer credits and US$298 million is a commercial loan, the interest on which is repayable after September 2012. It should bring 400 MW of electricity to Ghana's struggling grid and even allow some to be exported to West African neighbours. This revenue will be paid into an escrow account and funds used to service the debt. In addition there is a special arrangement with the Ghana Cocoa Board to supply cocoa as part payment of the debt.

Chinese corporations in general do not encourage trade unions, and originally did not allow for it at Bui. But a deputation from the Ghana TUC argued that it was enshrined both in Ghanaian law and the contract and so had to (Baah and Jauch 2009). More broadly this highlights an important issue for the developmental impacts of China in Africa. Where local laws are well elaborated and, more importantly, enforced then expropriation is more difficult although the trade-off may be lower levels of absolute investment. An example of weak adherence to the planning process and environmental standards around the Bui Dam reveals both obedience in some areas and noncompliance in others (Hensengerth 2011). This process suggests that where the Ghanaian state is determined to see a project realized then regulatory short cuts can be taken. While not confined to Chinese investments these large, elite-brokered projects are likely to encourage this flouting of due process in favour of the Chinese (Haglund 2009).

Sinohydro and other Chinese firms are looking to deepen their footprint in Ghana and Africa more broadly. Although the Chinese seemed to have got a foothold in Africa through these Chinese-government-supported projects they are now competing more openly for tenders and as one European aid official told us 'winning in straight fights' (see also Corkin 2011b). Furthermore, in terms of energy, oil reserves were discovered in 2007 in Ghana (McCaskie 2008). Estimates of revenue are difficult to determine but the IMF calculates around $20 billion over twenty years, peaking between 2011 and 2016. The oil producers soon began arriving. Initially the discovery was through a UK–US consortium—Tullow and Kosmos—but before long a range of applicants was seeking drilling blocks. Importantly in 2010 the Chinese state-owned enterprise China National Offshore Oil Corporation sought to purchase part of Kosmos' stake for a reported $5 billion on the basis of its Ghanaian and Ugandan oil discoveries.

The danger is that with a high budget deficit the government will be tempted to emulate the 'Angola model' by collateralizing the oil in return for credit. Major multilaterals are urging the government of Ghana to sort out its underlying structural problems first rather than simply use the windfall rents to shore up budget deficits which will re-emerge once the boom ends. Additionally there are worries about a 'Dutch-Disease' scenario where this resource exportation discourages investment and taxation in non-oil sectors (Oxfam 2009). Agriculture is one of the key sectors likely to suffer under this scenario.

Importantly, with the discovery of oil in Ghana the Chinese announced in 2010 a US$15 billion fund for oil-related infrastructure development which was negotiated at the highest levels, with Ghana's President Atta-Mills eschewing a high level meeting in New York about the future of aid to stay on in Beijing for the signing ceremony. This signals the changing power balance in African development relations and the established donors in Ghana have expressed concern about the transparency of these deals (Ghanaweb 2010). However, this situation appears to be changing with greater parliamentary scrutiny in Ghana over a $3 billion loan from China for an oil and gas corridor (Reuters 2011).

Sudan

Sudan is key to China's African oil interests but also a pariah regime. While the Chinese government may be an 'old friend' of Sudan based on the idea of non-interference, in practice China has played a deep and critical role in Sudan's politics. In late 1995 China's 'energy cooperation' with Sudan gathered momentum when President Bashir visited Beijing and secured a reduced rate loan with an agreement between China's Exim Bank and the Bank of Sudan to finance oil development (Ali 2007).

The turn to China by the National Islamic Front's (NIF), later re-named the National Congress Party, was born of necessity. Its renewed war against the Sudan People's Liberation Movement/Army (SPLM/A) continued, prosecuted as part of a project of Islamist transformation in Sudan. Having poor relations with the IMF and World Bank, Sudan also became the object of sanctions by the UN (1996) and the US (1997) so that turning to China was pragmatic given Beijing's political dependability and willingness to invest. China viewed Sudan as a friendly state with a more open oil market not, as elsewhere in Africa, dominated by established Western corporations.

From early 1997 the Chinese National Petroleum Company (CNPC) has operated a 40 per cent share in the Greater Nile Petroleum Operating Company (GNPOC), the main oil consortium in Sudan. However, oil production in southern Sudan had been constrained by the lack of a proper infrastructure. So, a CNPC subsidiary was involved in constructing a 1,600-km buried pipeline for GNPOC to connect oil production with the international market. The Khartoum oil refinery was built as a CNPC–Ministry of Energy joint venture with an investment of some $638 million and became operational in February 2000. Following GNPOC, the second major oil consortium in Sudan, Petrodar, was created in 2001. By 2006 China was by far the most important external economic actor in northern Sudan, whose oil-fuelled economic boom saw real GDP growing by 12 per cent in 2006.

The successful running of Sudan's oil industry by CNCP and other foreign oil companies amidst the civil wars demonstrated a willingness to side with Khartoum, despite the principle of 'non-interference'. China's 'blind-eye' support for the NIF has been the wellspring of grievances in many quarters in Sudan. Forced civilian displacement in southern Sudan continued, though largely overshadowed by Darfur, and the oil sector was targeted by the SPLA and other groups. Oil rich regions generate considerable revenue, but there have been negligible improvements in service delivery for affected civilian populations. Grievances concerning oil practices, the environmental impact of oil, and employment policies of oil companies abound. China has supplied arms to Sudan and helped develop northern Sudan's arms manufacturing industry in the late 1990s.

The Comprehensive Peace Agreement (CPA) of 2005 inaugurated a formal peace between northern and southern Sudan but the Chinese retained the ties they had built up over the years. Even before the CPA, the Chinese had identified its post-war reconstruction market as an area of expansion, especially given that sanctions restricted Western investment. Oil activity has expanded after the CPA and CNPC signed new concessions in 2007. Besides oil, key areas for expansion include construction, agriculture, mining, manufacturing, and importantly an assortment of transport infrastructure and energy projects. Most controversially, the Merowe Dam in northern Sudan being led by a Chinese consortium has generated conflict and displacement (Bosshard 2009).

China's diplomacy on Darfur became more publicly engaged from 2006 to the point where its efforts to 'influence' the Sudanese government on Darfur blurred the boundaries of non-interference. Beijing underestimated the political risk posed by Darfur to its interests within Sudan, as well as its standing in Africa and on the international stage. More proactive engagement on Darfur was evident before China's role in Sudan was connected to a 'genocide Olympics' campaign by activist groups in the US. The appointment of a new special ambassador, Liu Guijin, in May 2007 was part of China's efforts to bolster its image and contribute to solutions. For example, more aid was given to Darfur. Such moves also enabled China to promote its own interests through more vocal diplomacy and participation in multilateral forums and initiatives on Darfur. But China's more proactive diplomacy was accompanied by continuity in defending the sovereignty of Sudan and arguing against further sanctions, as well as deepening economic links. Thus, for this 'pariah state' the impact of oil has been to further concentrate wealth rather than achieve broader development, and this seems likely to worsen even if, as a result of diplomacy, it may lose some of its pariah status.

Discussion

Elites and Inclusion

The case studies suggest that regardless of the nature of the African state the dominant mode of engagement between China and Africa is at the elite level. State capacity on the African side clearly exists, even if it is not always in the form that Western liberal donors would wish for (see Kelsall 2013). It may even be that this selective and sometimes autocratic state capacity delivers forms of development—it may not be inclusive but it is effective by certain criteria.

China's preference for bilateralism encourages negotiations between senior officials which often occur outside of domestic accountability structures. In Ghana, for example, earlier Chinese investments such as the IT spine had very little discussion with telecommunications companies or within government and in Angola the GRN was effectively insulated from public scrutiny. In Ghana inputs to the Bui Dam were given to a company owned by a cabinet minister and in Namibia Chinese scholarships went to the children of high-ranking officials suggesting that China's entry may do little to alter existing forms of patrimonialism. That said, as Davies (2007) notes, the Chinese claim that their project focus as opposed to modalities like direct budget support reduces the chances of malfeasance since there is less free-floating cash to be siphoned off. Again, evidence of such arrangements is sparse and arguably part of the Chinese argument is to justify its tying of loans to Chinese SOEs.

Legitimacy and Policy Space

But whether these arrangements are elite-based and relatively unaccountable is somewhat different to whether they build legitimacy and contribute to a longer-term view of development. At one level the Angola and Sudan cases show that policy triangulation is possible with African states playing donors and investors off against one another. With resource security a global agenda, Africa's abundance of strategic minerals has given selected countries on the continent a degree of space to negotiate. And in this regard it is vitally important not to fixate on China since a raft of new investors are entering these markets (such as India in Sudan and Korea in Ghana). But as the Busan HLF noted that while these actors and economic relationships may provide enhanced markets for African exports they do not alter the structural position of these economies and do little to kick start broader industrialization. It is here that purposive policy on the African side is vital if developmental gains are to spread beyond mineral rents. Investment in training, for example, is important if more local employment is to be generated by this new investment.

In terms of regime legitimacy, Tull (2006) and Holslag (2011) note that Chinese investments have enhanced the legitimacy of recipient regimes. This is more than the aid-based vanity projects, such as ministries and stadia, but much-needed transport and energy infrastructure (Foster et al. 2008). While it is too early to say definitively, this infrastructural development might not only enhance the legitimacy of incumbent regimes but will have multiple, indirect benefits to citizens through such things as enhanced mobility and information flows. Moreover, effective transportation and communications can only increase the ability of the central state to reach and administer its territory, although how this plays out depends on the intentions of the regime that controls the system. In Sudan, for example, Chinese-owned infrastructure was used by the Sudanese army to mount attacks in the south so we need to be attuned to the progressive and regressive uses of technology and infrastructure that the Chinese bring.

Labour and Environment

The evidence around investment and labour suggests that labour importation varies according to the nature of the project, the Chinese firm involved, and the labour market conditions in Africa (Chen and Orr 2009). In Ghana, for example, Chinese labour was limited and firms had relatively little trouble finding semi-skilled labour, although the conditions and pay of this work are not high. That said, research by the author in Nigeria revealed that while local employees acknowledged the lower wages they were also grateful for the resilience of Chinese firms. Where a number of major Nigerian employers had gone bust the Chinese firms were still operating. By contrast the post-war labour market of Angola was poor so that labour importation is higher despite local content clauses (Corkin 2011b).

Moreover, the extension of the 'China Inc.' assumptions into Africa tends to suggest that ethnic economies are internally coherent and enclavic—the Chinese only look after their own. But this is clearly misplaced as our evidence showed hard capitalist logics determining business behaviour as opposed to favouring of co-ethnics. That is not to say that these business relationships are random, but that ethnicity and nationality are overdetermined in the literature on Chinese migrant businesses, which in turn diverts attention from the potential benefits to African economies. For example, recent research in Zambia (Fessehaie 2011) and Angola (Corkin 2011b) suggests that the Chinese are not as enclaved as earlier reports suggested and local firms have secured a growing number of contracts.

In all cases the environmental impacts are poorly understood and the focus has been on high profile cases, such as the Merowe Dam in Sudan. Again, there are issues around the contracts underpinning these investments, which go beyond a simple China–Africa logic. In the case of the Merowe Dam it is the German consulting firm that is being prosecuted which suggests that mitigating negative social and environmental impacts is a matter of complex arrangements between multiple actors, although as the Ghana and Angola cases show local laws are poorly enforced around these major projects though there is no evidence that this situation is worse regarding Chinese projects.

Emerging Issues and Research Gaps

The foregoing analysis suggests that China and other Asian powers are changing the political landscape of African states though not as drastically as Western sceptics would believe. As a recent report noted 'There is a clear opportunity for Africa to grab now, since both traditional and "new" players are in an important phase of reforming (e.g. Europe) and designing (e.g. China, India, and Brazil) their development policy towards Africa' (Rampa and Bilal 2011, p. VIII). To capitalize on this opportunity requires a series of coordinated responses across African, BRIC, and multilateral political spaces.

Changing China

China's domestic development has been the driver of its overseas engagements so as it changes there are likely to be implications for Africa. Kaplinsky and Farooki (2011) show that China's and India's high levels of commodity demand are likely to continue for at least twenty-five years which means that Africa will remain a strategic commercial interest. Despite the global recession and a slight drop in China's growth rate, China honoured its aid commitments to Africa. Yet the Chinese model is clearly imperfect with large and growing domestic inequality and environmental damage (Shirk 2007; Watts 2010). As international scrutiny and the influence of policy norms deepens it is likely that Chinese SOEs and policymakers will adopt more sustainable approaches and we are already seeing CSR agendas amongst some policy banks and SOEs. But as Chinese firms proliferate, diversify, and internationalize it becomes ever harder for the Chinese state to monitor and regulate them (Reilly and Na 2007), while the large numbers of smaller private firms never even enter these regulatory mechanisms. Hence, we are likely to see some high profile firms voluntarily adopting better practices but for the majority it will be business as usual unless and until African states have the capacity and willingness to regulate.

We are also seeing an evolution of Chinese firms, especially SOEs. Most come in under tied arrangements linked to state-backed concessional loans, which reduces the risk to these firms, even if the absolute levels of profit are thin. However, there is emerging evidence (Corkin 2011b) that once established in an African market these firms operate like any other TNC and tender for open contracts which they are increasingly winning.

The cases reviewed in the third section of this chapter showed that despite China branding itself as 'non-interfering' this has always been a flexible discourse. The Sudan case showed a growing involvement in domestic politics and the Libyan evacuation of 2011 suggested that a priority for China is ensuring the safety of its nationals, which is linked to stability of the political operating environment. Hence, we are likely to see growing direct involvement in African governance. This is likely to be below the radar rather than through public governance programmes.

Despite the long-standing discourse around 'South—South' cooperation and the distancing of China from mainstream donors, there is growing self-awareness of China as an international development actor. The White Paper on aid in May 2011 was relatively light on details (Provost 2011) but was significant for using the term 'aid' and acknowledging, despite its fragmentation, that China has an evolving aid 'system'. Other institutional reorganization identified in the White Paper and the establishment of the State Council Leading Group Office of Poverty Alleviation and Development (Davies 2007) suggest that a reflexive analytical move within China's aid system is under way and noises are being made about closer convergence around international development norms.

African States

Many of the issues that China in Africa raises are not unique to this specific relationship. As Broadman (2007) notes many of the issues around Africa's engagement with China concern long-standing problems of policy coherence, political stability, and border controls which pre-date China's entry. As such this raises a much wider series of questions about the African state and political economy, which are beyond the scope of this chapter.

One of the key issues at the interface of accumulation and inclusion is around the use of African labour. We noted that use of African labour varies according to labour market conditions and nature of the project, but that it is generally quite high. However, much of this African labour is relatively unskilled and so skills transfer is low and few African governments are investing in vocational training (Okonjo-Iweala 2010), which creates a self-fulfilling prophecy of the Chinese requiring the importation of skilled labour. However, we have seen companies like Huawei setting up training centres in Africa (Chang et al. 2009) as it is aware that local workers have certain advantages over Chinese staff. A similar issue is around linkages to local firms. We have seen in the cases of Angola and DRC that local content clauses were part of the agreements around loan packages but that adherence is uneven. There is emerging evidence that Chinese investment is creating local linkages to African firms though the jobs created in these firms tend to be relatively low skilled (Teka 2011) and in the case of Angola contracts are skewed towards firms owned by the ruling party (Soares de Oliveira 2007). These studies also show that local policy can make a difference and so while, for example, Angola has set up joint-venture clauses that encouraged foreign firms to partner with local firms much of the rest of the policy needed to kick start industrialization was poorly elaborated.

Multilateral Forums

The previous sub-section argued that it is long-standing structural issues within recipient states that need to be addressed rather than simply reforming the mode of entry of the new donors. While the Chinese White Paper on aid echoed some of the concepts and makes some concessions to international norms, it is unlikely that the Chinese state will wholeheartedly throw itself into these institutional processes. Their own development models are too powerful and different for them to, for example, suddenly start championing civil society, but as noted there is space for consensus around business-led growth (Chaponniere 2009). So, there is likely to be some convergence with Western donors around issues which do not threaten China's own growth or domestic political agendas, such as greener technologies and investments in technical capacity-building and social infrastructure. However, if the 'China model' is used ideologically by recipient states in Africa to oppose liberal reforms then this could become a site of conflict between Chinese, Western, and African actors.

The need for ongoing dialogue and learning (European Commission 2008; Davies 2010) between new donors, old donors, and recipients is still high on the agenda, as evidenced by debates at the 2011 Busan HLF on Aid Effectiveness. In comparison to the Paris and Accra meetings (these were the meetings of the HLF – High Level Forum on Aid Effectiveness) the new donors were much more prominent although the debates were salutary. While they recognized the benefits that South—South cooperation could bring to LDCs they noted that terms of trade are generally not altered by these relationships and Africa still largely imports manufactured goods while exporting raw materials. In the case of China they noted that the 2009 Forum on China–Africa Cooperation (FOCAC) meeting did pledge technical training and this might be one area where African states can use the commodities boom to upgrade skills levels, but this requires concerted and coordinated policy.

Research Gaps

The chapter will conclude with a series of research gaps in terms of the impacts of Chinese and Asian involvement on elite commitment to development and state effectiveness in Africa.

Development Discourses

A recurring theme within the major Chinese projects is that the Chinese get things done and that what they provide is important, notably infrastructure.

In terms of questioning notions of 'effectiveness' the issue for international development actors is more around development effectiveness than aid effectiveness per se (Rampa and Bilal 2011; Chaponniere 2009). The Paris Declaration usefully focuses on aid effectiveness but for recipient states the entry of China has refocused the debate around what is needed for development since the causal link between more/better aid and development is inconclusive. Sachs (2007) argues that China has forced the 'nuts and bolts' of development back on the agenda after a period in which liberal institutionalism fixated some policymakers. The China model, such that it exists, is one in which legitimacy is built on sustained growth and while its social and ecological effects are problematic it has recalibrated the wider debates around what development means.

Emerging issue: What is development effectiveness and how does China effect a change in this understanding? How do other actors respond to this changing discourse?

Elites and Inclusive Development

The analysis above suggests that recipient states and regimes can play a determining role in how relations with new donors play out, how far broader development priorities are negotiated with their respective polities, and who ultimately benefits from this new phase of development cooperation. Under all three regime types discussed in the second and third sections of this chapter we see elite compacts evolving in unaccountable ways. However, domestic and international scrutiny is growing as is China's own sense of 'social responsibility' for its development and investment projects. Despite this lack of accountability to domestic societies, these engagements with Africa do not necessarily make them anti-developmental if the effectiveness of these arrangements is directed at social and economic infrastructure which might benefit broader society. Moreover, if these investments stimulate economic growth and produce socially useful tax revenue then the developmental gains could spread further.

Emerging issue: Does China's preference for elite brokering undermine moves to democratic and open government? If new investments stimulate growth will these gains be channelled to broader developmental goals?

Governance Interventions

While the Chinese, for example, stress 'non-interference' we have seen that this was always something of a myth and is now breaking down. If this proves to be the case then this has major implications for politics in these countries, as well as for relations between the rising powers and 'established' powers that have long held trusteeship over these states (Kornegay and Landsberg 2009). At the same time as China's power within multilateral organizations grows we are likely to see influence brought to bear in more indirect ways that will affect pan-African and national policy processes.

Emerging issue: What forms of more direct and multilateral political intervention in Africa are the Chinese engaging in? To what extent does this conflict with established powers on the continent?

New Actors

Despite the importance of China in Africa there is a lack of analysis on countries operating in Africa besides China. Hence, we need much better data on who the new actors are, where they operate, how they operate, and with what impacts on development and politics in those countries. While we can hypothesize that new donors share certain characteristics and are different is some regards to DAC donors there is nothing substantive on how these play out on the ground in Africa.

Emerging issue: To what extent are new actors stepping up their African engagements? How is this organized and with what impacts?

Environmental Impacts

Another emergent issue noted in the analysis of the third section of this chapter is that we know very little about the environmental impacts and questions of land rights in Africa. In the past these have proven to be important political issues but have hardly been touched upon in the existing work on China and the Rising Powers in Africa. However, there is no primary or comparative work on these issues, with some rather sloppy causal analysis implying that the Chinese export the capitalism they know best and so overlook environmental consequences. Certainly, China's domestic environmental record is not good though neither have been the records of other countries that have industrialized in the past. And the Chinese have made a concerted and rapid shift to greener growth so it is not possible to simply project bad practices on to Chinese overseas operations. Rather we need systematic and comparative studies which assess whether Chinese firms are in fact worse than other nations' firms, which require a sample of different types of sizes of firms.

Emerging issue: What are the environmental impacts of Chinese activity in Africa and to what extent is this different to non-Chinese actors? What are the African responses to this?

Bibliography

Abdel-Latif, A., and H. Schmitz. 2010. 'Growth Alliances: Insights from Egypt'. *Business and Politics*, 12(4): 1–27.

Acemoglu, D. 2009. *Introduction to Modern Economic Growth*. Princeton, NJ: Princeton University Press.

Acemoglu, D., and J. Robinson. 2006. *Economic Origins of Dictatorship and Democracy*. New York, NY: Cambridge University Press.

Acemoglu, D., and J. Robinson. 2008. 'The Role of Institutions in Growth and Development'. Working Paper No. 10. Washington, DC: Commission for Growth and Development.

Acemoglu, D., and J. Robinson. 2012. *Why Nations Fail: The Origins of Power, Prosperity and Poverty*. New York, NY: Random House.

Acemoglu, D., S. Johnson, and J. Robinson. 2001. 'The Colonial Origins of Comparative Development: An Empirical Investigation'. *American Economic Review*, 91(5): 1369–401.

Acemoglu, D., S. Johnson, and J. Robinson. 2005. 'Institutions as the Fundamental Cause of Long-run Growth'. In *Handbook of Economic Growth*. Edited by Aghion, P., and S. Durlauf. Amsterdam: North-Holland.

Acharya, A., A. T. Fuzzo de Lima, and M. Moore. 2006. 'Proliferation and Fragmentation: Transaction Costs and the Value of Aid'. *Journal of Development*, 42(1): 1–21.

Adcock, R., and D. Collier. 2001. 'Measurement Validity: A Shared Standard for Qualitative and Quantitative Research'. *American Political Science Review*, 95(3): 529–46.

Adler, D., and M. Woolcock. 2010. 'Justice without the Rule of Law? The Challenge of Rights-based Industrial Relations in Contemporary Cambodia'. In *Human Rights at Work: Perspectives on Law and Regulation*. Edited by Fenwick, C., and T. Novitz. Oxford: Hart Publishing.

Adler, D., D. Porter, and M. Woolcock. 2008. 'Legal Pluralism and Equity: Some Reflections on Land Reform in Cambodia'. Justice for the Poor Briefing Note, 2(2). Washington, DC: World Bank.

Agarwal, B. 2011. *Gender and Green Governance*. Oxford: Oxford University Press.

Alden, C. 2007. *China in Africa*. London: Zed Books.

Alesina, A. 1999. 'Too Large and too Small Governments'. In *Economic Policy and Equity*. Edited by Tanzi, V., K.-Y. Chu, and S. Gupta. Washington, DC: International Monetary Fund.

Alesina, A., and D. Dollar. 2000. 'Who Gives Foreign Aid to Whom and Why?' *Journal of Economic Growth*, 5(1): 33–63.

Alesina, A., and G. Tabellini. 2004. *Bureaucrats or Politicians?* Cambridge, MA: NBER.

Alesina, A., R. Baqir, and W. Easterly. 1999. 'Public Goods and Ethnic Divisions'. *Quarterly Journal of Economics*, 114(4): 1243–84.

Algan, Y., C. Hémet, and D. D. Laitin. 2011. 'Diversity and Public Goods: A Natural Experiment with Exogenous Residential Allocation'. Discussion Paper Series No. 6053. Forschungsinstitut zur Zukunft der Arbeit (IZA).

Ali, A. A. 2007. 'The Political Economy of Relations between Sudan and China'. In *China in Africa: Mercantilist Predator or Partner in Development?* Edited by Le Pere, G. Johannesburg: Braamfontein Institute for Global Dialogue and South African Institute for International Affairs.

Ali, S. 2009. *Treasures of the Earth: Need, Greed and a Sustainable Future*. New Haven, CT: Yale University Press.

Amankwah, A. 2005. '23,000 Jobs Gone to the Wind'. AllAfrica.com, <http://www.modernghana.com/news/88758/1/23000-jobs-gone-with-the-wind.html> (accessed 20 October 2011).

Ambasta, P., P. S. V. Shankar, and M. Shah. 2008. 'Two Years of NREGA: The Road Ahead'. *Economic and Political Weekly*, 43: 41–50.

Amenta, E., N. Caren, E. Chiarello, and Y. Su. 2010. 'The Political Consequences of Social Movements'. *Annual Review of Sociology*, 36(1): 287–307.

Amenta, E. 2006. *When Movements Matter: The Townsend Plan and the Rise of Social Security*. Princeton, NJ: Princeton University Press.

Amsden, A. H., 2001. *The Rise of the Rest: Challenges to the West from Late-industrializing Economies*. Oxford: Oxford University Press.

Amsden, A. H., A. DiCaprio, and J. A. Robinson (eds.). 2012. *The Role of Elites in Economic Development*. New York, NY: Oxford University Press.

Ananth Pur, K., 2004. 'Rivalry or Synergy? Formal and Informal Local Governance in Rural India'. IDS Working Paper No, 226. Brighton: Institute of Development Studies.

Anderson, B. 1991. *Imagined Communities: Reflections on the Origin and Spread of Nationalism*, 2nd edn. New York, NY: Verso.

Anderson, M., A. Branchflower, M. Moreno-Torres, and M. Besançon. 2005. 'Measuring Capacity and Willingness for Poverty Reduction in Fragile States'. PRDE Working Paper No. 6. London: DFID.

Andre, P., and S. Mesple-Somps. 2009. *The Allocation of Public Goods and National Elections in Ghana*. Paris: AFD.

Andrews, K. T. 2004. *Freedom Is a Constant Struggle: The Mississippi Civil Rights Movement and its Legacy*. Chicago, IL: University of Chicago Press.

Andrews, M. 2008. 'Good Government Means Different Things to Different Countries'. *2008 Annual Meeting of the American Political Science Association*. Boston, MA 28–31 August 2008.

Andrews, M. 2010. 'How Far Have Public Financial Management Reforms Come in Africa? CID Working Paper No. 208, <http://www.hks.harvard.edu/centers/cid/publications/faculty-working-papers/cid-working-paper-no.-208> (accessed 4 June 2014).

Ansell, B., and J. Lindvall. 2013. 'The Political Origins of Primary Education Systems: Ideology, Institutions, and Interdenominational Conflict in an Era of Nation-Building'. *American Political Science Review*, FirstView: 1–18.

Araujo, C. 2010. 'The Limits of Women's Quotas: The Case of Brazil'. *IDS Bulletin*, 1, 41(5): 17–24.

Arellano-Yanguas, J. 2011. 'Aggravating the Resource Curse: Decentralisation, Mining and Conflict in Peru'. *Journal of Development Studies*, 47(4): 617–38.

Arellano-Yanguas, J. 2012. 'Mining and Conflict in Peru: Sowing the Minerals, Reaping a Hail of Stones'. In *Social Conflict, Economic Development and Extractive Industry: Evidence from South America*. Edited by A. Bebbington, 91–113. London. Routledge.

Arndt, C., S. Jones, and F. Tarp. 2009. 'Aid and Growth: Have We Come Full Circle?' Helsinki: UNU-WIDER Discussion Paper No. 2009/05.

Aron, A. 2003. 'Building Institutions in Post-conflict African Economies'. *Journal of Development*, 14: pp. 471–85.

Ascher, W. 2012. 'Mineral Wealth, Development and Social Policy in Indonesia'. In *Mineral Rents and the Financing of Social Policy: Opportunities and Challenges*. Edited by Hujo, K., 223–56. Basingstoke: Palgrave Macmillan.

Asian Development Bank. 2004. *Report on the Asian Development Bank's Law and Policy Reform Activities in Support of Poverty Reduction*. Manila: Asian Development Bank.

Askouri, A. 2007. 'China's Investment in Sudan: Displacing Villages and Destroying Communities'. In *African Perspectives on China in Africa*. Edited by Manji, F., and S. Marks, 71–86. London: Pambazuka Books.

Auld, G. 2012. 'Private Market-based Regulations: What They Are, and What They Mean for Land-Use Governance'. Background Paper for Ernst Strüngmann Forum, Frankfurt.

Auty, R. 1993. *Sustaining Development in Mineral Economies: The Resource Curse Thesis*. London: Routledge.

Auty, R. (ed.). 2001. *Resource Abundance and Economic Development*. Oxford: Oxford University Press.

Auty, R. 2008. 'From Mining Enclave to Economic Catalyst: Large Mineral Projects in Developing Countries'. *Brown Journal of World Affairs*, 13(1): 135–45.

Avritzer, L. 2002. *Democracy and the Public Space in Latin America*. Princeton, NJ: Princeton University Press.

Baah, A., and H. Jauch. 2009. *Chinese Investments in Africa: A Labour Perspective* Nambia: African Labour Research Network.

Baden, S., and A. M. Goetz. 1998. 'Who Needs [Sex] when you can have [Gender]? Conflicting Discourses on Gender in Beijing'. In *Feminist Visions of Development: Gender Analysis and Policy*. Edited by Jackson, C., and R. Pearson. London: Routledge.

Bakker, K., and G. Bridge. 2006. 'Material worlds? Resource geographies and the `matter of nature', Progress in Human Geography, 30(5): 5–27.

Baldwin, K., and J. D. Huber. 2010. 'Economic versus Cultural Differences: Forms of Ethnic Diversity and Public Goods Provision'. *American Political Science Review*, 104(4): 644–62.

Baldwin, R. 1963. 'Export Technology and Development from a Subsistence Level'. *Economic Journal*, 73(289): 80–92.

Banerjee, A., L. Iyer, and R. Somanathan. 2005. 'History, Social Divisions, and Public Goods in Rural India'. *Journal of the European Economic Association*, 3(2–3): 639–47.

Banerjee, A., L. Iyer, and R. Somanathan. 2007. 'Public Action for Public Goods'. In *Handbook of Development Economics*. Edited by Schultz, T. P., and J. Strauss, 3117–154. Amsterdam: North-Holland.

Banful, A. B. 2011. 'Old Problems in the New Solutions? Politically Motivated Allocation of Program Benefits and the 'New' Fertiliser Subsidies'. *World Development*, 39(7): 1166–76.

Banting, K., and W. Kymlicka. 2007. 'Introduction: Multiculturalism and the Welfare State: Setting the Context'. In *Multiculturalism and the Welfare State: Recognition and Redistribution in Contemporary Democracies*. Edited by K. Banting, and W. Kymlicka, 1–48. New York, NY: Oxford University Press.

Barker, R., R. W. Herdt, and B. Rose. 1985. *The Rice Economy of Asia*. Washington, DC: Resources for the Future.

Barrientos, A. 2007. 'Tax-financed Social Security'. *International Social Security Review*, 60: 99–117.

Barrientos, A. 2008. 'Cash Transfers for Older People Reduce Poverty and Inequality'. In *Institutional Pathways to Equity: Addressing Inequality Traps*. Edited by Bebbington, A. J., A. A. Dani, A. De Haan, and M. Walton. Washington, DC: World Bank.

Barrientos, A. 2011. *The Rise of Social Assistance in Brazil*. Manchester: BWPI.

Barrientos, A. 2013. *Social Assistance in Developing Countries*. Cambridge: Cambridge University Press.

Barrientos, A., and D. Hulme (eds.). 2008. *Social Protection for the Poor and Poorest*. Basingstoke: Palgrave.

Barrientos, A., M. Niño-Zarazúa, and M. Maitrot. 2010. 'Social Assistance in Developing Countries Database Version 5'. Manchester: Brooks World Poverty Institute.

Barron, P., R. Diprose, and M. Woolcock. 2011. *Contesting Development: Participatory Projects and Local Conflict Dynamics in Indonesia*. New Haven, CT: Yale University Press.

Barth, F. 1969. *Ethnic Groups and Boundaries: The Social Organization of Cultural Difference*. London: George Allen and Unwin.

Basinga. P., P. J Gertler, A. Binagwaho, A. L. B. Soucat, J. Sturdy, and C. M. J. Vermeersch. 2011. 'Effect on Maternal and Child Health Services in Rwanda of Payment to Primary Health-care Providers for Performance: An Impact Evaluation'. *The Lancet*, 377(9775): 1421–8.

Basu, A. 1995. *The Challenges of Local Feminisms: Women's Movement in Global Perspective*, Boulder, CO: Westview Press.

Basu, A. 2010. 'Introduction'. In *Women's movement in a Global Era*. Edited by Basu, A. Boulder, CO: Westview Press.

Bates, R. 1981. *Markets and States in Tropical Africa*. Boston: Little, Brown.

Bates, R. 1983. *Essays in the Political Economy of Rural Africa*. Cambridge: Cambridge University Press.

Bates, R. 2010. 'A Review of Douglas North, John Joseph Wallis and Barry Weingast's *Violence and Social Orders'. Journal of Economic Literature*, 48(3): 752–6.

Bates, R. H. 2005. *Markets and States in Tropical Africa: The Political Bias of Agricultural Policies*. Berkeley, CA: University of California Press.

Batley, R. 2004. 'The Politics of Service Delivery Reform'. *Development and Change*, 35(1): 31–56.

Batley, R. 2011. 'Structures and Strategies in Relations between Non-government Service Providers and Governments'. *Public Administration and Development*, 31(4): 306–19.

Batley, R., and G. Larbi. 2004. *The Changing Role of Government: The Reform of Public Services in Developing Countries*. Basingstoke: Palgrave Macmillan.

Batley, R., and C. Mcloughlin. 2010. 'Engagement with Non-State Service Providers in Fragile States: Reconciling State-Building and Service Delivery'. *Development Policy Review*, 28(2): 131–54.

Battistelli, S., and Y. Guichaoua. 2012. 'Diamonds for Development? Querying Botswana's Success Story'. In *The Developmental Challenges of Mining and Oil. Lessons from Africa and Latin America*. Edited by Thorp, R., S. Battistelli, Y. Guichaoua, J. C. Orihuela, and M. Paredes, 44–79. New York, NY: Palgrave Macmillan.

Bavister-Gould, A. 2011. 'Predatory Leadership, Predatory Rule and Predatory States'. Concept Brief 01, Developmental Leadership Program, <http://www.dlprog.org> (accessed 4 June 2014).

Baxi, U. 1982. *The Crisis of the Indian Legal System*. New Delhi: Vikas.

Bayly, C. A., V. Rao, S. Szreter, and M. Woolcock (eds.). 2011. *History, Historians and Development Policy: A Necessary Dialogue*. Manchester: Manchester University Press.

Beaman, L., R. Chattopadhyay, E. Duflo, R. Pande, and P. Topalova. 2008. 'Powerful Women: Does Exposure Reduce Bias?' NBER Working Paper, series 14198, Landon: Cambridge, MA.

Bebbington, A. 2009. 'The New Extraction? Rewriting the Political Ecology of the Andes?' *NACLA Report on the Americas*, 42(5): 12–20.

Bebbington, A. (ed.) 2012a. *Social Conflict, Economic Development and Extractive Industry: Evidence from South America*. London. Routledge.

Bebbington, A. 2012b. 'Underground Political Ecologies'. *Geoforum*, 43(6): 1152–62.

Bebbington, A., M. Connarty, W. Coxshall, H. O'Shaughnessy, and M. Williams. 2007. *Mining and Development in Peru: With Special Reference to the Rio Blanco Project, Piura*. London: Peru Support Group.

Bebbington, A., A. Dani, A. de Haan, and M. Walton. 2008. 'Inequalities and Development: Dysfunctions, Traps and Transitions'. In *Institutional Pathways to Equity: Addressing Inequality Traps*. Edited by Bebbington, A., A. Dani, A de Haan, and M. Walton, 3–44. Washington, DC: World Bank.

Bebbington, A., and D. Humphreys Bebbington. 2011. 'An Andean Avatar: Post-neoliberal and Neoliberal Strategies for Securing the Unobtainable'. *New Political Economy*, 15(4): 1311–45.

Bebbington, A., D. Humphreys Bebbington, J. Bury, J. Lingan, J. Muñoz, and M. Scurrah. 2008. 'Mining and Social Movements: Struggles over Livelihood and Rural Territorial Development in the Andes'. *World Development*, 36(12): 2888–905.

Bebbington, A., D. Humphreys Bebbington, L. Hinojosa, M. L. Burneo, and J. Bury. 2013. 'Anatomies of Conflict: Social Mobilization and New Political Ecologies of the Andes'. In *Subterranean Struggles: New Dynamics of Oil, Mining and Gas in Latin America*. Edited by Bebbington, A., and J. Bury. Austin, TX: University of Texas Press.

Bebbington, A., and U. Kothari. 2006. 'Transnational Development Networks'. *Environment and Planning*, A 38(5): 849–66.

Bebbington, A., and W. McCourt (eds.). 2007. *Development Success: Statecraft in the South*, Basingstoke: Palgrave Macmillan.

Bell, C. L. G. 1975. 'The Political Framework'. In *Redistribution with Growth*. Edited by Chenery, H., C. Bell, J. H. Duloy, and R. Jolly. Oxford: World Bank/Oxford University Press.

Benequista, N. 2009. 'Backed by Popular Demand: Citizen Actions for Accountability'. In *Citizenship DRC Case Study Series*. Brighton: Development Research Centre.

Benequista, N., and J. Gaventa. 2011. 'Blurring the Boundaries: Citizen Action across States and Societies: A Summary of Findings from a Decade of Collaborative Research on Citizen Engagement'. Brighton: Development Research Centre on Citizenship, Participation and Accountability.

Benson, P., and S. Kirsch. 2009. 'Corporate Oxymorons'. *Dialectical Anthropology*, 34: 45–8.

Benson, P., and S. Kirsch. 2010. 'Capitalism and the Politics of Resignation.' *Current Anthropology*, 51(4): 459–86.

Benton, L. 2002. *Law and Colonial Cultures: Legal Regimes in World History 1400–1900*. Cambridge: Cambridge University Press.

Berdegué, J., A. Bebbington, J. Escobal et al. 2012. 'Territorios en Movimiento. Dinámicas Territoriales Rurales en América Latina', Documento de Trabajo 110, Rimisp: Latin American Center for Rural Development.

Berg, A., J. Ostry, and J. Zettelmeyer. 2012. 'What Makes Growth Sustained?' *Journal of Development Economics*, 98(2): 149–66.

Bergamaschi, I. 2008. 'Mali: Patterns and Limits of Donor-driven Ownership'. In *The New Politics of Aid: African Strategies for Dealing with Donors*. Edited by Whitfield, L. 217–45. Oxford: Oxford University Press.

Berger, J. 2008. 'Litigating for Social Justice in Post-apartheid South Africa: A Focus on Health and Education'. In *Courting Social Justice: Judicial Enforcement of Social and Economic Rights in the Developing World*. Edited by Gauri V., and D. Brinks. New York, NY: Cambridge University Press.

Bergling, P., J. Ederlöf, and V. Taylor (eds.). 2009. *Rule of Law Promotion: Global Perspectives, Local Applications*. Uppsala: Lustu Forlag.

Bergström, L. 2005. 'Development of Institutions Is Created from the Inside'. *Sida Studies in Evaluation 05/04*. Stockholm: Sida.

Berthélemy, J.-C. 2005. 'Bilateral Donors' Interests vs Recipients' Development Motives in Aid Allocation: Do All Donors Behave the Same?' *Review of Development Economics*, 10(2): 179–94.

Besley, T., R. Burgess, and B. Esteve-Volart. 2004. 'Operationalising Pro-Poor Growth: A Country Case Study on India'. Final Report for the World Bank. [Mimeo.]

Besley, T., R. Burgess, and B. Esteve-Volart. 2005. 'The Policy Origins of Poverty and Growth in India'. In *Delivering on the Promise of Pro-Poor Growth: Insights and Lessons from Country Experiences*. Edited by Besley, T., and L. Cord. Washington, DC: World Bank.

Besley, T., and M. Ghatak. 2007. 'Reforming Public Service Delivery'. *Journal of African Economies*, 16(1): 127–56.

Besley, T., and T. Persson. 2009. 'The Origins of State Capacity: Property Rights, Taxation, and Politics'. *The American Economic Review*, 99(4): 1218–44.

Birdsall, N. 2004. 'Seven Deadly Sins: Reflections on Donor Failings'. Center for Global Development Working Paper No. 50. Washington, DC: Center for Global Development.

Birdsall, N. 2007. 'Do No Harm: Aid, Weak Institutions, and the Missing Middle in Africa'. Working Paper No.113. Washington, DC: Center for Global Development.

Birdsall, N., N. Lustig, and D. McLeod. 2011. 'Declining Inequality in Latin America: Some Economics, Some Politics'. Tulane University, New Orleans: Working Paper 1120.

Birner, R., S. Gupta, and N. Sharma. 2011. 'The Political Economy of Agricultural Policy Reform in India'. Washington, DC: IFPRI.

Birner, R., and D. Resnick. 2010. 'The Political Economy of Policies for Smallholder Agriculture'. *World Development*, 38(10): 1442–52.

Blaser, M. 2010. *Storytelling Globalization from the Chaco and Beyond*. Durham, NC: Duke University Press.

Blundo, G., and J.-P. Olivier de Sardan, and S. Cox. 2006. *Everyday Corruption and the State: Citizens and Public Officials in Africa*. London: Zed Books.

Boesen, N. 2004. 'Enhancing Public Sector Capacity: What Works, What Doesn't and Why?' Review for the OED Evaluation of World Bank Support for Capacity Building in Africa, unpublished paper, January.

Boix, C. 2008. 'Spain: Development, Democracy and Equity'. In *Institutional Pathways to Equity: Addressing Inequality Traps*. Edited by Bebbington, A., A. Dani, A de Haan, and M. Walton, 215–244. Washington, DC: World Bank.

Bond, P. 2010. 'South Africa's "Developmental State" Distraction'. *Mediations*, 24(1): 8–23.

Boone, C. 2003. *Political Topographies of the African State: Territorial Authority and Institutional Choice*. New York, NY: Cambridge University Press.

Booth, D. 2005. 'Missing Links in the Politics of Development: Learning from the PRSP Experiment'. ODI Working Paper 256. London: Overseas Development Institute.

Booth, D. 2009. 'Elite, Governance and the Public Interest in Africa: Working with the Grain?' Africa Power and Politics Programme (APPP) Discussion Paper No. 6. London: Overseas Development Institute (ODI).

Bibliography

Booth, D. 2010. 'Country "Ownership" When There Is No Social Contract: Towards a Realistic Perspective'. Third lecture in the SID-Netherlands series 'Global Values in a Changing World: Synergy of State and Society in a Globalized World'. Amsterdam 13 December 2010.

Booth, D. 2011a. 'Governance for Development in Africa: Building on What Works'. Africa Power and Politics Programme (APPP) Policy Brief No. 1. London: ODI.

Booth, D. 2011b. 'Towards a Theory of Local Governance and Public Goods Provision'. *IDS Bulletin*, 42(2): 11–21.

Booth, D. 2011c. 'Working with the Grain and Swimming against the Tide: Barriers to Uptake of Research Findings on Governance and Public Services in Low-income Africa', APPP Working Paper 18. London: Overseas Development Institute.

Booth, D. 2011d. 'Aid Effectiveness: Bringing Country Ownership (and Politics) Back In'. ODI Working Paper 336, <http://www.odi.org.uk> (accessed 4 June 2014).

Booth, D. 2012. 'Working with the Grain and Swimming against the Tide: Barriers to Uptake of Research Findings on Governance and Public Services in Low-income Africa'. *Public Management Review*, 14(2): 163–80.

Booth, D., and F. Golooba-Mutebi. 2009. 'The Political Economy of Roads Reform in Uganda: Aiding Economic Growth in Africa'. ODI Working Paper 307. London: Overseas Development Institute.

Booth, D., and F. Golooba-Mutebi. 2011. 'Developmental Patrimonialism? The Case of Rwanda'. Africa Power and Politics Working Paper 16. London: ODI.

Booth, D., A. Grigsby, and C. Toranzo. 2006. 'Politics and Poverty Reduction Strategies: Lessons from Latin American HIPCs'. ODI Working Paper 262. London: Overseas Development Institute.

Booth, D., and L.-H. Piron. 2004. 'Politics and the PRSP Approach: Bolivia Case Study'. ODI Working Paper 238. London: ODI.

Boserup, E. 1970. *Women's Role in Economic Development*. London: Allen and Unwin.

Bosshard, P. 2009. 'China Dams the World'. *World Policy Journal*, 26(4): 43–51.

Bourdieu, P. 1977. *Outline of a Theory of Practice*. New York, NY: Cambridge University Press.

Bowden, S., and P. Mosley. 2012. 'African Case Studies: Ghana, Uganda, Kenya, Zimbabwe'. In *The Politics of Poverty Reduction*. Edited by Mosley, P., 346–68. Oxford: Oxford University Press.

Bowles, S. 2008. 'Policies Designed for Self-interested Citizens May Undermine "the Moral Sentiments"'. *Science*, 320(5883): 1605–9.

Brady, D., and M. Spence. 2009. 'Leadership and Politics: A Perspective from the Growth Commission'. *Oxford Review of Economic Policy*, 25(2): 205–18.

Brass, P. R. 1994. *The Politics of India Since Independence*. New York, NY: Cambridge University Press.

Bratton, M., and E. Masunungure. 2011. 'The Anatomy of Political Predation: Leaders, Elites and Coalitions in Zimbabwe, 1980–2010'. Research Paper No. 9, Developmental Leadership Program, <http://www.dlprog.org> (accessed 4 June 2014).

Bräutigam, D. 2000. 'Aid Dependence and Governance'. *Expert Group on Development Issues 2000:1*. Stockholm: Almqvist and Wiksell International.

Bräutigam, D. 2008. 'Contingent Capacity: Export Taxation and State-building in Mauritius'. In *Taxation and State-building in Developing Countries: Capacity and Consent*. Edited by Bräutigam, D., O.-H. Fjeldstad, and M. Moore, 135–59. Cambridge: Cambridge University Press.

Bräutigam, D. 2009. *The Dragon's Gift: The Real Story of China in Africa* Oxford: Oxford University Press.

Bräutigam, D., O.-H. Fjeldstad, and M. Moore (eds.). 2008. *Taxation and State-building in Developing Countries: Capacity and Consent*, Cambridge: Cambridge University Press.

Bräutigam, D. A., and S. Knack. 2004. 'Foreign Aid, Institutions, and Governance in Sub-Saharan Africa'. *Economic Development and Cultural Change*, 52(2): 255–85.

Bräutigam, D., L. Rakner, and S. Taylor. 2002. 'Business Associations and Growth Coalitions in Sub-Saharan Africa'. *Journal of Modern African Studies*, 40(4): 519–47.

Brautigam, D., and X. Tang. 2011. 'African Shenzhen: China's Special Economic Zones in Africa'. *Journal of Modern African Studies*, 49(1): 27–54.

Bravo, A. 2002. 'The Impact of Improved Rural Roads on Gender Relations in Peru'. *Mountain Research and Development*, 22(3): 221–24.

Bridge, G. 2008. 'Global Production Networks and the Extractive Sector: Governing Resource-based Development'. *Journal of Economic Geography*, 8(3): 389–419.

Brinkerhoff, D. W., C. Fort, and S. Stratton. 2009. *Good Governance and Health: Assessing Progress in Rwanda*. USAID: Kigali.

Britto, T., and F. V. Soares. 2010. *Bolsa Família e Renda de Cidadania—um passo en falso?* Brasilia: IPEA.

Broadman, H. 2007. *Africa's Silk Road: China and India's New Economics Frontier.* Washington, DC: World Bank.

Brockerhoff, M., and P. Hewett. 2000. 'Inequality of Child Mortality among Ethnic Groups in Sub-Saharan Africa'. *Bulletin of the World Health Organization*, 78: 30–41.

Brown, G., and F. Stewart. 2006. 'The Implications of Horizontal Inequality for Aid'. CRISE Working Paper No. 36. Oxford: University of Oxford.

Brown, T., and A. Teshome. 2007. 'Implementing Policies for Chronic Poverty in Ethiopia, Background Paper for the Chronic Poverty Report 2008–09'. London: Chronic Poverty Research Centre.

Browne, S. 2007. 'Aid to Fragile States: Do Donors Help or Hinder?' UNU-WIDER Discussion Paper No. 2007/01. Helsinki: WIDER.

Brubaker, R. 2004. *Ethnicity without Groups*. Cambridge, MA: Harvard University Press.

Bryant, R., and S. Bailey. 1997. *Third World Political Ecology* London: Routledge.

Buira, A. 2003. 'An Analysis of IMF Conditionality'. G-24 Discussion Paper Series No.22, <http://www.unctad.org/en/docs/gdsmdpbg2420033.pdf> (accessed 4 June 2014).

Bukenya, B. 2013. 'Are Service-delivery NGOs Building State Capacity in the Global South? Experiences from HIV/AIDS Programmes in Rural Uganda'. ESID Working Paper No. 22. Manchester: ESID.

Bulkeley, H. 2005. 'Reconfiguring Environmental Governance: Towards a Politics of Scales and Networks'. *Political Geography*, 24: 875–902.

Burgess, R., R. Jedwab, E. Miguel, and A. Morjaria. 2010. 'Our Turn to Eat: The Political Economy of Roads in Kenya'. London: London School of Economics.

Burnet, J. E. 2008. 'Gender Balance and the Meanings of Women in Governance in Post Genocide Rwanda'. *African Affairs*, 107(428): 361–86.

Burnside, C., and D. Dollar. 2000. 'Aid, Policies and Growth'. *American Economic Review*, 90(4): 847–68.

Burton, M., and Higley, J. 2001. 'The Study of Political Elite Transformations'. *International Review of Sociology*, 11(2), 181–99.

Bury, J. 2005. 'Mining Mountains: Neoliberalism, Land Tenure, Livelihoods and the New Peruvian Mining Industry in Cajamarca'. *Environment and Planning*, A 37(2): 221–39.

Cammack, D., and E. Kanyongolo. 2010. 'Local Governance and Public Goods in Malawi'. In Africa Power and Politics Programme Working Paper No. 11. London: Overseas Development Institute.

Cammett, M. C. 2011. 'Partisan Activism and Access to Welfare in Lebanon'. *Studies in Comparative International Development*, 46(1): 70–97.

Campbell, B. 2003. 'Factoring in Governance Is Not Enough: Mining Codes in Africa, Policy Reform and Corporate Responsibility'. *Minerals and Energy*, 18(3): 2–13.

Campbell, B. 2008a. 'Reform Processes in Africa: Issues and Trends'. Presentation to the 2nd International Study Group Meeting, Economic Commission for Africa, 19–21 May 2008, Addis Ababa.

Campbell, H. 2008b. 'China in Africa: Challenging US Global Hegemony'. *Third World Quarterly*, 29(1): 89–105.

Campos, I., and A. Vines. 2008. 'Angola and China: A Pragmatic Partnership?' <http://www.csis.org/media/csis/pubs/080306_angolachina.pdf> (accessed 11 March 2009).

Carbone, G. 2009a. 'Does Democratisation Deliver Social Welfare? Political Regimes and Health Policy in Ghana and Cameroon'. Paper presented at the Annual Congress of the Societa Italiana di Scienza Politica (SISP), 17–19 September 2009.

Carbone, G. 2009b. 'The Consequences of Democratization'. *Journal of Democracy*, 20(2): 123–37.

Carmody, P. 2011. *The New Scramble for Africa*. London: Polity Press.

Carmody, P., G. Hampwaye, and E. Sakala. 2011. 'Globalisation and the Rise of the State? Chinese Geogovernance in Zambia'. *New Political Economy*, 17(2): 209–29.

Carmody, P., and I. Taylor. 2010. 'Flexigemony and Force in China's Geoeconomic Strategy in Africa: Sudan and Zambia Compared'. *Geopolitics*, 15(3): 495–515.

Carothers, T. (ed.). 2006. *Promoting the Rule of Law Abroad: In Search of Knowledge*. Washington, DC: Carnegie Endowment for International Peace.

Carothers, T. 2009. 'Rule of Law Temptations'. *Fletcher Forum of World Affairs*, 33(1): 49–61.

Carothers, T., and D. de Gramont. 2013. *Development Aid Confronts Politics: The Almost Revolution*. Washington, DC: The Carnegie Endowment for International Peace.

Carpenter, D. P. 2001. *The Forging of Bureaucratic Autonomy: Reputations, Networks, and Policy Innovation in Executive Agencies, 1862–1928*. Princeton, NJ: Princeton University Press.

Casely-Hayford, L. and A. Hartwell. 2010. 'Reaching the Underserved with Complementary Education: Lessons from Ghana's State and Non-state Sectors'. *Development in Practice*, 20(4–5): 527–39.

Cashore, B., G. Auld, and D. Newsom. 2004. *Governing Through Markets: Forest Certification and the Emergence of Non-state Authority*. New Haven, CT: Yale University Press.

Castellijo, C. 2011. 'Building a State That Works for Women: Integrating Gender into Post Conflict State-building'. Working Paper No. 107. FRIDE.

Cavarozzi, M. 1992. 'Beyond Transitions to Democracy in Latin America'. *Journal of Latin American Studies*, 24(3): 665–84.

Cecchini, S., and R. Martínez. 2011. *Protección social inclusiva en América Latina: Una mirada integral, un enfoque de derechos*, Santiago: CEPAL.

Cederman, L.-E., and L. Girardin. 2007. 'Beyond Fractionalization: Mapping Ethnicity onto Nationalist Insurgencies'. *American Political Science Review*, 101(1): 173–85.

Cederman, L.-E., N. B. Weidmann, and K. S. Gleditsch. 2011. 'Horizontal Inequalities and Ethnonationalist Civil War: A Global Comparison'. *American Political Science Review*, 105(3): 478–95.

Cederman, L.-E., A. Wimmer, and B. Min. 2010. 'Why Do Ethnic Groups Rebel? New Data and Analysis'. *World Politics*, 62(01): 87–119.

Centeno, M. A. 2002. *Blood and Debt: War and the Nation-State in Latin America*. University Park, PA: Pennsylvania State University Press.

Chabal, P., and J.-P. Daloz. 1999. *Africa Works: Disorder as Political Instrument*. Bloomington, IN: Indiana University Press.

Chandra, K. 2006. 'What Is Ethnicity and Does It Matter?' *Annual Review of Political Science*, 9: 397–424.

Chandra, K. 2007. *Why Ethnic Parties Succeed: Patronage and Ethnic Head Counts in India*. New York, NY: Cambridge University Press.

Chandra, K., and S. Wilkinson. 2008. 'Measuring the Effect of "Ethnicity"'. *Comparative Political Studies*, 41(4–5): 515–63.

Chan-Fishel, M. 2007. 'Environmental Impact: More of the Same?' In *African Perspectives of China in Africa*. Edited by Manji, F., and S. Marks, 139–152. Kenya: Fahamu.

Chang, C., A. Cheng, S. Kim, J. Kuhn-Osius, J. Reyes, and D. Turgel. 2009. 'Huawei Technologies: A Chinese Trail Blazer in Africa, <http://knowledge.wharton.upenn.edu/article.cfm?articleid=2211> (accessed 4 June 2014).

Chang, H.-J. 2002. *Kicking Away the Ladder: Development Strategy in historical Perspective*. London: Anthem Press.

Chanie, P. 2007. 'Clientelism and Ethiopia's Post-1991 Decentralisation'. *Journal of Modern African Studies*, 45(3): 355–84.

Chaponniere, J.-R. 2009. 'Chinese Aid to Africa, Origins, Forms and Issues'. In *The New Presence of China in Africa*. Edited by van Dijk, M., 55–82. Amsterdam: Amsterdam University Press.

Charlesworth, H. 2005. 'Not Waving but Drowning: Gender Mainstreaming and Human Rights in the United Nations'. *Harvard Human Rights Journal*, 18(Spring): 1–18.

Charness, G., R. Cobo-Reyes, and N. Jimenez. 2008. 'An Investment Game with Third Party Intervention'. *Journal of Economic Behaviour and Organisation*, 68(1): 18–28.

Chattopadhay, R., and E. Duflo. 2004. 'Women as Policymakers: Evidence from Randomized Policy Experiments in India'. *Econometrica*, 72(5): 1409–43.

Cheeseman, N., and M. Hinfelaar. 2009. 'Parties, Platforms and Political Mobilisation: The Zambian Presidential Election of 2008'. *African Affairs*, 109 (434): 51–76.

Chen, C., and R. Orr. 2009. 'Chinese Contractors in Africa: Home Government Support, Coordination Mechanisms, and Market Entry Strategies'. *Journal of Construction Engineering and Management*, 135(11): 1201–10.

Chen, D., J. Matovu, and R. Reinikka. 2001. 'A Quest for Revenue and Tax Incidence in Uganda'. IMF Working Paper 01/04. Washington, DC: IMF.

Chenery, H., C. Bell, J. H. Duloy, and R. Jolly. 1975. *Redistribution with Growth*. New York, NY: World Bank/Oxford University Press.

Chesterman, S. 2008. 'An International Rule of Law'. *American Journal of Comparative Law*, 56: 331–61.

Chhotray, V. 2011. 'The "Anti-Politics Machine" in India: State, Decentralisation and Participatory Watershed Development'. *South Asian Studies Series*. London: Anthem Press.

Chibwana, C., M. Fisher, and G. Shively. 2012. 'Cropland Allocation Effects of Agricultural Input Subsidies in Malawi'. *World Development*, 40(1): 124–33.

Childs, S., and M. L. Krook. 2009. 'Analysing Women's Substantive Representation: From Critical Mass to Critical Actors'. *Government and Opposition*, 44(2): 125–45.

China Africa Development Fund (CADFund). 2014. 'About CADFund', <http://www.cadfund.com/WebSite/cadf/Upload/File/201312/20131231154138105396.pdf> (accessed 13 June 2014).

China Daily (14 October). 2010. 'China-Africa Trade Volume Set to Hit New Record High'. <http://www.chinadaily.com.cn/china/2010-10/14/content_11412120.htm> (accessed 9 October 2011).

China Economic Review. 2011. 'Into Africa', <http://www.chinaeconomicreview.com/en/node/25346> (accessed 13 June 2014).

Chinese Academy of International Trade and Economic Cooperation (CAITEC). 2010. 'China-Africa Trade and Economic Relationship Annual Report 2010'. <http://www.focac.org/eng/zxxx/t832788.htm> (accessed 28 September 2011).

Chinese Customs. 2011. 'China-Africa Trade Statistics'. <http://www.e-to-china. com/2011/0823/96699.html> (accessed 1 September 2011).

Chinsinga, B. 2007. 'Reclaiming Policy Space: Lessons from Malawi's 2005/2006 Fertilizer Subsidy Programme'. Future Agricultures Policy Brief 13. Brighton: Institute of Development Studies (IDS).

Chinsinga, B. 2008. 'The Malawi Fertiliser Subsidy Programme: Politics and Pragmatism'. Future Agricultures Policy Brief 22. Brighton: Institute of Development Studies (IDS).

Chirwa, E. 2008. 'Land Reforms, Food Production and Maize Productivity in Malawi'. University of Manchester: unpublished paper for Institutions for Pro-Poor Growth Project.

Chirwa, E. W., J. Kydd, and A. Dorward. 2006. 'Future Scenarios for Agriculture in Malawi: Challenges and Dilemmas'. *Future Agricultures Consortium*. Sussex: Institute of Development Studies.

Chowdhury, N. 1994. *Women in Politics*. Dhaka: Women for Women.

Chowdhury, S., F. Yamauchi, and R. Dewina. 2009. 'Governance Decentralization and Local Infrastructure Provision in Indonesia'. International Food Policy Research Institute.

Christian Aid. 2009. 'Breaking the Curse: How to Increase Revenue and Transparency', Available at: http://www.christianaid.org.uk/Images/ breaking-the-curse.pdf, (accessed 7 June 2014).

Coady, D. 2008a. 'Human Capital Expenditures for the Poor'. In *Public Expenditures, Growth and Poverty*. Edited by Fan, S. Baltimore, MD: Johns Hopkins University Press for IFPRI.

Coady, D. 2008b. 'Social Safety Nets'. In *Public Expenditures, Growth and Poverty*. Edited by Fan, S., 147–83. Baltimore, MD: Johns Hopkins University Press for IFPRI.

Coffee, J. C. 2001. 'The Rise of Dispersed Ownership: The Roles of Law and the State in the Separation of Ownership and Control'. *Yale Law Journal*, 111: 1–82.

Collier, P. 2002. 'Making Aid Smart: Institutional Incentives Facing Donor Organizations and their Implications for Aid Effectiveness'. *Forum Series on the Role of Institutions in Promoting Growth*. Washington, DC: IRIS.

Collier, P. 2007. *Accountability in the Provision of Social Services: A Framework for African Research*. Oxford: Centre for the Study of African Economies.

Collier, P., and D. Dollar. 1999. 'Aid Allocation and Poverty Reduction'. Policy Research Working Paper No. 2041. Washington, DC: World Bank.

Collier, P., and A. Hoeffler. 2004. 'Greed and Grievance in Civil War'. *Oxford Economic Papers*, 56(4): 563–95.

Collier, P., and A. Hoeffler, 2005. 'Resource Rents, Governance, and Conflict'. *Journal of Conflict Resolution*, 49(4): 625–33.

Collier, P., and A. Venables. 2011a. *Plundered Nations? Successes and Failures in Natural Resource Extraction*. New York, NY: Palgrave Macmillan.

Collier, P., and A. Venables. 2011b. 'Key Decisions for Resource Management: Principles and Practice'. In *Plundered Nations? Successes and Failures in Natural Resource Extraction*. Edited by Collier, P., and A. Venables, 1–26. Basingstoke: Palgrave Macmillan.

Collins, P. H. 2000. 'Gender, Black Feminism, and Black Political Economy', *Annals of the American Academy of Political and Social Science*, 568: 41–53.

Commission for Growth and Development. 2008. *The Growth Report: Strategies for Sustained Growth and Inclusive Development*. Washington, DC: World Bank.

Committee of Inquiry into a Comprehensive System of Social Security for South Africa. 2002. 'Transforming the Present, Protecting the Future'. Pretoria: Committe of Inquiry into a Comprehensive System of Social Security for South Africa.

Cooksey, B. 2002. 'Can Aid Agencies Really Help to Combat Corruption?' <http://www.unodc.org/pdf/crime/publications/aid_agencies.pdf>.

Corbridge, S., G. Williams, M. Srivastava, and R. Véron. 2005. *Seeing the State: Governance and Governmentality in India*. Cambridge: Cambridge University Press.

Corkin L. 2011a. 'Uneasy Allies: China's Evolving Relations with Angola'. *Journal of Contemporary African Studies*, 29(2): 169–80.

Corkin, L. 2011b. 'Chinese Construction Companies in Angola: A Local Linkages Perspective'. MMCP Discussion Paper No. 2, March.

Cornia, A., R. Jolly, and F. Stewart. 1987. *Adjustment with a Human Face*. Oxford: Oxford University Press.

Cornwall, A. 2007. 'Buzzwords and Fuzzwords: Deconstructing Development Discourse'. *Development in Practice*, 17(4–5): 471–84.

Cornwall, A., and K. Brock. 2005. 'What Do Buzzwords Do for Development Policy? A Critical Look at "Participation", "Empowerment", and "Poverty Reduction". *Third World Quarterly*, 26(7): 1043–60.

Cornwall, A., and V. S. P. Coelho. 2007. 'Spaces for Change? The Politics of Participation in New Democratic Arenas'. In *Spaces for Change? The Politics of Citizen Participation in New Democratic Arenas*. Edited by Cornwall, A., and V. S. P. Coelho. London: Zed Books.

Coronil, F. 1997. *The Magical State: Nature, Money, and Modernity in Venezuela*. Chicago, IL: University of Chicago Press.

Correa Sutil, J. 1997. 'No Victorious Army Has Ever Been Prosecuted: The Unsettled Story of Transitional Justice in Chile'. In *Transitional Justice and the Rule of Law in New Democracies*. Edited by McAdams, A. J., 123–54. Notre Dame, IN: University of Notre Dame Press.

Costa, D. L., and M. E. Kahn. 2003. 'Civic Engagement and Community Heterogeneity: An Economist's Perspective'. *Perspectives on Politics*, 1(01): 103–11.

Craig, D., and D. Porter. 2006. *Development beyond Neoliberalism: Governance, Poverty Reduction and Political Economy*. London: Routledge.

Cress, D. M., and D. A. Snow. 2000. 'The Outcomes of Homeless Mobilization: The Influence of Organization, Disruption, Political Mediation, and Framing'. *American Journal of Sociology*, 105(4): 1063–104.

Crook, R. 2010. 'Rethinking Civil Service Reform in Africa: "Islands of Effectiveness" and Organisational Commitment'. *Commonwealth and Comparative Politics*, 48(4): 479–504.

Crook, R. C., K. Asante, and V. Brobbey. 2010. 'Ghana: Testing the Legitimacy of New or Hybrid Forms of State Justice'. Africa Power and Politics Programme Working Paper No. 14. London: ODI.

Crossley, N. 2000. *Making Sense of Social Movements*. Milton Keynes: Open University Press.

Cubero, R., and I. Vladkova Hollar. 2010. 'Equity and Fiscal Policy: The Income Distribution Effects of Taxation and Social Spending in Central America'. IMF Working Paper WP/10/112, Washington, DC:IMF.

Cueva, H. 2004. 'Women in Politics What Difference Does It Make? An Empirical Assessment of the Case of Abortion Law'. MPhil Thesis. Brighton: IDS (Mimeo).

Curtis, D. 2004. '"How We Think They Think": Thought Styles in the Management of International Aid'. *Public Administration and Development*, 24: 415–23.

Daelmans, B., J. Martines, and R. Saadeh. 2003. 'Update on Technical Issues Concerning Complementary Feeding of Young Children in Developing Countries and Implications for Intervention Programs'. Special issue of *WHO Food and Nutrition Bulletin*.

Dale, P. 2009. 'Delivering Justice to Sierra Leone's Poor: An Analysis of the Work of Timap for Justice'. In *Justice for the Poor Research Report, No. 1/2009*. Washington, DC: World Bank.

Dam, K. W. 2006a. China as a Test Case: Is the Rule of Law Essential for Economic Growth? John M. Olin Law and Economics Working Paper No. 275. Chicago, IL: The Law School, University of Chicago.

Dam, K. W. 2006b. *The Law-growth Nexus: The Rule of Law and Economic Development*. Washington, DC: Brookings Institute Press.

Daniel, P., M. Keen, and C. McPherson. 2010. *The Taxation of Petroleum and Minerals: Principles, Practices and Problems*. London: Routledge.

Daniels, R. J., and M. Trebilcock. 2004. 'The Political Economy of Rule of Law Reform in Developing Countries'. *Michigan Journal of International Law*, 26: 99–140.

Darden, K. 2008. 'The Integrity of Corrupt States: Graft as an Informal State Institution'. *Politics and Society*, 36: 35–59.

Darden, K. 2012. *Resisting Occupation: Mass Schooling and the Creation of Durable National Loyalties*. New York, NY: Cambridge University Press.

Davies, M., H. Edinger, N. Tay, and S. Naidu. 2008. *How China Delivers Development Assistance to Africa*. South Africa: Centre for Chinese Studies, University of Stellenbosch.

Davies, P. 2007. 'China and the End of Poverty in Africa: Towards Mutual Benefit?' Sweden: Diakonia and Eurodad. Diakonia, http://www.oefse.at/Downloads/veran staltungen/1011/Vienna_Penny%20Davies.pdf (accessed 7 June 2014).

Davies, P. 2010. 'Roles and Activities of the "New Development Partners"'. In *A Brave New World of 'Emerging', 'Non-DAC' Donors and their Differences from Traditional Donors*. Edited by King, K. *NORRAG News*, 44, September.

Davis, G. A. 1995. 'Learning to Love the Dutch Disease—Evidence from the Mineral Economies,' *World Development*, 23(10): 1765–79.

Davis, G. A., and J. E. Tilton. 2002. 'Should Developing Countries Renounce Mining? A Perspective on the Debate'. Report prepared for the International Council on Mining and Metals (ICMM). London: ICMM.

Davoodi, H., B. Clements, J. Schiff, and P. Debaere. 1999. 'Military Spending, the Peace Dividend and Fiscal Adjustment'. *IMF Staff Papers*, 48: 290–316.

de Britto, T. F. 2008. 'The Emergence and Popularity of Conditional Cash Transfers in Latin America'. In *Social Protection for the Poor and Poorest*. Edited by Barrientos, A., and D. Hulme. Basingstoke: Palgrave.

de Haan, A. 2009. *How the Aid Industry Works. An Introduction to International Development*. West Hartford, CT: Kumarian Press.

de Haan, A., and M. Everest-Phillips. 2007. 'Can New Aid Modalities Handle Politics?' UNU-WIDER Research Paper 2007/63. Helsinki: WIDER.

de Haan, A., and M. Everest-Phillips. 2010. 'Can New Aid Modalities Handle Politics?' In *Foreign Aid for Development*. Edited by Mavrotas, G. Oxford: Oxford University Press.

De Janvry, A., H. Nakagawa, and E. Sadoulet. 2009. *Pro-poor Targeting and Electoral Rewards in Decentralizing to Communities the Provision of Public Goods in Rural Zambia*. Berkeley, CA: University of California at Berkeley.

De La O, A. L. 2006. *Do Poverty Relief Funds Affect Electoral Behaviour? Evidence from a Randomized Experiment in Mexico*. Cambridge MA: MIT.

de Renzio, P., and J. Hanlon. 2007. 'Contested Sovereignty in Mozambique: The Dilemmas of Aid Dependence'. GEG Working Paper 2007/25.

de Renzio, P., L. Whitfield, and I. Bergamaschi. 2008. 'Reforming Foreign Aid: What Country Ownership Is and What Donors Can Do to Support It'. Global Economic Governance Programme Briefing Paper, June.

De Silva, S., and J.-W. Sum. 2008. 'Social Funds as an Instrument of Social Protection: An Analysis of Lending Trends, FY 2000-2007'. Social Protection Discussion Paper, HDNSP. Washington, DC: World Bank.

De Soto, H. 2000. *The Mystery of Capital: Why Capitalism Triumphs in the West and Fails Everywhere Else*. London: Bantam Press.

Deacon, B. 1997. *Global Social Policy: International Organizations and the Future of Welfare*. London: Sage.

Dennis, M. J., and D. P. Stewart. 2004. 'Justiciability of Economic, Social, and Cultural Rights: Should There Be an International Complaints Mechanism to Adjudicate the Rights to Food, Water, Housing, and Health?' *American Journal of International Law*, 98(3): 462–515.

Department for International Development (DFID). 2011. 'The Politics of Poverty: Elites, Citizens and States: Findings from Ten Years of DFID-funded Research on Governance and Fragile States 2001–2010'. DFID Research and Evidence Division Staff. London: DFID, <https://www. gov.uk/government/uploads/system/uploads/attachment_data/file/67679/ plcy-pltcs-dfid-rsch-synth-ppr.pdf> (accessed 4 June 2014).

Desai, D. 2010. '"Courting" Legitimacy: Democratic Agency and the Justifiability of Economic and Social Rights'. *Interdisciplinary Journal of Human Rights Law*, 4(1): 25–41.

Desai, D., D. Isser, and M. Woolcock. 2012. 'Rethinking Justice Reform in Fragile and Conflict-affected States: Lessons for Enhancing the Capacity of Development Agencies'. *Hague Journal on the Rule of Law*, 4(1): 54–75.

Dev, M. 1998. 'Government Interventions and Social Security for Rural Labour'. *In Empowering Rural Labour in India*. Edited by Radhakrishna, R. and A. N. Sharma. New Delhi: Institute for Human Development.

Devarajan, S., Khemani, S., and Walton, M. 2011. *Civil Society, Public Action and Accountability in Africa*. Washington, DC: World Bank.

Devarajan, S., and I. Widlund (eds.). 2007. *The Politics of Service Delivery in Democracies: Bettter Access for the Poor*. Stockholm: EGDI Secretariat.

Devereux, S. 2007. 'Social Pensions in Southern Africa in the Twentieth Century'. *Journal of Southern African Studies*, 33(3): 539–60.

Devereux, S. 2009. 'Agriculture and Social Protection in Malawi: Fertiliser Policies and Politics'. *Future Agricultures, Policy Brief 28*. Brighton: Institute of Development Studies (IDS).

Devine, T. M. 1995. 'Why the Highlands Did Not Starve: Ireland and Highland Scotland during the Potato Famine'. In *Conflict, Identity and Economic Development: Ireland and Scotland, 1600–1939*. Edited by Connolly, S., R. Houston, and R. J. Morris. Preston: Carnegie Publishing.

Dezalay, Y., and B. G. Garth. 1996. *Dealing in Virtue: International Commercial Arbitration and the Construction of a Transnational Legal Order*. Chicago, IL: Chicago University Press.

Dezalay, Y., and B. G. Garth. 2002. *The Internationalization of Palace Wars: Lawyers, Economists, and the Contest to Transform Latin American States*. Chicago, IL: University of Chicago Press.

DFID. 2010. *The Politics of Poverty: Elites, Citizens and States: Findings from Ten Years of DFID-funded Research on Governance and Fragile States 2000–2010*. London: DFID.

DFID. 2011. *Multilateral Aid Review: Ensuring Maximum Value for Money for UK Aid through Multilateral Organizations*. London: DFID.

Di John, J. 2006. 'The Political Economy of Taxation and Tax Reform in Developing Countries'. UNU-WIDER Research Paper No. 2006/74. Helsinki: WIDER.

Di John, J. 2008. 'Fiscal Reforms, Developmental State Capacity and Poverty Reduction'. Background paper for UNRISD Flagship Report on Poverty. Geneva: UN Research Institute for Social Development.

Di John, J. 2009. *From Windfall to Curse? Oil and Industrialization in Venezuela, 1920 to the Present*. University Park, PA: Pennsylvania State University Press.

Di John, J. 2010a. 'The Political Economy of Taxation and State Resilience in Zambia since 1990'. Crisis States Working Papers Series No. 2, Working Paper No. 78. London: LSE.

Di John, J. 2010b. 'Taxation, Resource Mobilization and State Performance'. Crisis States Working Papers Series No. 2, Working Paper No. 84. London: LSE.

Di John, J., and Putzel, J. 2009. 'Political Settlements: Issues Paper'. Governance and Social Development Resource Centre, University of Birmingham, June.

Diani, M., and I. Bison. 2004. 'Organizations, Coalitions, and Movements'. *Theory and Society*, 33(3–4): 281–309.

Dietrich, S. 2010. 'The Politics of Public Health Aid: Why Corrupt Governments Have Incentives to Implement Aid Effectively'. *World Development*, 39(1): 55–63.

Djurfeldt G., and M. Jirstrom. 2004. 'The Puzzle of the Policy Shift: The Early Green Revolution in India, Indonesia and the Philippines'. In *The African Food Crisis: Lessons from the Asian Green Revolution*. Edited by Djurfeldt, G., H. Holmen, M. Jirstrom, and R. Lersson, 43–63. Wallingford: CAB International.

Dodson, M. 2002. 'Review: Assessing Judicial Reform in Latin America'. *Latin American Research Review*, 37(2): 200–20.

Dollar, D., and V. Levin. 2006. 'The Increasing Selectivity of Foreign Aid, 1984–2003'. *World Development*, 34(12): 2034–46.

Dom, C., S. Lister, and M. Antoninis. 2010. 'An Analysis of Decentralization in Ethiopia'. Draft report for the World Bank PBS Implementation Completion and Results Report'. London: Mokoro.

Dorward, A., and E. Chirwa. 2011. 'The Malawi Agricultural Input Subsidy Programme: 2005/06 to 2008/09'. *International Journal of Agricultural Sustainability*, 9(1): 232–47.

Doucouliagos, H., and M. Paldam. 2005. 'The Aid Effectiveness Literature: The Sad Result of 40 Years of Research'. University of Aarhus, Department of Economics, Working Paper No. 2005-15.

Dovi, S. 2006. 'Making Democracy Work for Women?' Paper presented at Political Women and American Democracy Conference, Notre Dame University, Indiana.

Downing, B. 1992. *The Military Revolution and Political Change: Origins of Democracy and Autocracy in Early Modern Europe*. Princeton, NJ: Princeton University Press.

Dreher, A., P. Nunnenkamp, and R. Thiele. 2010. 'Are New Donors Different? In *A Brave New World of 'Emerging', 'Non-DAC' Donors and their Differences from Traditional Donors*. Edited by King, K. *NORRAG News*, 4, September.

Dreher, A., P. Nunnenkamp, and R. Thiele. 2011. 'Are "New" Donors Different? Comparing the Allocation of Bilateral Aid between Non-DAC and DAC Donor Countries'. *World Development*, 39(11): 1950–68.

Duncan, A., and G. Williams. 2010. 'Making Development Assistance More Effective by Using Political Economy Analysis: What Has Been Done and What Have We Learned?' A Presentation to the Carnegie Endowment for International Peace/USAID/DAI Workshop on 'Advancing Integration of the Political and Economic in Development Assistance: Sharing UK and US Experiences', The Policy Practice Ltd.

Duncan, A., I. Sharif, P. Landell-Mills, D. Hulme, and J. Roy. 2002. *Bangladesh: Supporting the Drivers of Pro-poor Change*. London: DFID.

Dunning, T. 2008. *Crude Democracy: Natural Resource Wealth and Political Regimes*. Cambridge: Cambridge University Press.

Dutta, P., S. Howes, and R. Murgai. 2010. 'Small But Effective: India's Targeted Unconditional Cash Transfers'. *Economic and Political Weekly*, 65: 63–70.

Dworkin, R. 1986. *Law's Empire*. Cambridge, MA: Harvard University Press.

Easterly, W. 2006. *The White Man's Burden: Why the West's Efforts to Aid the Rest Have Done so Much Ill and so Little Good*. New York, NY: Penguin Press.

Easterly, W., and R. Levine. 1997. 'Africa's Growth Tragedy: Policies and Ethnic Divisions'. *The Quarterly Journal of Economics*, 112(4): 1203–50.

Eaton, K. 2007. 'Backlash in Bolivia: Regional Autonomy as a Reaction against Indigenous Mobilization'. *Politics and Society*, 35(1): 71–102.

Eaton, K. 2011. 'Conservative Autonomy Movements: Territorial Dimensions of Ideological Conflict in Bolivia and Ecuador'. *Comparative Politics*, 43(3): 291–310.

Ebrahim, A., and S. Herz. 2007. 'Accountability in Complex Organizations: World Bank Responses to Civil Society'. Working Paper 08/27, http://www.hbs.edu/fac ulty/Publication%20Files/08-027_18c99232-358f-456e-b619-3056cb59e915.pdf> (accessed 7 June 2014).

EFA Global Monitoring Report. 2011. 'The Hidden Crisis: Armed Conflict and Education'. Paris: UNESCO.

Eggen, Ø. 2011. 'Chiefs and Everyday Governance: Parallel State Organisations in Malawi'. *Journal of Southern African Studies*, 37(02): 313–31.

Eisenman, J. 2008. 'China's Political Outreach to Africa'. In *China into Africa: Trade, Aid and Influence*. Edited by Rotberg, R. Washington, DC: Brookings Institution Press.

Elster, J. 1985. *Sour Grapes: Studies in the Subversion of Rationality*. Cambridge: Cambridge University Press.

Engel, J. 2011. *Ethiopia's Progress in Education: A Rapid and Equitable Expansion of Access*, Development Progress. London: Overseas Development Institute (ODI), <http://www.developmentprogress.org/sites/developmentprogress.org/files/ resource_report/ethiopia_report_-_master_0.pdf> (accessed 7 June 2014).

Engelbert, P. 2002. *State Legitimacy and Development in Africa*. Boulder, CO: Lynne Rienner.

Engerman, Stanley L., and Kenneth L. Sokoloff. 2002. 'Factor Endowments, Inequality, and Paths of Development among New World Economies'. *Economia*, 3: 41–88.

Enriquez, E., and M. A. Centeno. 2012. 'State Capacity: Utilization, Durability, and the Role of Wealth vs. History'. *RIMCIS. International and Multidisciplinary Journal of Social Sciences*, 1(2): 130–62.

Ertman, T. 1997. *Birth of the Leviathan: Building States and Regimes in Medieval and Early Modern Europe*. Cambridge: Cambridge University Press.

Esping-Andersen, G. 1990. *The Three Worlds of Welfare Capitalism*. Cambridge: Polity Press.

European Commission. 2008. 'EU, Africa and China Trilateral Dialogue', <http:// ec.europa.eu/development/icenter/repository/COMM_PDF_COM_2008_0654_F_ COMMUNICATION_en.pdf> (accessed 13 June 2014).

Evans, P., and J. Rauch. 1999. 'Analysis of "Weberian" State Structures and Economic Growth'. *American Sociological Review*, 64: 748–65.

Evans, P. 1995. *Embedded Autonomy: States and Industrial Transformation*. Princeton, NJ: Princeton University Press.

Evans, P. 2010. *The Challenge of 21st Century Development: Building Capability-Enhancing States*. New York, NY: United Nations Development Programme.

Evans, P. 2011. 'Constructing the 21st Century Developmental State'. [Mimeo.]

Evans, P., D. Rueschemeyer, and T. Skocpol (eds.). 1985. *Bringing the State Back In*. Cambridge: Cambridge University Press.

Everest-Phillips, M. 2007. 'Beyond "Constraints": Promoting the Politics of Growth in Developing Countries'. SPIRU Working Paper. London: ODI/DFID.

Everest-Phillips, M. 2010. 'State-building Taxation for Developing Countries: Principles for Reform'. *Development Policy Review*, 28(1): 75–96.

Eyben, R. 2008. 'Power, Mutual Accountability, and Responsibility in the Practice of International Aid: A Relational Approach'. IDS Working Paper 305. Brighton: IDS.

Eyben, R., and S. Ladbury. 2006. 'Building Effective States: Taking a Citizen's Perspective'. Development Research Centre: Citizenship, Participation and Accountability, <http://www.drc-citizenship.org/system/assets/1052734530/original/1052734530-eyben_etal.2006-building.pdf> (accessed 20 June 2014).

Faguet, J.-P., and Z. Ali. 2009. 'Making Reform Work: Institutions, Dispositions, and the Improving Health of Bangladesh'. *World Development*, 37(1): 208–18.

Fan, S. (ed.) 2008. *Public Expenditures, Growth and Poverty*. Baltimore, MD: Johns Hopkins University Press for IFPRI.

Fan, S., P. Hazell, and S. Thorat. 2000. 'Government Spending, Agricultural Growth and Poverty in Rural India'. *American Journal of Agricultural Economics*, 82(4): 1088–51.

Fan, S., and N. Rao. 2008. 'Public Investment, Growth and Rural Poverty'. In *Public Expenditures, Growth and Poverty*. Edited by Fan, S., 56–108. Baltimore, MD: Johns Hopkins University Press for IFPRI.

Fan, S., L. Zhang, and X. Zhang. 2002. *Growth, inequality and poverty in rural China: the role of public investment*. IFPRI Research Report 125. Washington DC: International Food Policy Research Institute.

Fan, S., L. Zhang, and X. Zhang. 2004. 'Reforms, Investment and Poverty in Rural China'. *Economic Development and Cultural Change*, 52(2): 395–421.

Fearon, J. D., and D. D. Laitin. 2003. 'Ethnicity, Insurgency, and Civil War'. *The American Political Science Review*, 97(1): 75–90.

Ferguson, J. 1990. *The Anti-politics Machine: 'Development', Depoliticization, and Bureaucratic Power in Lesotho*. Cambridge: Cambridge University Press.

Ferguson, J. 2006. *Global Shadows*. Durham, NC: Duke University Press.

Ferguson, J., and A. Gupta. 2002. 'Spatializing States: Toward an Ethnography of Neoliberal Governmentality'. *American Ethnologist*, 29(4): 981–1002.

Ferroni, M., and R. Kanbur. 1990. 'Poverty-conscious Restructuring of Public Expenditure'. Social Dimensions of Adjustment (SDA) in Sub-Saharan Africa. Working Paper No. 9. Policy Analysis. Washington, DC: The World Bank, <http://documents.worldbank.org/curated/en/1990/12/439287/poverty-conscious-restructuring-public-expenditure> (accessed 18 June 2014).

Fessehaie, J. 2011. 'Development and Knowledge Intensification in Industries Upstream of Zambia's Copper Mining Sector'. MMCP Discussion Paper No. 3, Cape Town, the University of Cape Town, and Milton Keynes, the Open University.

Fester, G. 2014. 'The South African Revolution: Protracted or Postponed?' In *Voicing Demands: Feminists' Activism in Transitional Contexts*. Edited by Nazneen, S., and M. Sultan. London: ZED books.

Fischer, P., and R. Kappel. 2005. 'Rent-seeking and Aid Effectiveness: The Case of Tanzania'. 11th EADI General Conference: Insecurity and Development. Bonn, 21–24 September 2005.

Fiszbein, A., and N. Schady. 2009. *Conditional Cash Transfers: Reducing Present and Future Poverty*, Washington, DC: World Bank.

Fjeldstad, O.-H. 2001. 'Taxation, Coercion and Donors: Local Government Tax Enforcement in Tanzania'. *The Journal of Modern African Studies*, 39(2): 289–306.

Flora, J. L., C. B. Flora, F. Campana, M. Garcia Bravo, and E. Fernandez-Baca. 2006. 'Social Capital and Advocacy Coalitions: Examples of Environmental Issues from Ecuador'. In *Development with Identity: Community, Culture and Sustainability.* Edited by Andes, R., and E. Rhoades, 287–97. Cambridge, MA: CABI Publishing.

Ford, J. 2001. *Former Soviet Union: U.S. Rule of Law Assistance Has Had Limited Impact.* Washington, DC: US General Accounting Office.

Foster, M. 2000. 'New Approaches to Development Co-operation: What Can We Learn from Experiences with Implementing Sector-wide Approaches'. Working Paper 140. London: Overseas Development Iinstitute.

Foster, M., and J. Leavy. 2001. 'The Choice of Financial Aid Instruments'. ODI Working Paper 158. London: Overseas Development Institute.

Foster, V., W. Butterfield, C. Chuan, and N. Pushak. 2008. *Building Bridges: China's Growing Role as Infrastructure Financier for sub-Saharan Africa*. Washington, DC: World Bank.

Foucault, M. 1984. 'Space, Knowledge and Power'. In *The Foucault Reader.* Edited by Rabinow, P. New York, NY: Pantheon.

Foucault, M. 1995. *Discipline and Punish: The Birth of the Prison.* New York, NY: Random House.

Foweraker, J., and R. Krznaric. 2002. 'The Uneven Performance of Third Wave Democracies: Electoral Politics and the Imperfect Rule of Law in Latin America'. *Latin American Politics and Society*, 44(3): 29–60.

Fox, J. 1996. 'How Does Civil Society Thicken? The Political Construction of Social Capital in Mexico'. *World Development*, 24(6): 1089–103.

Fraser, A. 2007. 'Zambia: Back to the Future'. GEG Working Paper 2007/30.

Fraser, A., and L. Whitfield. 2008. 'The Politics of Aid: African Strategies for Dealing with Donors'. Global Economic Governance Programme, Working Paper 2008/42.

Fraser, N. 1995. 'From Redistribution to Recognition? Dilemmas of Justice in a "Post-socialist" Age'. *New Left Review*, 212: 68.

Fraser, N. 2009. *Scales of Justice: Reimagining Political Space in a Globalizing World.* New York, NY: Columbia University Press.

Friedman, E., and B. Gilley (eds.). 2005. *Asia's Giants: Comparing China and India.* New York, NY: Palgrave.

Fritz, V., K. Kaiser, and B. Levy. 2009. *Problem-driven Governance and Political Economy Analysis.* Washington, DC: World Bank, PREM Network.

Frohman, A., and T. Valdez. 1995. 'Democracy in the Country and in the Home: The Women's Movement in Chile'. In *The Challenges of Local Feminisms: Women's Movement in Global Perspective.* Edited by Basu, A. Boulder, CO: Westview Press.

Bibliography

Fuentes, J. R. 2011. 'Learning How to Manage Natural Resource Revenue: The Experience of Copper in Chile'. In *Plundered Nations? Successes and Failures in Natural Resource Extraction*. Edited by Collier, P., and A. Venables, 79–113. Basingstoke: Palgrave Macmillan.

Fukuyama, F. 2010. 'Transitions to the Rule of Law'. *Journal of Democracy*, 21(1): 33–44.

Fukuyama, F. 2011. *The Origins of Political Order: From Prehuman Times to the French Revolution*. London: Profile Books.

Fukuyama, F. 2004. *State-building: Governance and World Order in the 21st Century*. Ithaca, NY: Cornell University Press.

Fung, A. 2003. 'Recipes for Public Spheres: Eight Institutional Design Choices and their Consequences'. *Journal of Political Philosophy*, 11(3): 338–67.

Furtado, X., and W. J. Smith. 2007. 'Ethiopia: Aid, Ownership, and Sovereignty'. GEG Working Paper 2007/28.

Gadzala, A., and M. Hanusch. 2010. 'African Perspectives on China–Africa: Gauging Popular Perceptions and their Economic and Political Determinants'. Afrobarometer Working Paper No. 117.

Galeano, E. 1998. *Open Veins of Latin America: Five Centuries of the Pillage of a Continent*. New York, NY: Monthly Review Press.

Gallie W. B. 1956. 'Essentially Contested Concepts'. *Proceedings of the Aristotelian Society*, 56: 167–98.

Garcia, M., and A. S. Rajkumar. 2008. 'Achieving Better Service Delivery through Decentralization in Ethiopia'. World Bank Working Paper No. 131. Washington, DC: World Bank.

Garth, B. 2002. 'American Civil Justice in a Global Context'. *DePaul Law Review*, 52: 383–400.

Gaspart, F., and J.-P. Platteau. 2006. 'The Perverse Effects of Cheap Aid Money'. UNU-WIDER Conference on Aid: Principles, Policies and Performance. Helsinki, 16–17 June.

Gauri, V. 2011. 'Redressing Grievances and Complaints Regarding Basic Service Delivery'. In World Bank Policy Research Working Paper No. 5699. Washington, DC: World Bank.

Gauri, V., and D. Brinks (eds.). 2008. *Courting Social Justice: Judicial Enforcement of Social and Economic Rights in the Developing World*. New York, NY: Cambridge University Press.

Gauri, V., M. Woolcock, and D. Desai. 2013. 'Intersubjective Meaning and Collective Action in Developing Societies: Theory, Evidence and Policy Implications'. *Journal of Development Studies*, 49(1): 160–72.

Gauthier, B., and R. Reinikka. 2007. 'Methodological Approaches to the Study of Institutions and Service Delivery: A Review of PETS, QSDS and CRCS'. Washington, DC: World Bank.

Gaventa, J., and G. Barrett. 2010. 'So What Difference Does It Make? Mapping the Outcomes of Citizen Engagement'. IDS Working Paper 347. Development Research Centre: Citizenship, Participation and Accountability.

Geddes, B. 1994. *Politician's Dilemma: Building State Capacity in Latin America*. Berkeley, CA: University of California Press.

Gelbach, J. B., and L. Pritchett. 1995. 'Does More for the Poor Mean Less for the Poor? The Politics of Targeting'. Washington, DC: World Bank.

Gellner, E. 1983. *Nations and Nationalism*. London: Oxford University Press.

Gemmell, N., and O. Morrissey. 2001. 'The Poverty Effects of Revenue Systems in Developing Countries'. Unpublished paper for DFID.

George, A. L., and A. Bennett. 2004. *Case Studies and Theory Development in the Social Sciences*. Cambridge, MA: MIT Press.

Gerring, J., S. C. Thacker, and C. Moreno. 2005. 'Centripetal Democratic Governance: A Theory and Global Inquiry'. *American Political Science Review*, 99(04): 567–81.

Gerschenkron, A. 1959. *Economic Backwardness in Historical Perspective*. Cambridge, MA: Harvard University Press.

Ghanaweb. 2010. 'Donors Question Transparency of STX Korea Housing Deal', <http://www.ghanaweb.com/GhanaHomePage/business/artikel.php?ID=194112> (accessed 4 June 2014).

Gibson, C., and M. Woolcock. 2008. 'Empowerment, Deliberative Development and Local-level Politics in Indonesia: Participatory Projects as a Source of Countervailing Power'. *Studies in Comparative International Development*, 43(2): 151–80.

Giddens, A. 1979. *Central Problems in Social Theory: Action, Structure, and Contradiction in Social Analysis*. Berkeley, CA: University of California Press.

Giddens, A. 1984. *The Constitution of Society*. Berkeley, CA: University of California Press.

Gill, J., and S. Hughes. 2005. 'Bureaucratic Compliance with Mexico's New Access to Information Law'. *Critical Studies in Media Communication*, 22(2): 121–37.

Ginsburg, T. 2010. 'The Politics of Courts in Democratization'. In *Global Perspectives on the Rule of Law*. Edited by Heckman, J. J., R. L. Nelson, and L. Cabatingan. London: Routledge.

Giovagnoli, P. 2005. 'Poverty Alleviation or Political Networking? A Combined Qual-quant Analysis of the Implementation of Safety Nets in Post-crisis Argentina'. London: DESTIN, London School of Economics.

Giraudy, A. 2012. 'Conceptualizing State Strength: Moving Beyond Strong and Weak States'. *Revista de Ciencia Política*, 32(3): 599–611.

Giraudy, A., and J. Luna. 2011. 'Weak Stateness vs. Challenged States: An Explanatory Typology'. In *APSA 2011 Annual Meeting Paper*. Edited by Glatzer, M., and D. Rueschemeyer. *Globalisation and the Future of the Welfare State*. Pittsburgh, PA: Pittsburgh University Press.

Glaeser, E., R. La Porta, and F. Lopez-de-Silanes. 2004. 'Do Institutions Cause Growth?' NBER Working Paper 10568.

Gloppen, S. 2008. 'Public Interest Litigation, Social Rights and Social Policy'. In *Inclusive States: Social Policy and Structural Inequalities*. Edited by Dani, A. A. and A. de Haan. Washington, DC: World Bank.

Glosny, M. 2006. 'Meeting the Development Challenge in the 21st Century: American and Chinese Perspectives on Foreign Aid National Committee on US–China Relations', <http://www.ncuscr.org/files/6.%20Foreign%20Aid%20(21).pdf> (accessed 18 November 2009).

Godoy, S., and J. E. Stiglitz. 2006. 'Growth, Initial Conditions, Law and Speed of Privatization in Transition Countries: 11 Years Later'. NBER Working Paper Series 11992. Cambridge, MA: National Bureau of Economic Research.

Goetz, A. M. 1995. 'The Politics of Integrating Gender to State Development Processes: Trends, Opportunities and Constraints in Bangladesh, Chile, Jamaica, Mali, Morocco and Uganda'. Occasional Paper 2. UNRISD/UNDP, Geneva.

Goetz, A. M. 1997. 'Local Heroes: Patterns on Field Worker Discretion in Implementing GAD Policy in Bangladesh'. In *Getting Institutions Right for Women in Development*. Edited by Goetz, A. M. London: ZED books.

Goetz, A. M. 2003a. 'The Problem with Patronage: Constraints on Women's Political Effectiveness in Uganda'. In *No Short Cuts to Power: African Women in Politics and Policy Making*. Edited by Goetz, A. M. and S. Hassim. London: Zed books.

Goetz, A. M. 2003b. 'Women's Political Effectiveness: A Conceptual Framework'. In *No Short Cuts to Power: African Women in Politics and Policy Making*. Edited by Goetz, A. M., and S. Hassim. London: Zed books.

Goetz, A. M., and S. Hassim (eds.). 2003. *No Short Cuts to Power: African Women in Politics and Policy Making*. London: Zed books.

Goetz, A. M., and R. Jenkins. 2005. *Reinventing Accountability: Making Democracy Work for Human Development*. New York, NY: Palgrave.

Goetz, A. M., and C. Nyamu-Musembi. 2008. 'Voice and Women's Empowerment: Mapping a Research Agenda'. Pathways Working Paper No. 2, Brighton: IDS.

Goldin, C., and L. F. Katz. 1999. 'The Shaping of Higher Education: The Formative Years in the United States, 1890–1940'. *Journal of Economic Perspectives*, 13: 37–62.

Golooba-Mutebi, F., and S. Hickey. 2009. 'Governing Chronic Poverty under Inclusive Liberalism: The Case of the Northern Uganda Social Action Fund'. Chronic Poverty Research Centre, Working Paper No. 150, Makerere University and University of Manchester, <www.chronicpoverty.org> (accessed 4 June 2014).

Golub, S. 2003. 'Beyond Rule of Law Orthodoxy: The Legal Empowerment Alternative'. Carnegie Endowment for International Peace Rule of Law Working Paper Series, No. 41. Washington, DC: Carnegie Endowment for International Peace.

Gordon, R. W. 1984. 'Critical Legal Histories'. *Stanford Law Review*, 36: 57–125.

Gorski, P. S. 1995. 'The Protestant Ethic and the Spirit of Bureaucracy'. *American Sociological Review*, 60: 783–6.

Gorski, P. 2003. *The Disciplinary Revolution: Calvinism and the Rise of the State in Early Modern Europe*. Chicago, IL: Chicago University Press.

Gough, I., and G. Wood (eds.). 2004. *Insecurity and Welfare Regimes in Asia, Africa and Latin America*. Cambridge: Cambridge University Press.

Graham, C. 1995. *Safety Nets, Politics, and the Poor: Transitions to Market Economies.* Washington, DC: Brookings Institute.

Graham, C. 2002. 'Public Attitudes Matter: A Conceptual Frame for Accounting for Political Economy in Safety Nets and Social Assistance Policies'. Social Protection Discussion Paper Series. Washington, DC: World Bank.

Green M. 2009. 'Thinking through Chronic Poverty and Destitution: Theorising Social Relations and Social Ordering'. In *Poverty Dynamics: Interdisciplinary Perspectives*. Edited by Addison, T., D. Hulme, and R. Kanbur. Oxford: Oxford University Press.

Greenaway, D., and C. Milner. 1993. *Trade and Industrial Policy in Developing Countries: A Manual of Policy Analysis*. Basingstoke: Macmillan.

Grimm, S., H. Höß, K. Knappe, M. Siebold, J. Sperrfechter, and I. Vogler. 2011. *Coordinating China and DAC Development Partners: Challenges to the Aid Architecture in Rwanda*. Bonn: Deutsches Institut für Entwicklungspolitik / German Development Institute.

Grindle, M. 2004. *Despite the Odds: The Contentious Politics of Education Reform* Princeton, NJ: Princeton University Press.

Grindle, M. 2005. 'When Good Policies Go Bad, Then What?' Paper presented at conference on Statecraft in the South. Manchester: University of Manchester.

Grindle, M. 2007. 'When Good Policies Go Bad, Then What? Dislodging Exhausted Industrial and Education Policies in Latin America' In *Development Success: Statecraft in the South*. Edited by Bebbington, A. and W. McCourt, 79–104. London: Palgrave Macmillan.

Grindle, M. S. 2004. 'Good Enough Governance: Poverty Reduction and Reform in Developing Countries'. *Governance: An International Journal of Policy, Administration, and Institutions*, 17(4): 525–48.

Grosh, M., C. Del Ninno, E. Tesliuc, and A. Ouerghi. 2008. *For Protection and Promotion: The Design and Implementation of Effective Safety Nets*. Washington, DC: World Bank.

Grossman, H. I. (1992), 'Foreign Aid and Insurrection'. *Defence Economics*, 3(4): 275–88.

Gu, J. 2009. 'China's Private Enterprises in Africa and the Implications for African Development'. *European Journal of Development Research*, Special Issue on China, India and Africa, 24(1): 570–87.

Gu, J., J. Humphrey, and D. Messner. 2008. 'Global Governance and Developing Countries: The Implications of the Rise of China'. *World Development*, 36 (2): 274–92.

Guajardo Beltrán, J. C. 2012. 'Mineral Rents and Social Development in Chile'. In *Mineral Rents and the Financing of Social Policy: Opportunities and Challenges*. Edited by Hujo, K., 185–222. Basingstoke: Palgrave Macmillan.

Guggenheim, S., T. Wiranto, Y. Prasta, and S. Wongm. 2004. 'Indonesia's Kecamatan Development Program: A Large-scale Use of Community Development to Reduce Poverty'. A case study from 'Reducing Poverty, Sustaining Growth: What Works, What Doesn't, and Why a Global Exchange for Scaling Up Success Scaling Up Poverty Reduction'. A Global Learning Process and Conference Shanghai, May 25–27, 2004.

Guhan, S. 1994. 'Social Security Options for Developing Countries'. *International Labor Review*, 133(1): 35–53.

Guhan, S. 1995. 'Social Expenditures in the Union Budget'. *Economic and Political Weekly*, 30(18/19): 1095–101.

Guichaoua, Y. 2012. 'Elites' Survival and Natural Resource Exploitation in Nigeria and Niger'. In *The Developmental Challenges of Mining and Oil: Lessons from Africa and Latin America*. Edited by Thorp, R., S. Battistelli, Y. Guichaoua, J. C. Orihuela, and M. Paredes, 131–67. New York, NY: Palgrave Macmillan.

Gulhati, R., and R. Nallari. 1990. 'Successful Stabilisation and Recovery in Mauritius'. Washington, DC: Economic Development Institute of the World Bank, EDI Development Policy Case Studies 5.

Gupta, A. 2007. 'Determinants of Tax Revenue in Developing Countries'. Working Paper 07/184. Washington, DC: International Monetary Fund.

Gupta, S., B. Clemens, A. Pivovarsky, and E. Tiongson. 2003. 'Foreign Aid and Domestic Response: Does the Composition of Aid Matter?' In *Helping Countries Develop: The Role of Fiscal Policy*. Edited by Gupta, S., G. Inchauste, and B. Clemens. Washington, DC: IMF.

Gurr, T. 1970. *Why Men Rebel*. Princeton, NJ: Princeton University Press.

Guthrie, D. 1998. 'The Declining Significance of Guanxi in China's Economic Transition'. *The China Quarterly*, 154: 254–82.

Haas, P. M. (1992). 'Introduction: Epistemic Communities and International Policy Coordination'. *International Organization*, 46(1): 1–35.

Haber, S., A. Razo, and N. Maurer. 2003. *The Politics of Property Rights: Political Instability, Credible Commitment and Economic Growth in Mexico, 1876–1929*, Cambridge: Cambridge University Press.

Habyarimana, J., M. Humphreys, D. N. Posner, and J. M. Weinstein. 2009. *Coethnicity: Diversity and the Dilemmas of Collective Action*. New York, NY: Russell Sage Foundation.

Haggard, S., and R. Kaufman. 2008. *Revising Social Contracts: The Political Economy of Welfare Reform in Latin America, East Asia, and Central Europe*. Princeton, NJ: Princeton University Press.

Haggard, S., J. Lafay, and C. Morrisson. 1996. *The Political Feasibility of Adjustment*. Paris: OECD.

Haglund, D. 2009. 'In It for the Long Term? Governance and Learning among Chinese Investors in Zambia's Copper Sector'. *The China Quarterly*, 199: 627–46.

Hagmann, T., and Peclard, D. 2010. 'Negotiating Statehood: Dynamics of Power and Domination in Africa'. *Development and Change*, 41(4): 539–62.

Hajer, M. A. 1995. *The Politics of the Environmental Discourse: Ecological Modernization and the Policy Process*. Oxford: Clarendon Press.

Hall, A. 2008. 'Brazil's Bolsa Família: A Double-Edged Sword?' *Development and Change*, 39: 799–822.

Hall, P. 2010. 'Historical Institutionalism in Rationalist and Sociological Perspective'. In *Explaining Institutional Change: Ambiguity, Agency, and Power*. Edited by Mahoney, J., and K. Thelen, 204–24. Cambridge: Cambridge University Press.

Hall, P., and D. Soskice (eds). 2001. *Varieties of Capitalism: The Institutional Foundations of Comparative Advantage*. New York, NY: Oxford University Press.

Hall, R., and C. I. Jones. 1999. 'Why Do Some Countries Produce So Much Output per Worker than Others?' *Quarterly Journal of Economics*, 114: 83–116.

Hammergren, L. 2002. 'Latin American Criminal Justice Reform: Evaluating the Evaluators'. *Sistemas Judiciales*, 3: 59–66.

Hammergren, L. 2003. 'International Assistance to Latin American Justice Programs: Towards an Agenda for Reforming the Reformers'. In *Beyond Common Knowledge: Empirical Approaches to the Rule of Law*. Edited by Jenson, E. G., and T. C. Heller. Stanford, CA: Stanford University Press.

Han, Y. 2011. 'Chinese Investment Boosts African Economic Development'. *China and Africa Journal*, 9 May, <http://www.focac.org/eng/zfgx/t821032.htm> (accessed 1 September 2011).

Hanlon J. 2004. 'Do Donors Promote Corruption? The Case of Mozambique'. *Third World Quarterly*, 25(4): 747–63.

Hanlon, J. 2010. 'Mozambique's Elite—Finding its Way in a Globalized World and Returning to Old Development Models'. UNU-WIDER, WP 2010-10.

Hanlon, J., A. Barrientos, and D. Hulme. 2010. *Just Give Money to the Poor: The Development Revolution from the South*. Sterling, VA: Kumarian Press.

Harman, D. 2007. 'Is Western Aid Making a Difference in Africa? Two US Economists Debate the Value of Antipoverty Efforts'. <http://www.globalpolicy.org/socecon/develop/oda/2007/0823westernaid.htm> (accessed September 2007).

Harrigan, J. 2003. 'U-turns and Full Circles: Two Decades of Agricultural Reform in Malawi, 1981–2000'. *World Development*, 31(5): 847–63.

Harris, D., and M. Foresti. 2011. 'Indonesia's Progress on Governance: State Cohesion and Strategic Institutional Reform, Development Progress'. London: Overseas Development Institute.

Harris, R. 2010. 'Comparing Legal and Alternative Institutions in Finance and Commerce'. In *Global Perspectives on the Rule of Law*. Edited by Heckman, J. J., R. L. Nelson, and L. Cabatingan. London: Routledge.

Harrison, G. 2004. *The World Bank and Africa: The Construction of Governance States*. London: Routledge.

Harrison, G., and S. Mulley. 2007. 'Tanzania: A Genuine Case of Recipient Leadership in the Aid System?' GEG Working Paper 2007/29.

Harriss, J. 2004. 'How Much Difference Does Politics Make? Regime Differences across Indian States and Rural Poverty Reduction'. London: LSE DESTIN.

Harriss, J. 2006. 'Notes on a Historical Institutionalist Approach to the IPPG Agenda'. IPPG Discussion Paper No. 1, University of Manchester, <http://www.ippg.org.uk/papers/dp1.pdf> (accessed 4 June 2014).

Harriss, J., Hunter, J., and Lewis, C. (eds.). 1997. *The New Institutional Economics and Third World Development*. London: Routledge.

Hartwell, A. 2006. 'Meeting EFA: Ghana School for Life', School Educational Quality Improvement Programme EQUIP2, Washington, DC: USAID.

Hassim, S. 2003. 'Representation, Participation and Democratic Effectiveness: Feminist Challenges to Representative Democracy in South Africa'.

In *No Short Cuts to Power: African Women in Politics and Policy Making*. Edited by Goetz, A. M. and S. Hassim. London: Zed Books.

Hausmann, R., L. Pritchett, and D. Rodrik. 2005. 'Growth Accelerations'. *Journal of Economic Growth*, 10: 303–29.

Hayman, R. 2007. '"Milking the Cow": Negotiating Ownership of Aid and Policy in Rwanda'. GEG Working Paper 2006/26.

Hayman, R. 2011. 'Budget Support and Democracy: A Twist in the Conditionality Tale'. *Third World Quarterly*, 32(4): 673–88.

He, W. 2008. 'China's Perspective on Contemporary China-Africa Relations'. In *China Returns to Africa: A Rising Power and a Continent Embrace*. Edited by Alden, C., D. Large, and R. Soares de Oliveira, 143–66. London: Hurst.

He, W. 2010. 'China's Aid to Africa: Policy Evolution, Characteristics and its Role'. In *Challenging the Aid Paradigm: Western Currents and Asian Alternatives*. Edited by Sorensen, J., 138–65. London: Palgrave.

Hedger, E., and Z. K. Agha. 2007. 'Reforming Public Financial Management When the Politics Aren't Right: A Proposal'. ODI Opinion No. 89. London: Overseas Development Institute, <http://www.odi.org.uk/sites/odi.org.uk/files/odi-assets/publications-opinion-files/566.pdf> (accessed 18 June 2014).

Hedström, P., and R. Swedberg. 1998. 'Social Mechanisms: An Introductory Essay'. In *Social Mechanisms: An Analytical Approach to Social Theory*. Edited by Hedström, P., and R. Swedberg, 1–31. New York, NY: Cambridge University Press.

Heller, P. 2001. 'Moving the State: The Politics of Democratic Decentralization in Kerala, South Africa, and Porto Alegre'. *Politics and Society*, 29: 131–63.

Helmke, G., and S. Levitsky. 2006. *Informal Institutions and Democracy: Lessons from Latin America*. Baltimore, MD: Johns Hopkins University Press.

Henderson, J. 2008. 'China and Global Development: Towards a Global Asian Era?' *Contemporary Politics*, 14(4): 375–92.

Hendrix, C. S. 2010. 'Measuring State Capacity: Theoretical and Empirical Implications for the Study of Civil Conflict'. *Journal of Peace Research*, 47(3): 273–85.

Henley, D. 2014. *Asia-Africa Development Divergence: A Question of Intent*. London: Zed Books.

Hensengerth, O. 2011. 'Interaction of Chinese Institutions with Host Governments in Dam Construction: the Bui Dam in Ghana'. Discussion Paper 3/2011. Bonn: German Development Institute / Deutsches Institut für Entwicklungspolitik (DIE).

Herbst, J. 2000. *States and Power in Africa: Comparative Lessons in Authority and Control*. Princeton, NJ: Princeton University Press.

Hesselbein, G. 2011. 'Patterns of Resource Mobilisation and the Underlying Elite Bargain: Drivers of State Stability or State Fragility'. CSRC Working Papers. London: Crisis States Research Centre (CSRC).

Hickey, S. 2006. 'The Politics of What Works in Reducing Chronic Poverty'. Chronic Poverty Research Centre Working Paper 91, University of Manchester, Manchester.

Hickey, S. 2007. 'Conceptualising the Politics of Social Protection in Africa'. Brooks World Poverty Institute, Manchester: University of Manchester.

Hickey, S. 2008a. 'The Return of Politics in Development Studies (I): Getting Lost within the Poverty Agenda?' *Progress in Development Studies*, 8(4): 349–58.

Hickey, S. 2008b. 'Conceptualising the Politics of Social Protection in Africa'. In *Social Protection for the Poor and Poorest: Concepts, Policies and Politics*. Edited by Barrientos, A., and D. Hulme, 247–63. London: Palgrave.

Hickey, S. 2009. 'The Politics of Protecting the Poorest: Beyond the Anti-Politics Machine'. *Political Geography*, 28: 473–83.

Hickey, S. 2010. 'The Government of Chronic Poverty: From Exclusion to Citizenship?' *The Journal of Development Studies*, 46(7): 1139–55.

Hickey, S., and Bracking, S. 2005. 'Exploring the Politics of Poverty Reduction: From Representation to a Politics of Justice?' *World Development*, 33(6): 851–65.

Hickey, S., and du Toit, A. 2007. 'Adverse-incorporation, Social Exclusion and Chronic Poverty'. CPRC Working Paper 81. Manchester: IDPM <www.chronicpoverty.org> (accessed 4 June 2014).

Hilbink, E. 2007. *Judges beyond Politics in Democracy and Dictatorship: Lessons from Chile*. New York, NY: Cambridge University Press.

Hilhorst, D., and B. J. Jansen. 2010. 'Humanitarian Space as Arena: A Perspective on the Everyday Politics of Aid'. *Development and Change*, 41(6): 1117–39.

Hill, H. 1996. *The Indonesian Economy since 1966: Asia's Emerging Giant*. Cambridge: Cambridge University Press.

Hilson, G., and S. M. Banchirigah. 2012. 'Are Alternative Livelihood Projects Alleviating Poverty in Mining Communities? Experiences from Ghana'. *Journal of Development Studies*, 45(2): 72–196.

Hilton, S. 1975. 'Vargas and Brazilian Economic Development, 1930–45: A Reappraisal of his Attitudes towards Industrialisation and Planning'. *Journal of Economic History*, 35(4): 754–78.

Hinojosa, L. (ed.) 2012. *Gas and Desarrollo. Dinámicas territoriales rurales en Tarija—Bolivia*. La Paz: Fundación Tierra—CERDET.

Hinojosa, L., A. Bebbington, and A. Barrientos. 2012. 'Social Policy and State Revenues in Mineral-Rich Contexts'. In *Mineral Rents and the Financing of Social Policy: Opportunities and Challenges*. Edited by Hujo, K., 91–121. New York, NY: Palgrave Macmillan.

Hirschl, R. 2004. *Towards Juristocracy: The Origins and Consequences of the New Constitutionalism*. Cambridge, MA: Harvard University Press.

Hirschmann, D. 1993. 'Institutional Development in the Era of Economic Policy Reform: Concerns, Contradictions and Illustrations from Malawi'. *Public Administration and Development*, 13: 113–28.

Hirway, I. 2003. 'Identification of BPL Households for Poverty Alleviation Programmes'. *Economic and Political Weekly*, 38: 4803–38.

Hobsbawm, E. J. 1990. *Nations and Nationalism since 1780: Programme, Myth, Reality*. Cambridge: Cambridge University Press.

Hobsbawm, E. J., and T. Ranger (eds.). 1983. *The Invention of Tradition*. New York, NY: Cambridge University Press.

Hofman, B., E. Gudwin, and K. W. Thee. 2007. 'Managing the Indonesian Economy: Good Policies, Weak Institutions'. In *Development Success: Statecraft in the South*. Edited by Bebbington, A. and W. McCourt, 52–78. London: Palgrave Macmillan.

Hoffman, B. D., and C. C. Gibson. 2005. 'Fiscal Governance and Public Services: Evidence from Tanzania and Zambia'. Annual meeting of the American Political Science Association. Washington, DC, 1 September.

Hoffman, F. F., and F. R. N. M. Bentes. 2008. 'Accountability for Social and Economic Rights in Brazil'. In *Courting Social Justice: Judicial Enforcement of Social and Economic Rights in the Developing World*. Edited by Gauri, V. and D. Brinks, 100–45. New York, NY: Cambridge University Press.

Hohfeld, W. N. 1917. 'Fundamental Legal Conceptions as Applied in Judicial Reasoning'. *The Yale Law Journal*, 26(8): 710–70.

Holslag, J. 2011. 'China and the Coups: Coping with Political Instability in Africa'. *African Affairs*, 110(440): 367–86.

Holston, J. 1991. 'The Misrule of Law: Land and Usurpation in Brazil'. *Comparative Studies in Society and History*, 33(4): 695–725.

Hook, S. W. 1995. *National Interest and Foreign Aid*. Boulder, CO: Lynne Rienner.

Horowitz, D. L. 1985. *Ethnic Groups in Conflict*. Berkeley, CA: University of California Press.

Hossain, N. 2005. *Elite Perceptions of Poverty in Bangladesh*. Dhaka: The University Press.

Hossain, N. 2009. 'The Local Politics of Public Action: Relationships, Bargains and the Question of "Impact"'. *IDS Bulletin*, 40(6): 87–98.

Hossain, N. 2010. 'Rude Accountability: Informal Pressures on Frontline Bureaucrats in Bangladesh'. *Development and Change*, 41(5): 907–28.

Hossain, N., and S. Akhter. 2011. 'Gender, Power, and Politics in Bangladesh: A Baseline for Upzilla Support Bangladesh'. Dhaka: UNDP.

Hossain, N., and F. Osman. 2007. 'Politics and Governance in the Social Sectors in Bangladesh, 1991–2006'. *Research Monograph Series* 34, November, Research and Evaluation Division, BRAC: Dhaka.

Hossain, S. M. 2003. 'Taxation and Pricing of Petroleum Products in Developing Countries: A Framework for Analysis with Application to Nigeria'. IMF Working Paper WP/03/42.

Hout, W. 2007. *The Politics of Aid Selectivity: Good Goverance Criteria in World Bank, US and Dutch Development Assistance*. London: Routledge.

Houtzager, P. and M. Moore (eds.). 2003. *International Development and the Politics of Inclusion*. Ann Arbor, MI: University of Michigan Press.

Hove, M., and A. Wynne. 2010. 'The Experience of Medium-term Expenditure Framework and Integrated Financial Management Information System Reforms in Sub-Saharan Africa: What Is the Balance Sheet?' Occasional Paper, African Capacity Building Foundation, Harare.

Hsiung, J. 2003. 'The Aftermath of China's Accession to the World Trade Organisation'. *Independent Review*, 8(1): 87–112.

Hsu, E. 2007. 'Zanzibar and Its Chinese Communities'. *Populations, Space and Place*, 13(2): 113–24.

Htun, M. 2004. 'Is Gender Like Ethnicity?' *Perspectives in Politics*, 2(3): 439–58.

Htun, M. 2004. 'From "Racial Democracy" to Affirmative Action: Changing State Policy on Race in Brazil'. *Latin American Research Review*, 39(1): 60–89.

Htun, M. 2005. 'Women, Political Parties, Electoral Systems in Latin America'. In *Women in Parliament and Beyond Number*. Edited by Ballington, J., and A. Karam. Stockholm: International Institute for Democracy and Electoral Assistance.

Htun, M., and S. C. Weldon. 2010. 'When Do Governments Promote Women's Rights? A Comparative Framework for Analysis of Sex Equality Policies'. *Perspectives in Politics* 8(1): 207–16.

Hubbard, M. 2003. *Developing Agricultural Trade: New Roles for Government in Poor Countries*. London: Palgrave Macmillan.

Hubbard, P. 2008. 'Chinese Concessional Loans'. In *China into Africa, Trade, Aid and Influence*. Edited by Rotberg, R., 217–30. Washington, DC: Brooking Institution Press.

Huber, E., and J. D. Stephens. 2001. *Development and Crisis of the Welfare States: Parties and Policies in Global Markets*. Chicago, IL: University of Chicago Press.

Huber, M. 2009. 'Energizing Historical Materialism: Fossil Fuels, Space and the Capitalist Mode of Production'. *Geoforum*, 40(1): 105–15.

Hudson, D., and A. Leftwich. 2013. 'From Political Economy to Political Analysis'. Working Paper for the Developmental Leadership Programme.

Hudson, J., P. Lenton, and P. Mosley. 2011. 'The "Social Efficiency Wage"; or, Poverty Reduction via Fiscal Signals'. Unpublished paper presented at DSA conference, York.

Hudson, J., and P. Mosley. 2008. 'Aid Volatility and Development Policy'. *World Development*, 36(10): 2082–103.

Hughes, C., and J. Hutchison. 2012. 'Development Effectiveness and the Politics of Commitment'. *Third World Quarterly*, 33(1): 17–36.

Hujo, K. (ed.) 2012. *Mineral Rents and the Financing of Social Policy: Opportunities and Challenges*. New York, NY: Palgrave Macmillan.

Hulme, D. 2010. *Global Poverty: How Global Governance Is Failing the Poor*. London: Routledge.

Human Rights Watch. 2011. ' "You'll Be Fired if You Refuse": Labor Abuses in Zambia's Chinese State-owned Copper Mines'. Human Rights Watch, <http://www.hrw.org/sites/default/files/reports/zambia1111ForWebUpload.pdf> (accessed 18 June 2014).

Humphreys Bebbington, D. 2010. 'The Political Ecology of Natural Gas Extraction in Southern Bolivia'. Doctoral thesis, University of Manchester.

Humphreys Bebbington, D. 2012a. 'Extraction, Inequality and Indigenous Peoples: Insights from Bolivia'. *Environmental Science and Policy*, 33: 438–46.

Humphreys Bebbington, D. 2012b. 'Consultation, Compensation and Conflict: Natural Gas Extraction in Weenhayek Territory, Bolivia'. *Journal of Latin American Geography*, 11(2): 49–72.

Humphreys Bebbington, D., and A. Bebbington. 2010a. 'Extraction, Territory and Inequalities: Gas in the Bolivian Chaco'. *Canadian Journal of Development Studies*, 30(1–2): 259–80.

Humphreys Bebbington, D., and A. Bebbington. 2010b. 'Anatomy of a Regional Conflict: Tarija and Resource Grievances in Morales' Bolivia'. *Latin American Perspectives*, 37(4): 140–60.

Humphreys, M., J. Sachs, and J. Stiglitz (eds). 2007. *Escaping the Resource Curse*. New York, NY: Initiative for Policy Dialogue, Columbia University Press.

Hutchful, E. 1989. 'From "Revolution" to Monetarism: The Economics and Politics of the Adjustment Programme in Ghana'. In *Structural Adjustment in Africa*. Edited by Campbell, B., and J. Loxley, 92–131. London: Macmillan.

Hyden, G. 2008. 'Institutions, Power and Policy Outcomes in Africa'. Power and Politics in Africa Discussion Paper No. 2.

Hyden, G. 2010. 'Political Accountability in Africa: Is the Glass Half-full or Half-empty?' Africa Power and Politics Programme Working Paper No. 6. London: ODI.

ICMM. 2006. *Resource Endowment Initiative—Synthesis of Four Country Case Studies*. London: International Council on Mining and Metals.

IDS. 2010. *An Upside-down View of Governance*. Brighton: Institute of Development Studies.

Ikenberry, J. 2008. 'The Rise of China and the Future of the West'. *Foreign Affairs*, 87(1): 23–37.

International Monetary Fund (IMF). 2011. 'Revenue Mobilisation in Developing Countries'. IMF: Fiscal Affairs Department, 8 March.

Ireland, P. 1994. *The Policy Challenge of Ethnic Diversity: Immigrant Politics in France and Switzerland*. Cambridge, MA: Harvard University Press.

Irish Aid, Advisory Board. 2008. 'Good Governance, Aid Modalities and Poverty Reduction: Linkages to the Millennium Development Goals and Implications for Irish Aid'. Research Project (RP-05-GG).

Jaccoud, L., P. D. E.-M. Hadjab, and J. R. Chaibub. 2009. 'Assistência social e segurança alimentar: Entre novas trajetórias, vehlas agendas e recentes desafíos (1988–2008)'. In *Políticas sociais: Acompanhamento e análise 17*. Edited by diretoría de etudos e políticas sociais, 175–250. SOCIAIS. Brasilia: IPEA.

Jaccoud, L., P. D. E.-M. Hadjab, and J. R. Chaibub. 2010. *The Consolidation of Social Assistance in Brazil and its Challenges, 1988–2008*. Brasilia: International Policy Centre.

Jackson, C. 1999. 'Social Exclusion and Gender: Does One Size Fit All?' *The European Journal of Development Research*, 11(1): 125–46.

Jackson, C., and R. Pearson. 1998. *Feminist Visions of Development: Gender Analysis and Policy*. London: Routledge.

Jackson, K. 2013. 'Diversity and the Distribution of Public Goods in Sub-Saharan Africa'. *Journal of African Economies*, 22(3): 437–62.

Jacoby, U. 2007. 'Getting Together'. *Finance and Development*, 44(2), <http://www.imf.org/external/pubs/ft/fandd/2007/06/jacoby.htm> (accessed 30 December 2007).

James, R., and R. Wrigley. 2007. 'Investigating the Mystery of Capacity Building: Learning from the Praxis Program'. *Praxis Paper 18*. Oxford: INTRAC.

Jayal, N. G. 2001. *Democracy and the State*. New Delhi: Oxford University Press.

Jenkins, R., and A. M. Goetz. 1999. 'Accounts and Accountability: Theoretical Implications of the Right-to-information Movement in India'. *Third World Quarterly*, 20(3): 603–22.

Jenkins, R. 1997. *Rethinking Ethnicity: Arguments and Explorations*. Thousand Oaks, CA: Sage.

Jerzmanowski, M. 2006. 'Empirics of Hills, Plateaus, Mountains and Plains: A Markov-switching Approach to Growth'. *Journal of Development Economics*, 81: 357–85.

John, M. E. 2007. 'Women in Power: Gender, Caste and Politics in Local Governance'. *Economic and Political Weekly*, 42(39): 3986–99.

Johnson, C. 1982. *MITI and the Japanese Miracle*. Stanford, CA: Stanford University Press.

Jones, B., and B. Olken. 2005. 'Do Leaders Matter? National Leadership and Growth since World War II'. *Quarterly Journal of Economics*, August: 835–64.

Jones, B., and B. Olken. 2008. 'The Anatomy of Start-Stop Growth'. *Review of Economics and Statistics*, 90(3): 582–87.

Joshi, A. 2010. 'Do Rights Work? Law, Activism, and the Employment Guarantee Scheme'. *World Development*, 38(4): 620–30.

Joshi, A., and J. Ayee. 2008. 'Associational Taxation: A Pathway into the Informal Sector?' In *Taxation and State-building in Developing Countries: Capacity and Consent*. Edited by Bräutigam, D., O.-H. Fjeldstad, and M. Moore, 183–213. Cambridge: Cambridge University Press.

Joshi, A., and P. P. Houtzager. 2012. 'Widgets or Watchdogs?' *Public Management Review*, 14(2): 145–62.

Joshi, A., and M. Moore. 2004. 'Institutionalised Co-production: Unorthodox Public Service Delivery in Challenging Environments'. *Journal of Development Studies*, 40(4): 31–49.

Junbo, J. 2011. 'The Myth of the "China Model" in Africa'. *Asia Times*, <http://atimes.com/atimes/China/MI14Ad01.html> (accessed 18 June 2014).

Kabeer, N. 1994. *Reversed Realities: Gender Hierarchies in Development Thought*. London and New York, NY: Verso.

Kabeer, N. 2000. 'Social Exclusion, Poverty and Discrimination: Towards an Analytical Framework'. *IDS Bulletin*, 31(4): 83–97.

Kaldor, N. 1963. 'Will Underdeveloped Countries Learn to Tax?' *Foreign Affairs*, 41(January): 410–19.

Kalk, A., F. A. Paul, and E. Grabosch. 2010. '"Paying for Performance" in Rwanda: Does It Pay Off?' *Tropical Medicine and International Health*, 15(2): 182–90.

Kalyvas, S. N. 2006. *The Logic of Violence in Civil War*. New York, NY: Cambridge University Press.

Kalyvitis, S., and I. Vlachiki. 2010. 'Democratic Aid and the Democratization of Recipients'. *Contemporary Economic Policy*, 28(2): 188–218.

Kaminski, J., and R. Serra. 2011. 'Endogenous Economic Reforms and Local Realities: Cotton Policy-making in Burkina Faso'. APPP Working Paper 17. London: ODI.

Kanbur, R. 2001. 'Economic Policy, Distribution and Poverty: The Nature of Disagreements'. *World Development*, 29(6): 1083–94.

Kanbur, R. 2000. 'Aid, Conditionality and Debt in Africa'. In *Foreign Aid and Development: Lessons Learnt and Direction for the Future*. Edited by Tarp, F., 409–22. Abingdon, UK and New York, NY: Routledge.

Kanyongolo, F. E. 2006. *Malawi: Justice Sector and the Rule of Law*. South Africa: Open Society Initiative.

Kaplinsky, R. 2008. 'What Does the Rise of China Do for Industrialisation in Africa'. *Review of African Political Economy*, 115: 7–22.

Kaplinsky, R., and M. Farooki. 2011. *How China Disrupted Global Commodities: The Reshaping of the World's Resource Sector*. Routledge Studies in Global Competition. London: Routledge.

Kaplinsky, R., and D. Messner. 2008. 'Introduction: The Impact of Asian Drivers on the Developing World'. *World Development*, 36(2): 197–209.

Kaplinsky, R., and M. Morris. 2009. 'The Asian Drivers and SSA: Is There a Future for Export-Oriented African Industrialisation?' *The World Economy*, 32(11): 1638–55.

Kar, S., L. Pritchett, S. Raihan, and K. Sen. 2013a. 'Looking for a Break: Identifying Transitions in Growth Regimes'. *Journal of Macroeconomics*, 38(Part B): 151–66.

Kar, S., L. Pritchett, S. Raihan, and K. Sen. 2013b. 'The Dynamics of Economic Growth: A Visual Handbook of Growth Rates, Regimes, Transitions and Volatility'. The University of Manchester, Manchester: Effective States and Inclusive Development (ESID).

Kardam, N. 1997. 'Making Development Organizations Accountable: The Organizational, Political and Cognitive Context'. In *Getting Institutions Right for Women in Development*. Edited by Goetz, A. M. London and New York, NY: Zed Books.

Karl, T. L. 1997. *The Paradox of Plenty: Oil Booms and Petro-States*. Berkeley and Los Angeles, CA: University of California Press.

Karl, T. L. 2007. 'Ensuring Fairness: The Case for a Transparent Fiscal Contract'. In *Escaping the Resource Curse*. Edited by Humphreys, M., J. Sachs, and J. Stiglitz. 256–85. New York, NY: Initiative for Policy Dialogue, Columbia University Press.

Kashi, E., and M. Watts. 2008. *The Curse of the Black Gold: 50 Years of Oil in the Niger Delta*. Brooklyn, NY: powerHouse Books.

Kastoryano, R. 2002. *Negotiating Identities: States and Immigrants in France and Germany*. Princeton, NJ: Princeton University Press.

Kaup, B. Z. 2010. 'A Neoliberal Nationalization: The Constraints on Natural Gas-Led Development in Bolivia.' *Latin American Perspectives*, 37(3): 123–38.

Kawamara-Mishambi, S., and I. Ovonji-Odida. 2003. 'The "Lost Clause": The Campaign to Advance Women's Property Rights in the Uganda 1998 Land Act'. In *No Short Cuts to Power: African Women in Politics and Policy Making*. Edited by Goetz, A. M. and S. Hassim. London: Zed Books.

Keck, M. E., and K. A. Sikkink. 1998. *Activists beyond Borders: Advocacy Networks in International Politics*. Ithaca, NY: Cornell University Press.

Keefer, P. 2007. 'Seeing and Believing: Political Obstacles to Better Service Delivery'. In *The Politics of Service Delivery in Democracies: Better Access for the Poor*. Edited by

Devarajan, S., and I. Widlund, 42–55. Southern Africa Regional Poverty Network, Stockholm: Swedish Ministry for Foreign Affairs.

Keefer, P., and S. Khemani. 2003a. *The Political Economy of Public Expenditures*. Washington, DC: World Bank.

Keefer, P., and S. Khemani. 2003b. *Democracy, Public Expenditures and the Poor, Development Research Group*. Washington, DC: World Bank.

Kelsall, T. 2011a. 'Development Patrimonialism? Rethinking Business and Politics in Africa'. Africa Power and Politics Programme Policy Brief No. 2. London: ODI.

Kelsall, T. 2011b. 'Rethinking the Relationship between Neo-patrimonialism and Economic Development in Africa.' *IDS Bulletin*, 42(2): 76–87.

Kelsall, T. 2013. *Business, Politics and the State in Africa*. London: Zed Books.

Kelsall, T., D. Booth, D. Cammack, and F. Golooba-Mutebi. 2010. 'Developmental Patrimonialism? Questioning the Orthodoxy on Political Governance and Economic Progress in Africa'. Africa Power and Politics Programme Working Paper No. 9. London: ODI.

Kemp, A., N. Madlala, A. Moodley, and E. Salo. 1995. 'The Dawn of a New Day: South African Feminisms'. In *The Challenges of Local Feminisms: Women's Movement in Global Perspective*. Edited by Basu, A., 131–62. Boulder, CO: Westview Press.

Kennedy, D. 2002. 'The Critique of Rights in Critical Legal Studies'. In *Left Legalism/Left Critique*. Edited by Brown, W. and J. E. Halley. Durham, NC: Duke University Press.

Kertzer, D. 1988. *Ritual, Politics, and Power*. New Haven, CT: Yale University Press.

Khan, M. 2006. 'Governance and Development'. Workshop on 'Governance and Development' organized by the World Bank and DFID, 11–12 November, Dhaka, Bangladesh, <http://eprints.soas.ac.uk/9957/> (accessed 4 June 2014).

Khan, M. 2010. 'Political Settlements and the Governance of Growth-enhancing Institutions'. London: School of Oriental and African Studies (SOAS). [Mimeo.]

Khemani, S. 2010. 'Political Capture of Decentralization: Vote-Buying through Grants-financed Local Jurisdictions'. Policy Research Working Paper 5350. Washington, DC: World Bank.

Khwaja, A. I. 2009. 'Can Good Projects Succeed in Bad Communities?' *Journal of Public Economics*, 93(7): 899–916.

Killick, T. 1997. 'Principals, Agents and the Failings of Conditionality'. *Journal of International Development*, 9(4): 483–95.

Killick, T. 1999. 'Making Adjustment Work for the Poor'. ODI Poverty Briefing 5. London: Overseas Development Institute, <www.odi.org.uk/publications/briefing/pov5.html> (accessed 25 February 2006).

Killick, T., and M. Foster. 2011. 'The Macroeconomics of Doubling Aid to Africa and the Centrality of the Supply Side'. *Development Policy Review*, 29(S1): S85–S108.

King, D., and R. C. Lieberman. 2009. 'Ironies of State-building: A Comparative Perspective on the American State'. *World Politics*, 61(3): 547–88.

King, K. 2010. '"New Actors: Old Paradigms?" In 'A Brave New World of "Emerging", "Non-DAC" Donors and their Differences from Traditional Donors'. Edited by King, K. *NORRAG News* 44, September.

Kirsch, S. 2012. 'Afterward: Mining Conflict in Bolivia, Ecuador and Peru'. In *Social Conflict, Economic Development and Extractive Industry: Evidence from South America*. Edited by Bebbington, A., 203–15. London. Routledge.

Kiser, E., and A. Sacks. 2011. 'African Patrimonialism in Historical Perspective'. *The ANNALS of the American Academy of Political and Social Science*, 636(1): 129–49.

Kitschelt, H. P. 1986. 'Political Opportunity Structures and Political Protest: Anti-Nuclear Movements in Four Democracies'. *British Journal of Political Science*, 16(1): 57–85.

Kitschelt, H. P. 1988. 'Left-libertarian Parties: Explaining Innovation in Competitive Party Systems'. *World Politics*, 40(2): 194–234.

Kjær, A. M., and O. Therkildsen. 2013. 'Elections and Landmark Policies in Tanzania and Uganda'. *Democratization*, 20(4): 592–614.

Knack, S. F., H. Rogers, and N. Eubank. 2010. 'Aid Quality and Donor Rankings'. Policy Research Working Paper 5290. Washington, DC: World Bank.

Knack, S., and P. Keefer. 2003. 'Institutions and Economic Performance: Cross-country Tests Using Alternative Institutional Measures'. In *Democracy, Governance, and Growth*. Edited by Knack, S., 56–77. College Park, MD: Center on Institutional Reform and the Informal Sector (IRIS).

Knight, M., N. Loayza, and D. Villanueva (1996) 'The Peace Dividend: Military Spending Cuts and Economic Growth'. *IMF Staff Papers*, 43: 1–37.

Kohli, A. 1989. *The State and Poverty in India*. Cambridge: Cambridge University Press.

Kohli, A. 2004. *State-Directed Development: Political Power and Industrialization in the Global Periphery*. Cambridge: Cambridge University Press.

Kornegay, F. A., and C. Landsberg. 2009. 'Engaging Emerging Powers: Africa's Search for a Common Position'. *Politikon*, 36(1): 171–91.

Kosack, S. 2003. 'Effective Aid: How Democracy Allows Development Aid to Improve the Quality of Life'. *World Development*, 31(1): 1–22.

Kosack, S. 2009. 'Realizing Education for All: Defining and Using the Political Will to Invest in Primary Education'. *Comparative Education*, 45(4): 495–523.

Kosack, S. 2012. *The Education of Nations: How the Political Organization of the Poor, not Democracy, Led Governments to Invest in Mass Education*. Oxford: Oxford University Press.

Kragelund, P. 2008. 'The Return of Non-DAC Donors to Africa: New Prospects for African Development?' *Development Policy Review*, 26(5): 555–84.

Krishna, A. 2006. 'Poverty and Democratic Participation Reconsidered: Evidence from the Local Level in India'. *Comparative Politics*, 38: 439–58.

Krishna, A. 2009. 'Why Don't "the Poor" Make Common Cause? The Importance of Subgroups'. *Journal of Development Studies*, 45(6): 947–66.

Krueger, A. 1979. 'The Political Economy of the Rent-seeking Society'. *American Economic Review*, 64(3): 291–303.

Kühl, S. 2009. 'Capacity Development as the Model of Development Aid Organizations'. *Development and Change*, 40(3): 551–77.

Kuhonta, E. 2011. *The Institutional Imperative: the Politics of Equitable Development in Southeast Asia*. Stanford, CA: Stanford University Press.

Kumar, R. 1995. *From Chipko to Sati: Contemporary Indian Feminist Movement: The Challenges of Local Feminisms: Women's Movement in Global Perspective*. Boulder, CO: Westview Press.

Kurlantzick, J. 2007. *Charm Offensive: How China's Soft Power Is Transforming the World*. New Haven, CT: Yale University Press.

Kurtz, M. J., and S. M. Brooks. 2008. 'Embedding Neoliberal Reform in Latin America.' *World Politics*, 60(2): 231–80.

La Porta, R., F. Lopez-de-Silanes, A. Shleifer, and R. Vishny. 1999. 'The Quality of Government'. *Journal of Law, Economics, and Organization*, 15(1): 222–9.

Lachmann, R. 2002. *Capitalists in Spite of Themselves: Elite Conflict and Economic Transitions in Early Modern Europe*. New York, NY: Oxford University Press.

Laitin, D., and D. Posner. 2001. 'The Implications of Constructivism for Constructing Ethnic Fractionalization Indices'. *APSA-CP: Newsletter of the Organized Section in Comparative Politics of the American Political Science Association*, 12(1): 13–17.

Lal, D. 1983. *The Poverty of 'Development Economics'*. Hobart Paperback 16. London: Institute of Economic Affairs.

Lamas, M., A. Martinez, M. L. Tarres, and E. Tunon. 1995. 'Building Bridges: The Growth of Popular Feminisms in Mexico'. In *The Challenges of Local Feminisms: Women's Movement in Global Perspective*. Edited by Basu, A., 324–47. Boulder, CO: Westview Press.

Lancaster, C. 2007. 'The Chinese Aid System'. Centre for Global Development, <http://www.cgdev.org/content/publications/detail/13953/> (accessed 26 December 2007).

Lancaster, C. 2007. *Foreign Aid: Diplomacy, Development, Domestic Politics*. Chicago, IL: University of Chicago Press.

Land, T., V. Hauck, and H. Baser. 2009. 'Capacity Change and Performance: Capacity Development: Between Planned Interventions and Emergent Processes'. Policy Management Brief No. 22. Maastricht: European Centre for Development Policy Management.

Lange, M., and D. Rueschemeyer (eds.). 2005. *States and Development: Historical Antecedents of Stagnation and Advance*. New York, NY: Palgrave Macmillan.

Lange, M., J. Mahoney, and M. vom Hau. 2006. 'Colonialism and Development: A Comparative Analysis of Spanish and British Colonies'. *American Journal of Sociology*, 111: 1412–62.

Lange, M. 2009. *Lineages of Despotism and Development: British Colonialism and State Power*. Chicago, IL: University of Chicago Press.

Lange, M. 2012. *Educations in Ethnic Violence: Identity, Educational Bubbles, and Resource Mobilization*. Cambridge: Cambridge University Press.

Langer, A. 2009. 'Living with Diversity: The Peaceful Management of Horizontal Inequalities in Ghana'. *Journal of International Development*, 21(4): 534–46.

Langton, M. 2012. 'The Quiet Revolution: Indigenous Peoples and the Resources Boom'. 2012 Boyer Lectures, Australian Broadcasting Company, <http://www.abc.net.au/radionational/programs/boyerlectures> (accessed 4 June 2014).

Large, D. 2008. 'China and the Contradictions of "Non-interference" in Sudan'. *Review of African Political Economy*, 115: 93–106.

Large, D. 2009. 'China's Sudan Engagement: Changing Northern and Southern Political Trajectories in Peace and War'. *The China Quarterly*, 199: 610–26.

Lashari, A., and R. Sharpe. 2011. 'IMF Policy, But Not Practice? Regressive Tax in Pakistan'. Action Aid briefing, <http://www.brettonwoodsproject.org/2011/06/art-568578/> (accessed 18 June 2014).

Le Billon, P. 2001. 'The Political Ecology of War: Natural Resources and Armed Conflicts'. *Political Geography*, 20(5): 561–84.

Lederman, D., and W. F. Mahoney (eds.). 2007. *Natural Resources: Neither Curse nor Destiny*. Washington, DC and Palo Alto, CA: World Bank and Stanford University Press.

Lee, C. 2009. 'Raw Encounters: Chinese Managers, African Workers and the Politics of Casualization in Africa's Chinese Enclaves'. *The China Quarterly*, 199: 647–66.

Leftwich, A. 1994. 'Governance, the State and the Politics of Development'. *Development and Change*, 25: 363–86.

Leftwich, A. 1995. 'Bringing Politics Back In: Towards a Model of the Developmental State'. *Journal of Development Studies*, 31: 400–27.

Leftwich, A. 2004. *What Is Politics? The Activity and its Study*. Cambridge: Polity Press.

Leftwich, A. 2005. 'Politics in Command: Development Studies and the Rediscovery of Social Science'. *New Political Economy*, 10: 573–607.

Leftwich, A. 2007. 'From Drivers of Change to the Politics of Development: Refining the Analytical Framework to Understand the Politics of the Places Where We Work'. Part 3: Final Report and Notes of Guidance for DFID Offices, <http://www.gsdrc.org/docs/open/doc104.pdf> (accessed 18 June 2014).

Leftwich, A. 2008. *Developmental States, Effective States and Poverty Reduction: The Primacy of Politics*. New York, NY: UNRISD Project on Poverty Reduction and Policy Regimes.

Leftwich, A. 2010. 'Beyond Institutions: Rethinking the Role of Leader, Elites and Coalitions in the Institutional Formation of Developmental States and Strategies'. *Forum for Development Studies*, 37(1): 93–111.

Leftwich, A., and K. Sen. 2010. *Beyond Institutions: Institutions and Organizations in the Politics of Economics and Growth and Poverty Reduction—a Thematic Synthesis of Research Evidence*. Manchester: Improving Institutions for Pro-Poor Growth.

Leftwich, A., and C. Wheeler. 2011. 'Politics, Leadership and Coalitions in Development: Findings, Insights and Guidance from the DLP's First Research and Policy Workshop'. Frankfurt 10–11 March 2011, Developmental Leadership Programme.

Lehmann, A. D. 1978. 'The Death of Land Reform: A Polemic'. *World Development*, 6(3): 339–45.

Leibbrandt, M., I. Woolard, A. Finn, and J. Argent. 2010. *Trends in South African Income Distribution and Poverty since the Fall of Apartheid*. Paris: OECD.

Leibbrandt, M., L. Poswell, P. Naidoo, and M. Welch. 2006. 'Measuring Recent Changes in South Africa Inequality and Poverty Using 1996 and 2001 Census Data'. In *Poverty and Policy in Post-Apartheid South Africa*. Edited by Bhorat, H., and R. Kanbur, 95–142. Cape Town: HSRC.

Lele, J., and F. Quadir. 2004. 'Introduction: Democracy and Development in Asia in the 21st Century: In Search of Popular Democratic Alternatives'. In *Democracy and Civil Society in Asia: Democratic Transitions and Social Movements in Asia*, ii. Edited by Lele, J., T. M. Shaw, and F. Quadir, 1–31. New York, NY: Palgrave Macmillan.

Lenton, P., and P. Mosley. 2011. 'Incentivised Trust'. *Journal of Economic Psychology*, 32(5): 890–7.

Leonard, D. 2008. 'Where are "Pockets" of Effective Agencies Likely in Weak Governance States and Why? A Propositional Inventory', IDS Working Paper 306, Brighton: IDS.

Levi, M., and Epperly, B. 2010. 'Principled Principals in the Founding Moments of Rule-of-law'. In *Global Perspectives on the Rule of Law*. Edited by Heckman, J. J., R. L. Nelson, and L. Cabatingan. London: Routledge.

Levi, M. 1988. *Of Rule and Revenue*. Berkeley, CA: University of California Press.

Levitsky, S. 2003. *Transforming Labor-Based Parties in Latin America: Argentine Peronism in Comparative Perspective*. New York, NY: Cambridge University Press.

Levkowitz, L., M. M. Ross, and J. R. Warner. 2009. 'The 88 Queensway Group: A Case Study in Chinese Investors Operations in Angola and beyond Washington'. US–China Economic and Security Review Commission, <http://china.usc.edu/App_Images/The_88_Queensway_Group.pdf> (accessed 18 June 2014).

Levy, B. 2012. 'Working with the Grain: Integrating Governance and Growth in Development Strategies'. Draft manuscript.

Lewis, D., and D. Mosse (eds.). 2006. *Development Brokers and Translators: The Ethnography of Aid and Agencies*. Bloomfield, CT: Kumarian.

Lewis, W. A. 1953. *Report on the Industrialisation of the Gold Coast*. Accra: Government Printer.

Li, F. 2009. 'Documenting Accountability: Environmental Impact Assessment in a Peruvian Mining Project'. *PoLAR* 32(2): 218–36.

Li, T. 2007. *The Will to Improve: Governmentality, Development, and the Practice of Politics*. Durham, NC: Duke University Press.

Lieberman, E. 2002. 'Taxation Data as Indicators of State-society Relations: Possibilities and Pitfalls in Cross-national Research'. *Studies in Comparative International Development*, 36(4): 89–115.

Lieberman, E. 2003. *Race and Regionalism in the Politics of Taxation in Brazil and South Africa*. New York, NY: Cambridge University Press.

Lieberman, E. S., and G. H. McClendon. 2013. 'The Ethnicity–Policy Preference Link in Sub-Saharan Africa'. *Comparative Political Studies*, 46(5): 574–602.

Lieberman, E., and P. Singh. 2012. 'Conceptualizing and Measuring Ethnic Politics: An Institutional Complement to Demographic, Behavioral, and Cognitive Approaches'. *Studies in Comparative International Development (SCID)*, 47(3): 255–86.

Lieberman, M. 1993. *Public Education: An Autopsy*. Cambridge, MA: Harvard University Press.

Lin, J. Y. and C. Monga. 2010. 'Growth Identification and Facilitation: The Role of the State in the Dynamics of Structural Change'. World Bank Policy Working Paper No. 5313. Washington, DC: World Bank.

Lindemann, S. 2008. 'Do Inclusive Elite Bargains Matter? A Research Framework for Understanding the Causes of Civil War in Sub-Saharan Africa'. Crisis States Research Centre Discussion Paper 15. London: LSE and SOAS.

Lindemann, S. 2011. 'Just Another Change of Guard? Broad-based Politics and Civil War in Museveni's Uganda'. *African Affairs*, 110(440): 387–416.

Lindert, K., A. Linder, J. Hobbs, and B. De La Brière. 2007. *The Nuts and Bolts of Brazil's Bolsa Família Program: Implementing Conditional Cash Transfers in a Decentralized Context*. Washington, DC: World Bank.

Lindert, P. H. 2004. *Growing Public: Social Spending and Economic Growth since the Eighteenth Century*. Cambridge: Cambridge University Press.

Lipton, M. 1977. *Why Poor People Stay Poor: A Study of Urban Bias in World Development*. London: Maurice Temple Smith.

Lister, R. 2008. 'Recognition and Voice: The Challenge for Social Justice'. In *Social Justice and Public Policy: Seeking Fairness in Diverse Societies*. Edited by Craig, D., T. Burchardt, and D. Gordon, 105–22. Bristol: Policy Press.

Little, A. 2010. 'Access to Basic Education in Ghana: Politics, Policies and Progress'. Research Monograph No. 42. Consortium for Research on Educational Access, Transitions and Equity (CREATE), London: Institute of Education, University of London.

Little, I., T. Scitovsky, and M. Scott. 1975. *Industry and Trade in Some Developing Countries*. London: Heinemann.

López-Alves, F. 2000. *State Formation and Democracy in Latin America, 1810–1900*. Durham, NC: Duke University Press.

López-Calva, L. F. and N. Lustig (eds.). 2010. *Declining Inequality in Latin America: A Decade of Progress?* Washington, DC: Brookings Institution and UNDP.

Loveman, M. 2005. 'The Modern State and the Primitive Accumulation of Symbolic Power'. *American Journal of Sociology*, 110: 1651–83.

Lund, F. 2008. *Changing Social Policy. The Child Support Grant in South Africa*. Cape Town: HSRC Press.

Lungu, J. 2009. 'The Politics of Reforming Zambia's Mining Tax Regime'. Johannesburg: Southern Africa Resource Watch, <http://www.sarwatch.org> (accessed 4 June 2014).

Luttmer, E. F. 2001. 'Group Loyalty and the Taste for Redistribution'. *Journal of Political Economy*, 109(3): 500–28.

Macauslan, I. 2008. *India's National Rural Employment Guarantee Act: A Case Study for How Change Happens*. Oxford: OXFAM.

MacLean, L. 2010. *Informal Institutions and Citizenship in Rural Africa: Risk and Reciprocity in Ghana and Côte d'Ivoire*. New York, NY: Cambridge University Press.

Maconachie, R., and G. Hilson. 2011. 'Artisanal Gold Mining: A New Frontier in Post-Conflict Sierra Leone?' *Journal of Development Studies*, 47(4): 595–616.

MacPherson, E. 2008. 'Invisible Agents: Women in Service Delivery Reform'. *IDS Bulletin*, 38(6): 38–46.

Madrid, R. L. 2012. *The Rise of Ethnic Politics in Latin America*. New York, NY: Cambridge University Press.

Mahdi, S. 2010. 'The Impact of Regulatory and Institutional Arrangements on Agricultural Markets and Poverty: A Case Study of Tanzania's Coffee Market'. In *IPPG Discussion Paper, No. 40*. Manchester: Improving Institutions for Pro-Poor Growth.

Mahmoud, Y. 2010. 'Chinese Foreign Aid: The Tale of a Silent Enterprise'. In *Challenging the Aid Paradigm: Western Currents and Asian Alternatives*. Edited by Sorensen, J., 186–213. London: Palgrave.

Mahmud, W., S. Ahmed, and S. Mahajan. 2008. 'Economic Reforms, Growth, and Governance: The Political Economy Aspects of Bangladesh's Development Surprise'. Working Paper No. 22. London: Commission on Growth and Development.

Mahoney, J. 2000. 'Path Dependence in Historical Sociology'. *Theory and Society*, 29(4): 507–48.

Mahoney, J., and K. Thelen. 2011. 'A Theory of Gradual Institutional Change'. In *Explaining Institutional Change: Ambiguity, Agency, and Power*. Edited by Mahoney, J., and K. Thelen, 1–37. Cambridge: Cambridge University Press.

Mahoney, J., and K. Thelen (eds.). 2010. *Explaining Institutional Change: Ambiguity, Agency, and Power*. New York, NY: Cambridge University Press.

Mahoney, J. 2010. *Colonialism and Postcolonial Development: Spanish America in Comparative Perspective*. Cambridge: Cambridge University Press.

Maiti, D. 2009. 'Institutions, Networks and Industrialisation: Field Level Evidence of Fragmentation and Flexibility from India'. In *IPPG Discussion Paper, No. 26*. Manchester: Improving Institutions for Pro-Poor Growth.

Mani, A., and S. Mukand. 2007. 'Democracy, Visibility and Public Goods Provision, *Journal of Development Economics*, 83 (2): 506–29.

Mann, M. 1984. 'The Autonomous Power of the State: Its Origins, Mechanisms and Results'. *Archives Européennes de Sociologie*, 25: 185–213.

Mann, M. 1986. *The Sources of Social Power, I: A History of Power in Agrarian Societies*. Cambridge: Cambridge University Press.

Mann, M. 1993. *The Sources of Social Power, II: The Rise of Classes and Nation States 1760–1914*. Cambridge: Cambridge University Press.

Manning, R. 2006. 'Will "Emerging Donors" Change the Face of International Cooperation?' *Development Policy Review*, 24(4): 371–85.

Manor, J. 2005. 'Introduction.' *IDS Bulletin*, 36(3): 1–7.

Mansbridge, J. 1999. 'Should Women Represent Women and Blacks Represent Blacks? A Contingent "Yes"'. *The Journal of Politics*, 61(3): 628–57.

Mansuri, G., and V. Rao. 2004. 'Community-based (and Driven) Development: A Critical Review'. Policy Research Working Paper Series 3209. Washington, DC: World Bank.

Maravall, J. M., and A. Przeworski. 2003. 'Introduction'. In *Democracy and the Rule of Law*. Edited by Maravall, J. M. and A. Przeworski, 1–17. Cambridge: Cambridge University Press.

Marks, S. 2006. 'China in Africa: The New Imperialism?' *Pambazuka News.* <http://www.pambazuka.org/en/category/features/32432> (accessed 10 November 2007).

Marx, A. 1998. *Making Race and Nation: A Comparison of South Africa, the United States, and Brazil.* Cambridge: Cambridge University Press.

Masaki, K. 2010. 'Rectifying the Anti-politics of Citizen Participation: Insights from the Internal Politics of a Subaltern Community in Nepal'. *Journal of Development Studies*, 46(7): 1196–215.

Matisonn, H., and J. Seekings. 2003. 'The Politics of a Basic-income Grant in South Africa, 1996–2002'. In *A Basic Income Grant for South Africa*. Edited by Standing, G., and M. Samson, 56–76. Cape Town: University of Cape Town.

Mazzuca, S. 2010. 'Access to Power versus Exercise of Power: Reconceptualizing the Quality of Democracy in Latin America'. *Studies in Comparative International Development*, 45: 334–57.

Mbatha, L. 2003. 'Democratizing Local Government: Problems and Opportunities in the Advancement of Gender Equality in South Africa'. In *No Short Cuts to Power: African Women in Politics and Policy Making*. Edited by Goetz A. M., and S. Hassim. London: Zed Books.

McAdam, D., J. D. McCarthy, and M. N. Zald (eds.). 2001.*Comparative Perspectives on Social Movements*. Cambridge: Cambridge University Press.

McAdam, D., S. G. Tarrow, and C. Tilly. 2001. *Dynamics of Contention*. New York, NY: Cambridge University Press.

McCarthy, J. D., and M. N. Zald. 1977. 'Resource Mobilisation and Social Movements: A Partial Theory'. *American Journal of Sociology*, 82(6): 112–24.

McCaskie, T. 2008. 'The United States, Ghana and Oil: Global and Local Perspectives'. *African Affairs*, 107(428): 313–32.

McDonald, O., and K. Jumu. 2008. 'Can Tax Challenge Bad Governance?' Christian Aid Occasional Paper No. 1, <http://www.christianaid.org.uk/images/OPS_one.pdf> (accessed 18 June 2014).

McGillivray, M., S. Feeny, N. Hermes, and R. Lensink. 2006. 'Controversies over the Impact of Development Aid: It Works, It Doesn't; It Can, but That Depends . . . ' *Journal of International Development*, 18: 1031–50.

Mcloughlin, C. 2011. 'Factors Affecting State–NGO Relations in Service Provision: Key Themes from the Literature'. *Public Administration and Development*, 31(4): 240–51.

Mcloughlin, C., with R. Batley 2012. 'The Effects of Sector Characteristics on Accountability Relationships in Service Delivery'. Working Paper 350. London: ODI.

McSweeney, C., and M. Remy. 2008. 'Building Roads to Democracy? The Contribution of the Peru Rural Roads Program to Participation and Civic Engagement in Rural Peru', *Social Development Notes, Participation and Civic Engagement*, No. 111. Washington, DC: World Bank

Meagher, K. 2010. *Identity Economics: Social Networks and the Informal Economy in Nigeria*. Rochester, NY: Boydell and Brewer.

Meessen, B., L. Musango, J.-P. Kashala, and J. Lemlin. 2006. 'Reviewing Institutions of Rural Health Centres: The Performance Initiative in Butare, Rwanda'. *Tropical Medicine and International Health*, 11(8): 1303–17.

Meltzer, A. M., and R. F. Scott. 1981. 'A Rational Theory of the Size of Government'. *Journal of Political Economy*, 89: 914–27.

Menon, N. 2000. 'Elusive Women: Feminisms and Women's Reservation Bill'. *Economic and Political Weekly*, 35: 43–4.

Merry, S. E. 1988. 'Legal Pluralism'. *Law and Society Review*, 22(5): 869–96.

Mesquita, A. C. S., L. Jaccoud, and M. P. G. Dos Santos. 2010. *Garantia de Renda na Política Social Brasileira: Entre a Proteçao aos Riscos Sociais e o Alivio à Pobreza*. Brasilia: IPEA.

Meyer, J. W., J. Boli, G. M. Thomas, and F. O. Ramirez. 1997. 'World Society and the Nation-State'. *American Journal of Sociology*, 103(1): 144–81.

Migdal, J. 2001. *State in Society: Studying How States and Societies Transform and Constitute One Another*. Cambridge: Cambridge University Press.

Migdal, J. S. 1988. *Strong Societies and Weak States: State-Society Relations and State Capabilities in the Third World*. Princeton, NJ: Princeton University Press.

Miguel, E., and M. K. Gugerty. 2005. 'Ethnic Diversity, Social Sanctions, and Public Goods in Kenya'. *Journal of Public Economics*, 89(11–12): 2325–68.

Ministry of Commerce (MOFCOM) PRC. 2008. Trade Statistics. <http://english.mof com.gov.cn/statistic/statistic.html> (accessed 17 July 2009).

Ministry of Foreign Affairs of the PRC. 2006. 'China's African Policy'. <http://www.fmprc.gov.cn/eng/zxxx/t230615.htm> (accessed 09 December 2009).

Minoiu, C., and S. Reddy. 2010. 'Development Aid and Economic Growth: A Positive Long-run Relation'. *Quarterly Journal of Economics and Finance*, 50(2): 27–39.

Mitchell, T. 2012. *Carbon Democracy: Political Power in the Age of Oil*. London: Verso.

Mitlin, D. 2008. 'With and Beyond the State: Co-Production as a Route to Political Influence, Power and Transformation for Grassroots Organizations'. *Environment and Urbanization*, 20: 339–60.

Mittelman, J. H. 2006. 'Globalization and Development: Learning from Debates in China'. *Globalizations*, 3(3): 277–91.

Mohan, G., and M. Tan-Mullins. 2009. 'Chinese Migrants in Africa as New Agents of Development? An Analytical Framework'. *European Journal of Development Research*, 21: 588–605.

Mohanty, R. 2007. 'Gendered Subjects, the State and Participatory Spaces: The Politics of Domesticating Participation in Rural India'. In *Spaces for Change? The Politics of Citizen's Participation in New Democratic Spaces*. Edited by Cornwall, A., and V. Coleho. London: Zed Books.

Molenaers, N., L. Cepinskas, and B. Jacobs. 2010. 'Budget Support and Policy/ Political Dialogue: Donor Practices in Handling (Political) Crises'. IOB, University of Antwerp, Discussion Paper 2010.06.

Molyneux, M. 1985. 'Mobilisation without Emancipation? Women's Interests, State and Revolution in Nicaragua.' *Critical Social Policy*, 4(10): 59–71.

Molyneux, M. 2001.*Women's Movement in International Perspective: Latin America and Beyond*. London: Palgrave.

Molyneux, M., and S. Razavi. 2005. 'Beijing Plus Ten: An Ambivalent Record on Gender Justice'. *Development and Change*, 36(6): 983–1010.

Montinola, G. R. 2010. 'When Does Aid Conditionality Work?' *Studies in Comparative International Development*, 45: 358–82.

Mookherjee, D. 2004. *The Crisis in Government Accountability*. New Delhi: Oxford University Press.

Moore, J., and T. Velásquez. 2012. 'Sovereignty Negotiated: Anti-mining Movements, the State and Multinational Mining Companies under "Correa's Twenty-First Century Socialism"'. In *Social Conflict, Economic Development and Extractive Industry: Evidence from South America*. Edited by Bebbington, A., 114–35. London: Routledge.

Moore, M. 1985. 'Economic Growth and Rise of Civil Society: Agriculture in Taiwan and South Korea'. In *Developmental States in East Asia: Report to the Gatsby Charitable Foundation*. Edited by White, G. and R. Wade. Brighton: IDS.

Moore, M. 1999. 'Death without Taxes: Democracy, State Capacity, and Aid Dependency in the Fourth World'. In *Towards a Democratic Developmental State*. Edited by White, G., and M. Robinson. Oxford: Oxford University Press.

Moore M. 2007. 'How Does Taxation Affect the Quality of Governance?' Working Paper 280. Brighton: IDS.

Moore, M., and J. Putzel. 2001. 'Thinking Strategically about Politics and Poverty'. IDS Working Paper 2001. Brighton: Institute of Development Studies (IDS).

Morgan, L. 2010. *Signed, Sealed, Delivered? Evidence from Rwanda on the Impact of Results-based Financing for Health*. Washington, DC: World Bank.

Morris, M., V. A. Kelly, R. Kopicki, and D. Byerlee. 2007. *Fertiliser Use in African Agriculture*. Washington, DC: World Bank.

Morss, E. R. 1984. 'Institutional Destruction Resulting from Donor and Project Proliferation in Sub-Saharan African Countries'. *World Development*, 12(4): 465–70.

Mosley, P. 2001. 'Microfinance and Poverty in Bolivia'. *Journal of Development Studies*, 37(4): 101–32.

Mosley, P. 2011. 'Fiscal Composition and Aid-effectiveness: A Political-economy Model'. Unpublished paper. Helsinki: WIDER.

Mosley, P. 2012. *The Politics of Poverty Reduction*. Oxford: Oxford University Press.

Mosley, P. 2013. 'Two Africas? Why Africa's "Growth Miracle" Is Barely Reducing Poverty'. Brooks World Poverty Institute Working Paper 191. Manchester: BWPI.

Mosley, P., and B. Chiripanhura. 2009. 'Liberalisation and Poverty in Africa since 2009: Why Is the Operation of the "Invisible Hand" Uneven?' *Journal of International Development*, 21(6): 749–56.

Mosley, P., J. Hudson, and A. Verschoor. 2004. 'Aid, Poverty Reduction and the "New" Conditionality'. *Economic Journal*, 114(496): 217–44.

Mosley, P., and A. Suleiman. 2007. 'Aid, Agriculture and Poverty in Developing Countries'. *Review of Development Economics*, 11(1): 139–58.

Moss, T., G. Pettersson, and N. van de Walle. 2006. 'An Aid–Institutions Paradox? A Review Essay on Aid Dependency and State-building in Sub-Saharan Africa'. Working Paper No. 74. Washington, DC: Center for Global Development.

Mosse, D. 2010. 'A Relational Approach to Durable Poverty, Inequality and Power'. *Journal of Development Studies*, 46(7): 1156–78.

Mosse, D., and D. Lewis. 2006. 'Theoretical Approaches to Brokerage and Translation in Development'. In *Development Brokers and Translators: The Ethnography of Aid and Agencies*. Edited by Lewis, D., and D. Mosse, 1–26. Bloomfield, CT: Kumarian.

Moyo, D. 2009. *Dead Aid: Why Aid Is not Working and How There Is Another Way for Africa*. London: Penguin.

Mridha, M. K., I. Anwar, and M. Koblinsky. 2009. 'Public-sector Maternal Health Programmes and Services for Rural Bangladesh'. *Journal of Health, Population and Nutrition*, 27(2): 124–38.

Mukhopadhyay, M., and N. Singh. 2007. *Gender Justice, Citizenship and Development*. New Delhi and Canada: Zuban and IDRC.

Mung, M. E. 2008. 'Chinese Migration and China's Foreign Policy in Africa'. *Journal of Overseas Chinese*, 4: 91–109.

Myint, H. 1976. The Economics of the Developing Countries. London: Hutchinson University Library.

Myrdal, G. 1967. *Asian Drama*. 3 vols. Harmondsworth: Penguin.

Nafziger, W., and Auvinen J. 2002. 'Economic Development, Inequality, War, and State Violence'. *World Development*, 30(2): 153–63.

Naim, M. 2007. 'Rogue Aid'. *Foreign Policy*, March/April 2007, 159: 95–6.

Natsios, A. 2010. 'The Clash of the Counter-bureaucracy and Development'. Essay. Center for Global Development, <http://www.cgdev.org> (accessed 4 June 2014).

Natsios, A. S. 2006. 'Five Debates on International Development: The US Perspective'. *Development Policy Review*, 24(2): 131–39.

Nattrass, N., and J. Seekings. 2001. 'Democracy and Distribution in Highly Unequal Economies: The Case of South Africa'. *Journal of Modern African Studies*, 39: 471–98.

Nattrass, N., and J. Seekings. 2010. 'State, Business and Growth in Post-apartheid South Africa'. IPPG Discussion Paper 34. Manchester: IPPG.

Nattrass, N., and J. Seekings. 2011. 'State–business Relations and Pro-poor Growth in South Africa'. *Journal of International Development*, 23(3): 338–57.

Nazneen, S., and M. Sultan. 2010. 'Reciprocity, Distancing and Opportunistic Overtures: Women's Organizations Negotiating Space and Legitimacy in Bangladesh'. *IDS Bulletin*, 41(2): 70–7.

Nazneen, S., and M. Sultan. 2014. *Voicing Demands: Feminist Activism in Transitional Contexts*. London: Zed Books

Nazneen, S., and S. Tasneem. 2010. 'A Silver Lining: Women in Reserved Seats in Local Government in Bangladesh'. *IDS Bulletin*, 41(5): 35–42.

Nelson, J. 2003. 'Grounds for Alliance? Overlapping Interests of the Poor and Not So Poor'. In: *International Development and the Politics of Inclusion*. Edited by

Houtzager, P., and M. Moore, 119–38. Ann Arbor, MI: University of Michigan Press.

Nelson, J. M. 1984. 'The Political Economy of Stabilization: Commitment, Capacity, and Public Response'. *World Development*, 12(1): 983–1006.

Nelson, J. M. 2007. 'Elections, Democracy and Social Services', *Studies in Comparative International Development*, 41(4): 79–97.

Nelson, R. L., and L. Cabatingan. 2010. 'A Preface and an Introduction'. In *Global Perspectives on the Rule of Law*. Edited by Heckman, J. J., R. L. Nelson, and L. Cabatingan. London: Routledge.

Neumayer, E. 2003. 'Do Human Rights Matter in Bilateral Aid Allocation? A Quantitative Analysis of 21 Donor Countries'. *Social Science Quarterly*, 84(3): 650–66.

Newell, P., and J. Wheeler. 2006. 'Rights, Resources and the Politics of Accountability: An Introduction'. In *Rights, Resources and the Politics of Accountability*. Edited by Newell, P., and J. Wheeler. London: Zed Books.

Ngome, I. 2009. 'Cameroonian Perceptions of the Chinese Invasion'. AfricaFiles, <http://www.africafiles.org/article.asp?ID=15986> (accessed 18 September 2011).

North, D. C. 1990. *Institutions, Institutional Change and Economic Performance*. Cambridge: Cambridge University Press.

North, D. C., and R. P. Thomas. 1973. *The Rise of the Western World: A New Economic History*. Cambridge: Cambridge University Press.

North, D.C., J. J. Walliss, S. B. Webb, and B. R. Weingast. 2013. *In the Shadow of Violence: Politics, Economics, and the Problems of Development*. Cambridge: Cambridge University Press.

North, D. C, J. J. Wallis, and B. R. Weingast. 2009. *Violence and Social Orders: A Conceptual Framework for Interpreting Recorded Human History*. Cambridge: Cambridge University Press.

Nsowah-Nuamah, N., F. Teal, and M. Awoonor-Williams. 2010. 'Jobs, Skills and Incomes in Ghana: How Was Poverty Halved?' Working Paper 2010-11. Oxford: Centre for the Study of African Economies.

Obiorah, N. 2007. 'Who's Afraid of China in Africa? Towards an African Civil Society Perspective on China–Africa Relations'. In *African Perspectives on China in Africa*. Edited by Manji, F., and S. Marks, 35–56. Cape Town: Fahamu/Pambazuka.

O'Donnell, G. A. 1993. 'On the State, Democratization and Some Conceptual Problems: A Latin American View with Glances at Some Postcommunist Countries'. *World Development*, 21: 1355–69.

OECD. 2003. 'Benefits and Employment, Friend or Foe? Interactions Between Passive and Active Social Programmes'. *OECD Employment Outlook 2003: Towards More and Better Jobs*, 171–235. Paris: OECD.

OECD. 2008. *Service Delivery in Fragile Situations*. Paris: OECD.

OECD. 2010. *Do No Harm: International Support for Statebuilding*. Paris: OECD.

OECD-DAC. 1995. 'Shaping the 21st Century: The Contribution of Development Co-operation'. Paris: OECD, <http://www.oecd.org/dataoecd/23/35/2508761.pdf> (accessed June 2007).

Okin, S. M. 1979.*Women in Western Political Thought*. Princeton, NJ: Princeton University Press.

Okonjo-Iweala, N. 2010. 'Africa: Promoting Smart and Responsible Investment in Africa', <http://allafrica.com/stories/201011160175.html> (accessed 4 June 2014).

Olivier de Sardan, J.-P. 2009. 'The Eight Modes of Local Governance in West Africa'. Africa Power and Politics Programme Working Paper Series, No. 4. London: ODI.

Olivier de Sardan, J.-P. 2011. 'The Eight Modes of Local Governance in West Africa'. *IDS Bulletin*, 42(2): 22–31.

Olivier de Sardan, J.-P., et al. 2010. 'Local Governance and Public Goods in Niger'. Africa Power and Politics Programme Working Paper No. 10. London: ODI.

Olken, B. 2007. 'Monitoring Corruption: Evidence from a Field Experiment in Indonesia, Unpublished Paper, Harvard University and National Bureau of Economic Research'. *Journal of Political Economy*, 115(2): 200–49.

Olken, B. 2010. 'Direct Democracy and Local Public Goods in Indonesia: Evidence from a Field Experiment in Indonesia'. *American Political Science Review*, 104(2): 243–67.

Olomola, A. S. 2010. 'Formal-informal Institutional Linkages in the Nigerian Agribusiness Sector and Implications for Pro-poor Growth'. In *IPPG Discussion Paper Series, No. 37*. Manchester: Improving Institutions for Pro-Poor Growth.

Olzak, S. 1983. 'Contemporary Ethnic Mobilization'. *Annual Review of Sociology*, 9: 355–74.

Orihuela, J. C. 2012. 'Building and Re-engineering "Good Governance" in Chile'. In *The Developmental Challenges of Mining and Oil: Lessons from Africa and Latin America*. Edited by Thorp, R., S. Battistelli, Y. Guichaoua, J. C. Orihuela, and M. Paredes, 19–43. New York, NY: Palgrave Macmillan.

Osei, R., O. Morrissey, and T. Lloyd. 2005. 'The Fiscal Effects of Aid in Ghana'. *Journal of International Development*, 17(8): 1037–54.

Osmani, S. R. 1991. 'Social Security in South Asia'. *In Social Security in Developing Countries*. Edited by Ahmad, E., J. Drèze, J. Hills, and A. Sen, 300–55. Oxford: Clarendon Press.

Østby, G. 2008. 'Polarization, Horizontal Inequalities and Violent Civil Conflict'. *Journal of Peace Research*, 45(2): 143–62.

Ostrom, E., C. Gibson, S. Shivakumar, and K. Andersson. 2002. 'Aid, Incentives, and Sustainability: An Institutional Analysis of Development Cooperation'. SIDA Studies in Evaluation 02/01:1, Commissioned by SIDA, Department for Evaluation and Internal Audit. Stockholm: SIDA.

Owen, B., and J. Portillo. 2003. 'Legal Reform, Externalities and Economic Development: Measuring the Impact of Legal Aid on Poor Women in Ecuador'. In *SIEPR Discussion Paper, No. 02-32*. Stanford, CA: Stanford University.

Oxfam America. 2009. 'Ghana's Big Test: Oil's Challenge to Democratic Development'. Boston: Oxfam America Headquarters. <http://www.oxfamamerica.org/files/ghanas-big-test.pdf> (accessed 2 June 2014).

Paredes, M. 2012. 'Extractive Dependence in Bolivia and the Persistence of Poor State Capacity'. In *The Developmental Challenges of Mining and Oil; Lessons from*

Africa and Latin America. Edited by Thorp, R., S. Battistelli, Y. Guichaoua, J. C. Orihuela, and M. Paredes, 80–109. New York. Palgrave Macmillan.

Parks, T., and W. Cole. 2010. *Political Settlements: Implications for International Development Policy and Practice*. Washington, DC: The Asia Foundation.

Pateman, C. 1988. *The Sexual Contract*. Cambridge: Polity Press.

Payne, A., and N. Phillips. 2010. *Development*. Key Concepts in Social Science series. Cambridge: Polity Press.

Pearson, L. 1969. *Partners in Development: Report of the Commission on International Development*. New York, NY: Praeger.

Pedley, D., and D. Taylor. 2009. 'Politics and Policy in Education in Ghana'. Paper presented to the 10th UKFIET International Conference on Education and Development.

Peerenboom, R. P. 2002. *China's Long March toward Rule of Law*. Cambridge: Cambridge University Press.

Peerenboom, R. P. (ed.) 2004. *Asian Discourses of Rule of Law: Theories and Implementation of Rule of Law in Twelve Asian Countries, France, and the US*. New York, NY: Routledge.

Peerenboom, R. P. 2008a. 'Are China's Legal Reforms Stalled?' The Foundation for Law, Justice and Society <http://www.fljs.org/uploads/documents/Peerenboom_pb5%231%23.pdf> (accessed 18 October 2011).

Peerenboom, R. P. 2008b. 'Law and Development in China and India: The Advantage and Disadvantages of Front-loading the Costs of Political Reform'. Legal Studies Working Paper Series, No. 2008/15. Melbourne: La Trobe University.

Peet, R., and M. Watts. 2004. 'Liberating Political Ecology'. In *Liberation Ecologies: Environment, Development and Social movements*. Edited by Peet, R., and M. Watts, 2nd edn, 3–47. London: Routledge.

Pegg, S. 2006. 'Mining and Poverty Reduction: Transforming Rhetoric into Reality'. *Journal of Cleaner Production*, 14(3–4): 376–87.

Pegg, S. 2012. 'Has Botswana Beaten the Resource Curse?' In *Mineral Rents and the Financing of Social Policy: Opportunities and Challenges*. Edited by Hujo, K. 257–84. Basingstoke: Palgrave Macmillan.

Pellissery, S. 2005. 'Local Determinants of Exclusion and Inclusion in Rural Public Work Programmes: A Political Economy Approach'. *International Journal of Rural Management*, 1: 167–84.

Pellissery, S. 2008. 'Process Deficits in the Provision of Social Protection in Rural Maharashtra'. In *Social Protection for the Poor and Poorest: Concepts, Policies and Politics*. Edited by Barrientos, A., and D. Hulme, 227–46. London: Palgrave.

Pellissery, S., and S. Sanju. 2011. 'NREGA to Bridge the Missing Link for Food Security: Improving the Natural Resource Access for Small Land Holders'. In *Millennium Development Goals and India: Case Assessing Performance, Prospects and Challenges*. Edited by Mishra, R. K., and R. Jayashree, 154–63. New Delhi: Allied Publishers.

Pérez-Perdomo, R. 2006. 'Rule of Law and Lawyers in Latin America'. *The ANNALS of the American Academy of Political and Social Science*, 603: pp. 179–191.

Perreault, T. 2006. 'From the Guerra del Agua to the Guerra del Gas: Resource Governance, Popular Protest and Social Justice in Bolivia'. *Antipode*, 38(1): pp. 150–172.

Perreault, T. 2008. *Natural Gas, Indigenous Mobilization and the Bolivian State*. Geneva: United Nations Research Institute for Social Development.

Perreault, T. 2013. 'Nature and Nation: Hydrocarbons, Governance and the Territorial Logics of "Resource Nationalism" in Bolivia'. In *Subterranean Struggles: New Dynamics of Mining, Oil and Gas in Latin America*. Edited by Bebbington, A., and J. Bury, 67–90. Austin, TX: University of Texas Press.

Phillips, A. 1991. *Engendering Democracy*. Cambridge: Polity Press.

Phillips, M. 2006. 'G-7 to Warn China over Costly Loans to Poor Countries'. *The Wall Street Journal* (15 September: pA2).

Plant, R. 2003. 'Citizenship and Social Security'. *Fiscal Studies*, 24: 153–66.

Porter, D., and D. Craig. 2004. 'The Third Way and the Third World: Poverty Reduction and Social Inclusion in the Rise of "Inclusive Liberalism"'. *Review of International Political Economy*, 11(2): 387–423.

Pose, R., and F. Samuels. 2011a. *Rwanda's Progress in Health: Leadership, Performance, Insurance, ODI Development Progress*. London: Overseas Development Institute.

Pose, R., and F. Samuels. 2011b. *Bangladesh's Progress in Health: Healthy Partnerships and Effective Pro-poor Targeting, ODI Development Progress*. London: Overseas Development Institute.

Post, L. A., A. N. W. Raile, and E. D. Raile. 2010. 'Defining Political Will'. *Politics & Policy*, 38(4): 653–76.

Poteete, A. 2009. 'Is Development Path Dependent or Political? A Reintepretation of Mineral-Dependent Development in Botswana'. *Journal of Development Studies*, 45(4): 544–71.

Poterba, J. M. 1997. 'Demographic Structure and the Political Economy of Public Education'. *Journal of Policy Analysis and Management*, 16(1): 48–66.

Powell, C. A., S. P. Walker, S. M. Chang, and S. M. Grantham-McGregor. 1998. 'Nutrition and Education: A Randomised Trial of the Effects of Breakfast in Rural Primary School Children'. *American Journal of Clinical Nutrition*, 68(4): 873–9.

Power, M. 2011. 'Angola 2025: The Future of the World's Richest Poor Country as Seen through a Chinese Rear-view Mirror'. *Antipode*, 44(3): 993–1014.

Power, M., G. Mohan, and M. Tan-Mullins. 2012. *China's Resource Diplomacy in Africa: Powering Development?* London: Palgrave Macmillan.

Prabhu, S., and S. Chatterjee. 1993. *Social Sector Expenditures and Human Development: A Study of Indian States*. New Delhi: Reserve Bank of India.

Pritchett, L. 2000. 'Understanding Patterns of Economic Growth: Searching for Hills among Plateaus, Mountains and Plains'. *World Bank Economic Review*, 14(2): 221–50.

Pritchett, L. 2002. '"When Will They Ever Learn?" Why *All* Governments Produce Schooling'. BREAD Working Paper No. 031. Kennedy School of Government and Centre for Global Development, <http://www.hks.harvard.edu/fs/lpritch/Education%20-%20docs/ED%20-%20Gov%20action/whenlearn_v1.pdf> (accessed 18 June 2014).

Pritchett, L., and E. Werker. 2012. 'Developing the Guts of a GUT (Grand Unified Theory): Elite Commitment and Inclusive Growth'. ESID Working Paper No. 16. Manchester: ESID.

Pritchett, L., and F. de Weijer. 2010. 'Fragile States: Stuck in a Capability Trap?' In *World Development Report 2011 Background Papers*. Washington, DC: World Bank.

Pritchett, L., and M. Woolcock. 2004. 'Solutions When *the* Solution Is the Problem: Arraying the Disarray in Development'. *World Development*, 32(2): 191–212.

Pronk, J. P. 2001. 'Aid as a Catalyst'. *Development and Change*, 32(4): 611–29.

Pronk, J. P. 2003. 'Aid as a Catalyst: A Rejoinder'. *Development and Change*, 34(3): 383–400.

Provost, C. 2011. 'China Publishes First Report on Foreign Aid Policy'. *The Guardian*, 28 April, <http://www.guardian.co.uk/global-development/2011/apr/28/china-foreign-aid-policy-report> (accessed 4 June 2014).

Przeworski, A., M. E. Alvarez, J. A. Cheibub, and F. Limongi. 2000. *Democracy and Development: Political Institutions and Well-being in the World, 1950–1990*. Cambridge: Cambridge University Press.

Putnam, R. 1993. *Making Democracy Work: Civic Traditions in Modern Italy*. Princeton, Princeton UP.

Putzel, J. 1997. 'Accounting for the "Dark Side" of Social Capital: Reading Robert Putnam on Democracy'. *Journal of International Development*, 9(7): 939–49.

Raabe, K., R. Birner, M. Sekher, K. G. Gayathrivedi, A. Shilp, and E. Schiffer. 2010. *How to Overcome Governance Challenges of Implementing NREGA*. Washington, DC: IFPRI.

Rai, S. 1996. 'Women and the State in the Third World: Some Issues for Debate'. In *Women and the State: International Perspectives*. Edited by Rai, S. and G. Livesevley, 5–22. London: Taylor and Francis.

Rai, S. 1997. 'Gender and Representation: Women MPs in the Indian Parliament 1991–96'. In *Getting Institutions Right for Women in Development*. Edited by Goetz, A. M. London: Zed Books.

Rajagopal, B. 2003. *International Law from Below: Development, Social Movements, and Third World Resistance*. Cambridge: Cambridge University Press.

Rajan, R., and A. Subramaniam. 2007. 'Does Aid Affect Governance?' *The American Economic Review*, 97(2): 322–7.

Rajan, R., and A. Subramaniam. 2008. 'Aid and Growth: What Does the Cross-country Evidence Really Show?' *Review of Economics and Statistics*, 90(4): 643–65.

Rajan, R., and A. Subramaniam. 2009. 'Aid, Dutch Disease and Manufacturing Growth'. Working Paper 196. Washington, DC: Center for Global Development.

Rampa, F., and S. Bilal. 2011. 'Emerging Economies in Africa and the Development Effectiveness Debate'. ECDPM Discussion Paper No. 107.

Randall, V. 1998.'Gender and Power: Women Engage the State'. In *Gender, Politics and the State*. Edited by Randall V., and G. Waylen, 185–205. London: Routledge.

Randall, V., and G. Waylen (eds.). 1998. *Gender, Politics and the State*. London: Routledge.

Rawls, J. 1971. *A Theory of Justice*, Cambridge, MA: Harvard University Press, repr. 1999.

Raz, J. 1977. 'The Rule of Law and Its Virtue'. *Law Quarterly Review*, 93: 195–202.

Razavi, S. 1997. 'Fitting Gender into Development Institutions'. *World Development*, 25(7): 1111–25.

Razavi, S. 2007. 'Does Paid Work Enhance Women's Access to Welfare? Evidence from Selected Industrializing Countries'. *Social Politics: International Studies in Gender, State and Society*, 14(1): 58–92.

Razavi, S., and C. Miller. 1995. 'Gender Mainstreaming: A Study of Efforts by the UNDP, the World Bank and the ILO to Institutionalize Gender Issues'. Occasional Paper No. 4. Geneva: UNRISD.

Reddy, M. G., K. A. Kumar, P. T. Rao, and O. Springate-Baginski. 2010. 'Obstructed Access to Forest Justice: An Institutional Analysis of the Implementation of Rights Reform in Andhra's Forested Landscapes'. In *IPPG Discussion Paper Series, No. 47*. Manchester: Improving Institutions for Pro-Poor Growth.

Reiling, D., L. Hammergren, and A. Di Giovanni. 2007. *Justice Sector Assessments: A Handbook*. Washington, DC: World Bank.

Reilly, J., and W. Na. 2007. 'China's Corporate Engagement in Africa'. In *Africa in China's Global Strategy*. Edited by Kitissou, M., 132–55. London: Adonis and Abbey Publishers.

Reinikka, R., and P. Collier. 2001. *Uganda's recovery*. Kampala: Fountain Press.

Reis, E., and M. Moore. 2005. *Elite Perceptions of Poverty and Inequality*. London: Zed Books.

Reisen, H., and S. Ndoye. 2008. 'Prudent versus Imprudent Lending in Africa: From Debt Relief to Emerging Lenders'. OECD Development Centre Working Paper No. 268. Paris: OECD.

Reuters. 2011. 'Ghana Parliament to Debate China's $3 bln Loan'. <http://af.reuters.com/article/investingNews/idAFJOE77L07H20110822> (accessed 4 June 2014).

Richards, E. 2002. *The Highland Clearances: People, Landlords and Rural Turmoil*. Edinburgh: Birlinn.

Riddell, R. C. 2007. *Does Foreign Aid really Work?* Oxford: Oxford University Press.

Robinson, J. A. 2010. 'The Political Economy of Redistributive Policies'. In *Declining Inequality in Latin America: A Decade of Progress?* Edited by López-Calva, L. F., and N. Lustig, 39–71. Washington, DC: Brookings Institution Press.

Robinson, J., and N. Parsons. 2006. 'State Formation and Governance in Botswana'. *Journal of African Economics*, 15(1): 100–40.

Robinson, M. 2008. 'Hybrid States: Globalization and the Politics of State Capacity'. *Political Studies*, 56: 566–83.

Robinson, W. I. 2010. 'Global Capitalism Theory and the Emergence of Transnational Elites'. UNU-WIDER WP 2010-02.

Rodrik, D. 2004. 'Growth Strategies'. [Mimeo.]

Rodrik, D., A. Subramanian, and F. Trebbi. 2004. 'Institutions Rule: The Primacy of Institutions over Geography and Integration in Economic Development'. *Journal of Economic Growth*, 9: 131–65.

Roodman, D. 'Macro Aid Effectiveness Research: A Guide for the Perplexed'. Working Paper 135. Washington, DC: Centre for Global Development, <http://www.cgdev.org/content/publications/detail/15003> (accessed January 2008).

Roque, S., and A. Shankland. 2007. 'Participation, Mutation and Political Transition: New Democratic Spaces in Peri-urban Angola'. In *Spaces for Change? The Politics of Citizen Participation in New Democratic Arenas*. Edited by Cornwall, A., and V. S. P. Coelho. London: Zed Books.

Rose, N. 1999. *Powers of Freedom: Reframing Political Thought*. Cambridge: Cambridge University Press.

Rose, P. 2009. 'NGO Provision of Basic Education: Alternative or Complementary Service Delivery to Support Access to the Excluded?' *Compare: A Journal of Comparative and International Education*, 39(2): 219–33.

Rose, P. 2011. 'Strategies for Engagement: Government and National Non-government Education Providers in South Asia'. *Public Administration and Development*, 31(4): 294–305.

Ross Schneider, B. 2004. 'Organising Interests and Coalitions on the Politics of Market Reform in Latin America'. *World Politics*, 56(3): 456–79.

Ross, M. 2001. *Extractive Industries and the Poor*. Boston, MA: Oxfam America.

Ross, M. 2008. 'Mineral Wealth, Conflict, and Equitable Development,' In *Institutional Pathways to Equity: Assessing Inequality Traps*. Edited by Bebbington, A. J., A. A. Dani, A. de Haan, and M. Walton, 193–216. Washington, DC: World Bank.

Ross, M. 2012. *The Oil Curse: How Petroleum Wealth Shapes the Development of Nations*. Princeton, NJ: Princeton University Press.

Rothstein, B. 2002. 'Cooperation for Social Protection: Explaining Variation in Welfare Programs'. *American Behavioral Scientist*, 45(5): 901–18.

Rothstein, B., and J. Teorell. 2008. 'What Is Quality of Government? A Theory of Impartial Government Institutions'. *Governance*, 21: 165–90.

Routley, L. 2012. 'Developmental States: A Review of the Literature'. ESID Working Paper No. 3. Manchester: ESID.

Rueschemeyer, D. 2009. *Useable Theory: Analytical Tools for Social Research*. Princeton, NJ: Princeton University Press.

Rueschemeyer, D., E. Huber Stephens, and J. D. Stephens. 1992. *Capitalist Development and Democracy*. Chicago, IL: University of Chicago Press.

Rusa, L., and G. Fritsche. 2007. 'Rwanda'. In *Performance-Based Financing in Health: Sourcebook on Emerging Good Practice*, 105–17. Washington, DC: World Bank.

Sachs, J. 2003. 'Institutions Matter, But Not for Everything: The Role of Geography and Resource Endowments in Development Shouldn't Be Underestimated'. *Finance and Development*, 40(2): 38–41.

Sachs, J. 2005. *The End of Poverty: Economic Possibilities for Our Times*. New York, NY: Penguin Press.

Sachs, J. 2007. 'China's Lessons for the World Bank'. *Economists View*, <http://economistsview.typepad.com/economistsview/2007/05/jeffrey_sachs_c.html/> (accessed 4 June 2014).

Sachs, J., and A. Warner. 1995. 'Natural Resource Abundance and Economic Growth'. National Bureau of Economic Research Working Paper Series, Working Paper No. 5398: 1–46.

Sacks, A., and M. Levi. 2010. 'Measuring Government Effectiveness and Its Consequences for Social Welfare in Sub-Saharan African Countries'. *Social Forces*, 88(5): 2325–51.

Sagbien, J., and N.-M. Lindsay (eds.). 2011. *Governance Ecosystems: CSR in the Latin American Mining Sector.* London: Palgrave Macmillan.

Sala-i-Martin, X., and A. Subramaniam. 2003. 'Addressing the Natural Resource Curse: An Illustration from Nigeria'. IMF Working Paper WP/03/139. Washington, DC: IMF.

Sandbrook, R., M. Edelman, P. Heller, and J. Teichman. 2007. *Social Democracy in the Global Periphery.* Cambridge: Cambridge University Press.

Santiago, M. 2006. *The Ecology of Oil: Environment, Labor, and the Mexican Revolution, 1900–1938.* Cambridge: Cambridge University Press.

Santos, A. 2006. 'The World Bank's Use of the "Rule of Law" Promise in Economic Development'. In *The New Law and Economic Development: A Critical Appraisal.* Edited by Trubek, D. M., and A. Santos, 253–99. Cambridge: Cambridge University Press.

Sardenberg, C., and A. Acosta. 2014. 'Feminisms in Brazil'. In *Voicing Demands: Feminists' Reflections on Strategies, Negotiations and Influence.* Edited by Nazneen, S., and M. Sultan. London: Zed Books.

Sarin, M., with O. Springate-Baginski. 2010. 'India's Forest Rights Act: The Anatomy of a Necessary but Not Sufficient Institutional Reform'. IPPG Discussion Paper, No. 45. Manchester: Improving Institutions for Pro-Poor Growth.

Sautman, B., and H. Yan. 2009. 'African Perspectives on China-Africa Links'. *The China Quarterly*, 199: 728–59.

Savun, B., and D. C. Tirone. 2011. 'Foreign Aid, Democratization, and Civil Conflict: How Does Democracy Aid Affect Civil Conflict?' *American Journal of Political Science*, 55(2): 233–46.

Saylor, R. 2013. 'Concepts, Measures, and Measuring Well: An Alternative Outlook'. *Sociological Research and Methods*, 42: 354–391.

Schiavo-Campo, S. 2008. 'Of Mountains and Molehills: "The" Medium-term Expenditure Framework'. Paper presented at the Conference on Sustainability and Efficiency in Managing Public Expenditures, East-West Center and Korea Development Institute. Honolulu, Hawaii, 24–25 July.

Schmitz, H. 2007. 'The Rise of the East: What Does It Mean for Development Studies?' *IDS Bulletin*, 38(2): 51–8.

Schneider, B. 2004. *Business, politics and the state in twentieth-century Latin America.* New York. Cambridge University Press.

Scott, J. C. 1998. *Seeing Like a State: How Certain Schemes to Improve the Human Condition Have Failed.* New Haven, CT: Yale University Press.

Scott, J. C. 2009. *The Art of Not Being Governed: An Anarchist History of Upland Southeast Asia.* New Haven, CT: Yale University Press.

Seekings, J. 2008. 'Deserving Individuals and Groups: The Post-apartheid State's Justification of the Shape of South Africa's System of Social Assistance'. *Transformation*, 68: 28–52.

Sen, G., and C. Grown. 1988. *Development, Crises and Alternative Visions: Third World Women's Perspective.* London: Earthscan.

Sen, K. 2012. 'The Political Determinants of Growth'. ESID Working Paper. Manchester: ESID.

Sen, K., and D. W. T. Velde. 2009. 'State–business Relations and Economic Growth in Sub-Saharan Africa'. *Journal of Development Studies*, 45(8): 1267–83.

Shambaugh, D. 2007. 'China's Quiet Diplomacy'. *China: An International Journal*, 5 (1): 26–54.

Shankar, S., and P. B. Mehta. 2008. 'Courts and Socioeconomic Rights in India'. In *Courting Social Justice: Judicial Enforcement of Social and Economic Rights in the Developing World*. Edited by Gauri, V., and D. Brinks, 146–82. New York, NY: Cambridge University Press.

Shankar, S., R. Gaiha, and R. Jha. 2011. 'Information, Access and Targeting: The National Rural Employment Guarantee Scheme in India'. *Oxford Development Studies*, 39: 69–95.

Shepherd, A., and G. Onumah. 1997. 'Liberalized Agricultural Markets in Ghana: The Roles and Capacity of Government'. The Role of Government in Adjusting Economies, Working Paper 12. Birmingham: University of Birmingham.

Shirk, S. 2007. *China—Fragile Superpower: How China's Internal Politics Could Derail Its Peaceful Rise*. Oxford: Oxford University Press.

Simatovic, M. I. 2008. *Impact of the Rural Roads Programme on Democracy and Citizenship in Rural Areas of Peru*. Washington, DC: World Bank.

Singh, P. 2011. 'We-ness and Welfare: A Longitudinal Analysis of Social Development in Kerala, India'. *World Development*, 39(2): 282–93.

Six, C. 2009. 'The Rise of Postcolonial States as Donors: A Challenge to the Development Paradigm?' *Third World Quarterly*, 30(6): 1103–21.

Skocpol, T. 1992. *Protecting Soldiers and Mothers: The Political Origins of Social Policy in the United States*. Cambridge, MA: Harvard University Press.

Skocpol, T. 2003. *Diminished Democracy: From Membership to Management in American Civic Life*. Norman, OK: University of Oklahoma Press.

Slack, K. 2012. 'Mission Impossible? Adopting a CSR-based Business Model for Extractive Industries in Developing Countries'. *Resources Policy*, 37(2): 179–84.

Slater, D. 2008. 'Can Leviathan Be Democratic? Competitive Elections, Robust Mass Politics, and State Infrastructural Power'. *Studies in Comparative International Development*, 43: 252–72.

Slater, D. 2010. *Ordering Power: Contentious Politics and Authoritarian Leviathans in Southeast Asia*. New York, NY: Cambridge University Press.

Smith, L. 2008. 'The Politics of Contemporary Language Policy in Ethiopia'. *Journal of Developing Societies*, 24(2): 207–43.

Soares de Oliveira, R. 2007. 'Business Success, Angola-Style: Postcolonial Politics and the Rise and Rise of Sonangal'. *Journal of Modern African Studies*, 45(4): 595–619.

Soares, V., A. A. Alcantara Costa, C. M. Buarque, D. D. Dora, and W. Sam'Anna. 1995. 'Brazilian Feminisms and Women's Movement: A Two-way Street'. In *The Challenges of Local Feminisms: Women's Movement in Global Perspective*. Edited by Basu, A. Boulder, CO: Westview Press.

Social Learning Group, W. C. Clark, J. Jaeger, J. V. Eijndhoven, and N. M. Dickson (eds.). 2001. *Learning to Manage Global Environmental Risks, I: A Comparative History of Social Responses to Climate Change, Ozone Depletion and Acid Rain.* Cambridge, MA: MIT Press.

Soeters, R., C. Habineza, and P. B. Peerenboom. 2006. 'Performance-based Financing and Changing the District Health System: Experience from Rwanda'. *Bulletin of the World Health Organization,* 84(11): 884–9.

Soifer, H. 2008. 'State Infrastructural Power: Approaches to Conceptualization and Measurement'. *Studies in Comparative International Development,* 43: 231–51.

Soifer, H. 2012. 'Measuring State Capacity in Contemporary Latin America'. *Revista de Ciencia Política,* 32(3): 585–98.

Soifer, H. 2013. 'Authority Over Distance: Institutions and Long-run Variation in State Development in Latin America'. Manuscript, Department of Political Science, Temple University.

Soifer, H., and M. vom Hau. 2008. 'Unpacking the Strength of the State: The Utility of State Infrastructural Power'. *Studies in Comparative International Development,* 43: 219–30.

Sowell, T. 2004. *Affirmative Action Around the World: An Empirical Study.* New Haven, CT: Yale University Press.

Stasavage, D. 2005. 'Democracy and Education Spending in Africa'. *American Journal of Political Science,* 49: 344–5.

Staudt, K. 1990. *Women, International Development, and Politics: The Bureaucratic Mire.* Philadelphia, PA: Temple University Press.

Staudt, K. 1997. 'Gender Politics in Bureaucracies: Theoretical Issues in Comparative Perspective'. In *Women, International Development, and Politics: The Bureaucratic Mire.* Edited by Staudt, K., 3–34. Philadelphia, PA: Temple University Press.

Stefanova, M., R. Porter, and R. Nixon. 2010. 'Leasing in Vanuatu: Findings and Community Dissemination on Epi Island'. Justice for the Poor Briefing Note, 5(4). Washington, DC: World Bank.

Steinmetz, G. 2007. *The Devil's Handwriting: Precoloniality and the German Colonial State in Qingdao, Samoa, and Southwest Africa.* Chicago, IL: Chicago University Press.

Stepan, A. 1978. *The State and Society: Peru in Comparative Perspective.* Princeton, NJ: Princeton University Press.

Stephens, M. 2009. 'Typologies, Risks and Benefits of Interaction between State and Non-state Justice Systems'. Paper presented at conference on 'Customary Justice and Legal Pluralism in Post-conflict and Fragile States', Washington, DC, 17–18 November. Washington, DC: World Bank and US Institute for Peace.

Stewart, F. 2010. 'Horizontal Inequalities as a Cause of Conflict: A Review of CRISE Findings'. World Bank: World Development Report 2011 background paper. <http://siteresources.worldbank.org/EXTWDR2011/Resour ces/6406082-1283882418764/WDR_Background_Paper_Stewart.pdf> (accessed 18 June 2014).

Stewart, F., G. Brown, and A. Langer. 2007. 'Policies Towards Horizontal Inequalities'. Working Paper 42. Oxford: CRISE.

Bibliography

Stigler, G. 1970. 'Director's Law of Public Income Distribution'. *Journal of Law and Economics*, 13(1): 1–10.

Stokes, S. C. 2004. *Is Vote Buying Undemocratic?* Chicago, IL: University of Chicago, Department of Political Science.

Stotsky, J., and A. Woldemariam. 1997. 'Tax Effort in Sub-Saharan Africa'. IMF Working Paper 97/107. Washington, DC: IMF.

Sultan, M. (n.d). 'Gender in Public Administration in Bangladesh'. UNDP [Mimeo].

Swidler, A. 2006. 'Syncretism and Subversion in AIDS Governance: How Locals Cope with Global Demands'. *International Affairs*, 82(2): 269–84.

Szreter, S. 2007. 'The Right to Registration: Development, Identity Registration and Social Security—A Historical Perspective'. *World Development*, 35: 67–86.

Tadros, M. 2010. 'Introduction: Quotas—Add Women and Stir?' *IDS Bulletin*, 41(5): 1–10.

Tadros, M. 2011. *Women Engaging Politically: Beyond Magic Bullets and Motorways*. Brighton: Pathways RPC.

Tamale, S. 1999. *When Hens Begin to Crow: Gender and Parliamentary Politics in Uganda*. Kampala: Fountain.

Tamanaha, B. Z. 2000. 'A Non-essentialist Version of Legal Pluralism'. *Journal of Law and Society*, 27(2): 296–321.

Tamanaha, B. Z. 2004. *On the Rule of Law: History, Politics, Theory*. Cambridge: Cambridge University Press.

Tamanaha, B. Z. 2011. 'The Primacy of Society and the Failures of Law and Development'. *Cornell International Law Journal*, 44: 216–47.

Tamanaha, B. Z. 2012. 'The Rule of Law and Legal Pluralism in Development'. In *Legal Pluralism and Development: Scholars and Practitioners in Dialogue*. Edited by Tamanaha, B. Z., C. Sage, and M. Woolcock. New York, NY: Cambridge University Press.

Tamang, S. 2004. 'The Politics of Conflict and Difference or the Difference of Conflict in Politics: The Women's Movement in Nepal'. *Feminist Review*, 91: 48–60.

Tang, J., and C. Zhang. 2011. 'SMEs Play "Big Role" in Africa'. *International Business Journal*, 29 August, <http://www.focac.org/eng/zfgx/jmhz/t859358.htm> (accessed 01 September 2011).

Tan-Mullins, M., G. Mohan, and M. Power. 2010. 'Redefining "Aid" in the China–Africa Context'. *Development and Change*, 41(5): 857–81.

Tavares, J. 2003. 'Does Foreign Aid Corrupt?' *Economic Letters*, 79: 99–106.

Taylor, I. 2006. 'China's Oil Diplomacy in Africa'. *International Affairs*, 82(5): 937–59.

Taylor, I. 2007. 'Governance in Africa and Sino-African Relations: Contradictions or Confluence?' *Politics*, 27(3): 139–46.

Teka, Z. 2011. 'Industrial Linkages in the Commodities Sector: The Case of the Angolan Oil and Gas Industry'. PhD thesis, The Open University.

Tendler, J. 1997. *Good Government in the Tropics*. Baltimore, MD: Johns Hopkins University Press.

Teshome, A. 2008. 'A Review of Education Policy, Strategy and Programmes'. In *Digest of Ethiopia's National Policies, Strategies and Programs*. Edited by Assefa, T., 47–93. Addis Ababa: Forum for Social Studies.

Therkildsen, O. 2008. 'Inequality, Elites and Distributional Coalitions in Tanzania'. Danish Institute for International Studies (DIIS), November, <http://www.diis.dk> (accessed 4 June 2014).

Thies, C. G. 2005. 'War, Rivalry, and State Building in Latin America'. *American Journal of Political Science*, 49: 451–65.

Thorp, R., S. Battistelli, Y. Guichaoua, J. C. Orihuela, and M. Paredes. 2012a. *The Developmental Challenges of Mining and Oil: Lessons from Africa and Latin America*. New York, NY: Palgrave Macmillan.

Thorp, R., S. Battistelli, Y. Guichaoua, J. C. Orihuela, and M. Paredes. 2012b. 'Introduction'. In *The Developmental Challenges of Mining and Oil: Lessons from Africa and Latin America*. Edited by Thorp, R., S. Battistelli, Y. Guichaoua, J. C. Orihuela, and M. Paredes, 1–18. New York, NY: Palgrave Macmillan.

Tilly, C. 1975. 'Reflections on the History of European State-making'. In *The Formation of National States in Western Europe*. Edited by Tilly, C., 3–83. Princeton, NJ: Princeton University Press.

Tilly, C. 1990. *Coercion, Capital, and European States, AD 990–1990*. Cambridge, MA: Basil Blackwell.

Tilly, C. 1992. *Coercion, Capital and European States*. Malden, MA: Blackwell.

Tilly, C. 1998. *Durable Inequality*. Berkeley, CA: University of California Press.

Tilly, C. 2001. 'Mechanisms in Political Processes'. *Annual Review of Political Science*, 4(1): 21–41.

Tilly, C. 2004. *Contention and Democracy in Europe, 1650–2000*. Cambridge: Cambridge University Press.

Torpey, J. C. 2000. *The Invention of the Passport: Surveillance, Citizenship and the State*. Cambridge: Cambridge University Press.

Toye, J. 1995. 'Ghana'. In *Aid and Power*, II. Edited by Mosley, P., J. Harrigan, and J. Toye. London: Routledge.

Toye, J., and R. Toye. 2004. *The UN and Global Political Economy: Trade, Finance, and Development*. Bloomington, IN: Indiana University Press.

Tradeinvest Africa. 2009. 'Development Fund Strengthens Sino-African Partnership', <http://www.tradeinvestafrica.com/feature_articles/224685.htm> (accessed 28 September 2011).

Trebilcock, M. J., and R. J. Daniels. 2008. *Rule of Law Reform and Development: Charting the Fragile Path of Progress*. Northampton: Edward Elgar.

Tripp, A. M. 2001. 'New Political Activism in Africa'. *Journal of Democracy*, 12(3): 141–55.

Tripp, A. M. 2003. 'The Changing Faces of Africa's Legislatures: Women and Quotas'. In IDEA Parliamentary Forum Conference, 11–12 November 2003, Pretoria, South Africa.

Tripp, A. M. 2004. 'Women's Movement, Customary Law and Land Rights in Africa: The Case of Uganda'. *African Studies Quarterly*, 1–19.

Tripp, A. M. 2012. *Women's Political Empowerment in State-building and Peacemaking: A Baseline Study*. Canada: IDRC.

Trofimov, Y. 2007. 'New Management: In Africa China's Expansion Begins to Stir Resentment: Investment Boom Fuels Colonialism Charges; a Tragedy in Zambia'. *The Wall Street Journal*, 2 February 2007, p A1.

Trounstine, J. 2013. *One for You, Two for Me: Support for Public Goods Investment in Diverse Communities*. Merced, CA: University of California, Merced.

Trubek, D. M. 2008. 'Developmental States and the Legal Order: Towards a New Political Economy of Development and Law'. In *University of Wisconsin Legal Studies Research Paper, No. 1075*. Madison, WI: University of Wisconsin Law School.

Trubek, D. M. 2009. 'The Political Economy of the Rule of Law: The Challenge of the New Developmental State'. *Hague Journal on the Rule of Law*, 1(1): 28–32.

Trubek, D. M., and A. Santos (eds.). 2006. *The New Law and Economic Development: A Critical Appraisal*. Cambridge: Cambridge University Press.

Trubek, D. M., and M. Galanter. 1974. 'Scholars in Self-estrangement: Some Reflections on the Crisis in Law and Development Studies in the United States'. *Wisconsin Law Review*, 4: 1062–102.

Tsai, L. L. 2007. *Accountability without Democracy*: Cambridge: Cambridge University Press.

Tull, D. 2006. 'China's Engagement in Africa: Scope, Significance and Consequences'. *Journal of Modern African Studies*, 44(3): 459–79.

UN Millennium Project. 2005. *Investing in Development: Millennium Development Goals*. London: Earthscan.

UN. 2002. Report of the International Conference on Financing for Development Monterrey. Mexico, 18–22 March, <http://www.un.org/esa/ffd/monterrey/MonterreyConsensus.pdf> (accessed 18 June 2014).

UNDP. Various years. *Human Development Report*. New York, NY: Oxford University Press.

UNESCO. 2011. *The Hidden Crisis: Armed Conflict and Education, EFA Education Monitoring Report*. Paris: UNESCO.

Unger, J., and A. Chan. 1999. 'Inheritors of the Boom: Private Enterprise and the Role of Local Government in a Rural South China Township'. *The China Journal*, 42: 45–74.

UNIFEM. 2008. *Progress of World's Women, Who Answers to Women?* New York, NY: UNIFEM.

United Nations Conference on Trade and Development. 2007. *Asian Foreign Direct Investment in Africa: Towards a New Era of Cooperation among Developing Countries*. New York, NY: United Nations.

United Nations. 1951. *Measures for the Economic Development of Underdeveloped Countries*. New York, NY: UN Economic and Social Council.

United Nations. 2007. *Asian Foreign Direct Investment in Africa: Towards a New Era of Cooperation among Developing Countries*. New York, NY: United Nations, <http://unctad.org/en/Docs/iteiia20071_en.pdf> (accessed 12 June 2014).

University of Manchester. 2011. 'Effective States and Inclusive Development Research Centre (ESID)'. Inception Report 1 January 2011 to 31 March 2012. Manchester: University of Manchester.

UNRISD/UN. 2005. *Gender Equality: Striving for Justice in an Unequal World*. New York, NY: UNRISD/UN Publication.

Unsworth, S. 2009. 'What's Politics Got to Do with It?' *Journal of International Development*, 21(6): 883–94.

Unsworth, S. 2010. *An Upside-down View of Governance*. Brighton: Institute of Development Studies.

Unsworth, S. 2010. 'Mobilising for Better Public Services'. In *An Upside-down View of Governance*. Brighton: Centre for the Future State, Institute of Development Studies.

Unsworth, S., and M. Moore. 2006. 'Critique of DFID White Paper on "Making Government Work for Poor People"'. *Development Policy Review*, 24(6): 707–15.

Unsworth, S. Undated. 'Is Political Analysis Changing Donor Behaviour?' [Mimeo].

USAID. 2008. *Pakistan Rule of Law Assessment: Final Report*. Washington, DC: USAID.

Uvin, P. 2004. *Human Rights and Development*. Bloomfield, CT: Kumarian Press.

Uvin, P. 2007. 'From the Right to Development to the Rights-based Approach: How Human Rights Entered Development'. *Development in Practice*, 17(4): 597–606.

Valdivia, M. 2010. 'Contracting the Road to Development: Early Impacts of a Rural Roads Program'. PPMA Working Paper 18. Poverty and Economic Research Network, World Bank.

Van Cott, D. L. 2005. *From Movements to Parties in Latin America: the Evolution of Ethnic Politics*. New York, NY: Cambridge University Press.

Van Cott, D. L. 2008. *Radical Democracy in the Andes: Indigenous Parties and the Quality of Democracy in Latin America*. New York, NY: Cambridge University Press.

Van de Walle, S., and Z. Scott. 2011. 'The Political Role of Service Delivery in State-building: Exploring the Relevance of European History for Developing Countries'. *Development Policy Review*, 29(1): 5–21.

Van Der Berg, S. 1997. 'South African Social Security under Apartheid and Beyond'. *Development Southern Africa*, 14: 481–503.

Van Der Berg, S., and K. Siebrits. 2010. *Social Assistance Reform during a Period of Financial Stress*. Stellenbosch: University of Stellenbosch Department of Economics.

Vandemoortele, M., and K. Bird. 2011. 'Progress in Economic Conditions: A Recent Example of Progress in Malawi'. *Development Progress*. London: Overseas Development Institute (ODI).

Varshney, A. 2003. *Ethnic Conflict and Civic Life: Hindus and Muslims in India*. New Haven, CT: Yale University Press.

Vera Institute of Justice. 2004. *Charting Justice Reform in Chile: A Comparison of the Old and New Systems of Criminal Procedure*. New York, NY: The Vera Institute of Justice.

vom Hau, M. 2008. 'State Infrastructural Power and Nationalism: Comparative Lessons from Mexico and Argentina'. *Studies in Comparative International Development*, 43 (3–4): 334–54.

vom Hau, M. 2012. 'State Capacity and Inclusive Development: New Challenges and Directions'. ESID Working Paper No. 3. Manchester: ESID.

Vu, T. 2007. 'State Formation and the Origins of Developmental States in South Korea and Indonesia'. *Studies in Comparative International Development*, 41(4): 27–56.

Vu, T. 2010. 'Studying the State through State Formation'. *World Politics*, 62: 148–75.

Wade, R. 2011. 'Emerging World Order? From Multipolarity to Multilateralism in the G20, the World Bank and the IMF'. *Politics and Society*, 39(3): 347–77.

Waldner, D. 1999. *State Building and Late Development*. Ithaca, NY: Cornell University Press.

Waldron, J. 2002. 'Is the Rule of Law an Essentially Contested Concept (in Florida)?' *Law and Philosophy*, 21(2): 137–64.

Walton, M. 2010. 'Capitalism, the State, and the Underlying Drivers of Human Development'. Human Development Reports Research Paper, UNDP.

Warmerdam, W., and A. de Haan. 2011. 'The Roles of Aid in Politics: Putting China in Perspective'. Annotated Biliography, <http://www.iss.nl/fileadmin/ASSETS/iss/Documents/Academic_publications/Bibliography_The_Roles_of_Aid_in_Politics_February_2011.doc> (accessed 4 June 2014).

Watts, J. 2010. *When a Billion Chinese Jump: How China Will Save Mankind—Or Destroy It*. London: Faber and Faber.

Watts, M. 2003. 'Development and Governmentality'. *Singapore Journal of Tropical Geography*, 24(1): 6–34.

Watts, M. 2004. 'Antinomies of Community: Some Thoughts on Geography, Resources and Empire'. *Transactions of the Institute of British Geographers* NS 29(2): 195–216.

Waylen, G. 1996. *Gender in Third World Politics*. Buckingham: Open University Press.

Waylen, G. 1997. 'Women's Movement, the State, Democratic Transition: The Establishment of SERNAM'. In *Getting Institutions Right for Women in Development*. Edited by Goetz, A. M. London: Zed Books.

Waylen, G. 2007. *Engendering Transitions*. Oxford: Oxford University Press.

Wayne Nafziger, E., and J. Auvinen. 2002. 'Economic Development, Inequality, War, and State Violence'. *World Development*, 30(2): 153–63.

Weber, M. 1978. *Economy and Society: An Outline of Interpretive Sociology*. Berkeley, CA: University of California Press.

Weber-Fahr, M. 2002. *Treasure or Trouble? Mining in Developing Countries*. Washington, DC: World Bank and International Finance Corporation.

Weiss, L. (ed.) 2003. *States in the Global Economy: Bringing Domestic Institutions Back In*. New York, NY: Cambridge University Press.

Weldon, S. L. 2002. 'Beyond Bodies: Institutional Sources for Women in Democratic Policymaking'. *Journal of Politics*, 64(4): 1153–74.

Wen, J. B. 2009. Full text of Wen Jiabao Speech at FOCAC IV, <http://www.china.org.cn/world/2009-11/09/content_18849890.htm> (accessed 18 June 2014).

Weyland, K. 1996. *Democracy without Equity: Failures of Reform in Brazil*. Pittsburgh, PA: University of Pittsburgh Press.

Whitfield, L. 2006. 'Aid's Political Consequences: The Embedded Aid System in Ghana'. GEG Working Paper 2006/24.

Whitfield, L. (ed.) 2008. *The Politics of Aid: Africa Strategies for Dealing with Donors*. New York, NY: Oxford University Press.

Whitfield, L., and E. Jones. 2007. WP 2007/32 'Ghana: The Political Dimensions of Aid Dependence'. Global Economic Governance Programme, WP 2007/32, Oxford University.

Whitfield, L., and O. Therkildsen. 2011. 'What Drives States to Support the Development of Productive Sectors? Strategies Ruling Elites Pursue for Political Survival and their Policy Implications'. DIIS Working Paper 15. Copenhagen: DIIS.

Wiggins, S., and H. Leturque. 2011. 'Ghana's Sustained Agricultural Growth: Putting Underused Resources to Work'. *Development Progress*. London: Overseas Development Institute.

Williams, T. 2009. 'An African Success Story: Ghana's Cocoa Marketing System'. IDS Working Paper 318. Brighton: Institute of Development Studies.

Wilson, F. 2004. 'Towards a Political Economy of Roads: Experiences from Peru'. *Development and Change*, 35(3): 525–46.

Wimmer, A. 1997. 'Who Owns the State? Understanding Ethnic Conflict in Post-Colonial Societies'. *Nations and Nationalism*, 3(4): 631–66.

Wimmer, A. 2002. *Nationalist Exclusion and Ethnic Conflict: Shadows of Modernity*. Cambridge: Cambridge University Press.

Wimmer, A. 2008. 'The Making and Unmaking of Ethnic Boundaries: A Multilevel Process Theory'. *American Journal of Sociology*, 113(4): 970–1022.

Wimmer, A. 2012a. *Ethnic Boundary: Institutions, Power, Networks*. New York, NY: Cambridge University Press.

Wimmer, A. 2012b. *Waves of War: Nationalism, State Formation, and Ethnic Exclusion in the Modern World*. New York, NY: Cambridge University Press.

Wimmer, A., L.-E. Cederman, and B. Min. 2009. 'Ethnic Politics and Armed Conflict: A Configurational Analysis of a New Global Data Set'. *American Sociological Review*, 74(2): 316–37.

Wolfe, A., and J. Klausen. 1997. 'Identity Politics and the Welfare State'. *Social Philosophy and Policy*, 14: 231–55.

Wong, S. 2010. 'Elite Capture or Capture Elites? Lessons from the "Counter-elite" and "Co-opt-elite" Approaches in Bangladesh and Ghana'. UNU-WIDER, WP 2010-82.

Woo-Cummings, M. 1999. *The Developmental State*. Ithaca, NY: Cornell University Press.

Woods, N. 2007. 'The Shifting Politics of Foreign Aid'. Global Economic Governance Programme, Working Paper 2007/36, <http://www.l20.org/publications/18_I7_ODA_Woods.pdf> (accessed 18 June 2014).

Woolard, I., and M. Leibbrandt. 2010. *The Evolution and Impact of Unconditional Cash Transfers in South Africa*. Cape Town: University of Cape Town.

World Bank Operations Evaluation Department. 2003. 'Toward Country-led Development: A Multi-partner Evaluation of the Comprehensive Development Framework'. Washington, DC: World Bank, <http://www.worldbank.org/evaluation/cdf/> (accessed 4 June 2014).

World Bank Social Development Department. 2006. 'Understanding Socio-economic and Political Factors to Impact Policy Change'. Report No. 36442-GLB. Washington, DC: World Bank.

World Bank. 1981. *Accelerated Development in sub-Saharan Africa: An Agenda for Action*. Washington, DC: World Bank.

World Bank. 1989. *Sub-Saharan Africa: From Crisis to Sustainable Growth, a Long-term Perspective*. Washington, DC: World Bank.

World Bank. 1990. *World Development Report 1990: Poverty*. Washington, DC: World Bank and Oxford: Oxford University Press.

World Bank. 1991. *World Development Report 1991: The Challenge of Development*, Washington, DC: World Bank and Oxford University Press.

World Bank. 1994. *Governance: The World Bank's Experience*. Washington, DC: World Bank.

World Bank. 1995a. *Priorities and Strategies for Education: A World Bank Review*. Washington, DC: World Bank.

World Bank. 1995b. 'Towards Gender Equality: The Role of Public Policy'. World Bank Discussion Paper 292. Washington, DC: World Bank, <http://dx.doi.org/10.1596/0-8213-3337-2> (accessed 18 June 2014).

World Bank. 2001. *Engendering Development through Gender Equality in Rights, Resources, and Voice*. Washington, DC: World Bank and Oxford University Press.

World Bank. 2002. *Legal and Judicial Sector Assessment Mannual: Issues on Legal and Judicial Reform*. Washington, DC: Legal Vice Presidency, World Bank.

World Bank. 2003. *Making Services Work for Poor People: World Development Report 2004*. Washington, DC: World Bank.

World Bank. 2004. *Striking a Better Balance—The World Bank Group and Extractive Industries: The Final Report of the Extractive Industries Review*. World Bank Group Management Response. Washington, DC: World Bank.

World Bank. 2005a. *Extractive Industries and Sustainable Development: An Evaluation of World Bank Group Experience*. Washington, DC: World Bank, IFC, MIGA.

World Bank. 2005b. *Maintaining Momentum to 2015? An Impact Evaluation of Interventions to Improve Maternal and Child Health and Nutrition in Bangladesh*. Washington, DC: World Bank.

World Bank. 2007. 'Strengthening World Bank Group Engagement on Governance and Anticorruption', <http://siteresources.worldbank.org/EXTGOVANTICORR/Resources/3035863-1281627136986/GACReport2.pdf> (accessed 18 June 2014).

World Bank. 2008. The Political Economy of Policy Reform: Issues and Implications for Policy Dialogue and Development Operations. Report No 44288-GLB. Washington, DC: World Bank.

World Bank. 2008a. *The Growth Report: Strategies for Sustained Growth and Inclusive Development*. Washington, DC: World Bank.

World Bank. 2008b. *Public Sector Reform: What Works and Why? An IEG Evaluation of World Bank Support*. Washington, DC: World Bank.

World Bank. 2010. 'Empowering Indonesian Communities through Direct Participation in Developing Infrastructure and Services'. IBRD Results,

March 2010:1–5, <http://siteresources.worldbank.org/NEWS/Resources/ Indonesia_Direct_Participation_4-11-10.pdf accessed 20 June 2014.

World Bank. 2011. *Social Protection for Changing India*. Washington, DC: World Bank.

World Bank, 2011b. *World Development Report 2012: Gender Equality and Development*. Washington, DC: The World Bank.

Xinhua. 2011. 'China's Foreign Aid', <http://news.xinhuanet.com/english2010/ china/2011-04/21/c_13839683.htm> (accessed 4 June 2014).

Yadav, Y., and S. Palshinkar. 2009. 'Between Fortuna and Virtu: Explaining the Congress' Ambiguous Victory in 2009'. *Economic and Political Weekly*, 44(39): 33–46.

Yashar, D. 2005. *Contesting Citizenship in Latin America: The Rise of Indigenous Movements and the Postliberal Challenge*. Cambridge: Cambridge University Press.

Yeğen, M. 2006. 'Turkish Nationalism and the Kurdish Question'. *Ethnic and Racial Studies*, 30(1): 119–51.

Younas, J. 2008. 'Motivation for Bilateral Aid Allocation: Altruism or Trade Benefits'. *European Journal of Political Economy*, 24(3): 661–74.

Young, I. M. 1990. *Justice and the Politics of Difference*. Princeton, NJ: Princeton University Press.

Zucco, C. 2008. 'The President's "New" Constituency: Lula and the Pragmatic Vote in Brazil's 2006 Presidential Elections'. *Journal of Latin American Studies*, 40: 29–49.

Index

bold=extended treatment or term highlighted in text;
f=figure; n=footnote; t=table;
[-]=intermediate page skipped

Index

Index